Simple
MODEL LOCOMOTIVE
BUILDING introducing
LBSC's TICH

Curly's own version of "Tich", which departs in many particulars from the "standard" version. It is shown here pulling the wagon devised by LBSC to carry additional supplies of coal and water as well as fireman's tools.

Simple
Model Locomotive
Building

introducing
LBSC's TICH

LBSC describes the construction of
his famous TICH for $3\frac{1}{2}$ in. gauge

MODEL & ALLIED PUBLICATIONS
ARGUS BOOKS LTD
Station Road, Kings Langley, Herts,
England

Printed in England by
Clarke, Doble and Brendon Ltd, Plymouth
for the publishers, Argus Books Ltd, Station Rd,
Kings Langley, Herts

Contents

Foreword

THERE CAN BE FEW model locomotive designs which have introduced more novices to the pleasures of building and driving their own live steamers than L.B.S.C.'s famous *Tich*! Based on a contractor's shunting locomotive its description appeared issue by issue in the *Model Engineer* many, many years ago. In response to demand the series appeared in book form in 1968 and has since progressed through a further two editions and now appears for the first time in paperback guise.

This new lease of life would have delighted "Curly" Lawrence the ex-footplateman who wrote under the name of L.B.S.C.—initials of the London, Brighton and South Coast Railway where he spent so many working years. L.B.S.C. had the happy knack of making the most difficult parts of model locomotive construction seem easy when he had broken them up into progressive steps, which may be the secret behind his immense popularity with all but the "experts", who deplored the success of his devotees who so often achieved success going the wrong way about it—according to the pundits!

The sketches provided in the book are taken from the set of full-size (or sometimes twice full-size) drawings which we recommend the serious builder to acquire. By keeping small drawings near to the descriptive text we have lightened the task of the diligent "armchair builder" who will we trust be inspired to get up and don overalls and join the many thousands who have now built and steamed a *Tich* of their own!

This edition incorporates some minor amendments to a few of the drawings and also includes corrections to some stated dimensions reported or suggested by readers who have actually built the model. We wish to thank those who passed on information. To make an actual model the complete set of *Model Engineer* drawings is required and these (11 sheets) can be had by post from M.A.P. Plans Service, 13–35 Bridge Street, Hemel Hempstead, Herts. Full details and prices are given in *M.A.P. Plans Handbook No. 3.*

Introduction — "Tich" by LBSC

QUITE A NUMBER of enthusiasts who started with 2½ in. gauge locomotives, and then switched to 3½ in. gauge may still have some of the smaller castings and parts on hand; it occurred to me, therefore, that it might be possible to describe a small and easily-built type of contractors' shunting locomotive, that would run on a 3½ in. gauge line, but utilise the "surplus". In my articles in *Model Engineer*, I once mentioned that Mr. Leslie Clarke, late of Swindon Works, G.W.R. and now in Johannesburg, South Africa, was building a small 3½ in. gauge contractors' engine, and his engine was built entirely from 2½ in. gauge castings and material.

Here is my version of such an engine: I called her *Tich* because—well, she just is. She is the weeniest coal-fired steam locomotive I have ever seen specified for this gauge, and I can just imagine the roars of derisive laughter that the mere suggestion of such an engine would have conjured up in the days gone by. Thank goodness, we know better now; not only will the tiny engine steam and run, but she will give you a ride, no matter what your size and weight. The few folk who have seen my old 2-2-2 *Ancient Lights* in action, wouldn't need any assurance on that score! Incidentally, this old girl did an astounding thing not so long ago. A friend up in Lancashire built a 3½ in. gauge *Royal Scot* which proved a "Royal Spot"—of bother!—instead, and I tested it on my road, to diagnose the trouble. His son came to collect it, and to show what the big engine should be capable of doing, if in first-class order, I steamed up old *Ancient Lights*, which has a boiler not very much bigger than specified for *Tich*.

A "Three-legged Race"

Ancient Lights has a very big dome, with the regulator right up in the top of it; and I usually run with the boiler almost full, on account of its small capacity, relying on the dome for steam space. She got up steam in the usual three minutes or so; and after a warm-up, running light, I took my seat on the car and did about half-a-dozen laps, to show her paces. When my visitor took over, he tapped at the regulator handle instead of holding it and opening up like a full-size driver; and the engine made a sudden dart forward, pulling up with a jerk as a coupling-chain became tight. The boiler was pretty full, and the jerk sent some of the water over, down the steam pipe; the piston banged it up against the cylinder cover, and the shock must have sheared the cotter-pin holding the piston rod to the crosshead. We didn't know that at the time, as the engine got the load under way, and proceeded to run as usual; but I noticed that the beats were uneven and that she appeared to jerk a bit on the curves. Anyway, she did a few laps, blowing off all the time, and my visitor expressed amazement at the way she pulled. Then I took over, and "ran out" the remains of the fire, travelling at the usual speed, with apparently nothing amiss, save that a blow had appeared at one of the cylinder covers; occasionally a gasket ring will split, especially if of oiled paper, and cause a blow.

After my visitor's departure, when I had dropped the fire and wiped the engine down (always clean before putting away), I was astonished to find that the right-hand piston rod was clean out of the crosshead, and the pin sheared; that she had only been getting power on the outward stroke of the piston. On the return-stroke, as soon as the valve uncovered the back port, the piston had shot to the front cover, as the rod was detached from the crosshead, the repeated concussions loosening the screws and causing the blow. The engine running on "three legs", in a manner of speaking, was only developing 75 per cent of her power, yet she made short work of a heavy adult, and maintained normal speed easily. It is hardly necessary to add that I fitted a larger pin, and a new joint, and she was soon O.K. once more.

Brief Specifications

Returning to little *Tich*, she is just a plain four-wheeled job with all the "works" outside, except the feed pump, and can be built with the minimum of tools and equipment. She would be an interesting and quick job even for anybody with a fleet of larger engines, and just the "Cat's whiskers" for anyone who is just making a start, and wants something inexpensive, easy, and simple. The main frames are $2\frac{1}{2}$ in. deep, and made from $\frac{3}{32}$ in. steel, the blue ductile sheet or strip for preference; and no filing to outline is needed, as they could be cut out straight away in a few minutes on a bench shear. If a shear is not available, they could be sawn, using the tops of the vice jaws for a guide; but a file would be needed to remove the saw-marks, although there are no curved lines, the bottom and ends being straight. The hornblock openings would be made to suit whatever hornblock castings or pressings you happened to have in stock. The hot-pressed type sold by advertisers in *Model Engineer* would do fine; but those who supply castings and material for "L.B.S.C." engines, produce cast hornblocks very nearly as clean. I have samples here now, as sold for *Austere Ada* and other $2\frac{1}{2}$ in. gauge jobs, that only need a little attention with a file. The centre of the leading axle is $4\frac{3}{8}$ in. from end of frame; the coupled wheels are $4\frac{1}{4}$ in. apart, and the overhang at the trailing end is $4\frac{1}{4}$ in. The buffer beams are made from $\frac{3}{4} \times \frac{3}{4} \times \frac{1}{8}$ in. flat bar, attached to frames by angles, or by brazing.

The axleboxes are fitted with overhead springs. The coupled wheels are 2 in. diameter on tread, but it would make no odds if they are a shade larger, to bring in stock castings. *Ada* wheels turned as small as the castings would allow, would do very well. The axles are $\frac{3}{8}$ in. diameter, same as for $2\frac{1}{2}$ in. gauge, but turned to the correct length for $3\frac{1}{2}$ in. gauge, viz. $3\frac{9}{32}$ in. between shoulders. The driving crankpin should be $\frac{1}{4}$ in. diameter, and the leading one $\frac{3}{16}$ in., the length being same as *Ada* or *Dyak*. The distance from centre of axle to centre of crankpin is $\frac{9}{16}$ in.

Cylinders and Motion

Cylinder castings as used for *Dyak* and *Ada*, *Green Arrow*, etc. could all be utilised, the bore being made about $\frac{11}{16}$ in., stroke $1\frac{1}{8}$ in. and with the ports and passages, slide-valves, etc., all as specified for the engines mentioned. The single guide-bar of the *Green Arrow*, with the same type of box cross-head, would fit in with Mr. Clarke's layout. The outer end of the bar is supported by a simple angle-bracket attached to the main frames, and this carries a triangular bracket with the link bearing on it, same as the *Dyak*. A single bearing can be used as on the *Dyak*, or an additional bearing can be added on the inner side, just as you prefer, as there is room for it. The Walschaerts' gear is also very similar to the *Dyak*'s, except for the lifting arrangement for the radius rod; this is attended to by a swinging link on the end of the lifting arm attached to the usual type of weighbar shaft, running in flanged bushes attached to the frame by screws. In connection with this, here is a tip which beginners might like to know. The valve gear is, of course, arranged for outside admission, the cylinders having ordinary slide valves; Mr. Clarke showed the return crankpin leading the main pin, which means that the engine goes ahead with the dieblock in the lower part of the link. Therefore, if the reverse arm on the weighbar shaft is pointing upwards and connected to the lever in the cab above, the fulcrum pin, the engine will run the opposite way to the inclination of the lever.

To get over this, there are three easy ways. First, the reverse arm could hang down instead of pointing upwards. Secondly, the lever in the cab could be extended below the fulcrum pin, and the reach rod is connected to the extension, so that the arm on the weighbar shaft worked in the opposite direction. Thirdly—easiest of all—set the return crankpin to follow the main crank instead of leading it, and let the engine use the top half of the link for going ahead, same as all the Maunsell 2-6-0's on the Southern, and the American "Austerities". This doesn't make the slightest difference to the efficiency of the engine.

The steam and exhaust pipes could be the same as on *Dyak* or *Ada*, and there is room for a $2\frac{1}{2}$ in. gauge size mechanical lubricator between frames, behind the buffer-beam. The ratchet lever could be operated by an eccentric on the leading axle. The ram should be $\frac{3}{32}$ in. with a stroke of $\frac{3}{16}$ in. full, the oil being fed into the tee on the steam pipe.

Boiler

I made a separate drawing of the kind of boiler I should specify for such an engine. The barrel is the same diameter as shown on Mr. Clarke's drawing, but I made the firebox wrapper $\frac{3}{8}$ in. longer, for two reasons; one, it gives a little more grate area, and two, it brings the boiler a little farther back into the cab, with consequently better counterbalancing effect. The weight of the cylinders ahead of the leading axle, would put the engine "down on her knees" if she didn't have a counterbalance at the back end, and we might as well take advantage of it, instead of putting a dead weight under the footplate.

The barrel, wrapper, firebox, crown-stays, and firebox tubeplate can be made from 18 gauge copper sheet; the smokebox tubeplate and throatplate from 16 gauge, and the backhead from 13 gauge. The method of construction is exactly the same as I described for larger boilers, and a $2\frac{1}{2}$ pint blowlamp would make short work of the whole doings. There are six $\frac{3}{8}$ in. by 24 gauge tubes, and a single $\frac{3}{4}$ in. flue, of 20 gauge copper, for the superheater; the element should be made from $\frac{1}{4}$ in. by 20 gauge tube, with a brazed-on block return bend coming within $\frac{1}{2}$ in. of the firebox. This little "kettle" will be most exceedingly lively, and a very fast steamer; also with the big flue and element, the steam will be plenty hot, which is needed for the greater efficiency. Nine $\frac{1}{8}$ in. copper stays will be needed in each side of the firebox, and two in the ends; these, plus the two longitudinal stays (one of $\frac{5}{32}$ in. copper rod, and the other of tube) will make the boiler quite safe for a working pressure of 80 lb. Either Sifbronze, easy-running strip, or Johnson-Matthey's "B6" alloy, which is a coarse-grade silver-solder, and makes a sound job at low temperature, can be used for the first operations. The tubes, foundation ring, backhead and bushes can be treated to a dose of "Easyflo", or ordinary best grade silver-solder.

A circular smokebox, made of brass tube, of a diameter that will just fit over the boiler barrel, can be fitted, and covered with a wrapper made of sheet brass, and bent to the outline shown in the front view of the engine. The front could be cut to the same outline, from $\frac{3}{32}$ in. sheet brass, and have a ring silver-soldered to it, which would press into the smokebox barrel. I have fitted the front of *Grosvenor's* smokebox in similar manner, and it is quite O.K. The door and hinges, dart, handles, etc. need no comment. The chimney could be made from a piece of $\frac{11}{16}$ in. brass tube, the cap and base being turned from pieces of brass previously silver-soldered on. No liner is needed.

Boiler Fittings

The boiler being so weeny, you would need to do the same as I do on *Ancient Lights*, viz. run with a high water-level and use the dome as steam space. The inner dome could be made from a piece of 1 in. copper tube with a flange silver-soldered on, and a top turned from 1 in. brass rod, or a cast disc, in which is formed the seating for a safety valve. The latter should be a genuine spring-balance, which is easy enough to make, as the dome is bigger than *Grosvenor*'s. If a dummy balance is used, with a direct-acting spring-valve inside the dome cover, it means restricting the height of the inner dome and getting the regulator too close to water level. By the same token (says Pat) it would not be advisable to put safety valves on the boiler barrel or they would be blowing water best part of the time.

The regulator can be Stroudley pattern, but a single port would be plenty. Mr. Clarke connected the top of the water gauge by a pipe to the turret; this is O.K., but the steam gauge was shown apparently directly connected to the top of the turret by a union, whereas it should be attached to a $\frac{1}{8}$ in. syphon, and set toward the side. As to boiler feeds, a pump $\frac{5}{16}$ in. bore and $\frac{3}{8}$ in. stroke can be placed between frames and operated by an eccentric on the front axle, out of the way of grit from the ashpan. A small hand pump could be installed in one of the side tanks, which should be made from 20 gauge sheet brass, and carry water. An injector could also be fitted if desired; although the smallest size I recommend, with 78 delivery nozzle, would put the feed in rather too fast for the small size of the boiler. Mr. Clarke's own design of donkey-pump could also be fitted.

Accessories

The superstructure can be made from 20 gauge brass or steel sheet. The engine having only a plain bent-over weatherboard, makes the footplate easily accessible; but a piece would have to be cut out of the bunker, to render the firehole get-at-able. A supply of coal would have to be carried on the flat car. As brake-gear is a prominent feature of these contractors' engines, and if left out is conspicuous by its absence, the brake shown by our friend should be fitted. I note, however, that he has shown the bearing carrying the brake shaft, fixed in the step. I would prefer it fixed to the frames. The shaft could project through the bearing, far enough to carry the arm which is operated by the brake screw and nut, as the brake would not be used for service stops, being more or less an ornament only. The engine would be too light to make a service stop with its own brake when hauling a passenger. Buffers, couplings and other oddments would be the same as on any normal type of $3\frac{1}{2}$ in. gauge engine, as it would naturally be used with the same type of rolling-stock.

Well, I guess that about completes a "quick survey" of *Tich*. Sets of full-size blueprints are available for those who prefer working to them.

CHAPTER ONE

Making a start

Main Frames

FOR THE MAIN FRAMES, two pieces of 13 gauge or $\frac{3}{32}$ in. soft blue steel plate 13 in. long and $2\frac{5}{8}$ in. wide, will be required. Having tried all kinds of sheet steel for making frames, I use this kind exclusively now. The trouble with *hard-rolled* bright steel is that it invariably buckles and twists when the openings for the hornblocks are cut out; if the steel is soft, it is, of course, quite O.K. I was fortunate in getting a nice bit of ductile steel, dull finish, for the frames of *Tugboat Annie*, and they remained true after being cut, milled, and generally "mauled about", although they are exceptionally long. I should never dream of using rustless steel for frame plates—I've yet to see a full-sized engine with rustless steel frames!—because ordinary steel frames can be painted if desired, as soon as they are erected, thus preventing any chance of rusting; and once the engine goes into service, they will always be more or less oily, which effects a further "insurance policy". Incidentally, if you happen to have a small piece of rustless steel sheet handy, try drilling a few holes in it, and see how you—or your drills—like it. I don't! I made a cover for the water-tank by the side of my railway, from a piece of rustless steel sheet, and that was quite enough for your humble servant.

How to Mark Out the Frames

Now, brother tyros, this is how you mark out your frames, as easy a job as ever was. Test one long edge of the plate against a steel rule, and see that it is dead straight; if it isn't, file away the high-spots. Then put your try-square against the end, stock to top of frame plate, and blade to the edge, as near as you can get it. Scribe a line down, using blade as guide. Along the top edge, starting from the scribed line, make a mark $4\frac{3}{8}$ in. away, another mark $4\frac{1}{4}$ in. beyond that, and finally another $4\frac{1}{4}$ in. beyond the last one, which will come pretty close to the edge of the plate, as the overall length of the finished frame is $12\frac{7}{8}$ in. Now, with the stock of your square resting on top of frame, set the blade to all the marks, and scribe a line clean across the plate at each mark. You'll have to reverse the direction of the stock of the try-square to do the last one.

Now test if the bottom edge of the plate is parallel with the top edge; if all four scribed lines are exactly the same length, it is O.K. These lines should be $2\frac{5}{8}$ in. long, if the width of the material is correct. If not, mark off a point $2\frac{5}{8}$ in. from the top, on first and last lines; join them, and cut off or file the metal away to the line. At bottom of frame plate, mark off a point $\frac{3}{8}$ in. each side of the two centre-lines. Using your square with stock against the bottom edge of the frame, draw a line $1\frac{1}{4}$ in. high at each point; then connect the tops with another straight line across each pair. That gives you the correct location of the openings for the hornblocks.

At $\frac{5}{8}$ in. from the bottom of the third vertical line, make a mark, and centre-pop it. That is the running position of the driving axle. On the first line, at the front edge of frame, mark a point at $1\frac{11}{32}$ in. from the top. Draw a line from that point to the centre-dot just made; that gives you the centre-line of the motion, from which the location of the cylinders has to be set out. On this line, at $1\frac{1}{4}$ in. and $1\frac{3}{4}$ in. respectively, scribe two lines at right-angles to the inclined line. Mark off a point on each one, $\frac{3}{8}$ in. below the inclined line, and join them. Mark off two similar points $1\frac{3}{8}$ in. above the inclined line, and join them also. The enclosed space gives you the exact location of the cylinder bolting face. Scribe a line exactly down the centre of this, that is, $\frac{7}{8}$ in. from each side; easily done if you keep the stock of the square set to the long inclined line. That gives you the vertical centre-line of the cylinders.

Now for the cylinder stud holes, and the holes for steam and exhaust pipes. At $\frac{3}{16}$ in. below the inclined line (centre-line of motion), also at $\frac{1}{2}$ in. above it, draw two lines parallel with it. Make centre-pops at the points where these lines cross the vertical centre-line. The upper one indicates the hole for the exhaust pipe; the lower one is the middle stud hole of the bottom row. At $\frac{11}{16}$ in. on either side of these pops, make four more, and there are your stud holes. Next, at $\frac{1}{2}$ in. above the upper row, and $\frac{1}{2}$ in. ahead of the vertical centre-line of the cylinders make another pop mark, and that settles the position of the hole for the steam pipe.

Next, we want the shape of the frame. On the vertical line nearest to the left-hand side of the plate, set out a point $\frac{3}{4}$ in. from the top and corner of the rectangle indicating the cylinder bolting face. Then, on the bottom line of the frame, mark off a point $\frac{7}{8}$ in. ahead of the centre-line of the front hornblock opening, and draw a line from that, also to the front corner of the cylinder location. On the bottom of the frame, $1\frac{5}{16}$ in. behind the centre-line of the rear hornblock opening, mark a point, and draw a line from this, to a point $\frac{3}{4}$ in. below the top line of frame, on the vertical line at the back end, and there is your frame outline. Simple enough, sure-lie, as they say down in Sussex.

Next item, screw holes for pump stay. At $1\frac{1}{8}$ in. behind the centre-line of front hornblock opening, scribe a vertical line with your try-square stock held against bottom of frame; and on it set out and make three centre-pops, $\frac{3}{16}$ in., $\frac{7}{16}$ in. and $\frac{7}{16}$ in. again, measuring from bottom of frame. At $\frac{1}{4}$ in. from each end of top of frame, scribe a short vertical line, and another $\frac{1}{4}$ in. from that. On the ones nearest the end, make centre-pops $\frac{5}{16}$ in. from top, and $\frac{5}{16}$ in.

below that. On the other one, make a centre-pop halfway between the two first marked; and that completes your marking out. You can do it as quickly as I wrote the instructions.

How to Cut the Frames

If you own, or have the use of a bench shear, all you have to do is to cut the outline with five snips of the shear along the two ends and the three diagonal lines. If not, drill the three No. 40 holes, already marked out, at each end of the frame plate. Temporarily clamp the plates together, and make certain they line up all ways; then drill one hole at each end of the lower plate, using one of the already-drilled holes in the upper ones as a guide, and temporarily rivet them together with a couple of $\frac{3}{32}$ in. rivets. Drill all the holes through both plates at once, with No. 40 drill; then open out the larger ones with the drill sizes specified on the drawing.

To cut the frames to outline when a shear isn't available, just catch the frames in the bench vice with the marked line showing level with the vice jaws. Put a fine-toothed hacksaw blade, say about 22 teeth per inch, sideways in the saw frame, and saw along the marked line with the side of the blade resting on top of the vice jaws, which thus guide the cut straight. A drop of cutting oil, as used for lathe turning, helps the saw to walk through the steel. Next, put the frames vertically in the vice, with the line marking side of horn-block slot showing at the jaws, and saw as far as the cross line. Drill a few holes just under the cross line, and break out the piece by grabbing it with a pair of pliers, and bending back and forth like a National Health Service dentist doing a bit of overtime. Finally, smooth out all the saw-marks with a file; knock out the temporary rivets, and there are your finished frame plates. The whole job shouldn't take more than one evening. Next stage, hornblocks, buffer-beams, and frame erection.

Buffer-Beams

The buffer-beams are made from $\frac{3}{4}$ in. by $\frac{1}{8}$ in. angle; steel for preference, but brass will do as a substitute if steel angle cannot be easily obtained. Two pieces long enough to finish to an overall length of $6\frac{3}{8}$ in. will be needed. Mark them off with your try-square; saw just a weeny bit longer than finished size, and trim up the ends by filing to the marked line. Then saw away half of the angle for a distance of $\frac{5}{8}$ in. at each end, as shown in the top-and-underside view, filing away the saw-marks. Next, using the try-square again, carefully mark off the position of the two slots, into which the frames fit. The best way to do this is to find the centre of the shorter side of the angle, then set out a line $1\frac{15}{32}$ in. each side of it. Another $\frac{3}{32}$ in. away from this, will give you the exact position of the slots, and they will be equi-distant from the ends of the beam.

Find the centre of the longer side of the angle, and on it mark off a $\frac{1}{8}$ in.

Plate 1

Mr. F. E. Levett in action with his "Tich" on the Tonbridge Society's
track at Tonbridge, Kent

Plate 2

Underside of the chassis of a "Tich" built by Edgar Richardson of Handsworth Wood. Note the axlebox springs below the axles

A fine example of the small-boilered "Tich" by J. H. Balleny of Birmingham

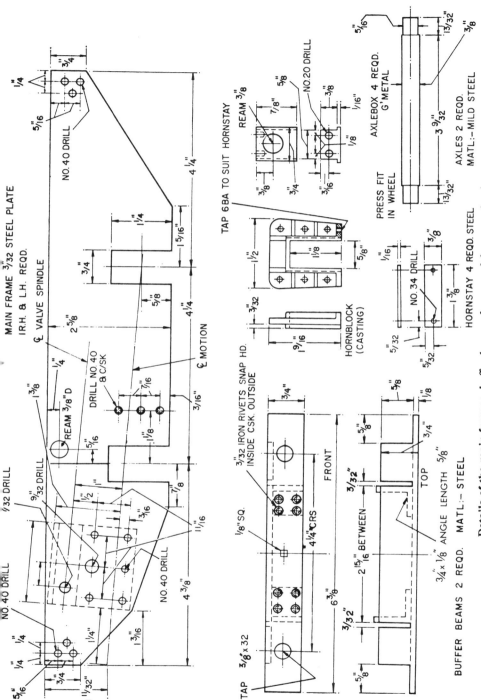

Details of the main frames, buffer beams, horns, axleboxes and axles.

square for the drawbar hole. At $2\frac{1}{8}$ in. from the centre of this, on each side, and on the horizontal centre-line of the angle, mark off two points, and make a heavy centre-dot on each. These are for the buffer holes. Also, centre-dot the drawbar hole. At $\frac{7}{8}$ in. from each side of the drawbar centre, scribe a vertical line down the angle, and another a full $\frac{5}{16}$ in. farther on. Next, on these two pairs of lines, make centre-dots $\frac{1}{8}$ in. from the bottom, and two more at $\frac{5}{16}$ in. above them. These are for the rivet holes. That finishes the marking-out.

Drill all the marked spots with a No. 41 drill; then open out the buffer holes with a $\frac{3}{8}$ in. drill, and the drawbar hole with $\frac{1}{8}$ in. drill. File this hole square using a watchmaker's small square file, until a piece of $\frac{1}{8}$ in. square rod will slide into it, easily. Countersink the rivet holes on the outside of the angle with a $\frac{5}{32}$ in. drill. Let the drill cut until the full diameter is just showing at the edge of the hole; no more.

The next job is to cut the slots; they can be cut speedily and also to "guaranteed" accuracy, if the job is done in the lathe, the process being very simple; but a milling cutter of the "circular saw" type is needed for the job. This should be $\frac{3}{32}$ in. thick, and not less than 2 in. diameter; $2\frac{1}{8}$ in. is preferable. It is mounted either on a spindle between lathe centres, or on a short spindle held in the chuck. In the days gone by, when my equipment was limited, I got a bolt just big enough to fit the hole in the cutter, and two nuts. The head of the bolt was sawn off, and the nuts were then run right down to the end of the thread on the headless bolt; the cutter was put on, and then the other nut, which was well tightened up, to prevent the cutter shifting. The plain part of the bolt was then gripped in the three-jaw chuck, and the cutter was then all ready to operate. If the hole was big, and I had to use a fairly big bolt, both ends of it were centred in the lathe, after beheading it; and the bolt was then run between centres, being driven by a carrier clamped on to the plain part. If I had no bolt big enough to suit the cutter, I put a washer in the hole, and a suitable bolt through the hole in the washer; and another washer, larger than the hole in the cutter, was placed at each side of same, between nut and cutter, just like the way an emery wheel is mounted.

To cut the slots, the piece of angle is clamped under the slide-rest tool holder, parallel to the lathe bed. You can set the angle true in a brace of shakes, by putting the faceplate on the lathe mandrel nose, holding the stock of the try-square against it, and setting the angle to the blade. Tighten the tool clamp, and Bob's your uncle. Now, very carefully set the marked-out slot to the edge of the cutter; run the lathe at its slowest speed, and feed the beam on to the cutter very slowly. Apply some cutting oil with a brush. I use Edgar Vaughan & Co.'s "Cutmax", diluted with half its bulk of paraffin; this gives a lovely finish and keeps the lathe free from rust—my machines are all silvery bright. However, any good cutting compound, or even soapy water, can be used; but if using the latter, or any cutting oil which is soluble in water, be sure to give the lathe a good wipe down when the job is finished. Otherwise you will have the unpainted parts going rusty, and the painted parts will be covered by a sticky mess which clings like fish glue.

Angles for Frame Attachment

Cut four pieces of the same kind of angle used for the beams, and finish them to a length of $\frac{5}{8}$ in., with nicely squared ends. If the bits are sawn over length, they can be gripped together in the three-jaw chuck, and faced off with a round-nose tool set cross-wise in the rest. It doesn't matter about them running "axially" true; as long as the jaws are in contact with the sides, the ends will be at right-angles to the sides after facing off.

These pieces have to be riveted in the beams, flush with the inside edge of the frame slots; another easy job. To locate them correctly, all you have to do is to jam a piece of $\frac{3}{32}$ in. sheet steel in the slot; put the bit of angle tightly up against it, and hold it there, either with a toolmaker's clamp or a small hand-vice; then run the No. 41 drill through it, using the holes already in the beam for a guide. Smooth any burrs off which may be left from the drilling; put $\frac{3}{32}$ in. snaphead iron rivets through (one at a time, naturally!) and if they project more than $\frac{3}{32}$ in. beyond the beam, snip off the stems to leave that amount. Then carefully hammer down the stems into the countersinks on the outside of the beam, resting the head of the rivet on top of a small piece of steel bar (any convenient size you have handy will do) held vertically in the bench vice.

If you wish to preserve the shape of the rivet head, make a depression in the "dolly", or "holder-up", by drilling a countersink in it with a $\frac{3}{16}$ in. drill, placing a $\frac{3}{16}$ in. cycle ball in the depression, and giving it a few hearty cracks with a heavy hammer. This will form a cup, into which the head of the rivet will fit, whilst you commit assault and battery on the stem. When through, file off any projections on the face of the beam, and give it a final rub on a sheet of emery-cloth laid on something flat. The rivets, if steel or iron, should then be invisible. Note—if the builder intends to braze the frames to the beams, no angles are needed, so don't drill any rivet holes in the beams.

Hornblocks

The hornblocks for this engine are the "standard" hornblocks I specify on normal type engines for $2\frac{1}{2}$ in. gauge. If hot-pressed alloy hornblocks are procurable, they save work, all filing or milling of the contact faces being eliminated. However, some of the castings I have seen are very nearly as clean; one set in particular, which was sent to me many years ago by Mr. W. Bryden of Sydney, N.S.W., I used without touching the contact faces at all. If you buy castings and they are reasonably clean, judicious application of a file will be all that is needed to fit them to the openings in the frame. Hornblocks can easily be machined in the lathe, an easy enough method, when a vertical-slide is available. I have said before, and have no hesitation in repeating, that a vertical-slide should form part of the regular equipment of every home-workshop lathe worthy of the title; and if manufacturers concentrated more on a heavy substantial construction, with a few useful necessaries, instead of

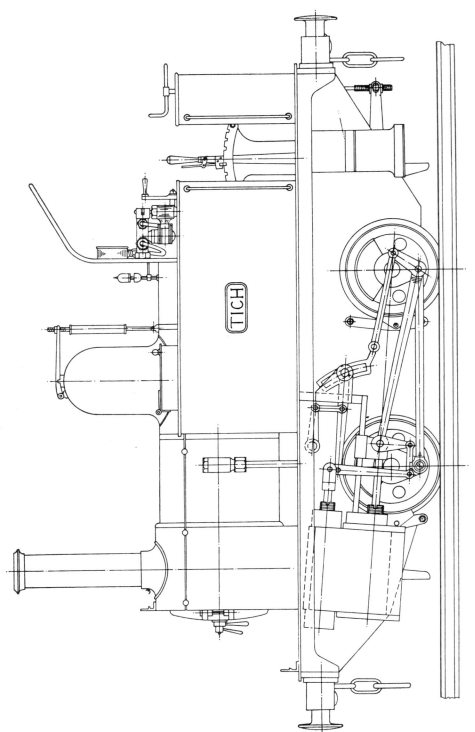

General arrangement of the small-boiler Tich.

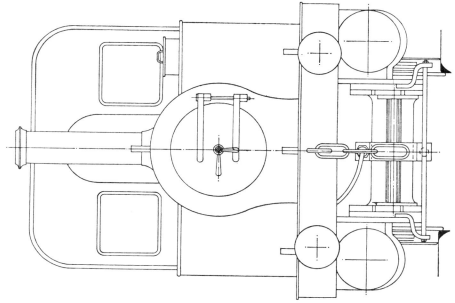

Front elevation of the small Tich.
(NB. Check valves and left-hand tank filler omitted.)

a more or less flimsy machine with a lot of fallals that are seldom or never required on our job, the said machines would be far more useful, and turn out better work in less time.

To bolt the casting to the slide (or to the milling-machine table, if one is available) you need a little block of metal about $\frac{3}{4}$ in. square, and about $\frac{3}{8}$ in. thick. This is sawn and filed, or milled, to the shape shown in the illustrations, the narrower part being easy to fit in the hornblock jaws. A hole about $\frac{5}{16}$ in. diameter is drilled through it. The head of a short $\frac{5}{16}$ in. bolt is turned down until it will slide easily in the tee-slot in the slide or table; and the hornblock can then be clamped down to the face of the slide, or milling-machine table, as shown in the illustration, which explains better than any words. Incidentally, I've often thought, with a smile, when looking at one of the "Dick Tracy", "Kit Conquest", or similar type of picture story strip in daily's and periodicals, that I could do a locomotive-building serial by a similar strip—and you'd then see what Inspector Meticulous, Ken Knowitall, Tommy Tyro, Milly Amp, and the rest of "the gang" looked like!

Once the hornblock casting is set up, with the sides of the little flange (the part that fits in the opening in the frame) at right-angles to the lathe centre-line, the job is easy. To set the hornblock right, simply put the stock of your try-square on the lathe saddle, and set one side of the flange to the blade; then tighten the bolt. See that the sides of the holding-down block do not project beyond the flange. Now put an end-mill, or a slot-drill, not less than $\frac{3}{8}$ in. diameter, in the three-jaw as shown. Feed the hornblock casting on to it, by the aid of the saddle screw or top-slide screw; then, by careful manipulation of the handles of the cross-slide and the vertical-slide, you can traverse the casting up, down and across the cutter, which should revolve at a good speed. The cutter will clean up the contact faces, and leave a nice sharp corner between contact face and side of flange, which will fit snugly into the opening of the frame. I do this job on my vertical milling machine, which is exactly the same process "turned sideways" as the kiddies would say; the cutter operates vertically, and the slide horizontally, the slide being the miller table, which is operated by the two handles (longitudinal and cross feeds) to let the cutter cover the whole of the contact face. I use a piece of metal, with an opening in it exactly the same as those in the frames, as a gauge; you can do the same.

Drill six No. 41 holes in each hornblock as shown in the illustration, then fit one to the frame. Hold it in position with a toolmaker's clamp; this can be home-made, from a couple of pieces of $\frac{1}{2}$ in. square bar and a couple of $\frac{1}{4}$ in. screws. Run the drill through all the holes, carrying on right through the frame. Countersink the holes outside frame, and rivet the hornblock in place, as described for the buffer-beam angles. A dolly, in which to rest the rivet heads while hammering down the shanks, can be made from a bit of $\frac{1}{2}$ in. square rod about 4 in. long. Turn one end to a blunt cone, leaving the end about $\frac{3}{16}$ in. across; make a cup-shaped depression in the end, as described above, with a $\frac{3}{16}$ in. drill and cycle ball, and put it vertically in the bench vice. After riveting in the hornblocks file off any projections, flush with outside of frames.

Before proceeding to erect the frames for *Tich*, the jaws of the hornblocks must be cleaned up all ready for fitting the axleboxes. Now to ensure that the axleboxes are exactly opposite one another, the obvious thing to do, is to bolt the frames together and clean out each pair of hornblock jaws at one fell swoop; so we will proceed to do that. Put the frames together in the way the kiddies would call "inside out"; that is, with the hornblocks outside, and fix them together temporarily with a couple of screws and nuts through the holes at each end.

I don't suppose there are many beginners who own a milling machine; but any lucky person who does, won't need detailed instructions on how to mill out the hornblock jaws, as all that is needed is to catch the frames in the machine vice, and run them under a suitable side-and-face milling cutter mounted on the arbor. Probably there may be a few who own a planing or shaping machine; in that case, the frames are mounted in the machine vice, and a bent tool in the clapper box, fed downwards, will clean out the sides. The bottom is cleaned off with a straight tool. However, there is really no need for machining at all, as the humble but necessary file will do the job quite well, if the operator exercises just ordinary care. You will need a gauge; this is a simple piece of $\frac{5}{8}$ in. square bar about $1\frac{1}{2}$ in. long. Grip the frames in the bench vice, end-up, with the hornblock as close to the vice jaws as possible; then, with a wide, flat second-cut file, held horizontally, smooth off one side

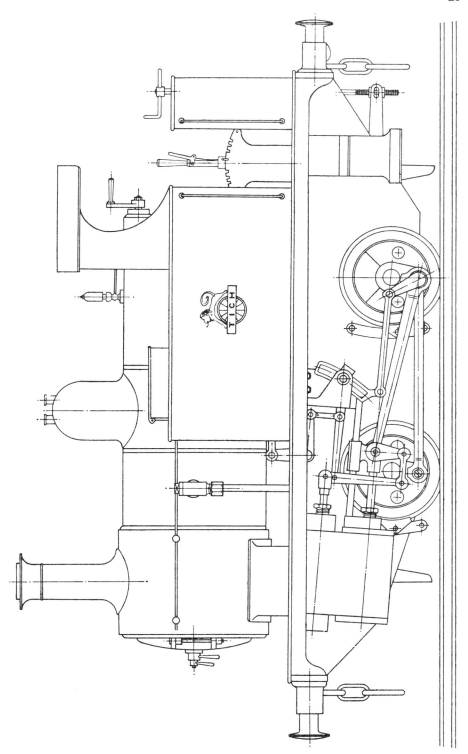

General arrangement of the large-boiler Tich.

of the jaws, taking off about $\frac{1}{32}$ in. Now turn the pair of frames up the other way, and repeat the operation; but this time, try your piece of bar in the opening, and continue filing, very carefully, until the piece of bar is an exact fit in the hornblock jaws, sliding in easily to the full depth, but without any appreciable shake. Then turn the frames horizontally in the vice, and clean out the ends of the jaws; no gauge is, of course, needed for that. The axleboxes, when fitted, should now be dead in line, each with its opposite mate on the other side of the frame, if same is erected properly.

How to Erect Frames

Part the frames again, then put the ends in the two slots in each of the buffer-beams. See that the frames go right to the ends of the slots, so as to form a perfect rectangle; the frames must be exactly at right-angles to the beams. This can be checked by applying your try-square. The top edges of the frames, and the tops of the beams, must all be what engineers call "in the same plane" that is, perfectly level; and this state of affairs can be achieved in two wags of a happy dog's tail, simply by laying the whole bag of tricks upside down on something true and flat such as the lathe bed, and pressing both frames and both buffer-beams into contact with it. Hold them thus by any means available; personally, I use a toolmaker's clamp at each corner, placed over frame end, and the angle attached to buffer-beam. For those with shallow pockets there is not the slightest need to buy the clamps; they can be home-made in a few minutes apiece. They can be made in any size.

To fix the frames to the angles, run the No. 40 drill into all the holes in the ends, using the hand brace, and make countersinks on the bits of angle. Follow up with No. 48 drill, then tap the holes with either a $\frac{3}{32}$ in. or 7 BA taper tap. Work same backwards and forwards, using some cutting oil on the threads. Warning to those who haven't used small taps in steel: *don't* use a big tap-wrench, and *don't* force the tap. As soon as it tries to stop, "reverse engines" and turn backwards half-a-turn or so. No sense in wasting money when it can be avoided, and it is fairly expensive to replace broken taps. When you have tapped the three holes in one corner, put the screws in before you do any more drilling and tapping; then check the frames to see that it hasn't got "out of plumb". If it has shifted, reset before proceeding.

Beginners often ask why I don't stick to fraction-size drills, $\frac{1}{16}$ in., $\frac{3}{32}$ in., and so on, instead of giving numbers. Well, it is for the very simple reason that there is too big a jump between fraction sizes, for many of our jobs; one size would be too small, the next too large. For example, a $\frac{3}{32}$ in. pin would flop about in a $\frac{7}{64}$ in. hole, and such "fitting" would be useless for valve gears. In the number sizes, there are six drills between $\frac{3}{32}$ in. and $\frac{7}{64}$ in., viz. 41 to 36 (the bigger the drill the lower the number) and the No. 41 drill is the exact clearing size for a $\frac{3}{32}$ in. pin. Number drills are as readily obtainable as fraction drills. Beginners should, if possible, buy a complete set 1 to 60 and a few extra of the most commonly used sizes—55 and 51 for $\frac{1}{16}$ in. or 10 BA tapping and clearing; 48 and 41 for $\frac{3}{32}$ in. or 7 BA ditto; 40 and 30 for $\frac{1}{8}$ in. or 5 BA and so on.

Ordinary cheesehead steel screws can be used to hold the frames to the buffer-beam angles, apart from the fact that they are out of sight, a full-size Chief Mechanical Engineer would not hesitate to use the most handy and suitable screws for his engine, and if he thought cheeseheads would do, in they would go. Actually there are plenty of slotted screws in many full-sized engines. When all the screws are tight, the frames should be true and rigid; they will be more rigid still when the pump stay has been fitted.

Brazed Frame Assembly

For years past, I have brazed or Sifbronzed all my frames to the buffer-beams, entirely dispensing with screws; and welding is now used in full-size, to a large extent. If any beginner wants to braze up his frame assembly, the job is easy. As previously mentioned, no angles are needed on the buffer-beams; the frames are jammed into the plain slots and the whole job levelled on the lathe-bed or other flat surface, a distance-piece, or spacer the exact width between frames, is placed between them, and a big cramp (a carpenter's cramp would do) placed over the lot and tightened up. If the frames are long, I use two spacers and cramps, one at each end. To prevent the beams moving, some iron wire is wound right round the lot, and the ends twisted together. All four corners are then given a dose of wet Sifbronze flux, and the assembly placed upright in the brazing-pan, which need only be a big tin lid, or an old tea tray, or even the lid of the domestic ash-bin, if nothing else is available. You won't hurt it! Bend a bit of sheet-iron, about 9 in. wide, into a half circle, and stand it in the pan; this prevents the coke or breeze falling off the back, and provides a rest for the frame assembly to lean against. I use an oxy-acetylene blowpipe with a small "tip" or nozzle in it (say 150 litre), and the flame from this heats the joint to bright red in a matter of seconds. The end of a Sifbronze rod is applied to the joint, leaving a nice fillet, and the job is done. It is far easier than soldering up a leak in the domestic kettle.

I don't expect many beginners will have an oxy-acetylene blowpipe, but they should have either a paraffin blowlamp, or an air-gas blowpipe operated by a fan or bellows, and this will do the job. The only difference is, that the flame isn't concentrated enough to heat just the joint only; you'll have to heat up the whole buffer-beam to red. Use easy-running brazing-strip, which can be purchased from most tool merchants. The best flux to use is Boron Compo, a blue powder sold in tins of 1 lb. and upwards. Mix some to a paste with water, and put a good smear over each joint. Then heat the beam to bright red, and apply the stick of brazing material to the joint; if a little doesn't melt off and run into the joint, it isn't hot enough. When the melted metal has run in and formed a nice smooth fillet, give the other beam a dose of the same medicine. Then let the whole issue cool to black, finally quenching in water, and removing all traces of burnt flux with an old file.

Frame Stay

To support the frames, a cross-stay is fitted just behind the leading horn-blocks, and as it serves a double purpose by carrying the boiler feed pump as well, it is usually known as the pumpstay. It may either be a casting, or bent up from a piece of $\frac{1}{8}$ in. brass plate. Our "approved" advertisers can supply suitable castings. The ends will require machining off to fit between the frames. This can be done by clamping the casting under the lathe toolholder, and traversing across an end-mill, or slot-drill, held in the three-jaw chuck. To set the stay right for machining, put the faceplate on the lathe nose, run up the rest with the stay on it, then apply your try-square to the job, the stock resting on the faceplate. Set the edge of the stay to the blade, tighten the clamp, and you're all set. Replace chuck, put the end-mill in it, start the lathe, and traverse the stay across the cutter by means of the cross-slide handle, feeding into cut with the top-slide handle. Do the other end same way; and if you haven't a slide-gauge with which to measure the correct overall width, just cut a gap $2\frac{15}{16}$ in. wide in a bit of sheet metal (bit of tin would do) and use that for a gauge. Both ends could, of course, be carefully hand-filed, and the try-square used to make certain the sides were at right-angles to the top and bottom.

To make the stay from $\frac{1}{8}$ in. sheet or plate, saw out a piece $3\frac{11}{16}$ in. long and $1\frac{1}{8}$ in. wide. Scribe a line across this, $\frac{1}{2}$ in. from each end; then put it in the bench vice with one of the lines just showing at the jaws, and hammer the projecting $\frac{1}{2}$ in. over to a right-angle. The $\frac{1}{8}$ in. thickness of metal forming the angles, will bring the overall width to $2\frac{15}{16}$ in., which is correct. File away $\frac{1}{8}$ in. at top and bottom, as shown in drawing.

In either cast or plate stay, find the centre; make a pop-mark, drill it first $\frac{1}{8}$ in., then open out with a $\frac{15}{32}$ in. drill and tap the hole $\frac{1}{2}$ in. by 32 T for the pump. Then place the stay between the frames, at the point where the three holes are drilled each side, the flanges overlapping the holes so that the screws will be central. The bottom of the stay should be $\frac{1}{16}$ in. above the bottom of frames, and the stay itself exactly vertical; test with the try-square. Then put the big clamp across the frames, to hold them tightly against the stay; run the No. 40 drill into the three holes each side, making countersinks on the stay. Follow up with No. 48 drill, tap $\frac{3}{32}$ in. or 7 BA, and put in countersunk screws to suit. That completes the frame erection, and the next job will be the axleboxes and springs, and the hornstays.

CHAPTER TWO

Building the running gear

Axleboxes

THE AXLEBOXES FOR *Tich* may be made from castings, from bar material or built up from bar and sheet. In the case of castings, the four will be cast in a stick; a piece of bar the same length, approximately 4 in. long, $\frac{3}{4}$ in. wide and $\frac{7}{16}$ in. thick, will also do quite well. Our suppliers will see that the metal in the castings will be of the right quality. Bar material should be good hard bronze or gunmetal; not soft brass, or the alloy frequently sold as brass and known in the trade as "screw-rod". Either of these would rapidly wear. Good tough brass would be satisfactory. The first item is to mill the rebates, as they are called; that is, the part which slides in the hornblock jaws. It will be noticed that these axleboxes have a single flange only, which is for two reasons; one, it is easier for beginners than making axleboxes with flanges both sides. Two, it automatically allows the boxes to tilt a little in the frames when following the " 'umps and 'ollers", as the p-way gang might say, of an uneven line, thus preventing running off the road.

If a regular milling machine is available, all that is needed is to put a side-and-face cutter on the arbor, set the piece of bar horizontally in the machine vice and traverse it under the cutter which will take out the rebate at one fell swoop; but milling machines are only just beginning to find their way into home workshops, so the lathe has to do the needful. There are two ways of doing the job on the lathe. The first is to copy the above procedure, putting a cutter not less than $\frac{3}{8}$ in. wide and about 2 in. diameter on an arbor or spindle between lathe centres. The piece of bar is held in a machine vice on the lathe saddle and traversed under the cutter by means of the cross-slide screw. Note—very important this—that the movement of the slide must be against the cutter teeth, otherwise the cutter will catch up and probably wrench the arbor from between the centres, damaging the lathe in the process. Either run the lathe in the usual direction and feed by pulling the cross-slide toward you, or run the lathe backwards and feed in the cross-slide in the usual way, according to which way the cutter is mounted on the arbor.

The work must be set in the machine vice at such a height that the cutter will take out the correct amount of metal. Here is where those who own an old 4 in. Drummond round-bed lathe will score, because the slotted table which forms the cross-slide may be raised and lowered, giving the facility of a regular milling machine. A simple form of vertical saddle adjustment would add enormously to the usefulness of certain much-advertised small lathes on the market.

Simple Tool-making

Did I hear some beginner say he had no machine vice and they were expensive? Well, don't let that worry you! It didn't worry young Curly, whose finances were nearly always at rock-bottom. Curly sawed two pieces of angle from the broken kitchen fender, and with a couple of long stove screws he had a nobby machine vice in very little time. Any convenient and available bits of angle and screws may be used; to bolt it down to the lathe saddle or cross-slide, simply drill holes as required in the horizontal members.

Somebody else has no milling cutters; they, too, are expensive. In that case, try another method. Make a slot drill, put it in your three-jaw chuck, mount the piece of bar on the slide-rest, clamp it down with the toolholder clamp, and traverse it across the slot drill. To make the slot drill or slotting cutter you need about 2 in. of round cast steel $\frac{7}{16}$ in. diameter. File away each side of this until it looks like a glorified screwdriver; then file a nick across the middle and back off each side of the nick. Use a fine file for this job. Then harden and temper the cutter. Heat to medium red and plunge into clean cold water. Brighten up the business end of the cutter with fine emery cloth, or similar abrasive, taking care not to destroy the cutting edges; then hold the shank end of the cutter in a blowlamp or gas flame. Watch the colours travel down the bright part, and as soon as the dark yellow reaches the cutting edges, drop the cutter into the cold water again. Give the cutting edges a rub on an oilstone and the cutter is ready for use. Personally, I prefer these home-made cutters to any commercial end-mill, as I find they cut faster, cleaner and much more freely. I made lots of them in the old days before I had a milling machine.

Another Method

The slot drill is another method which could be used. Put it in the three-jaw chuck and put the piece of bar under the slide-rest toolholder, packing up if necessary to allow the cutter to leave $\frac{1}{16}$ in. of the bar the full width. Then traverse the bar across the cutter by turning the cross-slide handle. Run the lathe at a good speed. An ordinary end-mill may, of course, be used instead of the home-made cutter. When one side is cut, reverse the piece of bar and cut the other side, but use a gauge to get the milled part the exact width. I use a spare hornblock, but an opening the exact width of the hornblock jaws, made in a piece of sheet metal, does just as well.

To set the piece of bar truly for the operation is simplicity itself. Take off the chuck and put on the faceplate. Run the slide-rest up to the faceplate and press the bit of bar against it whilst you tighten the clamp screws. If it won't reach, put your steel rule between the bar and faceplate; both sides of the rule being parallel, the effect is just the same as if bar and faceplate were in contact. When both sides of the bar are milled, either hold it in the four-jaw and part off four $\frac{7}{8}$ in. portions, or saw it up, chuck each piece separately and face off each end with a round-nose tool set crosswise in the rest, until each piece is exactly $\frac{7}{8}$ in. long.

Built-up Axleboxes

Axleboxes can also be made without any milling. Get a piece of bar 4 in. long $\frac{5}{8}$ in. wide and $\frac{3}{8}$ in. thick. Cut a strip of $\frac{1}{16}$ in. or 16 gauge sheet brass same length and approximately $\frac{7}{8}$ in. wide. Lay this in a tin lid, tray or pan of any kind available on top of a layer of small coke, breeze or cinders. Smear it over with a paste made from "Easyflo" flux and water or ordinary powdered borax and water, and put the piece of bar on top of it. Heat the whole to medium red with a blowlamp or blowpipe, then touch the joint with a strip of "Easyflo" or ordinary best-grade silver-solder. Only a very little is required; it will melt and flow into the joint. Let it cool to black, then drop it into a pickle made by adding one part of commercial sulphuric acid to about fifteen parts of water. Warning: don't on any account add the water to the acid; if you do, you'll either need to take quick advantage of the National Health Service or have to buy some more clothes or overalls, or both. After a few minutes in the pickle, fish out the piece, wash well in running water, clean up with a scratch brush or fine emery cloth and serve the bar as directed for the milled one. The side flanges can be filed to $\frac{1}{16}$ in. width.

How to Drill for Axles

Fit the axleboxes to the hornblocks and mark one side 1 and 2 and the other 3 and 4 on both horns and boxes, so you can always put them back correctly. Also mark which is the top. Now, on boxes 1 and 2, set out the position of the axle hole $\frac{3}{8}$ in. from the top and dead in the middle. Make a heavy centre-dot, then drill through the box with a $\frac{1}{8}$ in. or No. 30 drill. As the hole *must* go through squarely, use a drilling machine: if you haven't one, use the lathe. Put the drill in the chuck, take out the tailstock centre and, if you have a drilling pad, put it in and hold the axlebox against it with a pair of pliers, putting a true piece of wood between. Feed up by turning the handwheel. If you haven't any drilling pad, put the piece of wood against the end of the tailstock barrel.

As the axles must lie square across the frame use each axlebox as a guide to drill its opposite mate. Take No. 1 and No. 3 boxes and place them face to face; then put a piece of strip in the channel formed by the two flanges. Grip the lot in the machine vice, then drill the second box by putting the drill through the hole in the first one, using either drilling machine or lathe as described above. Then, even if the first box is very slightly "off-centre", the second one will be just the same, and the axle will still lie square across the frames. Serve No. 2 and No. 4 boxes in like manner and then open out all the holes with a $\frac{23}{64}$ in. drill, using drilling machine or lathe as before. Leave the reaming until the axleboxes are finally fitted to the frames.

Springs and Hornstays

Each axlebox has two springs housed in pockets drilled in the top; these are located $\frac{1}{8}$ in. from each end, $\frac{3}{16}$ in. from the narrower side, and are $\frac{3}{16}$ in. deep. Drill these pockets with a No. 20 drill, then with a $\frac{1}{16}$ in. or No. 52 drill, drill an oil hole from the bottom of each pocket into the axle hole.

The hornstays are $1\frac{3}{8}$ in. lengths of $\frac{3}{8}$ in. by $\frac{1}{16}$ in. strip steel, or they may be cut from $\frac{1}{16}$ in. sheet. Each one has two screwholes drilled with No. 34 drill located $\frac{5}{32}$ in. from each end and $\frac{5}{32}$ in. from one side. Put each hornstay in place, holding the frames upside down, with the screwholes on the side of the hornblock away from the frames. Run the No. 34 drill through the holes and make countersink marks in the feet or lugs of the hornblock; remove the hornstay, drill the marked pieces with No. 44 drill and tap 6 BA. Ordinary cheesehead screws may be used to attach the stays to the hornblocks, the bottom of the lugs being filed flush with the frame.

To make the springs, put a piece of $\frac{1}{8}$ in. round steel rod in the three-jaw. Take a length of 22 gauge tinned steel wire and bend about an inch or so at right-angles. Poke this between the chuck jaws, then carefully pull the lathe belt with your left hand, guiding on the wire with your right until three or four equally-spaced coils are wound on the rod. Then, if you press your thumb on them and continue to pull the belt steadily, a nice even spring will form on the rod. Cut off eight pieces about $\frac{5}{16}$ in. long and touch the ends on your emery wheel whilst it is running full speed—but mind your fingers! These springs are placed in the pockets and the axleboxes can then be erected as shown with the flanges outside the frames. See that each one is in its proper hornblock. Finally, poke a $\frac{3}{8}$ in. parallel reamer through each pair of boxes, using a tap wrench to turn it, and whilst turning, work the boxes up and down the hornblocks. This ensures that the axles will still be quite free when the engine runs over an uneven road. I have yet to see the small railway which is as level and even as a full-size line! Next stage, wheels and axles.

The Wheels

As the coupled wheels for *Tich* are only 2 in. diameter, they can be turned on practically any average home workshop lathe. They can easily be done even on a baby lathe of the "Adept" type, by rigging up a handle on the end of the mandrel. If you have nothing larger, and turn them thus, try to get a friend to act as "motor", so that you can concentrate on the actual turning. Some builders have managed to turn *Juliet* wheels on these tiny machines, using a handle, and going to work like a housewife or girl friend operating a

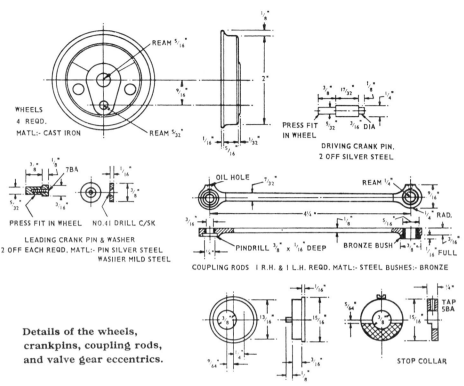

WHEELS
4 REQD.
MATL:- CAST IRON

REAM 5/16"

REAM 5/32"

2"

9/16"

1/8"

1/16" 5/16" 1/32"

PRESS FIT 5/32"
IN WHEEL

3/8" 17/32" 1/8"
1/4"
5/32" 3/16" DIA

DRIVING CRANK PIN.
2 OFF SILVER STEEL

7BA
3/8" 1/8"
5/32" 3/16"
3/16"
1/16"
3/8"

PRESS FIT IN WHEEL   NO.41 DRILL C/SK

LEADING CRANK PIN & WASHER
2 OFF EACH REQD. MATL:- PIN SILVER STEEL
WASHER MILD STEEL

OIL HOLE 7/32"

REAM 1/4"

9/16"

1/4" RAD.

3/16"

4 1/4"

5/16"

1/8"

PINDRILL 3/8" x 1/16" DEEP

BRONZE BUSH 3/8"

3/16"
1/16" FULL

1/4"

COUPLING RODS 1 R.H. & 1 L.H. REQD. MATL:- STEEL BUSHES:- BRONZE

Details of the wheels,
crankpins, coupling rods,
and valve gear eccentrics.

1/16"

3/8" 13/16"

15/16"

9/64" 4

3/16"

1/8"

5/64"

3/8" 15/16"

1/4"
TAP
5BA

STOP COLLAR

VALVE GEAR ECCENTRIC & STOP COLLAR (FOR INSIDE MOTION ONLY)

hand-driven sewing machine; but it is much better to "see what toucan do", as the Guinness advertisements put it.

Perhaps I had now better say a word about turning cast-iron. Well, first of all, you need slow and even speed to turn the wheels; not faster than fifty revolutions per minute, at the outside. A back-geared lathe is very nearly essential, if the drive is by motor or treadle. The only satisfactory alternative is a very large pulley on the lathe mandrel. Another thing very essential is a good turning tool, preferably of high-speed steel, though you don't use it at high speed. This kind of steel gets under the skin of a casting much better than ordinary carbon steel, and lasts much longer on one grinding. If you get tungsten-carbide tipped tools, such as "Wimet" or similar brands, you will really be in the clover. With a "Wimet" tool, I can turn a 5 in. driving wheel tread on my Milnes lathe in two cuts; one roughing and one finishing. Ordinary steel tools should have a fair amount of top rake, as the chippings come away much more easily.

The following method of machining wheel castings is one which I always use; it is fairly quick, easy, and what is more important, the wheels finish to exactly the same diameter without measuring each one. Coupled wheels *must* be the same diameter, otherwise one pair will be always slipping; and on a curve, where one side must of necessity slip a little, as the rails are of different lengths, you might have only one solitary wheel biting the railhead and taking the whole of the driving stress.

If there is any moulding-sand sticking to the castings, brush it off with a wire brush; then chuck the wheel in the three-jaw, back outwards, gripping by the tread in the outside jaws of the chuck. Set it so that the back runs as truly as possible, and leave the flange clear of the jaws; just far enough away to allow the point of the turning tool to pass. Now put your tailstock chuck in the tailstock barrel, with a size A or B centre-drill in it. A tailstock chuck, which is just a small drill chuck with a taper shank to fit the tailstock barrel, is one of the most useful accessories one could have for any lathe. The most convenient size to get is one taking from 0 to $\frac{3}{8}$ in. Run up the tailstock to the job, lock it to the bed by whatever means is provided on the lathe, then feed the centre-drill into the boss of the wheel, until it has penetrated to the end of the countersink; that is, full diameter of the centre-drill. For this job, and the drilling and reaming to follow, run the lathe quite fast, with the belt on the smallest pulley, and feed the drills with the wheel or handle on the tailstock barrel.

Next, put a $\frac{19}{64}$ in. drill in the tailstock chuck, and drill clean through the wheel boss. After that, put a $\frac{5}{16}$ in. parallel reamer in the chuck; and this time, instead of using the handwheel or handle, slack the tailstock locking nut, grip the tailstock bodily with both hands, and slide it along the bed, so that the reamer enters the hole to the full depth of the flutes. Then with the lathe still running the same way, pull it out again by sliding the tailstock back. You now have a hole truly in the middle, and dead to size required.

Put a round-nose tool crosswise in the slide-rest; then, with the lathe running at medium speed, face off the boss, starting with the tool in the reamed hole, and feeding toward you. Take a cut deep enough to clean the hard skin on the casting right off; if the cutting edge of the tool rubs on this hard skin, it is goodbye to the edge right away, and the tool will need re-grinding before you do any more.

Now put the back gear in, if the lathe has one; if not, put the belt on the lowest speed; using the same tool, bring it back to the rim of the wheel, and take a cut right across back of rim and flange, still feeding toward you, and getting under the skin of the casting. When you have cleaned it up, take a finishing cut at a little higher speed, right across the back of rim and flange, and boss as well, at the same setting of the tool, as rim and boss are flush at the back. Finally, turn the tool around and reset it at right-angles to the lathe bed; then take a cleaning-up cut over the edge of the flange, just sufficient to clean all the skin off. Mind you don't let the tool run into the revolving chuck jaws, otherwise the tool, chuck, and even the machine itself might suffer serious damage.

Give the other three wheels a dose of the same medicine; then reverse one of them in the chuck, gripping by the flange, and letting the turned back rest up hard against the chuck jaws. Now, with the tool set crosswise in the rest

Plate 3

A "Tich" chassis built by Mr. G. F. Collins of Brighton

Below: Mrs. Ruth Daltry's "Tich" chassis

Near side of Mr. Collins' "Tich" chassis

Plate 4

Bolting up the cylinders to the frames on a small-boilered "Tich"

Below: Mrs. Ruth Daltry's "Tich" chassis, with a partly-built "Juliet" to the rear

again, face off the boss until the distance from the back to the face of the boss is $\frac{13}{32}$ in. The easiest way for a beginner to gauge this is to cut a strip of metal bar $\frac{5}{16}$ in. wide, which will just fit the reamed hole, and file a notch in it $\frac{13}{32}$ in. long. Face off the boss until, when the gauge is put in the hole, the notch just goes over the thickness, and the job is complete. Young Curly used to make all sorts of "patent" gauges—you'd have laughed to see some of them, especially bent wire "calipers", but they all worked fine. I made two nobby pairs of adjustable calipers by filing up the legs from bits cut out of the discarded broken kitchen fender (the bottom plate of this was good steel of about 18 gauge) with two of the screws and nuts for pivots. There wasn't much of the old fender left when I had done with it; the material it provided was of untold value to a poor kid who had to earn every copper.

Next, on the slow speed again, face off the rim, until the thickness of the wheel is $\frac{3}{8}$ in. overall. This can be gauged, either by a home-made one as mentioned above, or else by an ordinary slide-gauge, the jaws of which are previously set $\frac{3}{8}$ in. apart, as indicated by the scale. Face off all four wheels thus; then, when the last one is still in the chuck, take out the round-nose tool, and put in a parting-tool. With this, still on low speed, cut a tiny rebate about $\frac{1}{16}$ in. wide and deep, at the inner edge of the rim, where the spokes would join the rim if the wheel had any spokes. This indicates the joint between the wheel and tyre.

Turning the Treads

The treads and flanges of the wheels are turned by mounting each wheel on an improvised faceplate. Anything circular, a little under 2 in. diameter, will do fine for this; an iron disc, a discarded or spoilt wheel casting, an old chuck back, or anything similar. Chuck this in the three-jaw, and set it to run as truly as possible; then centre and drill it, exactly as described for drilling the wheels, but use a drill to suit whatever $\frac{3}{8}$ in. tap you may possess. This would be $\frac{19}{64}$ in. for $\frac{3}{8}$ in. Whitworth thread, $\frac{5}{16}$ in. for $\frac{3}{8}$ in. by 26 and so on. Then put a $\frac{3}{8}$ in. tap in the tailstock chuck, and tighten it well; use a taper tap for preference. Run up the tailstock so that the tap enters the hole as far as it will go; then pull the belt with your left hand, and push the tailstock towards the chuck with your right. The tap will then start to cut a true thread in the hole; and by working the mandrel back and forth, by pulling first one side of the belt and then the other, you can get the tap to enter to its full depth. Note: cast-iron is drilled and tapped dry; wrought iron or steel should be lubricated with cutting oil diluted with paraffin.

Next, with a round-nose tool set crosswise in the rest, face off the old wheel, disc or whatever it is you are using, exactly the same as the wheels were faced, starting from centre, and working outwards, running the lathe at slow speed. When faced truly all over, face out the centre, just $\frac{1}{32}$ in. more, to a diameter of 1 in., so as to leave a little recess that size in the middle.

We now need a peg on which to mount the wheels; so take a piece of $\frac{3}{8}$ in.

round mild steel, put it in the bench vice, and screw it down for about $\frac{1}{2}$ in. length, to the same pitch thread as the hole in the disc. This can be done with the stocks and dies in the usual way, a job so simple that it needs no describing; but a better way still, for a raw recruit or a very inexperienced worker, would be to get a $\frac{3}{8}$ in. bolt about $1\frac{1}{2}$ in. long, or longer would do, provided that the threaded part is not more than about 1 in. long. Saw off either the piece of screwed rod, or the bolt, as the case may be, at $\frac{3}{4}$ in. from the end of the threads, and screw it as tightly as possible into the hole in the disc or wheel forming the improvised faceplate. Using a knife-tool, set in the rest so that it inclines a little toward the lathe mandrel, carefully turn the peg until the wheels will just slide on to it without shake; then screw the end $\frac{5}{16}$ in. by 32 (or any other fine thread for which you may have a die and tap) leaving about $\frac{5}{16}$ in. of the peg plain. The screwing should be done with a die in the tailstock holder.

Most commercial tailstock die-holders have a taper shank, to fit in the hole in the tailstock barrel, but I prefer a parallel shank which can be held in the tailstock chuck, as it is quicker. My Boley lathe has a lever-operated tailstock, in addition to the ordinary screw pattern, and this has had a $\frac{3}{8}$ in. Jacobs-type chuck attached to it for so long that I forget when it last came off! I use this lathe for making all my boiler fittings, and other blobs and gadgets needing screwing and tapping, and the chuck has a sort of season-ticket on that job If you have no tailstock die-holder, purchase or make one at the earliest opportunity; I made one of mine from a discarded cast-iron valve guide off a Tilling-Stevens bus engine, with a bit of a valve spindle for the stem—a bit of improvisation inherited from my childhood days. Meanwhile, the peg could be screwed by aid of the ordinary die-stock, same being applied carefully, and held as squarely as possible, whilst the lathe belt is pulled by hand.

You will need a nut to fit the peg; well, get an ordinary $\frac{1}{4}$ in. nut, any thread, run a $\frac{1}{4}$ in. drill through it to clean the old thread out, and re-tap it to suit the threads on the peg.

Don't remove the disc or old wheel "faceplate" under any circumstances after facing it truly, but put a wheel on the peg, boss outwards, and tighten the nut. The friction between the back of the rim against the "faceplate", will be quite sufficient to drive the wheel around against the cutting tool. Use a round-nose tool with a rather pointed end. Running the lathe at slow speed, first turn the flange to $2\frac{1}{4}$ in. diameter. If the cross-slide has a "mike" collar, note the reading, and when turning the other three wheels, set it at the same number. If no collar, note the position of the handle, and turn the other flanges with the handle in the same position. Then carefully turn the tread to a shade over 2 in. diameter, again noting position of cross-slide collar or handle. The shape of the tool will attend to the contour of the flange; keep turning until the edge of the flange is $\frac{1}{16}$ in. wide.

Treat the other three wheels in precisely the same manner; then, after the last one has been roughed out, take out the tool and re-grind it, or if it is not too bad (good grey cast-iron doesn't spoil the tool very much) maybe a few rubs on the oilstone will restore the keen edge. Replace it, and turn the last few thousandths off the wheel tread, to bring it to size. If it is a shade over, or under, it doesn't matter a bean, as the rest will be exactly the same. Now, don't shift the cross-slide handle—very important, that!—just run the top-slide back, and take off the wheel. Replace it by No. 2, taking the finishing skim off that, ditto Nos. 3 and 4. As all four wheels are finished without shifting the cross-slide, they must of necessity all be exactly the same diameter on the tread.

After each one is turned, apply an old smooth file to the sharp edge of the tread, with the lathe still running, and hold it there until it has formed a little bevel or chamfer. Then apply it to the flange, rounding this off, as shown in the side view of the wheel. This point is very often entirely neglected, even among professional builders; not so long ago, I saw a $3\frac{1}{2}$ in. gauge 4-6-0, costing well into a three-figure price, on which the flanges had been left with sharp edges, and had cut grooves in the boiler barrel and firebox wrapper. As the engine "bounced" on a road with undulations and bad joints, the excessive axlebox movement had enabled the flanges to touch the boiler.

It will be noticed that I have said nothing about tapering or coning the treads; they are left parallel. I have long since found out that it enables the engine to run more freely on curves, if the treads are parallel or cylindrical, especially in the case of a locomotive having six or more rigid wheels. All the Stroudley engines of the L.B. & S.C. Ry. had cylindrical treads to the driving wheels; and Sir William Stanier, when C.M.E. of the L.M.S., conducted a series of tests which proved very conclusively that the old idea of a 1 in 20 taper was a myth, after which the wheels of the engines were given just the weeniest bit of taper, merely sufficient to keep the flanges from rubbing on one side or the other, when the engine was on a straight line. On our little engine, the radius at the root of the flange serves the same purpose.

Beginners should now know how to turn wheels, and the knowledge will come in useful for future jobs, as all kinds of wheels, bogie, pony, radial, tender, carriage and wagon wheels, may all be machined in similar manner. Don't on any account attempt to polish, or otherwise put a posh finish, on wheel treads; just leave them as finished by the tool. The slight roughness of the turned surfaces, affords the driving wheels a much better grip on the railheads; anyway, they wear smooth quickly enough, as they adapt themselves to the railheads in a very short time.

Drilling for Crankpins

It is imperative that the holes for the crankpins carrying the coupling rods should all be drilled exactly the same distance from the centre of the axle hole, otherwise the rods will bind, unless the holes in the coupling rod bushes are drilled so large as to be "sloppy". Like everything else, the job is dead easy when you know how; all that is needed is a simple drilling jig made in a few minutes. Get a piece of steel bar, say of $\frac{1}{2}$ in. by $\frac{1}{4}$ in. section, and about $1\frac{1}{4}$ in. long. Scribe a line down the centre of this; and on the line, set out two points

$\frac{9}{16}$ in. apart. Make a heavy centre-pop on each. Drill them both with $\frac{5}{32}$ in. drill, as described for drilling axleboxes, using either lathe or drilling machine; hand-drilling won't be true enough. Open out one of the holes with a $\frac{19}{64}$ in. or letter N drill. Next, chuck a piece of $\frac{5}{16}$ in. round steel rod in the three-jaw, and take a weeny skim off it with a round-nose tool, so that it just goes into the reamed holes in the wheel bosses. Part off at about $\frac{5}{8}$ in. from the end. Re-chuck this in the three-jaw, and turn down $\frac{1}{4}$ in. of the end until it will almost, but not quite, push into the larger hole in the piece of bar. With the lathe running fast, ease the end with a file, until it will just enter the hole for about $\frac{1}{16}$ in.; then remove from chuck, and squeeze it into the hole, using the bench vice as a press. The jig is then ready for use.

Scribe a line down the centre of each wheel boss. Insert the peg in the jig, into the hole in the boss, and adjust it so that you can see the scribed line passing across the bottom of the $\frac{5}{32}$ in. hole in the jig. Clamp the jig in this position, by aid of a toolmaker's clamp; then poke the $\frac{5}{32}$ in. drill down the hole in the jig, and drill right through the wheel boss. Repeat operation on the other wheels, and all the small holes can't help being exactly the same distance from the big ones. Use either a drilling machine, or the lathe, as before, because the crankpin holes must be dead square with the wheels; otherwise you'll never get the connecting and coupling rods to fit properly.

Crankpins

The best material for the crankpins is silver-steel. The "natural" finish on commercial ground silver-steel enables pins made from it to run with a minimum of friction, and they resist wear to an extraordinary degree; especially if running in correctly-reamed bronze bushes. To make the leading wheel crankpin of *Tich*, chuck a piece of $\frac{3}{16}$ in. round silver-steel truly in the three-jaw. If the chuck doesn't hold truly of its own accord, put a piece of thin foil, or even paper, between the steel and the offending jaw. Alternatively, you can use a split bush, which is equivalent in many respects to a collet chuck, and can be used an indefinite number of times. To make it, chuck a piece of $\frac{3}{8}$ in. round brass rod about $\frac{1}{2}$ in. long, in the three-jaw. Face the end, centre, drill it with an $\frac{11}{64}$ in. or No. 16 drill, and ream it $\frac{3}{16}$ in. by exactly the same process as described above, for drilling and reaming the whole bosses. Make a centre-dot on it, opposite No. 1 chuck jaw. Remove from chuck, and split it down one side with a fine hacksaw. Replace with dot opposite No. 1 jaw in its original position; don't screw up the chuck jaws too tightly, but only enough to prevent it turning when the reamer is run through again to clean out any burr left by the saw. If the silver-steel is placed in the bush, and the chuck jaws tightened, the bush will grip the rod and hold it quite truly for turning.

With a knife-tool in the slide-rest, turn down $\frac{3}{8}$ in. length to a diameter of $\frac{5}{32}$ in. which should be a tight press fit in the hole in the wheel boss. Now I've tried many ways of making this a soft job for any beginner, and I fancy the following is the best. With a $\frac{5}{32}$ in. taper broach (you can get one at any tool stores) fixed in a small file or bradawl handle, broach the hole in the face of the boss, just the weeniest bit. Just take the merest scrape out of it, which will extend about $\frac{1}{8}$ in. into the hole. Now very carefully turn the spigot until it will just enter the broached part of the hole; it will then be a tight press fit for the rest.

Part off the steel at $\frac{1}{8}$ in. full from the shoulder; reverse, and grip in chuck by the turned part. Centre, and drill through with No. 48 drill; tap $\frac{3}{32}$ in. or 7 BA, guiding the tap by aid of tailstock chuck thus. Put a tap wrench on the tap shank close to the threads; put the shank in the tailstock chuck, and close the jaws just tight enough to allow the tap to slide. Run the tailstock up to the job, enter the tap in the hole, and work the lathe belt back and forth by left hand, whilst you hold the tap wrench with your right. Use cutting oil for turning, drilling and tapping. If the tap shows signs of jamming, withdraw it and brush off all chippings. Choked flutes break taps.

For the washer, just chuck a piece of $\frac{3}{8}$ in. round mild steel in three-jaw, and take a $\frac{1}{16}$ in. skim off it. Centre-drill down about $\frac{3}{8}$ in. with No. 41 drill; countersink the hole with $\frac{5}{32}$ in. or No. 20 drill, and part off a $\frac{1}{16}$ in. slice. Repeat countersink and parting for second washer.

For the driving crankpins, chuck a piece of $\frac{1}{4}$ in. round silver-steel making a $\frac{1}{4}$ in. split bush if necessary, to hold it truly. Turn a $\frac{3}{8}$ in. by $\frac{5}{32}$ in. spigot as above, then part off at a bare $\frac{11}{16}$ in. from the shoulder. Reverse in chuck, face the end, and turn down $\frac{1}{8}$ in. length to $\frac{3}{16}$ in. diameter, using a piece of steel with a $\frac{3}{16}$ in. hole in it, for a gauge. The hole in this should be drilled No. 14, and reamed; and the turned pip on the end of the pin should fit it very tightly.

The spigots can then be pressed home in the wheels by using the bench vice as a press. Warning: don't overdo the "Sunny Jim", if the spigots are extra tight, ease them with a file very slightly, otherwise you will split the wheel bosses. Next stage, axles and erection.

Axles

The next job is a simple bit of plain turning; but for raw recruits, it involves a lesson in accuracy, as the ends of the axles must be a press fit in the wheel bosses. They must not be too tight, or the said bosses will split; whilst if the least bit slack, they will shift in the bosses under heavy turning strain, and jam up the whole works. Two pieces of $\frac{3}{8}$ in. round mild steel rod are needed $4\frac{1}{8}$ in. long. Chuck truly in three-jaw, with about 1 in. projecting. If the chuck is slightly out of true, as most of the cheaper kind are, put a piece of foil, or even paper, between the offending jaw and the rod. To test, simply run up the slide-rest to the work, with a knife-tool in the holder, and pull the belt by hand. If the tool makes a faint scratch completely round the rod, it is set truly. If not, the side that isn't scratched, shows which way the adjustment must be made, to bring the rod O.K.

Use a knife-tool with the extreme sharp point taken off by a rub on an oil-stone; this prevents the wheel seat being left scratchy. Face off the end of the rod, then set your slide-gauge or calipers to $\frac{21}{64}$ in. and turn down $\frac{13}{32}$ in. length until the gauge or calipers just slips over. Next, if you have a $\frac{5}{16}$ in. taper reamer, enter it into the hole in the wheel boss, from the back, and take the merest scrape off the end of the hole, just a thousandth or so. If you haven't the reamer, you can take a scrape out of the end of the hole with a scraper; only the tiniest bit, to give the end of the axle a start. Now carefully turn down the end of the axle, until it will just enter the slightly enlarged end of the hole; it should then be a press fit for the rest of the hole.

An alternative way is to turn the end of the axle until it just won't go into a boss which has not been slightly reamed or scraped. That sounds like Pat's way of giving instructions; but when you come to do it, you'll get my meaning easily enough. Then with a smooth file, ease the turned part until you can push it very tightly about halfway. The lathe should be run fast for this job; and the wheel, of course, used for a gauge. The distance between shoulders is $3\frac{9}{32}$ in.

If you haven't a three-jaw chuck, or one which is badly worn or very inaccurate, turn the axles between centres. For this job you need two pieces of round steel same length, but of slightly larger diameter, say $\frac{7}{16}$ in. or $\frac{1}{2}$ in. It doesn't matter about the chuck being wibbly-wobbly for making the centre holes; just grip the bits of steel in it, and centre each end with a centre-drill in the tailstock chuck, same as for the wheels. Put the centre points in mandrel and tailstock, and mount one of the pieces of steel between them, with a carrier on the headstock end. Turn the other end to a press fit in the wheel boss, as described above; then reverse the piece of rod between centres, putting the carrier on the reduced part. Turn down the other end to correct diameter, as above; then turn the centre part to $\frac{3}{8}$ in. diameter. The axles will then be true with the wheel seats. For the centre part use a round-nose tool, and plenty of cutting oil. When operating the lathe, don't stand in line with the revolving carrier, or you will get well and truly splashed, as the excess cutting oil runs along the axle, and the carrier throws it off.

Press one wheel on each axle, same way as you pressed in the crankpins. Put a bit of soft sheet metal between the vice jaws, wheel, and end of axle. If your vice is small, don't forget you can increase its capacity by taking out the steel insets of the jaws, If the vice jaws won't open wide enough even then, a wheel press can be improvised by two pieces of bar, with a bolt at each end. The bottom bar is held in the bench vice, level with the tops of the jaws, and the wheel is placed on it, with the axle held vertically over the hole in the boss. The top bar is then placed on top of the axle, with a piece of soft metal between the bar and the end of the axle; alternatively, a hole can be drilled halfway through the top bar, and the end of the axle placed in it. Then screw the nuts on the bolts until they just touch the bar, using finger pressure only; put a spanner on each nut, and screw down both nuts together, turning the spanners exactly in unison. That will do the trick all right.

As a last resource, the axle could be driven into the wheel, using a lead or copper hammer, but I don't recommend it. It is more liable to split the boss than a "squeeze"; also there is a risk of slightly bending the axle. Incidentally, in the days of the *Rocket*, when there were no hydraulic presses, wheels were driven on to axles by aid of sledge-hammers operated by hefty specimens of manhood with muscles of the "village blacksmith" type—something you couldn't develop on the meat rations we had in 1947-49! Warning—whichever method you adopt, if the axle doesn't want to go into the wheel, don't force it too much, or the boss will split. Take it out again and ease it slightly. Castings are expensive, and time is valuable!

Pump Eccentric

Before pressing on the second wheel, the pump eccentric must be fitted to the driving axle. Builders who are intending to fit loose-eccentric valve gear, will also have to fit the eccentrics and stop collars to the driving axle. I strongly recommend the loose-eccentric gear to all beginners who are hazy on valve gear subjects, for two reasons. First, it is so simple to understand, and so easy to make and erect, that the veriest Billy Muggins is assured of economical and efficient working of his engine; secondly, it is the only valve gear that gives equal port-openings at each end of the cylinder in both directions, plus absolutely correct timing.

The wheelbase of the engine being so short, she will run on a continuous line in the limits of the average suburban back garden, so that there is no need for constant reversing. The valves may be set with a fixed early cut-off, combining easy starting with reasonable expansion, speed being controlled entirely by the regulator. The parts can be made much more robust than the Walschaerts' gear without being clumsy and unsightly, so that the gear has a much longer working life, besides retaining accurate setting.

A piece of 1 in. round steel rod will be needed for the pump eccentric; a stub end of mild steel shafting is about the best material. Chuck it in the three-jaw chuck, face off the end, and then turn about $\frac{5}{8}$ in. length to $\frac{15}{16}$ in. diameter, using a round-nosed tool. Now with a parting tool, form a groove $\frac{1}{16}$ in. deep and $\frac{3}{16}$ in. wide, starting at $\frac{1}{16}$ in. from the end. Anybody who has a lathe with plenty of "meat" in it, and a good solidly-built headstock, won't have the slightest difficulty in turning a perfect groove, but the majority of small lathes, even the much advertised types, will probably chatter like nobody's business, leaving the metal at the bottom of the groove looking like the waves of the Danube. Well, don't worry. Just pull the belt very slowly by hand, feeding in with a very light cut, and slapping on a good dose of cutting oil. This treatment will soon lop off the crests of the waves, and leaves a smooth shiny surface. The parting tool should be about $\frac{3}{32}$ in. wide, and you can take three overlapping cuts to obtain the full width. The wider the parting tool, the greater the tendency for it to chatter. When turning eccentrics on my Milnes lathe, there isn't a vestige of chatter; the turnings come off in the form of a closely-coiled watch-spring, with a sound just like frying bacon, though the smell of the cutting oil isn't quite as appetising. The tool leaves a perfectly smooth surface; I grind it with plenty of top rake. Incidentally, the **front** bearing of the mandrel is $2\frac{1}{2}$ in. diameter.

Having obtained a smooth groove, part off at $\frac{1}{2}$ in. from the end. Now if you take a look at the faced end, you'll see that the tool has left a mark indicating the true centre; scribe a line through the centre, cutting right across the end, and on this line, at $\frac{3}{16}$ in. from the true centre, make a heavy centre-dot. This will be the "eccentric centre", as our Hibernian friend would remark. Chuck in four-jaw and adjust until this centre-pop runs truly. Leave about $\frac{1}{4}$ in. projecting from chuck jaws; then open out the centre-pop with a centre-drill (size E for preference), drill a $\frac{1}{8}$ in. or No. 30 pilot hole right through, open out again with $\frac{23}{64}$ in. or letter T drill, and ream $\frac{3}{8}$ in. to be a good fit on the axle. Beginners note, that drilling a pilot hole first, usually prevents the bigger drill making a hole larger than its diameter, especially when the drill has been ground by somebody who has had no previous experience.

Put a short piece of rod, any diameter over $\frac{3}{8}$ in., in the three-jaw and turn about $\frac{1}{2}$ in. of it to a tight drive fit in the hole in the embryo eccentric; squeeze this into the hole, same way as the crankpins were pressed into the wheels, entering it on the grooved side. Chuck the projecting rod in the three-jaw. When the lathe starts running, the eccentric will commence to "tumble" (many enginemen call eccentrics "tumbling blocks" or just "tumblers"). Face off the end; then very carefully turn $\frac{3}{16}$ in. length to $\frac{9}{16}$ in. diameter, that is, flush with the edge of the flange. Use a knife-tool, and be careful when feeding in, as the cut is intermittent, on account of the eccentric bobbing up and down. Drive the spindle out of the eccentric, and drill a No. 40 hole in the newly-turned boss, tapping it $\frac{1}{8}$ in. or 5 BA. The eccentric should now fit fairly tight on the axle.

Valve Eccentrics for Inside Motion

If loose eccentric gear is being used, the valve eccentrics are turned next, and they are easier than the pump eccentrics, as they have only one flange, and no bosses. Chuck a piece of 1 in. round steel rod in the three-jaw, and face the end as before, but this time, turn down $\frac{3}{16}$ in. length to $\frac{13}{16}$ in. diameter with a knife-tool, and have the surface as smooth as possible. Turn down about $\frac{1}{2}$ in. length to $\frac{15}{16}$ in. diameter (size over eccentric flanges) then part off $\frac{1}{4}$ in. from the end; this will leave $\frac{1}{16}$ in. flange. Repeat operation for second eccentric, and then hold them in turn by the $\frac{13}{16}$ in. part whilst you take a finishing skim off the flange side, Some parting tools leave a rough surface; it all depends on the way they have been ground.

The true centre will be marked on the flanged side, as before; so scribe a line right across it. On one side of the centre, make a centre-pop $\frac{9}{64}$ in. away, and on the other side, make another $\frac{1}{4}$ in. away. Chuck the eccentric in the four-jaw, holding by the $\frac{13}{16}$ in. part and set the $\frac{9}{64}$ in. pop-mark to run truly. Open out with a centre-drill, then with $\frac{1}{8}$ in. or No. 30, follow up with $\frac{23}{64}$ in. or letter T drill, and finally put a $\frac{3}{8}$ in. parallel reamer through. Note that these eccentrics must be free on the axle, but without shake. Before taking the eccentrics out of the chuck, try one of the axles in the hole; if it does not push in easily, put the reamer through again, with a piece of wire in one of the flutes, just large enough in diameter to make the reamer tight at the leading end. This dodge will cause the reamer to cut a hole that is slightly oversize, and the axle should then fit easily.

Drill a hole with a No. 32 drill, right through the eccentric, at a point $\frac{1}{4}$ in. from centre. This hole should be drilled either on a machine, or in the lathe, in the same manner as described for axleboxes. Put a short piece of $\frac{1}{8}$ in. round silver-steel in the three-jaw, and apply a file at the end, whilst the lathe is running fast, to reduce the diameter sufficiently to allow it to enter the No. 32 hole, then drive it into the eccentric on the side opposite the flange, cut it off $\frac{1}{8}$ in. from the surface, and smooth the end with a file. Serve the second eccentric in like manner.

Stop Collars

A stop collar is fixed to the axle next to each eccentric. This is a wide collar or boss, with part of one side cut away, leaving two shoulders, which catch against the stop pin in the eccentric, and drive it around, according to the direction in which the engine is desired to travel. Any beginner or raw tyro who does not understand the first principles of steam distribution—we were all in the same boat, at one time!—will readily grasp the whole sequence of events later on, when I describe the erection and setting of the valve gear. Meanwhile, follow instructions carefully. The stop collars may be either brass or steel. Chuck a piece of 1 in. round rod in three-jaw, and turn down about $\frac{3}{4}$ in. length to $\frac{15}{16}$ in. diameter. Face off the end, centre and drill down about $\frac{3}{4}$ in. depth, first with a $\frac{1}{8}$ in. drill then with $\frac{23}{64}$ in. or letter T drill. Part off two $\frac{1}{4}$ in. slices; but after parting off the first one, take a skim off the end of the rod, to make sure it is absolutely true, before parting off the second one. On the faced sides of these two collars, scribe a line exactly across the middle, and then another one $\frac{5}{64}$ in. below it. Half of the collar then has to be cut away to this line.

The best way to do this is to mill it, either on a regular machine if available, or else in the lathe, exactly as described in one method of milling axleboxes, viz. with the collar held in a machine vice bolted to the lathe saddle, the cutter being mounted on an arbor or spindle between the lathe centres. The surplus metal could also be cut away in a planing or shaping machine, the collar being gripped in a machine vice on the planer table, or on the cross-slide of the shaper. A straight-edged tool in the clapper box would soon remove the necessary metal, and leave the shoulders exactly on the marked line, to engage the stop in the eccentric.

The metal may also be removed by sawing and filing. First of all, saw straight across the collar, and halfway through it, just below the marked line, then carefully saw down the middle of the thickness, to meet the cross saw-cut, when the piece should fall out. Smooth out the saw marks with a flat smooth file, and be careful to file exactly to the marked line, also to have the surface at right-angles. In the thick part of the collar, drill a No. 40 hole from the edge to the hole in the centre, and tap it ⅛ in. or 5 BA. The latter is preferable, as the finer-pitch threads give the screw a tighter grip without increasing the pressure on them.

Quartering the Wheels

This is a job that sometimes puzzles a beginner, but it is easily and simply done. First of all, put the wheels in place in the frame. Poke the driving axle through one of the rear axleboxes—doesn't matter which side of the frame— then mount the blobs and gadgets on it in the following order. First, a valve eccentric, flanged side first. Second, a stop collar, with the cut-away next to the eccentric. Third, the pump eccentric, boss first or last, as you like. Fourth, a stop collar, plain side first. Fifth and last, the other eccentric, with the pin first, pointing to the cut-away in the stop collar. Then push the axle through the other axiebox, and put the wheel on as far as it will go by hand pressure, setting the cranks at right-angles, as near as you can "by eye". If you are going to use the outside valve gear, there will only be the pump eccentric to go on the axle. Push the leading axle through the axleboxes, and put that wheel on likewise; don't forget that the short crankpin is the leader.

On this engine, the right-hand crank leads; that is, the left-hand crank is right at the highest point, when the right-hand one is in the forward horizontal position. I might here remind raw beginners that the right-hand side of the engine is to the driver's right-hand when he is standing on the footplate and looking towards the chimney. To set the cranks at the exact right-angle, all you need is your try-square and scribing block (or surface gauge, to give it the posh title). Stand the engine on something flat, such as the lathe bed. Set the try-square with the stock on the flat surface, and adjust the wheels until the edge of the blade passes exactly over the centres of the axle and crankpin. Now set your scribing-block needle to the centre of the axle on the other side, and adjust the wheel on the axle, until the centre of the crankpin is exactly the same height, the needle pointing to the centre of the pin. The setting is O.K. when both these conditions obtain at the same time; have a good look at each side, without touching anything, to make certain it is so, and then the wheel can be squeezed right home. I have read much about making special jigs, fixtures and what-have-you, to get this quartering right; there is nothing against any of them, as they all do the job, but for my own part, I always use the method described above, and it never fails. Next items will be the coupling rods, and the boiler feed pump, the pump being easier to erect if fitted before the motion work.

CHAPTER THREE

Coupling rods and feed pump

Coupling Rods

THE COUPLING RODS FOR *Tich* are cut from steel bar $\frac{3}{16}$ in. thick and $\frac{9}{16}$ in. or $\frac{5}{8}$ in. wide, two pieces $4\frac{7}{8}$ in. long being needed. Mark out one of them to the outline shown; but before centre-popping to drill the crankpin holes, check off the axle centres on your own chassis. If they are $4\frac{1}{4}$ in. apart, all serene; but if not, mark the centres of your coupling rods to correspond, otherwise they will bind at certain parts of the revolution. Drill a $\frac{1}{8}$ in. hole at each centre-pop, then use the drilled rod as a jig to drill the second one. Rivet temporarily together with bits of $\frac{1}{8}$ in. wire, so that both rods can be operated on at once, if they are to be milled.

Anybody owning a milling machine, can clamp the bits of rod in the machine vice on the table, and traverse them under a small slabbing cutter, not less than $\frac{1}{2}$ in. wide, feeding into cut by raising the table. If the machine is in-clined to be flimsy, and the cutter chatters, take two or more cuts. Use plenty of cutting oil. The front faces are recessed by screwing the rods to a bit of steel bar, anything over $\frac{5}{8}$ in. square, held in the machine vice. This allows the cutter to do its job without causing the rods to spring. However, milling machines being scarce in home workshops, the lathe can be used, or even the common but useful hacksaw.

For hand-sawing, clamp the piece of bar in the bench vice, with the marked line level with top of jaws. File a slot at the end; just wide enough to let the hacksaw blade pass. Put a blade on its side in the hacksaw frame, insert in slot, and saw along, using top of vice jaws as guide. Slap on some cutting oil with a brush; it makes sawing easier, the blade lasts longer, and the cut comes out nice and straight. Saw down to meet the horizontal cut, when you reach the boss. Cut the bottom bit out in like manner, then finish with a file. Be careful when rounding off the bosses.

The bulk of the unwanted metal can be turned off, by mounting the piece of bar between centres, with a carrier on one end. This method leaves the centre part of the rod rounded at top and bottom, and it has to be finished off with a file; but the method saves a lot of "donkey work". A simple

43

jig can be made, to obtain nicely-rounded bosses. Chuck a bit of $\frac{1}{2}$ in. round silver-steel in the three-jaw, turn a pip on the end to fit the holes in the bosses, and a bare $\frac{3}{32}$ in. long. Part off at $\frac{1}{4}$ in. from the end, and repeat operation. Harden the two pieces right out, by heating to red and dropping into water. Put one at each side of the boss, with the pips in the holes; grip the lot in the bench vice, and file away the superfluous metal projecting beyond the "buttons"—but don't file away the bit which stands out at the top and represents the oil box on a full-size rod!

Open out the hole at the front end of each rod with a $\frac{3}{8}$ in. pin-drill to a depth of $\frac{1}{16}$ in. The pin-drill you can make as easily as the slotting cutter: in fact, it is the same thing plus a pin where the nick was filed. Chuck a bit of $\frac{3}{8}$ in. round silver-steel in the three-jaw; face the end, centre, and drill down with a No. 32 drill for about $\frac{1}{4}$ in. depth. Now proceed exactly as described for the slotting cutter, filing away the sides, backing off, hardening and tempering. Put a bit of $\frac{1}{8}$ in. round silver-steel, $\frac{1}{2}$ in. long in your three-jaw; and with the lathe running as fast as possible without rocking the workshop, ease the end very slightly with a file, for about $\frac{1}{4}$ in. length, so it will just push tightly into the hole in the cutter. Press it in, and there is your pin-drill. Use it the same as an ordinary drill, lubricate with cutting oil, and don't run it too fast. Put something with a hole in it, either under the coupling rod boss, if you are using a drilling machine, or between it and the tailstock drilling-pad, if using the lathe. Mind the drill doesn't penetrate too far; $\frac{1}{16}$ in. is plenty.

Put a $\frac{1}{4}$ in. drill through the hole at the opposite end, and a $\frac{3}{16}$ in. drill through the pin-drilled one, and try the rods on the crankpins. The wheels should turn without the least sign of binding anywhere; if they do bind, then either the rods haven't been drilled correctly, or the wheels are not properly quartered. Try one at a time. If they bind when tried singly, the fault is in the rods; if O.K. singly, but bind when tried together, it is the wheels at fault. Correct by easing the holes with a rat-tail file, or shifting the wheels, as the case may be. When corrected, open out the pin-drilled ends to $\frac{1}{4}$ in., and the plain ends to $\frac{5}{16}$ in. ready for bushing.

Bushing the Rods

For the pin-drilled ends, chuck a bit of $\frac{5}{16}$ in. round rod in three-jaw. Use good hard bronze or gunmetal; soft brass soon wears away on a little engine intended for a real job of hard work. Face the end, centre, and drill down about $\frac{3}{8}$ in. depth with No. 15 drill. Turn down the outside to a press fit in the hole in the rod, same as described for turning the crankpins, and the ends of the axles. If you "read, mark, learn and inwardly digest"—as we used to at school 60 years ago—previous lessons in turning and fitting, it saves you time, and saves your humble servant a lot of needless repetition. Part off two $\frac{1}{8}$ in. slices, and press them into the holes in the bosses.

For the driving ends, chuck a bit of $\frac{3}{8}$ in. rod; face, centre, and drill down a full $\frac{5}{8}$ in. with a letter C drill, if you have one; if not, use $\frac{15}{64}$ in. Turn down

$\frac{3}{16}$ in. length of the outside, to a press fit in the $\frac{5}{16}$ in. hole; part off a full $\frac{1}{16}$ in. from the shoulder, or a full $\frac{1}{4}$ in. from the end. Repeat operation, then reverse each bush in the chuck, take a slight skim off the face, and just slightly chamfer the edge, that is, take the sharp edge off. A square-ended tool with the left-hand corner ground off at an angle of about 45 degrees is just the boy for skimming, chamfering, and light facing; I have one in all my turrets. I always use a four-tool turret (home-made) on each side of my lathe, as it saves such a lot of tool changing; they are simply slewed around against a stop on the top-slide, to bring any of the four tools into business position. A nut with a handle sticking out of the side, holds the turret to the top-slide, and a flick of the handle either way, releases or locks the turret.

Press the bushes into the holes in the bosses, not forgetting that the flange goes on the same side as the recessed part of the rod. Drill a $\frac{1}{16}$ in. oil hole clean through each boss and bush, opening out for about $\frac{1}{8}$ in. depth with a $\frac{1}{4}$ in. drill, to hold a drop of oil; see dotted lines in the illustration. Finally, ream the driving end with $\frac{1}{4}$ in. reamer, and either ream the pin-drilled end $\frac{3}{16}$ in. or put a $\frac{3}{16}$ in. drill through the bush. The leading end should be a little easier on the pin than the driving end. The rods can be put on the wheels, securing the leading bosses with the specially-turned washers, held in place by ordinary commercial countersunk steel screws. No fixing is needed for the driving end, as the connecting rod keeps that in place.

Boiler Feed Pump

Locomotives doing real work need plenty of water, so a pump is needed to keep the boiler well supplied. This is a simple gadget, driven by an eccentric on the driving axle, which has already been made and fitted. Three small castings are required for the pump, and one for the eccentric strap; the parts can be made from rod material, silver-soldered together, but castings save work, so I advise beginners to use them.

First chuck the body casting by one end of the valve box, keeping the barrel part right up close to the chuck jaws, and setting the opposite end of the valve box to run truly. Leave the jaws slightly slack; tap the end with something light, such as a spanner head, until it runs truly when the lathe belt is pulled by hand, then tighten the jaws. Face off the end, centre, drill clean through with No. 33 drill, open out to $\frac{1}{4}$ in. depth with $\frac{7}{32}$ in. drill, and bottom the hole with a $\frac{7}{32}$ in. D-bit, to $\frac{5}{16}$ in. depth, to form a true seat for the ball valve. D-bits are easily home-made; you might try one. All you need for the $\frac{7}{32}$ in. merchant, is a couple of inches of silver-steel of that size. File away about $\frac{3}{4}$ in. length to half the diameter, back off the end as shown, harden and temper exactly as described for the slot drill, and give the flat face a rub on an oilstone. Put it in the tailstock chuck, and feed it into the drilled hole until it cuts out the coned end left by the drill, and forms a flat $\frac{5}{16}$ in. from the end. Now tap the hole $\frac{1}{4}$ in. by 40, operating the tap from the tailstock chuck, as I described in a previous lesson. Warning—don't run the tap in far enough to catch the D-bitted seating and spoil it. Finally, take a weeny skim off the end, to remove any burring, and slightly countersink the hole with a $\frac{5}{16}$ in. drill.

The easiest way to set the opposite end to run truly, is to mount it on a screwed spigot like a gauge "O" mandrel nose. Chuck a bit of round rod of any diameter over $\frac{3}{8}$ in. in the three-jaw. Face the end, and turn down $\frac{3}{16}$ in. of the end to $\frac{1}{4}$ in. diameter, using a knife tool, so as to leave a shoulder. Screw $\frac{1}{4}$ in. by 40 with a die in the tailstock chuck, operating as per previous instructions. Don't remove this from the chuck, but screw the machined and tapped end of the valve box on to it; the outer end will then run truly.

Face off the end, open out to $\frac{5}{16}$ in. depth with $\frac{7}{32}$ in. drill, tap $\frac{1}{4}$ in. by 40, countersink, and skim off any burrs, exactly the same as the previous end, except that the D-bit is not needed. Instead, make a couple of nicks at the entrance of the small hole, with a little chisel made from a bit of $\frac{1}{8}$ in. silver-steel. File the end like a screwdriver, harden and temper same as described for slot-drill. Put a $\frac{1}{8}$ in. parallel reamer through the remnants of the No. 33 drill hole; this may be done by hand, using a tap wrench to turn the reamer. On the back of the valve box there will be a chucking-piece cast on, for gripping in the chuck whilst machining the barrel; put this in the three-jaw, and if the barrel doesn't run truly, give it a gentle tap or two with something light, until it does, then tighten chuck jaws. Face the end, centre, and drill clean through into the valve box with a $\frac{5}{32}$ in. or No. 21 drill. Open out to $\frac{3}{4}$ in. depth with a $\frac{5}{16}$ in. drill. Turn down $\frac{5}{8}$ in. of the outside, to $\frac{1}{2}$ in. diameter, and screw it $\frac{1}{2}$ in. by 26 or 32, to suit the tapped hole in the pump stay, which is already fitted to the chassis. Saw off the chucking piece, and file away the stub, smoothing it off to the outline of the valve box. That completes the body machining.

We now need the top and bottom caps for the valve box. The valves themselves are $\frac{5}{32}$ in. balls, either rustless steel or phosphor-bronze. If you are using the former, drop one into the D-bitted end of the valve box; rest the other end on a block of lead, or something else that won't damage the faced end. Put a short bit of $\frac{3}{16}$ in. round brass rod on top of the ball, and give it just one sharp crack with a hammer. This takes the sharp arris off the edge of the reamed hole, and the ball thus forms its own watertight seating. If you are using bronze balls, form the seating as above, with a $\frac{5}{32}$ in. cycle bearing ball; not the bronze ball. The latter isn't nearly so hard as the steel ball, and the seating will cut a weeny grove in it, if you try to seat it direct. The bronze ball will seat watertight on a seating formed by a cycle ball of similar size.

Now take the distance from the top of the ball, to the top of the valve box, with a depth gauge. Young Curly's depth gauge was one of mother's hat-pins stuck through a tram ticket. You can make one by drilling a No. 41 hole through an inch or so of $\frac{3}{16}$ in. square brass rod, putting a $\frac{3}{32}$ in. or 7 BA set screw in the side, and using a piece of $\frac{3}{32}$ in. silver-steel, about 3 in. long, for the sliding part. Put the rod across the top of the valve box; push the pin down until it touches the ball, and tighten the screw. You'll need this in a few minutes, all being well.

The top cover of the valve box is in the form of a T, the stem screwing into the valve box, and the two ends of the head carrying unions for connecting to the boiler clack and the by-pass valve respectively. It can be made from a casting, or built up. If cast, it will look like a cross, as it will have a chucking piece on top. First, chuck in three-jaw by one side of the head, and set the other end to run truly, gently tapping with a lead hammer, or something else that won't damage the casting, until it doesn't wobble when the lathe is running. Then tighten the chuck. Face off the end carefully; for nearly all facing jobs on small fittings I use a square-ended tool, with the point nearest the chuck, ground off to an angle of about 30 deg. An ordinary knife-tool sometimes catches up and knocks the job clean out of the chuck, damaging the soft casting beyond recall. The tool above mentioned, never plays that trick, and is also useful for chamfering the corners of union nuts and similar fittings.

Centre the end, same as you centred the wheels, letting the centre-drill penetrate until it has sunk in far enough to leave a countersink which measures a full $\frac{3}{16}$ in. across. Then turn the outside for $\frac{1}{4}$ in. length to $\frac{1}{4}$ in. diameter, using a knife-tool as when turning wheel seats, and screw it $\frac{1}{4}$ in. by 40, with a die in tailstock holder. You obviously can't reverse the job in the chuck, to turn and screw the other end, as the chuck jaws would have to be tightened enough to ruin the threaded part; so use a tapped bush. Chuck a short bit of $\frac{1}{2}$ in. round rod in three-jaw, any odd scrap, brass or steel, about $\frac{1}{2}$ in. long will do fine. Face the end, centre, drill right through with $\frac{7}{32}$ in. drill, slightly countersink the end with $\frac{1}{4}$ in. drill, tap $\frac{1}{4}$ in. by 40, using the tailstock chuck to guide the tap, as previously described, and skim off any burr left from drilling and tapping. Don't remove from chuck, but screw the threaded end of the tee into it. The outer end will run quite truly. Give that end a dose of the same medicine as the first end and then drill right through it with a No. 40 drill, as shown in the section of the complete pump. Make a centre-pop opposite No. 1 jaw on the bush, before taking it out of the chuck.

Now chuck the casting by the spigot on top, provided for the purpose. Set the stem to run truly, as above. Face off the end; centre, and drill it with a No. 40 drill until you break into the cross-hole at the top. The next bit is where you need the already-set depth gauge; turn the stem to $\frac{1}{4}$ in. diameter, to the same length as indicated by the projecting part of the depth gauge pin. Screw it $\frac{1}{4}$ in. by 40, and then face just $\frac{1}{32}$ in. off the end, to allow the ball that much lift. Finally, file two nicks across the end, with a thin flat file, so that when the ball rises off its seating on the forcing stroke of the pump, and seats against the hole, the water can get out through the nicks. An old friend forgot these nicks on one of his engines, and spent about a fortnight looking for the tight spot, error in valve gear, etc., which he imagined was causing the wheels to lock as soon as the engine tried to make a start! Cut off the chucking piece, and file away the stub, making the fitting as neat as possible; then drop the ball in the valve box, and screw the fitting home, with a touch of plumbers' jointing ("Boss White", or any similar preparation, sold at all ironmongery stores) on the threads; but be careful not to get any inside the valve box. The union screws should point fore and aft, as our nautical friends would remark; see sectional drawing.

The bottom fitting is somewhat similarly machined, but it has only one union screw, and the ball seats on the stem. The fitting will have two chucking pieces, so chuck in three-jaw by one of them; set the other end to run truly, then face, centre, turn and screw it, exactly as described for the union ends of the tee above. Then drill halfway through it with No. 40 drill. Next, chuck by the other chucking piece, and set the other end to run truly. Face off, centre, and drill down with No. 32 drill until you break into the hole already drilled; see section of complete pump. Put a $\frac{1}{8}$ in. parallel reamer into this hole, as far as it will go, then carefully face off the end.

Turn the pump upside down, and drop a $\frac{5}{32}$ in. ball into the lower part of the valve box. Take the distance from the top of the ball, to the end of the valve box as before, and tighten the set screw of the depth gauge. Now turn the stem of the fitting in the chuck, to $\frac{1}{4}$ in. diameter, for a distance approximately $\frac{1}{16}$ in. less than the length indicated by the gauge pin, and screw it $\frac{1}{4}$ in. by 40. As the ball sinks into the seating a little, this will give the ball a shade over $\frac{1}{32}$ in. total lift. Saw off both chucking pieces, and smooth the stubs away with a file; put the ball (if steel) on the end of the stem, apply the brass rod to it, and give it a crack with a hammer as above. The fitting can be held in the bench vice for this job. Then drop the ball in the hole in the valve box, and screw in the fitting, with the union screw pointing towards the pump barrel, as shown in the section of the complete pump.

Built-up Fittings

Instead of using castings, the top and bottom fittings may be built-up. For the top one, chuck a piece of $\frac{5}{16}$ in. round brass rod in the three-jaw. Face the end, centre deeply, and turn and screw it exactly as described for the casting; part off at 1 in. from the end. Reverse in chuck, and serve the other end the same, drilling a No. 40 hole clean through. Drill a $\frac{5}{32}$ in. hole in the side, halfway along, breaking into the middle hole.

Chuck a piece of $\frac{3}{8}$ in. brass rod in three-jaw; face, centre, and drill down $\frac{3}{4}$ in. depth with No. 40 drill. Face off the end until any countersinking has been removed; then turn the end to $\frac{1}{4}$ in. of ball to top of box, as indicated by the depth from the end. Put the tapped bush in the chuck, with the centre-pop opposite No. 1 jaw, and screw the fitting into it. Turn $\frac{1}{16}$ in. of the end to a tight fit in the side hole in the other piece; then turn the rest to the shape shown in the illustration. Squeeze it in, and silver-solder the joint, afterwards cross-nicking it, same as the casting.

Silver-soldering Fittings

This is one of the easiest jobs going. I use "Easyflo" silver-solder in wire form (supplied commercially by Johnson-Matthey's) and the special flux that

Plate 5

Mr. F. Raw, of the Stockport Model Engineering Society, at the regulator of his "Tich"

Plate 6

A view of the frame, showing lubricator drive and brake standard: G. F. Collins

A view inside the frames of the "Tich" built by Michael Holt of Lytham. Note the slip-eccentrics

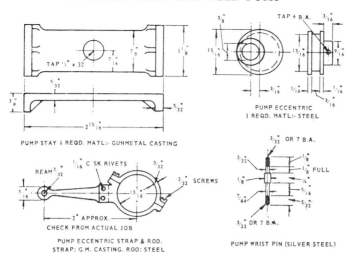

Details of the pump stay, pump eccentric, strap, rod and wrist pin.

goes with it; but best-grade silver-solder cut in thin strips, with jewellers' borax (powdered and mixed to a paste with water) does very well. You can use a little blowlamp, or a small gas blowpipe can be made in a few minutes from a bit of ⅜ in. brass or copper tube, which is self-blowing. A small tin lid with a few bits of small coke or asbestos cubes in it, makes a small forge; it need not be bigger than a soap dish. Simply anoint the joint with the wet flux, blow to medium red, and touch the joint with the silver-solder wire or strip. It immediately melts and runs in. Don't use too much—it not only spoils the appearance, but is expensive. Quench out when it has cooled to black, in a drop of acid pickle in a jam jar. The acid pickle is composed of 1 part commercial sulphuric acid to about 16 of water, or 1 part old accumulator acid to 4 of water. Let the fitting stay in for about ten minutes, then fish it out, wash under the kitchen tap, wipe dry and clean up. For cleaning up, I use a circular wire brush on a spindle stuck in a taper hole in the end of my electric grinder; but it does as well if held in the lathe chuck. Run the lathe as fast as possible without causing an earthquake.

The bottom fitting is easier still to build up. Simply chuck a bit of ⅜ in. brass rod in three-jaw, and proceed to machine up the end exactly as described for the casting, when forming the ball seat. Part off at 5⁄16 in. from the shoulder, and drill a 3⁄32 in. hole in the side. Chuck a piece of ¼ in. round rod in the three-jaw; face the end, centre deeply, and drill down to a full ½ in. depth with No. 40 drill. Screw the outside ¼ in. by 40, for ¼ in. length, and part off at ⅜ in. from the end. Re-chuck in the tapped bush; turn about 3⁄32 in. of the end to a tight squeeze fit in the side hole of the other part. Squeeze it in, silver-solder it, pickle, wash and clean up. Seat a ball on the faced end, and assemble as previously explained.

The Pump

We left off with the body machined and valves fitted, so now we need a gland and ram. The gland may be made from a hexagon-shaped casting, or from a piece of hexagon bronze or gunmetal rod measuring $\frac{5}{8}$ in. across the flats. This can be sawn or parted off from a longer piece of bar; if sawn, allow enough for facing both ends, to bring the finished length to $\frac{1}{2}$ in. The machining of either the casting or the piece of rod, is exactly the same. Chuck in three-jaw; it doesn't matter if the chuck is slightly out of truth in this case, as all the machining is done at the same setting. Face the end, centre, and drill a $\frac{1}{8}$ in. or No. 30 pilot hole right through. Open out with a $\frac{19}{64}$ in. or letter N drill, letting it go right through. Further open out to $\frac{3}{8}$ in. depth with a $\frac{29}{64}$ in. drill, and tap $\frac{1}{2}$ in. by 26 or 32, to suit the thread on the pump barrel. Note, the gland should not be too easy a fit on the pump barrel, otherwise it will try to slack back when the engine is working; and if it does, it will release the packing, and allow water to escape at the gland instead of being forced into the boiler. No gland of any sort should be too easy on the threads. Several cases have occurred, where piston glands have worked out, and on the return stroke, have been caught between crosshead and stuffing box, causing considerable damage to the engine.

It may possibly happen that some beginners have a tailstock chuck that won't take a $\frac{1}{2}$ in. drill or tap. This will call for a bit of judicious wangling.

General arrangement of the feed pump.

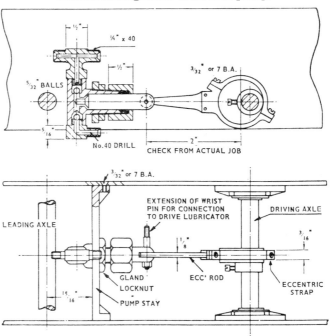

Details of the pump ram, the body and the top and bottom connections.

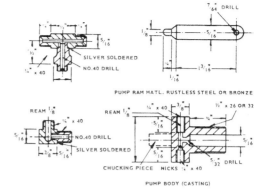

Most of the larger sizes of drills and taps have a centre-hole in the end. In that case, put the centre point in the tailstock, and clamp a tool crosswise in the slide-rest with the shank end projecting, or use a piece of bar. Let the tail of the carrier rest on it, to prevent the drill or tap turning; run up the centre so that it engages with the hole in the end of the drill or tap, and holds same truly; then go ahead as if using a tailstock chuck.

If the drills and taps haven't any centre-holes in the end, and are too hard to be held in three-jaw and centred with an ordinary centre-drill of the Slocomb type, the only thing to do, is to make sockets. They are easy enough to make. A piece of round rod is required; any metal, even soft brass will do. First centre both ends; then with the piece mounted between lathe centres, either turn the outer end taper, to fit the taper in the tailstock barrel, or turn it parallel, to the biggest size your tailstock chuck will accommodate. Then put it either in tailstock barrel or chuck, as the case may be. Put a drill in the three-jaw, run up the tailstock with the socket blank in it, and drill a hole in the end, working very carefully; the size of the hole, of course, should be to accommodate the size of drill or tap you want to use in the socket. A set-screw can be fitted, for holding drills. For different sized shanks, all you need is a set of sleeves, home-made in a few minutes. If, for example, you make the "master" socket $\frac{1}{2}$ in. bore, you can use bits of $\frac{1}{2}$ in. rod in it, each one drilled out for a smaller size of drill. A hole can be made in each, for the set-screw to pass, and get to the drill. This is how the old craftsmen managed in the days before three-jaws, tailstock chucks, and other modern conveniences came into general use.

Returning to our gland, chamfer the corners of the hexagon and put a $\frac{5}{16}$ in. parallel reamer through the small hole; then reverse it in the chuck, face off the other end, and chamfer; also whilst you have the drills and tap handy, make the lock-nut. This is either a casting, or a piece of hexagon rod, same as the gland, but only a full $\frac{3}{16}$ in. long. Chuck in three-jaw; face, centre, drill a small pilot hole right through, then open out and tap exactly the same as the gland, putting the $\frac{29}{64}$ in. drill, and the $\frac{1}{2}$ in. tap clean through. Reverse in chuck, setting to run truly, and take a cleaning-up skim off the other side.

Pump Ram

If a piece of $\frac{5}{16}$ in. ground rustless steel, or phosphor-bronze rod is available, very little machining will be needed on the pump ram. If you haven't a bit this size, chuck a piece the nearest size larger, and turn $1\frac{3}{8}$ in. length to $\frac{5}{16}$ in. diameter, using the gland as a gauge, and turning to an exact sliding fit. You'll find that easier than turning wheel seats! Part off at $1\frac{11}{16}$ in. from the end. The ground rustless, or drawn bronze, if either is used, should be the same length. Now reverse in chuck, turn $\frac{1}{4}$ in. length to $\frac{1}{8}$ in. diameter, and bevel off the shoulder as shown in the illustration, to match the drilled end of the pump barrel. This pin, which I call the anti-airlock pin, is to prevent air being trapped in the pump barrel, and causing the pump either to deliver short measure, or fail altogether. Eccentric-driven pumps, in the past, were stated to be "not altogether satisfactory". It wasn't any fault of the pumps, but the designs, which allowed air pockets. Air is, as everybody knows, freely compressible, while water isn't. If you have an air space in the pump barrel, air will be compressed into it, up to boiler pressure on the inward stroke of the pump ram. On the outward stroke, the air simply expands again, fills the pump barrel, or partly fills it, as the case may be, according to the clearance between the ram and the end of the barrel.

As no water will get past the inlet valve whilst the pressure on it exceeds that of the atmosphere, it is easy to see why the pump is a partial or complete failure. In this pump, the pin left on the end of the ram, goes through the small hole at the end of the barrel, right into the valve box; and even when the pump is set to work for the first time, with a barrel full of air, the first inward stroke of the ram expels it all past the delivery valve, the close clearances, and the pin, ensuring that there wouldn't be enough air left in the pump barrel on front dead centre, to supply the lungs of a gnat for a couple of minutes. The instant that the ram starts its outward stroke, a partial vacuum is created in the pump barrel, sucking in a charge of water via the inlet or suction valve. Beginners should now be able to see why the pump will always "fill the pot", as an old engineman used to say before injectors came into general use.

At $1\frac{3}{16}$ in. from the shoulder, drill a $\frac{7}{64}$ in. hole through the pump ram. The best way to do this is to make a heavy centre dot at the location of the hole, and drill the hole with the ram resting in a vee-block, either on the drilling machine, or held against a drilling pad on the lathe tailstock barrel. I have already explained how a serviceable vee-block can be made with two pieces of sheet metal held parallel, $\frac{1}{2}$ in. or so apart, by spacers; but a pair of regular mechanics' vee-blocks are not very expensive, and are exceedingly useful. After drilling, chuck the ram in the three-jaw again, and round off the drilled end.

The next job is to slot the end of the ram for the eccentric rod. The easiest way is to clamp it under the lathe toolholder, and run it up to a $\frac{1}{8}$ in. saw-type slotting cutter, mounted on a spindle held in the three-jaw, or between centres.

Use plenty of cutting oil, feed very slowly, and run the lathe at a slow speed. The slot can also be cut by hand, using a couple of hacksaw blades in the frame, side by side, to make a fairly wide rough slot to start with. This is then trued up, and finished to size, by aid of a thin flat file, as used for cutting wards in keys. Use a piece of $\frac{1}{8}$ in. flat rod for a gauge. Now screw the gland on the pump barrel, and try the ram in it. The ram should slide freely the full length of barrel, whatever the position of the gland on the barrel.

Next, screw the pump barrel into the pumpstay until it projects about $\frac{1}{2}$ in.; the valve box caps will have to be slacked back half-a-turn, to enable this to be done. Then put on the lock-nut, and screw it up tightly against the stay, so that the pump barrel cannot become slack. Don't forget that the end with the T-piece goes at the top! The gland can then be packed with a few strands of packing, unravelled from a bit of full-size hydraulic packing, for preference. If not available, use graphited yarn, or soft hemp well tallowed. Plaited lamp wick, unravelled, and soaked in black cylinder oil, does well.

The Eccentric Strap

It is surprising how often beginners go to work the wrong way on a simple job, and get into a tangle. Eccentric straps are a case in point. I know of several beginners who have cheerfully bored and faced a strap, sawn it across, screwed the two halves together, and then found that not only was the hole oval, but the two halves joined on an angle, so that the strap wouldn't fit the groove in the tumbler. The proper way is easy enough. In the present instance, centre-pop both lugs first, and drill them No. 48, clean through where the screws will go. Next, mark a line across the centre of both lugs on the casting. Put it in the bench vice with this line just showing above the jaws. With a thin fine-toothed blade mounted sideways in your hacksaw frame, saw right across both lugs, keeping the blade pressed down on the top of the vice jaws. By this means you get a fine straight cut, and the two halves of the strap will line up properly when screwed together. Give each half a rub on a smooth flat file laid on the bench, to take the roughness off the saw-cuts. Open out the holes in the upper half, with No. 41 drill; tap those in the lower half, $\frac{3}{32}$ in. or 7 BA, then screw the halves together with a couple of cheeseheaded screws.

Now chuck the strap in the four-jaw, with the hole running as truly as possible; you won't get it perfectly true, as it is oval. Leave about $\frac{1}{16}$ in. of the strap standing clear of the chuck jaws; and with a round-nose tool set cross-wise in the rest, face it off. Next, with an ordinary boring tool, carefully bore the strap until it is an easy fit, without any shake, on the eccentric. If you have an accurate slide gauge, you can set the outside jaws to the eccentric, and use the inside jaws to gauge the hole, as the jaws should register exactly when adjusted; but a lot of them don't. I've only one small slide-gauge that is absolutely accurate on both inside and outside jaws at once, and that is, sad to say, one of Jerry's productions. I have two big ones, a Swiss and an American, that are both O.K.

The best way for a beginner, is to chuck a stub of round steel, or any other odd bit of metal of suitable diameter, and turn $\frac{1}{4}$ in. of it to exactly the same diameter as the eccentric at the bottom of the groove. This can not only be used to gauge the hole in the strap, boring out same until the turned piece fits exactly, but it can be used as a mandrel for finishing off the other side of the eccentric strap. Chuck it in the three-jaw, put a thin strip of paper round the turned part, and put the eccentric strap on it over the paper, rough side outwards, just overhanging the end of the mandrel. Secure the eccentric strap by its own two screws; the paper will allow it to grip tightly. Then carefully face off the rough side, with a round-nose tool set crosswise in the rest, until the strap is reduced sufficiently to fit in the groove in the eccentric; the actual measurement is $\frac{3}{16}$ in. bare.

The lug for attaching the eccentric rod can be slotted by gripping the strap in a machine vice (regular or improvised) on the lathe saddle, and traversing under a $\frac{1}{8}$ in. slotting cutter of saw type; same one as used for slotting the pump ram. It can be done by clamping the strap on its side under the slide-rest toolholder, and traversing across a little $\frac{1}{8}$ in. slot drill, made as previously described in earlier instalments. As a last resort, it could be formed by hand, as mentioned for the slot in the pump ram.

Eccentric Rod and Pin

The eccentric rod is a simple filing job, made from a piece of $\frac{1}{8}$ in. mild steel, $\frac{3}{8}$ in. wide and $1\frac{5}{8}$ in. long. The larger end is fitted into the lug in the strap, and riveted in by two $\frac{1}{16}$ in. rivets, or pieces of domestic blanket pins would do. Countersink the holes both sides of the lug, rivet the ends of the pins into both countersinks, and file flush. If the rod is soldered into the lug before putting in the rivets, it makes the job easier. Round off the small end roughly, but don't drill the hole yet.

This pump needs a special gudgeon pin, or wrist pin as it is sometimes called, as the drive for the mechanical lubricator will be taken off it, obviating the use of a separate eccentric. To make it, chuck a piece of $\frac{1}{8}$ in. round steel in the three-jaw, and turn down a bare $\frac{1}{2}$ in. length to $\frac{7}{64}$ in. diameter, a sliding fit without shake, in the cross-hole in the pump ram. Turn down $\frac{5}{32}$ in. of the end of this, to $\frac{3}{32}$ in. diameter, and screw it $\frac{3}{32}$ in. or 7 BA. Part off at 1 in. from the end; reverse in chuck, turn down $\frac{1}{4}$ in. length to $\frac{3}{32}$ in. diameter, and screw a bare half of this either $\frac{3}{32}$ in. or 7 BA.

Erecting the Pump

Replace the pumpstay in the frames, with pump attached, securing by screws already fitted. Attach the eccentric strap to the tumbler by means of the two screws in the lugs, and see that the strap is quite free on it, able to revolve easily, without binding either on the bottom or sides of the groove. A tight eccentric strap acts as a very efficient "band brake" on the engine. Adjust the eccentric on the axle until the rod can be fitted easily into the slot in the pump ram, without having to strain it either way. Now push the pump ram right in as far as it will go; then put the end of the eccentric rod in the slot, with the eccentric on front dead centre. Put the business end of a bent scriber through one of the holes in the ram, and make a little circle on the eccentric rod, denoting position of hole. Take off the strap and rod; note the centre of the little marked circle, at the end of the rod, and at $\frac{1}{32}$ in. nearer to the straps make a centre-pop. Drill this with a $\frac{7}{64}$ in. drill, and file the end of the rod to shape around the hole. This will give the correct clearance between the ram and the end of the barrel.

To prevent undue wear, this eye may be case-hardened; a simple job. Just heat the eye to redness, and dip it in some good case-hardening powder such as "Kasenit", "Pearlite", or any other similar brand. Make certain the hole is well filled up; then reheat until all the powder has fused, and the yellow flame died away, leaving the whole eye bright red. Quench in clean, cold water; scrape off any residue, and clean up. This treatment leaves a hard surface on the steel, which will resist wear indefinitely; but it must not be allowed to run without oil.

All that remains, is to replace the eccentric strap on the tumbler, and put the little end of the eccentric rod in the slot in the pump ram, securing it by poking the $\frac{7}{64}$ in. end of the long pin through the holes in ram and rod, and securing with an ordinary commercial nut. The long end of the pin should project to the right-hand side, as shown in the plan view. The eccentric should be set on the axle in such a position that it is in step with one of the crankpins in the wheels. This ensures that it will get the full power of one of the cylinders, to force a barrelful of water into the boiler at each stroke, when the bypass valve is closed. We shall fit a bypass valve in due course. To test the pump, all you need do is to slip a bit of rubber pipe over the suction union, drop the other end in a can of water and turn the wheels. If you try to stop the flow by putting your thumb and finger over the union on the tee, you'll be astonished at the power behind the water!

CHAPTER FOUR

Machining the cylinders

THE CYLINDERS DIFFER SLIGHTLY in detail from the kind I have hitherto specified, though the principles are the same. The bore and stroke, $\frac{11}{16}$ in. by $1\frac{1}{8}$ in., are suited to the equivalents of a full-sized locomotive of this type, and to the average steaming capacity of the little boiler. I might mention here, that bigger bore cylinders may be used if desired, and I describe an alternative boiler of larger size in a later chapter. However, "sufficient for the day is the evil (?) thereof", so we will see about these, first of all. There is no need to have an excess of metal in cylinders, so I have specified a steamchest just large enough to accommodate a slide valve of suitable dimensions; and the bolting face of the cylinder castings may be recessed, enabling the cylinders to warm up quickly when starting from cold. As this recess is not open to the atmosphere when the cylinders are erected, cooling will be very slow.

The ports are of ample size, and the passages are large enough to pass easily all the steam needed, but not large enough to cause waste, and produce a too-violent blast. The big slide valves are driven by a long nut working in a slot in the back of the valve; the spindle of each goes through a U-shaped slot in the back of the valve gear one side, and screws into the nut. No tail guides are needed; the long gland gives sufficient bearing surface to the valve spindle, without any additional support, making it an easier job for beginners. The cylinder casting is long enough to allow of a piston $\frac{7}{16}$ in. wide, enabling a packing ring of $\frac{3}{16}$ in. square braided graphited yarn to be used. This is easily put on; much more easily than winding ordinary strands of yarn into the groove, and it works with little friction, whilst remaining quite steam tight. The oft-presented idea of a divided piston, with a groove which is filled with packing crushed tightly against the cylinder wall by screwing the two halves of the piston together, is what our transatlantic cousins would call "boloney". Pistons should be steam-tight, but not mechanically tight. You want the power delivered at the engine drawbar, not all mopped up in overcoming internal friction in the moving parts of the engine.

Machining the Casting

The following method is one which I have personally used ever since I first owned a lathe with a slide-rest, faceplate and angle-plate. This, incidentally,

56

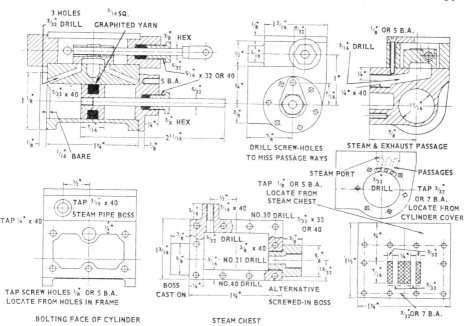

Details of the cylinders and steam chests.

was one of the first $3\frac{1}{2}$ in. Drummonds ever turned out of the original shop at Rydes Hill, Guildford; it cost £13 10s., and was purchased on the "never-never", as my pay as a young fireman on the L.B. & S.C. Ry. wouldn't permit of cash purchase. This was about the turn of the century.

First, measure up the distance from the centre of the corehole in the casting to the bolting face and the port face. If the former is more than $\frac{7}{8}$ in., and the latter more than $\frac{3}{4}$ in., you can start operations from the corehole, and save a lot of marking out and measuring; but if less, then the corehole is not true with the block, and provision must be made accordingly. Plug the corehole with a bit of wood at one end; scribe a line parallel with the bolting face at $\frac{15}{16}$ in. away, and one parallel with the port face at $\frac{15}{16}$ in. away. Where the lines cross is the true centre of the bore. Make a centre-pop at the crossing, and scribe a circle from it, $\frac{11}{16}$ in. diameter.

Next, attach your angle-plate to the faceplate by aid of a couple of bolts. Smooth off the port face of the cylinder casting with a file; no need for a posh job—you needn't touch it if there are no knobs or excrescences on it—just make certain it will bed down on the angle-plate reasonably flat. Then mount it on the angle-plate, just overhanging the edge, fixing it with a bar across its back, held down by a bolt at each end. Now a little patience is called for. If you are locating from the corehole, set a scribing block in the lathe bed, or put a pointed tool, or even a bit of pointed wire, in the slide-rest. Now adjust cylinder casting and angle-plate, until, when the lathe belt is pulled by hand, the edge of the corehole runs truly. This can be gauged by applying the scriber needle, or tool point to it. Gauge whether the casting is square with the face-plate, by applying your try-square to it, stock to faceplate, and blade to cylinder. When the casting is square with the faceplate, and the corehole runs truly, it is set O.K., so the bolts can all be tightened up. Warning—don't overdo the tightening and distort either the casting, the angle-plate, or both. You'd be surprised how even a heavy lump of metal will "spring"!

If locating from a marked-off centre, as mentioned above, all you need do is to run up the tailstock, with the centre point in it, and adjust the casting and angle-plate until the point will enter the centre-pop. Start the lathe; if it runs steadily, all well and good. If it rocks the workshop, as it most likely will, bolt a balance-weight to the faceplate directly opposite. I use an old circular cistern weight for a heavy casting, or one or two of my lathe change-wheels for a lighter one; anything handy will do.

Facing and Boring Operations

Set a round-nose tool cross-wise in the rest at centre height, and take a facing cut right across the end of the casting, same as you faced the rims of the wheels. The amount to take off is easily ascertained. Measure the overall length of the casting; from this, subtract the finished length, viz., $1\frac{3}{4}$ in., and turn away half the difference; thus, if the casting is $1\frac{7}{8}$ in. long it needs just $\frac{1}{16}$ in. turning off each end. Take a good cut, say a full $\frac{1}{32}$ in. deep, at slow speed, to get the skin off the casting; if the tool rubs on the skin, the cutting edge will be dulled in a matter of seconds. The final cut should be just a skim, with the lathe running fairly fast.

Now set up your boring-tool in the rest. I use a boring-tool with plenty of top rake—that is, sloped well back from the cutting edge—and set a little above centre, which precludes any chance of the lower part rubbing. Set your change wheels to move the saddle at the slowest possible speed (that is, as if you were going to cut the finest thread that the lathe would produce) and take a cut, at fairly slow speed, and about $\frac{1}{32}$ in. deep, clean through the corehole. Another warning, if the corehole isn't true, and you have had to find the true centre, adjust the tool to cut deep enough to clean out the corehole completely; if it cuts one side and rubs on the other, away goes the cutting edge at once. Set your slide gauge, or inside calipers to a shade under $\frac{11}{16}$ in., and ditto repeat the boring operation until the tips just enter.

But supposing we haven't a screw-cutting lathe, not even a self-act, says a beginner; what then? Nothing at all to worry about! Before setting up the casting in the first place, put your three-jaw on the mandrel nose, with a piece of brass rod in it about $\frac{1}{2}$ in. diameter, projecting about 2 in. from the jaws. With a round-nose tool in the rest, take a very slight cut, only a few thousandths deep, along the rod. Gauge both ends, with a micrometer or caliper gauge, or even an ordinary pair of calipers. If the "mike" indicates less than half a thousandth difference at each end of the cut, or if you can detect no appreciable difference in the feel of the calipers, the top-slide is set O.K. for boring. If there is a difference, simply adjust the top-slide, have another go, and keep on by trial and error until you get the slide set right. Then set up your cylinder casting as above; and when boring, simply turn the top-slide handle very slowly, to feed the tool steadily through the bore.

Reaming

If you have no $\frac{11}{16}$ in. parallel reamer, finish to size by boring only. Regrind the boring tool, and give the cutting edge a rub on an oilstone, to make certain it won't scratch; then take out the final few thousandths in the same way as the boring operation. To get a posh finish, take the final two or three traverses of the tool through the bore without moving the cross-slide; then, when the tool ceases to cut, you should have a bore as smooth as glass, and perfectly true. I finished *Jeannie Deans*'s big low-pressure cylinder that way, as I had no reamer as large as $1\frac{7}{8}$ in. and sometimes I finish a smaller one in similar manner, as my Milnes lathe bores truly.

To ream in the lathe, first make sure there is sufficient room between the cylinder casting and the faceplate, for the full diameter of a parallel reamer to come through; if not, you'll have to ream by hand. If there is room, first make certain that the bore is all right for reaming. Try the "lead" end of the reamer in it; it should just enter nicely. If it won't, then take another cut through the casting with a boring-tool, until it will. A reamer is a finishing tool only; it isn't intended for removing a lot of metal, only just a scrape.

Now watch your step. Put a carrier on the reamer shank, and hold the reamer against the tailstock centre, with your left hand. Grip the tailstock with your right, run it up to the casting, enter the end of the reamer in the bore, and with the lathe running at medium speed, push the reamer clean through the bore, as far as it will go, by sliding the tailstock bodily (and steadily!) along the bed. Don't stop until you get to the end of the movement; then reverse, and make a non-stop journey back again. This operation has never, in my own case, failed to produce a clean smooth bore. A drop of cutting oil on the reamer is a help; and it is advisable to rub your finger-nail along each cutting edge, to see if there are any rough places to scratch the bore. If you find any, apply your oilstone along the edges. If the reamer is stopped at any point in the bore the result will be scratches and rings, so be sure to make a non-stop run both ways. Make the reversing pause as short as possible.

If there is no room to ream in the lathe, do it by hand after facing off the other end of the casting. Catch the casting in the bench vice, put a big tap wrench on the reamer shank, and carefully work it through by hand. When hand-reaming, it doesn't matter about stopping the forward movement of the reamer, if you stop turning it at the same time. Don't reverse the reamer, but when the flutes have passed right through the bore, take off the tap wrench, and push the shank of the reamer right through. If you reverse, and "screw" the reamer out, it is a million dollars to a pinch of snuff that you will bell-mouth the end of the bore.

To face off the other end of the casting, put a bit of $\frac{3}{4}$ in. round rod in your three-jaw, and turn it down until the cylinder will just push on very tightly; if you have turned the crankpins and wheel seats to press fits, that job shouldn't cause any worry! Then push the cylinder on, and face off the end by the same method as you faced off the first end; the total length over the flanges should be $1\frac{3}{4}$ in. If the cylinder slips on the mandrel, a bit of tissue paper between mandrel and bore, will teach it better manners without doing any damage to the finished surface.

Before I had a milling machine, I faced the flat surfaces of all cylinders by the following method, which I still employ sometimes, by way of a change. First of all, mark out on the finished ends of the cylinder, the limits of the port and bolting faces. The former is $\frac{3}{4}$ in. from centre of bore, so the distance between edge of bore, and port-face, will be $\frac{13}{32}$ in. By the same token, as Pat would say, the bolting face will be $\frac{17}{32}$ in. from edge of bore. Scribe the lines as shown, and you'll see how much there is to come off.

Now up-end the cylinder on the angle-plate and hold it in position by a long bolt through the bore. Put a piece of soft metal, such as copper or aluminium, between faced end and angle-plate, to prevent marking; put another piece on top, a big washer on top of that, and finally the nut. Adjust the angle-plate so that the cylinder is as near the centre of the faceplate as you can get it; then set the bolting face right for machining, by putting your try-square with the stock to the faceplate, and adjusting the casting until the line indicating the port face limit, is level with the blade. Tighten the bolt, and with a round-nose tool set cross-wise in the rest, face off the bolting face until you reach the marked line. Check with slide gauge or caliper, making sure the bolting face is exactly $\frac{17}{32}$ in. from the edge of the bore.

Slack the bolt, and slew the casting around a quarter turn, to bring the port face right for machining off. This time, set truly by applying the stock of your try-square to the faceplate and the blade to the machined bolting face. Tighten the bolt again, and tool off the port face until it is exactly $\frac{13}{32}$ in. from the edge of the bore. Both faces should now be exactly at right-angles to each other, also at right-angles to the ends of the cylinder, and both should be parallel to the bore, which itself should be perfectly true.

Cutting the Ports

The easiest way I know of cutting long smooth straight ports, is by aid of a dental burr. The way those little instruments of torture walk through even hard cast-iron, is just nobody's business; no wonder they give you a "two-penny one" when you are in the operating chair. I don't know how things go under the National Health Service; but at one time, dentists used a fresh one for each client (my friend did, anyway) and then threw them away. I could get all I required merely by asking; all they needed were the remnants of tooth brushed out of the flutes with a wire brush, and they were all set to cut several sets of ports. I use them in a Wolf-Jahn precision vertical milling machine, but they can be used in the lathe, just as well, as described below.

The first job is to mark out the location of the ports; and to make the lines stand out like those at Crewe on a sunny day, coat the port face with marking-out fluid. A good one can be made by dissolving some shellac in methylated spirit, and adding a little blue or violet aniline dye or other colouring matter. This, applied with a soft brush, dries in a minute or so; and any residue left after the job is finished, can be rubbed off with a rag wetted with spirit. The location of the ports is given on the accompanying illustration, and all you have to do is copy it. The two steam ports can be cut with a dental burr, and the exhaust port with a $\frac{1}{4}$ in. slot-drill. It doesn't matter a continental about the ends being left rounded; many big engines' ports have rounded ends. If you can't get a dental burr, make a weeny slot-drill from a bit of $\frac{3}{32}$ in. silver-steel, or else cut the ports by hand, as explained later.

Put the dental burr or slot drill in the three-jaw. If you have a vertical-slide, bolt the angle-plate to it, and mount the cylinder end-up on it, in the same way as when machining the port face. If you haven't a vertical-slide, clamp the casting to the saddle or slide-rest, packing it up so that one of the marked ports is level with the cutter. Then run the lathe as fast as you can, without causing an earthquake. Feed the casting on the cutter, by moving either the top-slide or the saddle; let the cutter enter about $\frac{1}{16}$ in. and then traverse the casting across the cutter by aid of the cross-slide. Warning—don't "overshoot the platform" and make the ports too long. Beginners can easily fix a temporary stop on the cross-slide to prevent over-running; the kind of stop depends on what type of lathe you have. Some lathes only need something like a toolmaker's clamp clipped on the slide. Cut the port to about $\frac{1}{4}$ in. depth; if you use a vertical-slide, you only have to turn the handle, to bring up another port ready for cutting; but if not, you'll have to adjust the height with packing. Use the $\frac{1}{4}$ in. cutter, naturally, for the exhaust port.

To cut ports by hand, drill a row of holes down each marked-out steam port with a $\frac{5}{64}$ in. drill, and $\frac{7}{64}$ in. for the exhaust port. Then make a couple of weeny chisels, one from $\frac{1}{4}$ in. silver-steel, and one from $\frac{3}{32}$ in. Just file to shape, harden and temper, same as I described for the slot-drills, etc., and give each a rub on the oilstone. With these, a light hammer, a bit of "common savvy" and the bench vice, you will find it easy enough to chip each row of holes into a rectangular port. Don't drill the holes more than $\frac{1}{4}$ in. deep; in fact, they only need be deep enough to meet the slanting passage-ways coming up from the bore, and the exhaust passage.

The Passages

On the centre-line of the bolting face, at $\frac{1}{4}$ in. below the port face, drill a $\frac{7}{32}$ in. hole about $\frac{3}{8}$ in. deep and tap it $\frac{1}{4}$ in. by 40. To connect this with the exhaust port, you can either poke a $\frac{3}{16}$ in. drill into the end of it, canting upwards, and drill up into the port, or put the $\frac{3}{16}$ in. drill down the port, drilling through the bottom corner until the drill breaks into the tapped hole. The other holes are a little more tricky. What I usually do, is to make deep centre-pops close to the bore, then put the drill in my drilling machine, and the casting in a machine vice, end up, sighting it with the drill outside the casting, and slanting same in the machine vice until the drill forms a line from the lip of the bore, to the bottom of the port. I then go right ahead, knowing that the drill will break into the bottom of the port. This, however, would be awkward to emulate on a lathe, because the machine vice and casting would have to be held by hand against the drilling pad; so if you have no drilling machine, do the job by hand. Simply catch the casting in the bench vice, but hold it at such an angle that the drill, if the drill brace is held horizontally, will go straight from the centre-pop at the edge of the bore, to the bottom of the steam port. Very important tip, this—grind the drill slightly off centre (that is, with one cutting edge longer than the other; I might add that most beginners do this automatically) and the drill will then cut a bigger hole than its diameter. If you are unlucky, and break it, the bits are easy to get out. The fatal moment is just as the drill goes through into the port. Whilst drilling through the solid metal, withdraw it every $\frac{1}{8}$ in. or so, and clear the chips off.

Cylinder Covers

Before machining and fitting the cylinder covers, there is one little filing job to do, viz. establish communication (as the radio announcer would say) between the drilled passageways and the cylinder bore. This is a simple job; all you have to do is to file a bevel about $\frac{3}{32}$ in. deep, in the edge of the bore, at each end of the cylinder, extending the full width of the three holes. This is shown in the longitudinal section, and also in the end view showing the passageways. The great thing to avoid, when filing, is hitting the bore with the tip of the file; and to make certain of this, a good wheeze is to bend a bit of thin tin, brass, or anything else handy, into a half circle, and slip it into the bore, opposite the passageways. Then, if you are a wee bit too vigorous on the forward stroke of the file, the point of it will hit the shield, and the bore won't be damaged.

Now for the covers. Do the front covers first. They should have a chucking-piece cast on the outside. Grip this in the three-jaw, and set the cover to run as truly as possible; a gentle tap with a small hammer will do the needful, as bronze or gunmetal castings are quite ductile. Face off the rough skin with a round-nose tool set cross-wise in the rest; then put a knife tool in. The cutting edge of the tool shouldn't be exactly at right-angles to the lathe centres; because if it is, on the average small lathe, it will chatter like Old Nicko if the full length of the cutting edge makes contact with the cover. Slant it slightly towards the lathe headstock, so that only the point and a little of the edge, will cut. Set your slide gauge or calipers to a little over $\frac{11}{16}$ in. opening, and very carefully turn a full $\frac{1}{16}$ in. length of the cover, until the gauge jaws or caliper tips will just slide over. If you take off about $\frac{1}{16}$ in. at a "bite", and run the lathe at medium speed only, there won't be any chattering, neither will the tool try to dig in. When the little projection has been turned to a diameter that the calipers or gauge will slide over, very carefully turn off a shade more, until it will enter the cylinder bore without the least bit of shake. This projection is known as the register, because it registers the cover truly with the cylinder bore. Now watch your step again: on the last cut, when you have got the register to dead size, feed the tool in a weeny bit, so as to make a slight under-cut, or groove, at the end of the register; then draw it back, which will take a skim off the face of the flange part, which makes contact with the cylinder casting, and leave it perfectly true. The edge of the cover can then be turned to $1\frac{1}{8}$ in. diameter, and the operations repeated on No. 2. Face $\frac{1}{64}$ in. or so off each register, before removing from chuck.

The way I hold the covers to face off the outside is by gripping them in a home-made step chuck held in the three-jaw. Old-time craftsmen used wood chucks for jobs like these, and young Curly followed their example on his first tiny lathe. A piece of hardwood was either gripped in the chuck, or screwed to the faceplate by woodscrews through the back; then a recess was turned in the face of the wood, just big enough to allow the cover to be pressed in tightly. The outside was then faced off with a round-nose tool. This method is still quite good, and beginners who haven't a bit of metal to make the step chuck, can use it with advantage. A piece of metal $1\frac{1}{2}$ in. diameter and about $\frac{1}{2}$ in. thick, is needed; chuck this in the three-jaw, and turn down about $\frac{3}{8}$ in. length to a little over 1 in. diameter. Exact measurement doesn't matter. Reverse in chuck; face, centre, drill a pilot hole right through, and open it out to about $\frac{3}{4}$ in. diameter. If you haven't a drill that size, use the biggest you have, and finish with a boring-tool, same as boring cylinders. Next, with a knife-tool set cross-wise in the rest, and starting from the edge of the hole, form a recess $\frac{3}{32}$ in. deep in the face; this should be an exact fit for the cover. Make a centre-dot in the edge, or face, opposite No. 1 jaw of the chuck; take out the step chuck, as the piece of metal has now become, and make a hacksaw cut through one side of it. Then put it back in the three-jaw, with the dot opposite No. 1 jaw; put the cover in the recess, tighten the chuck jaws and the cover will be gripped firmly, and dead true, whilst you face off the outside. Saw off the chucking-piece first.

The Back Covers

The back covers are a little more tricky, as they carry the gland bosses, and the guide bars. The first part of the operation is to turn the registers, and the diameter, exactly as for the front covers; it is important that the registers fit the bores exactly, without a vestige of shake. Before removing from chuck, centre each cover carefully with a size E centre-drill in the tailstock chuck, and drill about $\frac{1}{2}$ in. depth with No. 21 drill. This is the clearing size for the $\frac{5}{32}$ in. piston rod. Now put your step chuck in the three-jaw, and set a cover in it, with the gland boss outwards. Saw off the chucking-piece, and face off the boss with a round-nose tool to the dimensions shown in the illustration. The metal of the cover below the boss cannot, of course, be faced off in the lathe, so it will have to be hand filed when the machining is finished. There is a way of getting a machined surface over the whole of the cover, but this involves fitting a separate gland boss, and we needn't bother about such refinements on a job like little *Tich*.

Where many beginners fall out of the cart, in a manner of speaking, is in getting the gland concentric, or dead true, with the stuffing box; yet it is so easy when you know how. If a tyro opens out the piston rod hole with an ordinary drill, in 99 cases out of 100 the bigger drill won't line up properly with the smaller hole. The error is usually exaggerated when tapping. Then, when he makes the gland, there is a chance that the piston rod hole in that won't be dead central either; so we have then the combination of an eccentric gland in an eccentric stuffing box. The holes in gland and stuffing box only line up in one position of the gland; a fraction of a turn either way, throws them out of line, and the piston rod promptly jams or binds in both.

All you need do, to prevent this untoward happening, is to open out the piston rod hole with a pin-drill. I have already explained how these are made; so make one a weeny shade under $\frac{9}{32}$ in. diameter, using a piece of $\frac{5}{32}$ in. round silver-steel for a pilot pin. After facing off the boss, put this pin-drill in the tailstock chuck, and open out the hole in the boss with it, to a depth of $\frac{5}{16}$ in. Then tap it $\frac{5}{16}$ in. by 32, using a tap guided by the tailstock chuck, in exactly the same way that I described for tapping the ends of the valve box on the pump casting. Go very steadily to work, as it is essential that the threads be clean and true. The unturned part of the cover can then be cleaned up with a file; to hold the cover, screw the end of a piece of $\frac{5}{16}$ in. brass rod $\frac{5}{16}$ in. by 32, screw it into the tapped stuffing box, and you have a nobby handle.

The next job is to drill and tap the holes for the guide bars. Make a plug to fit in the stuffing box, and show the true centre of same, and scribe a line across the centre, down the middle of the gland box. At exactly $\frac{7}{16}$ in. above the centre, make a centre-pop on the line; drill it about $\frac{1}{4}$ in. deep with No. 40 drill, and tap $\frac{1}{8}$ in. or 5 BA. Use the drilling machine or lathe, because if the hole isn't dead square with the face of the boss, the guide bar won't line up with the piston rod, and you will be in a nice old mess when assembling the crossheads.

Drilling the Covers

There isn't the slightest need to mark out all the screw holes separately on each cover; life's too short! Use a simple jig. Get a washer, or a brass disc, the size of the cylinder cover, or a weeny bit larger. Chuck this truly in the three-jaw, and drill and bore the centre hole until it is the same size as the cylinder bore, so that it will fit on the register of each cover. Set out the location of the screwholes on this, as shown in the end view of the cylinder illustrated; make a centre-pop at each location, and drill No. 40. Put this drilled

Plate 7

Two views of the "Tich" chassis by Mr. J. H. Balleny

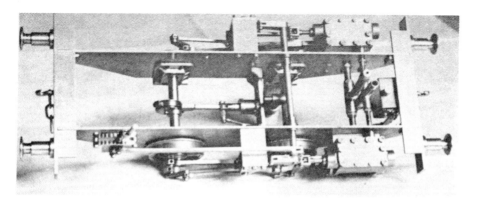

Cylinders, connecting rods, crossheads and slide-bars by G. F. Collins of Brighton

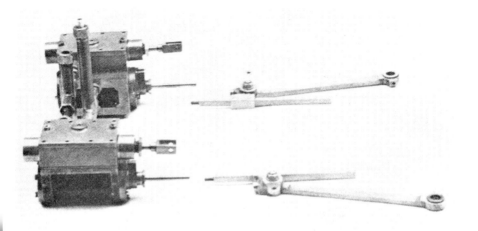

Plate 8

Two views of the cylinders, with steam and exhaust pipes for the "Tich" built
by Mr. G. F. Collins of Brighton

washer over the register of each cylinder, and hold it in place with a tool-maker's clamp; then run the drill through all the holes, carrying on clean through the cover. Warning: the back covers have to be attached to the cylinders, so that the hole for the guide bar in the gland boss is exactly above the piston rod hole. By the same token, as Pat would say, the screw holes have to be drilled to miss the passageways. Therefore, when attaching the jig to the back covers, make certain that the holes in it correspond to the holes shown in the end view of the assembled cylinder; also, don't forget that one cylinder (the one shown) is right-hand, and the other left-hand, and the offset of the holes in the left-hand cylinder, will incline the opposite way.

As the machining of the two cylinder castings was carried out in the same way, they should be exactly alike, and up to this stage there is nothing to distinguish right from left, or back from front; so now mark one right, and one left. I use a set of letter punches and figures for marking. These may be obtained in all sizes from $\frac{1}{32}$ in. characters upwards. The $\frac{1}{16}$ in. size is about the best for our job, with normal eyesight; they don't disfigure the parts, and the letters or figures are easily readable. You could also use one dot for right, and two dots for left, putting the dots at the front end. Then proceed to drill and tap the holes for the front cover screws. Put a cover on the front end, with the blank space in between two screw holes covering the bevel at the end of the passageways. Hold it temporarily in place with a toolmaker's clamp; then run the No. 40 drill through all the holes in the cover, and make counter-sinks on the cylinder flange. Remove cover, drill out all the countersinks with No. 48 drill, and tap $\frac{3}{32}$ in. or 7 BA. This job should also be done on the drilling machine or lathe, so that the screws go in nice and square. If they go in on the slant—what the kiddies would call lopsided or cockeyed—one side of the head touches the cover before the other. You go to tighten it down, and—click! off comes its noddle!

To set the back covers truly, put one in place with the guide bar hole as nearly direct above the piston rod centre as you can judge by eye. Leave the centre plug in the stuffing box. Hold the cover to the cylinder with a clamp. Lay the cylinder, bolting face down, on the lathe bed or drilling machine table. Set the needle of your scribing block to the centre of the plug; then adjust the cover until the centre of the hole for the guide bar is at the same height, and you can run the scriber needle along, with the point touching the marked line on the gland boss, for its full length. Tighten the clamp, and proceed to locate, drill and tap the screw holes, as described for the front covers.

It is quite possible that the flanges of the cylinder castings will now project beyond the edges of the covers; mine usually do, as my own patterns allow for plenty of metal. If so, run the point of an ordinary scriber around the edges of the covers, which can be temporarily fixed by two screws in each, for this purpose. Then remove covers, and file the flanges until the lines just disappear; this will permit a thin sheet of lagging to be put around each cylinder between the covers, and flush with the edges of them. Don't forget to mark which covers belong to right- and left-hand cylinders.

The Pistons

The success, or otherwise, of a locomotive, frequently depends on the fit of the pistons in the cylinders. I have often said, and emphasise again for beginners' benefit, that pistons should be perfectly steam-tight, yet not mechanically tight. The old school of thought considered this to be impossible, and got up to all sorts of weird and wonderful antics to squeeze the packing into close contact with the cylinder bores, irrespective of how much internal friction was caused. My own engines never suffer from blowing pistons, and they work with such little friction that quite a moderate push will send the engine running down the line; whilst the distance they will coast with steam shut off is amazing. The secret of success, is to have the piston rod dead in the middle of the piston, so that when the cover is on, and the piston rod projecting through the gland, you can twirl the rod between thumb and finger, without feeling a tight place anywhere in the bore; yet the piston itself is an exact fit in the bore. A precision job, says the beginner; however can I manage it on my not-so-precision lathe? Easy enough, as you will see.

First of all, make the rods. These can be rustless steel or phosphor-bronze, cut to the length shown in the illustration. Either ground or drawn rod of $\frac{5}{32}$ in. diameter, will do fine. Chuck each piece in the three-jaw, and put a bare $\frac{1}{8}$ in. length of $\frac{5}{32}$ in. by 40 thread on one end, with the die in the tail-stock holder.

The pistons can be made from $\frac{3}{4}$ in. round bronze or gunmetal rod, or from castings or cast stick bronze. Chuck the rod or stick in the three-jaw; turn down about $1\frac{1}{8}$ in. length to $\frac{1}{64}$ in. over finished diameter, as measured by slide-gauge or caliper. Face the end, centre, and drill down $\frac{1}{2}$ in. depth with No. 30 drill. At $\frac{1}{8}$ in. from the end, form a groove $\frac{1}{16}$ in. wide, and $\frac{3}{16}$ in. deep, with a parting tool; then part off at a full $\frac{7}{16}$ in. from the end. Repeat operation for piston No. 2. Chuck each piston blank in the three-jaw, parted-off side outwards, and take a truing-up skim off it, as some parting-tools leave a scored surface; then open out the centre hole for half its depth, with a No. 23 drill. Tap the rest of the hole $\frac{5}{32}$ in. by 40. Put one of the piston rods in the tailstock chuck, threaded end outwards, and tighten well up, so that the smooth rod cannot slip. Run the tailstock up to the head end, and enter the screwed end of the piston rod into the hole in the piston. Carefully pull the belt by hand, and the screw will draw a part of the plain rod into the enlarged end of the hole in the piston. This way of fitting, part by screw, and part plain, is the way all chucks of precision lathes are fitted to the mandrel noses, and is the finest way I know of ensuring that the piston is quite true on the rod. Keep going until the rod has entered the piston for its full width.

Finally, the piston has to be fitted to the cylinder. I don't suppose that many beginners have a precision lathe fitted with collet chucks, but if there are any such lucky persons, all they have to do is to grip the piston rod in a $\frac{5}{32}$ in. collet, and turn the piston to a sliding fit in the cylinder. Users of ordinary lathes with only a three-jaw chuck of doubtful veracity, can, however, make quite an accurate job by using a split bush. Chuck a piece of rod (brass will do quite well) in the three-jaw, any small scrap end will do, a convenient size being $\frac{3}{8}$ in. diameter and about $\frac{1}{2}$ in. long. Face the end, centre, and drill through with No. 24 drill. Make a D-bit from a piece of the same sized steel as the diameter of the piston rods, and put this through the bit of brass, by aid of the tailstock chuck. Be careful when starting it at the entrance of the hole, and it will bore a hole dead true with the centre-line of the lathe mandrel, even if the chuck is out of true. Now make a centre-pop opposite No. 1 jaw. Remove bush, split it lengthwise with a hacksaw from side to centre hole; rechuck, and run the D-bit through again, to remove any burring. If you put the piston rod in the hole, and tighten the chuck jaws on the bush, both rod and piston should run truly. Now, with very fine cuts, little more than mere scrapes, and a keen tool, like a pointed one with a rounded-off end (says Pat) turn down the two flanges or "lands" of the piston, until they are an exact sliding fit in the cylinder, without any shake. Use the cylinder itself for a gauge. If your cross-slide has a micrometer collar, turn the piston to a very tight fit first, then advance the cross-slide a bare half-a-division of the collar. That will enable you to finish-turn the piston to a size that will be perfectly steamtight without relying on the packing, when the cylinder is at working temperature, and the oil supply is working properly. Take great care over fitting your pistons; it doesn't need much of a blow-by to waste more steam than the little *Tich* boiler can generate. Next stage, steam chests and valves.

Glands for Cylinders

The glands for both piston rods and valve spindles are the same, except for length. The best material to use is $\frac{3}{8}$ in. hexagon rod, either drawn or cast bronze. Gunmetal also does well, but soft brass should only be used if nothing better is available. Although there isn't much stress on the piston rod gland owing to the crosshead and guide bars doing the needful, the long spindle gland has to do the guiding as well, so should be made from wear-resisting material. Whatever material is used, the job is done the same way. Chuck the piece of rod in the three-jaw; the chuck will hold the hexagon metal as well as it will hold round stock. Face off the end, and centre with a Slocomb-type drill, making the countersink deep enough to allow a No. 24 drill to enter. This is important, because the holes for piston rod and spindle must be dead in the middle of the gland, otherwise the rods will bind when the gland is tightened. If the drill just enters the countersink, it will make a hole slap-bang in the middle; but if the countersink is shallow, and the drill starts to cut on the sharp edge, the odds are 99 to 1 that it will take off more from one side than the other, and the hole will be out of truth. Beginners should bear this in mind; even our more experienced friends have slipped up on the same point, on occasions! Drill down about $\frac{5}{8}$ in. for the spindle gland, and about $\frac{1}{2}$ in. for the piston gland. Face off the end, just sufficiently to take out all traces of the countersink; then turn down the end to $\frac{5}{16}$ in. diameter, $\frac{3}{8}$ in. length for the spindle gland, and $\frac{5}{16}$ in. length for the piston gland. Screw $\frac{5}{16}$ in. by 32 or 40, to match the threads in the stuffing box. The steam chest bosses will be tapped same pitch as the stuffing box on the back cylinder cover already described. Part off $\frac{1}{8}$ in. from the shoulder. You need two piston rod and two spindle glands, so make the lot whilst at it.

Make a tapped bush to hold in the three-jaw. A bit of $\frac{1}{2}$ in. round rod, about $\frac{1}{2}$ in. long, will do nicely. Chuck it, face, centre, drill right through with letter K or $\frac{9}{32}$ in. drill, countersink the end slightly with letter O or $\frac{5}{16}$ in. drill, and tap $\frac{5}{16}$ in. by 32 or 40, to match the glands. Skim off any burring on the face; then screw each gland into it, skim the faces, chamfer the corners of the hexagon, and run a $\frac{5}{32}$ in. parallel reamer through the hole. Before removing the tapped bush from the chuck, make a centre-pop opposite No. 1 jaw, or mark it with a figure punch, so that you can keep it handy for use in holding screwed fittings, and can replace it truly any time it is needed. I have a box full of these tapped bushes; and very handy they are too!

Steam Chests

The steam chests may either have the bosses cast on, or they may be separate, and screwed in. Both kinds are shown on the drawings. If a planing, shaping or milling machine is available, the cast-on bosses are best, but beginners who have only a small lathe and not much equipment, may find the separate bosses the better proposition, for reasons you will see below. Chuck the first-mentioned type of casting in the three-jaw, holding by one of the bosses, and set the other boss to run truly. Leave the chuck jaws slightly slack, and tap the outer boss with a small spanner or anything light, until it ceases to wobble. Tighten chuck jaws, and centre the boss deeply with a centre-drill. The tailstock, with the centre point in the barrel, can then be run up to support the boss, whilst you turn same, and face off the end of the steam chest. This is done with a knife-tool set in slightly towards the headstock, which prevents chattering; and don't have the tool projecting from the rest farther than necessary to reach the boss, without the steam chest fouling the rest as it revolves. Repeat operation to turn the other boss, gripping the turned one in the chuck. When the second one is turned, drill, counterbore, and tap it exactly as already described for the stuffing box on the back cylinder cover. Don't forget that the tapped boss is the one farthest away from the little boss at the side of the steam chest, which is for attachment of the steam pipe, and will be cast on in any case.

The sides of the steam chest can be smoothed off with a file. Careful filing would also do for the contact faces, if no method of machining is available; but they can be milled or planed. If you own, or have the use of a milling machine, it is a simple job to hold the casting in the machine vice, and run it under a small slabbing cutter on the arbor, taking sufficient cuts to cover the whole surface of the contact face of the casting, without altering the height adjustment of the table. I do all mine that way, if they have cast-on bosses. The casting could also be held in a machine vice on the table of a planing or shaping machine, and the contact faces cleaned off by aid of a round-nose tool in the clapper box, using a square-nose for finishing off the extreme edges next to the bosses. If your lathe is a good stout one with plenty of "meat" in it, so that it doesn't spring, the contact faces could be milled, as given above, with the casting set at correct height in a machine vice on the saddle, and the cutter on an arbor between centres.

If separate bosses are used, all you have to do is to set up the casting in the four-jaw chuck, contact face outwards, and face it off with a round-nose tool; reverse in chuck, and repeat process on the other face, leaving the steam chest $\frac{1}{2}$ in. from top to bottom. The sides and ends can be filed up; a nice little exercise in the use of that humble, but very necessary metal-disintegrator. On the centre-line of each end, at the side farthest away from the little boss, and $\frac{13}{32}$ in. from the edge, make a heavy centre-pop at each end. Then put a $\frac{1}{8}$ in. drill in the three-jaw; hold the casting against it, with the drill point in one centre-pop. Bring up the tailstock, set the point in the other centre-pop, and turn the wheel or handle. The drill must of necessity go through in line with the other pop. Then reverse the steam chest, and ditto repeato, the centre this time entering the first hole. Both holes will then be in line. Repeat operations with $\frac{11}{32}$ in. or letter R drill, and tap $\frac{3}{8}$ in. by 32 or 40. The steam-pipe boss is drilled $\frac{5}{32}$ in. and tapped $\frac{3}{16}$ in. by 40. For the plain boss, merely chuck a piece of $\frac{5}{8}$ in. round rod in three-jaw; face the end, turn down $\frac{1}{4}$ in. length to $\frac{3}{8}$ in. diameter, screw $\frac{3}{8}$ in. by 32 or 40, and part off $\frac{3}{8}$ in. from shoulder. Reverse in chuck, skim off any burr, and slightly chamfer. For the gland boss, face, turn and screw as above; but before parting off, centre, and drill down to about $\frac{3}{4}$ in. depth with No. 21 drill. After parting, reverse in chuck, and grip by the plain part; then open out, drill, and tap, exactly as described for the stuffing box on the back cylinder cover.

Set out the position of the screw holes in the wall of the steam chest, as shown in the recent illustration; drill them either on the drilling machine, or in the lathe, as per previous drilling instructions. Screw the bosses into place with a taste of plumbers' jointing on the threads, and another good job is done. Next, covers, valves and spindles, and assembly.

I have not hurried the description of the cylinders, because I know from correspondence how long it takes the average tyro to machine up a pair of cylinder castings, and make a proper job of it; but by this time I should imagine most of our beginner friends are ready to carry on, so here we go. The flat covers for the steam chests may either be castings, or merely a piece of $\frac{1}{8}$ in. brass plate for each. If castings are supplied, they should have a chucking-piece cast on, in the centre of the rectangle; all you have to do is to grip this in the three-jaw, give the cover a little gentle persuasion with a light hammer if it doesn't run truly, and then face off with a round-nose tool set cross-wise in the slide-rest. File the sides and ends to the same dimensions as the steam chest, cut off the chucking-piece with a hacksaw, file the stub flush, and smooth off the unturned side with a file. There is no need to machine both sides.

The plate cover is merely a piece of $\frac{1}{8}$ in. brass plate, or thick sheet, sawn to a little over the size of the steam chest, and finished to exact size with a file. It must, of course, be perfectly flat, so that when screwed down, it makes a steam-tight joint with the contact face of the steam chest. If you are lucky enough to own a finisher, or emery-band surface grinder, a minute or so on the fast-running emery-band will iron out any small " 'umps and 'ollers" on the cover. A similar effect can be obtained by laying a sheet of medium-grade emery cloth, or other abrasive, on something flat and true, such as the drilling machine table, and rubbing the cover on it, keeping it well pressed down. Temporarily clamp the finished cover, plate or cast, to the steam chest with a toolmaker's clamp; drill the screw holes by running the drill through the holes in the steam chest, carrying on right through the cover, and clean off any burring around the holes.

Slide Valves

The slide valves may be made either from castings, or bar material. If cast, the metal should be of a different grade from that of the cylinders, as like metals don't "work together" so well as unlike ones. If bar material is used, I recommend drawn bronze or gunmetal. Drawn phosphor-bronze is pretty tough stuff to machine; but once it is done, it IS done, if you get my meaning! I've never had to reface a hard bronze slide valve yet, in any of my locomotives. Drawn gunmetal is a little easier to machine, and lasts what the kiddies would call "donkey's years" before needing a reface, so that may be used with all confidence. Rustless steel also works very well on a cast bronze port face, and so does monel metal; but both of these are about as tough as phosphor-bronze, as far as machining is concerned. The advantage of using castings, is that the cavity and maybe the slots in the back also, would be cored out, so that not much machining would be needed. Although careful filing would bring the casting to size, it makes a better job if the casting is chucked in the four-jaw, with one end or side projecting, and faced off with a round-nose tool set cross-wise in the rest; repeat operation for the other end and side. Leave the valve a shade full on the length, to allow of a slight adjustment when setting the valves later on. You can easily shorten a valve, but lengthening it isn't quite so easy! The cavity should be trued up to the sizes given, by aid of a small chisel, which can be home-made from a bit of silver-steel, say $\frac{3}{8}$ in. diameter. Make it the same way as the one I suggested for hand-cutting the ports.

The round-bottomed slot for the valve spindle can be smoothed out with a file; but the wider flat-bottomed one for the nut, needs to be "about right", so should be machined. This can be done thus; either clamp the valve on its side, under the slide-rest holder, or attached to an angle-plate, or to the vertical-slide, and traverse it across a $\frac{1}{4}$ in. end-mill or slot-drill held in the chuck; or else hold it at the proper height in a machine vice (regular or improvised) on the lathe saddle, and traverse it under a $\frac{1}{4}$ in. wide saw-type cutter mounted on a spindle between centres. Of course, if any beginner owns, or has the use of a milling machine, planer or shaper the job is just a piece of cake; merely grip the valve in the machine vice on the table, and traverse it under a $\frac{1}{4}$ in. side-and-face cutter on the arbor of the milling machine, or under a square-ended tool in the clapper-box of a planer. On a shaper, naturally, the valve would remain stationary, the tool being operated by the ram.

To make the valve from bar material, you would need a $\frac{3}{8}$ in. square bar about $1\frac{3}{4}$ in. long, to allow enough for facing the ends and parting off. Chuck it in the four-jaw—doesn't matter a bean if it isn't dead true—face the end, and part off a $\frac{3}{4}$ in. full length. By "full", I mean leave enough to allow for facing off the parted end. Some parting tools part off truly, and some don't. It isn't always the fault of the tool, at that! I gave somebody a parting tool which did the job perfectly on my Milnes lathe, because he said he could never get a satisfactory part-off, the cut being always "on the skew-whiff". With the tool I gave him, the result was the same. The lathe was one of the "all-fallals-and-no-meat" variety, and sprung under a decent cut. He eventually managed to get good results by rigging up a toolholder to take pieces of broken hacksaw blades, ground at the ends like parting tools. The narrow cut didn't spring the machine. The tip may be useful; anyway, it is a good wheeze for making use of the remnants of broken blades!

Face off both pieces of bar to the correct length, then mark out the slots and cavities. The cavity can be end-milled out by the same process as described for port cutting. Mount the valve end-up on the vertical-slide, and feed it up

Details of the slide valves, valve spindles and valve crossheads.

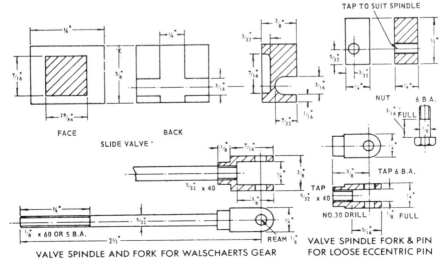

to an end-mill or slot-drill in the three-jaw; use the one that cut the exhaust port. By careful manipulation of the cross-slide and vertical-slide handles, the marked-out space denoting the cavity, can be manoeuvred across the cutter over its entire area, and the cavity formed quite easily. When it is the required depth, viz. $\frac{3}{32}$ in., remove the exhaust-port cutter, substitute the dental burr, and reduce the radius at the corners. It doesn't matter about the corners of the cavity being rounded, as long as they are the same radius as the ports, or within a little of it.

If you haven't a vertical-slide, do the job by hand. In the middle of the marked-out cavity, either make a shallow countersink with a $\frac{13}{32}$ in. drill, or else drill a number of blind holes $\frac{3}{32}$ in. deep, all over the enclosed space. Then chip away the superfluous metal with a chisel, made as described above, for finishing the cavity of a cast valve. Although much of the efficiency of the engine depends on the accuracy of the exhaust cavities, there is nothing difficult about doing the job. Anybody who can hold the business end of a chisel on a marked line, whilst they assault the butt end with a hammer, should be able to cut the cavity to the correct size. All it needs is care and patience.

The slots in the back are cut by the same process, with the same rig-up, as described above for truing up the slots in a casting; the only difference is, that you have to cut away more metal in chewing from the solid. If any beginner has a $\frac{3}{16}$ in. milling-cutter with rounded teeth, he can cut the slot for the valve spindle at one fell swoop. If not, don't bother to mill it at all, just drill a $\frac{3}{16}$ in. hole lengthwise through the valve, the centre of it being $\frac{1}{8}$ in. from the top, and $\frac{1}{32}$ in. from the side; then, with the hacksaw and file, cut away the bit of metal left at the top, leaving the round-bottom channel, as shown in the cross section. To get a true face on the valve, lay a piece of fine emery cloth, or similar abrasive, on a flat surface, as mentioned for the cover job; give the valve a few rubs on it, pressing well down all the time, and moving the valve with a partly circular motion. This will do the trick in two wags of a dog's tail. The rubbing surface of the valve should show a matt surface, covered with minute scratches. These hold a film of oil, which makes the valve slide easily over the ports, and prevents any steam getting under it. If you belong to a club, and the usual "know-all-the-answers" merchant who is found in every club, starts in to tell you about my big valves being all wrong, due to the great pressure on the back, and so on and so forth, don't take any notice. It isn't the size of the valves that matters, but the friction between the valve and port face; and by maintaining a film of oil between the rubbing parts (*Tich*'s mechanical lubricator will see to this) friction is reduced to a minimum.

Nut and Spindle

The nut should require no machining at all, being simply a $\frac{1}{2}$ in. length of $\frac{1}{4}$ in. square brass rod, with No. 40 hole drilled through it at the position shown in the illustration, and tapped $\frac{1}{8}$ in. by 60, if you have a tap, and die for this fine thread. If not, tap it 5 BA. The object of this fine thread is to give a finer adjustment, enabling a more perfect valve setting to be obtained. Be sure that the hole goes squarely through the nut, because if the nut cants on the spindle, the valve will not seat truly on the port face; so drill the nut on lathe or drilling machine and not by hand. The nut should fit easily in the wider slot in the valve but must not shake. If it is tight, give one side a few rubs on a flat file laid on the bench, and ease it just sufficiently to drop into the slot; no more.

The valve spindle is a piece of $\frac{5}{32}$ in. round rustless steel or drawn bronze rod $2\frac{1}{4}$ in. long. Chuck in three-jaw with a little over $\frac{3}{4}$ in. projecting from the jaws, and carefully turn down $\frac{3}{4}$ in. length to $\frac{1}{8}$ in. diameter. Beginners note: if your lathe is at all "suspicious", leave only $\frac{1}{8}$ in. projecting from the chuck jaws, for a kick-off. Face the end with a knife-tool, and centre it with a small centre-drill in the tailstock chuck. Then pull it out about $\frac{7}{8}$ in. or so; put the centre point in the tailstock, and run it up until the point will enter the centre hole in the end of the rod, and support it. Don't forget a drop of oil! Then turn as above, using a round-nose tool with plenty of top rake; replace tailstock chuck, and with a die in the tailstock holder, screw the turned part to match the hole in the nut. Reverse the rod in the chuck, and put about $\frac{3}{16}$ in. or $\frac{5}{32}$ in. by 40 thread on the other end.

The fork, or clevis, is made from $\frac{1}{4}$ in. by $\frac{3}{8}$ in. mild steel. At a full $\frac{1}{8}$ in. from the end, in the middle of the narrower side, make a centre-pop, and drill a No. 33 hole right through the thickness, same as you did the nut. Ream it $\frac{1}{8}$ in. Now mount the piece of rod on the slide-rest, under the toolholder, and form a slot in it, $\frac{1}{4}$ in. wide and $\frac{3}{8}$ in. deep, by exactly the same method as was previously described for slotting the pump ram; but use the $\frac{1}{4}$ in. cutter that did the slot in the slide valve. If you haven't a cutter, file the slot by hand; care and a little patience will do the trick. Chuck in four-jaw, and part off at $\frac{5}{8}$ in. from the end. Reverse in chuck, set to run truly, face the end, centre, drill No. 30 until the drill breaks through into the bottom of fork, tap $\frac{5}{32}$ in. by 40, and turn down $\frac{1}{8}$ in. of the outside to $\frac{7}{32}$ in. diameter. Round off the ends of the jaws, same as described for the coupling rods, and screw in the $\frac{5}{32}$ in. end of the valve spindle. Next stage, how to pack the pistons and glands, and make the joints.

Cylinder Assembly

The cylinder components being all made, we can put them together. First, pack the pistons. Now, the easiest and most satisfactory way I know of packing small pistons—and I have tried about every possible variation—is to use a kind of piston-ring made from square braided graphited yarn. This is a commercial article, which can be obtained at any stores, in most towns, who sell engineers' supplies. Some model advertisers sell it. For *Tich*'s cylinders, you need a short piece of $\frac{3}{16}$ in. square section. All you have to do is to cut a piece about $\frac{1}{4}$ in. longer than the circumference of the groove in the piston; cut off both ends at an angle, as neatly as you can manage, and put the piece of packing in the groove in the piston, with the wedge-shaped ends interlocking. Although the nominal size is $\frac{3}{16}$ in. square, the actual size is a weeny bit larger; so roll the piston on something smooth (the lathe bed will do, you won't hurt it) pressing on the piston with a piece of perfectly smooth bar. This will press down the surface of the packing, level with the piston, or nearly so.

Now insert the piston into the cylinder, with the joint away from the passageways. It probably won't want to go in, the packing springing out a little from the groove in the piston; but it can be easily coaxed by judicious prodding all around with a small screwdriver, or a pocket-knife blade which isn't sharp enough to cut the packing. Press the piston in, at the same time as you prod all around, and a little care and patience will do the trick. When the piston is in the cylinder, it should be quite free to move up and down, yet by virtue of the "spring" in the packing, no steam will be able to blow past, the packing forming a perfect seal. Now you see what I mean by a piston being steam-tight, but not mechanically tight. If a piston is properly packed in the first place, and kept properly lubricated, it will remain steam-tight for an amazing length of time.

Cover Joints

The cover joint can be made from $\frac{1}{64}$ in. "Hallite", or any other good brand of steam jointing; or oiled paper may be used. Beginners frequently have trouble with joints blowing badly, due to gaskets cracking or splitting, but they won't do either if you make them the following simple way. Whether using regular jointing material, or paper, the method is the same, but if paper is used, it should not be crumpled up, and the best kind to use is strong wrapping paper with a matt surface. Lay the cover on the bench, register upwards, and put a piece of jointing, or dry paper, over it; then rub your finger on the paper, which will "print" the outline of the cover on the surface of it. Cut out the inner circle (outline of register) exactly to the line, with a pair of small nail scissors (ask your wife or girl friend if she would like her nail scissors sharpened up a little, and it will be a good excuse for testing them by cutting the jointing material!) then slip the hole over the register, and cut the jointing all around, level with edge of cover. If using paper, put a smear of cylinder oil all around the cover flange before putting the paper over it. Put the cover, with gasket attached, over the cylinder flange, smearing same with cylinder oil first, if paper is used; then poke your scriber down each screw hole, holding the cover on tightly, and make a puncture in the gasket under each hole. Put two opposite screws in, tightening sufficiently to hold the cover; the screws will enlarge the "puncture", but the gasket will be steam-tight around the screws. Then put the rest in, and tighten the lot in much the same order as those in a motor cylinder head, when replacing same after decarbonising; opposite screws in turn. Joints put in thus, won't split, crack, or blow in what the kiddies call "donkey's years" and will prevent possible failures on the track.

The rectangular steam chest joints are cut out and applied the same way, but don't do them yet; just put three or four screws in temporarily, to hold the parts together. The steam-chest covers will have to be taken off, for valve-setting purposes; and the joints can be made permanently after that is done.

The glands are packed with loose graphited yarn, another commercial product obtainable from the same sources as the jointing and braided material. It looks like thick black string, as sold. Cut off a few inches, and unravel it into separate strands; a dirty job, but if you rub some grease into your fingers first, the graphite will easily wash off, instead of becoming "grimed in", as my old granny used to say. Wind a few turns loosely around piston rod and valve spindle, then prod it into the stuffing boxes with a bit of stiff wire, flattened at the end. The stuffing boxes should be almost full; cut off any surplus, then screw the glands in until the yarn starts to compress. The glands must not be too tight, or the packing will go hard, and score the rods. It is surprising how little pressure is needed to keep the steam in, when the packing is soft and springy. I have dilated on cylinders at length, as they are the heart of the engine; and all beginners should aim at putting their very best efforts into making them up.

CHAPTER FIVE

Guide bars and crossheads

Guide Bars

BEFORE ERECTING THE CYLINDERS on the frames, we need the guide bars, crossheads and connecting rods; the whole lot go up together. The guide bars are only two bits of $\frac{1}{8}$ in. by $\frac{3}{16}$ in. silver-steel with a screw at one end, for attaching to the gland boss, and the countersunk hole at the other end, to take the screw holding the outer ends to the link bracket. Saw off the two pieces a shade over length; then chuck truly in the four-jaw. This job seems a bit of a headache to many beginners, yet it is easy enough when done as follows: set it as near as you can "by eye", closing the jaws on the piece of rod so that each one comes, as near as you can judge, to the centre of the width of the metal. One of my own four-jaw chucks has jaws just $\frac{1}{8}$ in. wide at the gripping end; so if I want to chuck a piece of rod that width, all I do is to set it flush with the jaws. Pull the belt by hand, and run up the end of your knife-tool in the slide-rest until it touches the rod. If it touches all four corners, the rod is set O.K. If it only touches one, slack the two opposite jaws very slightly, and tighten up the two on the "touching side", which will throw the work over a shade. If the tool touches two corners, slack the opposite jaw only, and tighten up the one between the touched corners. You'll get the knack of setting truly, after a few shots, and probably need only one or two adjustments in each direction, after that. Incidentally, one of my old "Kaiser's War" munition girls had a marvellous eye for four-jaw chucking, and could set a dozen pieces "spot-on" one after the other. Whether the fact that she could play any piece of music on the piano, at sight, had anything to do with it, I don't know; but anyway, there it was. Some folk are "gifted" that way.

Cutting Fluids

Face the end of the rod, then turn down $\frac{3}{16}$ in. length to $\frac{1}{8}$ in. diameter, and screw it 5 BA to match the tapped hole in the gland boss. Old-time tool-makers who had occasion to turn cast steel always reckoned that turps was the finest cutting fluid for that metal; but personally, I just use the same kind of cutting oil ("Cutmax" diluted with paraffin) as for ordinary steel, both for turning and screwing, and get an excellent finish. Use the tailstock holder for

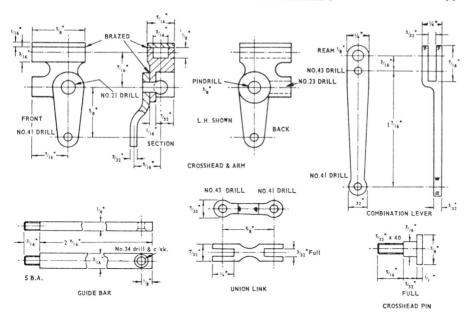

The crosshead, combination lever, guide bar and union link.
Crosshead arm not required if slip eccentric valve gear fitted.

the die; don't be tempted to use the hand die-stock, as I've known plenty of "L-card merchants" to do. If the threads aren't true, the guide bars won't come parallel with the piston rods. After screwing, reverse the bar in the chuck, and face the other end until it is exactly $2\frac{9}{16}$ in. from shoulder to end. If you slack No. 1 and 2 jaws, and re-tighten the same two after reversing, the bar will still run truly.

Now screw the bar into the gland boss, and note which is the underside when the bar is right home. Remove bar, make a centre-pop at $\frac{1}{8}$ in. from the end, in the middle of the underside, drill it No. 34, and countersink with a $\frac{3}{16}$ in. drill. If you don't screw in the bar, but drill and countersink "on the off-chance", the chances are 1,000 to 1 that the countersink will come on top; and when you try to get the other half-turn, the screw breaks off in the hole, and you've had it. If the bars are now screwed home, they should be parallel with the piston rods.

Crossheads

Though the crossheads on full-size engines are made from steel, it would be easier for beginners to make these from bronze or gunmetal; but steel may, of course, be used if preferred. A piece of metal $\frac{5}{16}$ in. thick, $\frac{3}{4}$ in. wide, and $1\frac{1}{2}$ in. long, will make the two of them. Now, in making these crossheads, beginners will be able to put to good use the lessons they have already learned in making the previously described components. The first thing to do, is to mill a groove the full length of one of the narrow edges. This groove is $\frac{3}{16}$ in. wide and $\frac{1}{8}$ in. deep, to fit the guide bar. It can be machined by any of the methods described for milling the rebates at each end of the axleboxes. The way I personally prefer is "straight" milling. If you own, or have the use of a milling machine the job is the proverbial "piece of cake"; for all you have to do, is to put the piece of metal in the machine vice on the miller table, adjust the table so that the $\frac{3}{16}$ in. saw-type cutter on the arbor will cut a groove $\frac{1}{8}$ in. deep, slap in the centre of the narrow side of the bit of bar and go right ahead.

Incidentally, I never measure my depth of cut; always trust the machine, and it never fails. This is how: the spindle operating the vertical movement of the table has 10 threads per inch and is bevel-geared 2-to-1, to the operating handle. This has a collar divided into 50 parts, so that moving the handle one division raises or lowers the table one-thousandth of an inch. To mill a $\frac{1}{8}$ in. crosshead groove I just put the blank in the machine vice on the table; a bit of parallel packing between the blank, and the bottom slide of the vice, ensures the blank being level. Then I raise the table, and pull the belt by hand backwards, until the teeth of the cutter just scrape the blank. The table is then traversed so that the blank is clear of the cutter; the handle lifting the table is turned $2\frac{1}{2}$ revolutions, equal to 125 thousandths, or $\frac{1}{8}$ in., and the table traversed under the cutter, which takes out the metal to a depth of $\frac{1}{8}$ in. exactly.

This method of milling can be reproduced on the lathe by mounting the cutter on a spindle, between centres, and clamping the vice to the saddle; but the right height to set the piece of metal in the vice will, of course, have to be measured, as the saddle won't have any vertical adjustment, unless it happens to be on that very useful machine, the 4 in. Drummond. A modernised version of this, with back gear, would easily lick any of the "fancy" lathes now on the market, for versatility.

The groove can also be formed with a $\frac{1}{8}$ in. end-mill, or home-made slot-drill held in the three-jaw, the blank being clamped on its side under the slide-rest toolholder, as described previously for milling axleboxes. The groove should be an exact sliding fit for the guide bar; test with a bit of the same section of steel, and if it doesn't slide, rub the blank up and down a $\frac{3}{16}$ in. square file held in the bench vice, keeping the groove pressed well down on the file. A very few rubs will do the needful. The blank can then be sawn in half, and each half chucked in the four-jaw. Face off the ends, so that the pieces are each $\frac{5}{8}$ in. long.

Next, at $\frac{3}{8}$ in. from the bottom of the groove, or $\frac{1}{2}$ in. from the top, and $\frac{7}{16}$ in. from the end, make a centre-pop. Drill right through with No. 21 drill, using either drilling machine or lathe, as the hole must go through dead square. Pin-drill this to a depth of $\frac{7}{32}$ in. with a $\frac{3}{8}$ in. pin-drill having a $\frac{5}{32}$ in. pilot pin; something else I have already described how to make, in detail. Don't forget to pin-drill block No. 2 from the opposite side to which you pin-drilled No. 1, so that one crosshead is right hand, and one left hand. The blocks can then be filed to the above shape shown, a job needing no description, but merely care and patience. Take $\frac{1}{32}$ in. off the side opposite to the pin-drilled one, starting at $\frac{3}{16}$ in. from the top, as shown in the section.

Trim off the outer end of each, level with the pin-drilled recess; see back view. The part into which the piston rod fits can be rounded off if you wish, but it isn't essential.

The next job is the crosshead arm, which operates the combination lever of the valve gear. Note, this isn't needed if you are using loose eccentrics; it is only for Walschaerts' gear. It is filed up from $\frac{3}{8}$ in. by $\frac{3}{32}$ in. flat steel, and bent to the shape shown in the section of the crosshead; drill as shown. Don't bother about exact measurement of the bent part, until the arm is attached to the crosshead. It is best to braze or silver-solder it in place, so that it cannot shift and upset the valve setting. The easiest way to make it "stay put" during the brazing process, is to fix with a hollow rivet. Chuck a bit of $\frac{5}{32}$ in. round rod in three-jaw; this should be of the same kind of metal as the crosshead. Centre, and drill down for about $\frac{1}{2}$ in. depth with No. 40 drill; part off two pieces a full $\frac{5}{32}$ in. long. Put the drop-arm against the crosshead, put one of the pieces through the holes, put the business end of a centre-punch in the hole at each end of the hollow rivet, and give it a crack with a hammer. This will spread the ends, and the arm will be held securely to the crosshead. Set it at right-angles, as shown in the illustrations.

The tops are made from two bits of the same kind of material as the crossheads, $\frac{1}{16}$ in. thick, and a little bigger than $\frac{3}{8}$ in. long, and $\frac{5}{16}$ in. wide; they are brazed or silver-soldered on at the same heating as the drop arms. A small tin lid makes a nobby brazing pan for jobs like these, also boiler fittings and other small components. Put some coke breeze or asbestos cubes in it. To prevent the lot falling down among the contents of the pan, lay a piece of asbestos millboard on the coke and put the pieces forming the tops of the crossheads on it. For brazing, use Boron compo for flux; for silver-soldering, powdered borax or "Easyflo" flux. Steel can be brazed or silver-soldered, as you prefer; bronze or gunmetal, silver-soldered only. Smear some wet flux on the two strips, also around the joint between drop arm and crosshead. Stand the crossheads upside down in the centre of the strips. Heat up to bright red for brazing, medium for silver-soldering, and touch the joints either with a bit of 16 gauge soft brass wire (if steel) or a narrow bit of silver-solder, or "Easyflo" wire, if bronze. Warning: don't use too much, or it will flow inside the joint, and the guide bar won't go through the hole; you'll have a dickens of a job filing it out, yet retaining the "all-along" fit for the bar. If you should be unlucky, however, one good method of cleaning the hole is to square off the end of a couple of inches of silver-steel, same section as used for the bars; harden and temper it, as described for pin-drills, cutters, etc., and drive it through the hole. This will cut away most of the unwanted brazing material inside the hole, and a watchmaker's square file will finish the job if judiciously applied. Steel crossheads can be quenched out in clean water, and bronze or gunmetal ones in acid pickle, either kind being cleaned up afterwards, and the top filed flush with the sides and ends; also drill out the hollow rivet with a No. 21 drill.

To drill the piston rod hole in the right place, beginners proceed as follows. Take off the back cylinder cover. Slip the crosshead over the guide bar, and run it back to the gland, holding it tightly against the gland whilst you poke a No. 22 drill through the gland and stuffing box, making a deep countersink on the crosshead boss. Remove crosshead and drill out the countersink with No. 23 drill, using either milling machine or lathe, and holding the crosshead in a machine vice either on the drill table or against a drilling pad in the tailstock barrel. Set the crosshead in the vice by aid of your try-square, so that the hole is drilled dead parallel with the top of the crosshead.

The pins are turned from a piece of $\frac{3}{8}$ in. round mild steel; just a kiddy's practice job. Chuck in the three-jaw, face the end, turn down $\frac{15}{32}$ in. length to $\frac{3}{16}$ in. diameter, further reduce a bare $\frac{5}{16}$ in. length to $\frac{5}{32}$ in. diameter, and screw $\frac{5}{32}$ in. by 40. Part off to leave a head $\frac{1}{16}$ in. wide, as shown in the illustration. For the nuts, chuck a piece of $\frac{1}{4}$ in. hexagon rod in three-jaw; face, centre, drill down about $\frac{1}{2}$ in. with No. 30 drill, tap $\frac{5}{32}$ in. by 40, and part off two $\frac{5}{32}$ in. slices. Rechuck each and chamfer the corners of the hexagons. Run the tap through again to clear out any burring.

Connecting Rods

As these are made by exactly the same process as described for the coupling rods, the lesson learned when making those is simply applied to the job in hand. The material needed will be two pieces of $\frac{5}{8}$ in. by $\frac{3}{16}$ in. flat steel. Whereas the coupling rods are parallel, the connecting rods are slightly tapered, from $\frac{3}{16}$ in. width at the little end, to $\frac{1}{4}$ in. at the big end. The big end bush is made and fitted exactly as described for the coupling rod bush at the back end of the rod; but on the inside of the rod it projects $\frac{3}{64}$ in. to form a distance-piece or spacer, keeping the connecting and coupling rods the right distance apart. The boss or flange on the outside of the rod is $\frac{1}{32}$ in. thick only, as the return crank for driving the valve gear fits outside it. Drill the hole in the big end of the rod, with an $\frac{11}{32}$ in. drill, and turn the bush to a tight squeeze fit.

The little end should be just large enough to fit in the recess in the crosshead. It is also reduced in thickness, $\frac{1}{32}$ in. being filed or milled off the outside, so that when the rod is fitted in the crosshead, and erected, it will be parallel with the coupling rod. The hole for the bush is drilled $\frac{1}{4}$ in. and the bush itself is filed flush each side, and does not project at all. Drill an oil hole in each big end, as shown by the dotted lines; again, don't forget you need one right-hand and one left-hand rod. When finished, put the little end of each connecting rod into the recess in the proper crosshead, poke the crosshead pin through, and put the nut on outside the drop arm. The large head of the crosshead pin fills the end of the pin-drilled recess, and gives the same effect as if the crosshead were double-sided.

Plate 9

There is no reason why the ladies should not build model locomotives, or for that matter, milk tanks! Here is Mrs. Ruth Daltry, a well-known Rugby enthusiast, with her "Tich" and United Dairies milk wagon

Plate 10

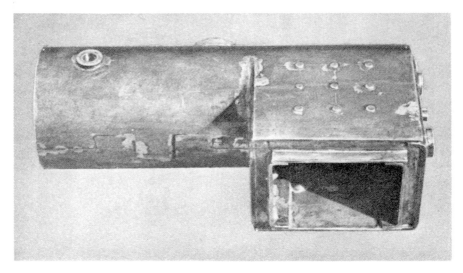

A fine "Tich" boiler built by Mr. Alec Farmer of Birmingham: note the barrel joint

Boiler shell and inner firebox and tubes made by Edgar Richardson of Handsworth Wood. This is not a "Tich" boiler but shows a similar type.

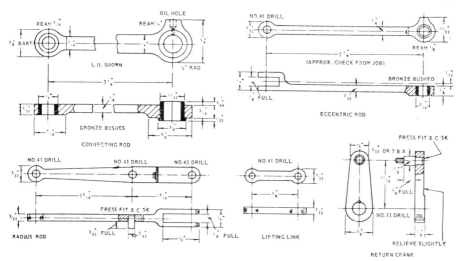

Details of connecting rod, eccentric rod, radius rod return crank and lifting link.

Erecting the Cylinders

Erecting cylinders correctly is a job that tangles up many a tyro, and even some of the more experienced builders; a friend managed to get the cylinders of a 4-6-0 erected in such a manner that one was $\frac{3}{16}$ in. higher than the other. If you follow the simple procedure set forth here you'll find the job easy. The tools needed for the job consist of a big toolmaker's clamp, which can be home-made, and a hand-brace with a long No. 30 drill in it. The drill must project not less than $3\frac{3}{8}$ in. from the chuck. These long drills are commercial articles; I have some of various sizes, but there is no need to buy one specially for the job. Any odd No. 30 drill that you already have can be lengthened as follows. File a step in the end of the shank, half through the diameter, and $\frac{1}{4}$ in. long, like making a short D-bit. File the end of a piece of $\frac{1}{8}$ in. steel rod, in the same way. Put the two together to form a continuous rod, with the steps interlocking; tie in position with a bit of thin iron binding wire and braze the joint. The wire binding will probably stick, but it can easily be filed off, and the extension rod cut to proper length.

Put the crossheads over the guide bars and enter the piston rods a little way in the crossheads; then put the cylinder up against the frame, slipping the big ends over the crankpins at the same time. Put the big clamp in position over cylinder and frame. Now adjust the cylinder until the bottom corner of the bolting face is right against the obtuse angle at the front end of the frame; see dotted line in the erection illustration. Tilt the cylinder away from the buffer-beam, until the front edge of the steam chest cover is $1\frac{11}{32}$ in. from the front of frame, behind the buffer-beams. Tighten the clamp, and then turn the wheels until the piston rod and connecting rod are in a straight line. The axlebox should be in correct running position, that is, with the centre of axle

$\frac{5}{8}$ in. above the bottom edge of frame. If the connecting rod passes exactly over the centre of the axle, the cylinder is set O.K. If not, then adjust cylinder until you get the desired result.

See that the clamp is tight; then poke the drill through the stud or screw holes in both frames (which was the idea of the long drill) and make countersinks on the bolting face of the cylinder. Remove cylinder, drill out the countersinks with No. 40 drill, and tap $\frac{1}{8}$ in. or 5 BA. Repeat the whole operation on the other cylinder; then temporarily secure both to the frame, with three screws in each. Pull the piston rods out of the crosshead bosses, and push them back into the cylinders as far as they will go, until the pistons hit the front covers. Now put each crank on front dead centre. The crosshead bosses will go over the piston rods again. Keeping the crank on the centre, advance each piston rod $\frac{1}{32}$ in. more, into the crosshead boss; the easiest way of doing this, is to take off the front cover and gently tap the piston. If you make a scratch around the piston rod, $\frac{1}{32}$ in. from the crosshead boss, and tap until the scratch is level with the boss, you can't very well fail to get the correct movement. Finally, drill a No. 43 hole clean through crosshead boss and piston rod; squeeze in a little bit of $\frac{3}{32}$ in. silver-steel, or 13 gauge spoke-wire, with one end very slightly tapered to give it a start, and the job is done. Front covers can then be replaced, and the pistons will just clear the covers by $\frac{1}{32}$ in. at each end of the stroke, so no steam will be wasted in filling up large open spaces and blowing to waste. Next stage, the *pons asinorum* of all beginners, the valve gear; but if you follow the words and music, there will be no difficulty in singing the tune!

CHAPTER SIX

Making the valve gear

Valve Gear

AS MENTIONED EARLIER, I propose to give alternative valve gears for *Tich*; the simple loose-eccentric, and the full Walschaerts'. As the engine will run around a circular track of suitable dimensions for any suburban back garden, there is no need for constant reversing; and for this, the loose-eccentric gear is the most desirable for locomotives made by inexperienced workers. It is easily made, easily set, and easily understood by the veriest Billy Muggins; the working parts are cut to the minimum, and there is nothing to go wrong. With the valves set as I shall specify, steam consumption is very low, yet the power and acceleration are all-present-and-correct-sergeant. Even on a straight up-and-down line, the slight push needed to reverse the engine—half-a-turn of a 2 in. wheel—is nothing to fret about. Still, I fully realise that there are lots of more experienced workers who are building the little engine as a "break" from bigger and more complicated types, and prefer a gear which can be reversed from the footplate, and notched up on a non-stop run; and so the description of the Walschaerts' gear will fill their needs. I might add, for beginners' benefit, that the Walschaerts' gear can be substituted for the loose-eccentric at any time during the lifetime of the engine; and some beginners might care to fit the loose-eccentric gear for a kick-off, and change over at some later date, when they have had more experience.

The accompanying illustrations show the layout of the gear. Mid-way between the centre-lines of the piston rod and valve spindle, and almost half-way between the axles, a rocking shaft works in a substantial bronze bearing attached to the frame by an oval flange. This carries two arms or levers. The outside one points upwards and is made like a crank, the pin of which is connected to the valve spindle fork by an offset valve rod. The offset is unavoidable, because the crank arm must be set close enough to the frames to allow the coupling rod to clear it, which it does by $\frac{1}{32}$ in. The centre-line of the valve spindles could, of course, be brought into line with the rocker arm, and a straight valve rod used, by adopting the Great Western type of cylinder; but if this were done special patterns would be needed, and the cylinder could not be used for Walschaerts' gear. However, offset valve rods make no difference to the working of the engine; and as they are used in some types of

83

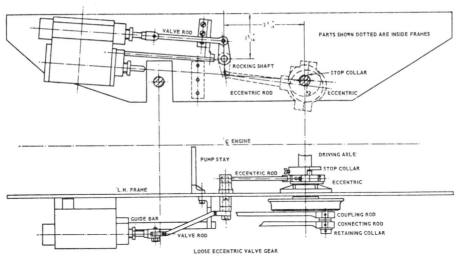

General arrangement of the slip-eccentric valve gear.

full-size locomotives, nobody need lose any sleep through worrying about them.

The inside arm of the rocking shaft hangs downwards and is slotted to take the end of the eccentric rod. The eccentric itself is mounted on the driving axle, close to the hornblock, and is not fixed to it in any way (hence the term "loose-eccentric"), but is driven by the shoulder of the stop-collar catching against the pin in the side of the eccentric. This is the only type of valve gear that gives equal port openings at both ends of the cylinders in either direction of running. Now to construction.

Rocking Shaft and Bearing

First of all, mark out and drill the holes for the rocking shaft bearings. Scribe a vertical line on each frame, $2\frac{5}{16}$ in. ahead of the centre-line of the driving axle, using your try-square, with the stock resting against the top edge of the frame. If you have difficulty in measuring from the driving axle centre, take the distance from the extreme end of the frame, at the point where it touches the back buffer-beam. This comes out at $6\frac{9}{16}$ in. On this line, at $1\frac{5}{16}$ in. from the top of the frame, make a centre-pop, and drill it first with a $\frac{1}{8}$ in. drill, then open out with $\frac{5}{16}$ in. drill. File off any burr. On the vertical line, at $\frac{5}{16}$ in. above and below the centre of the hole, drill two holes with No. 41 drill, for the fixing screws.

Little castings are probably available for the bearings. Chuck by the shorter end, holding in three-jaw; if the other end doesn't run truly, a gentle tap with a hammer, with the chuck jaws slightly slack, will teach it better manners. Tighten the chuck jaws and turn down the longer end to $\frac{5}{16}$ in. diameter for a full $\frac{3}{8}$ in. length, using a knife-tool, and facing the oval flange at the same time. Face off the end, to bring the distance from flange to end, exactly $\frac{3}{8}$ in., then centre, drill right through with No. 14 drill, and put a $\frac{3}{16}$ in. parallel reamer through. If you don't possess a $\frac{3}{16}$ in. parallel reamer, an excellent substitute for the job in hand can easily be made. Get a piece of $\frac{3}{16}$ in. round silver-steel, say about 3 in. long, and file off one end on the slant, like the old-time provision merchant, or the cooked meat vendor sliced a fat German sausage. Harden and temper the end; give the oval face a rub on the oilstone, and use it in the tailstock chuck, same way as I have described for ordinary reaming. This gadget will leave a true hole which will be an exact fit for the rocking-shaft spindle. Then reverse the casting in the chuck and turn down the outer end, as shown, to approximately the same diameter, leaving the flange about $\frac{1}{8}$ in. thick. Note the distance from the inner side of the flange must be $\frac{5}{16}$ in. bringing the overall length to $\frac{11}{16}$ in.

If, by any chance, a casting should not be available, a piece of $\frac{7}{8}$ in. round rod, bronze or gunmetal for preference, can be used. Chuck it in three-jaw, face the end, centre, and drill to about $\frac{3}{4}$ in. depth with No. 14 drill. Turn down $\frac{3}{8}$ in. length to $\frac{5}{16}$ in. diameter, and part off at $\frac{11}{16}$ in. from the end. Reverse in chuck, and turn enough away to leave a flange about $\frac{1}{8}$ in. thick; then put the $\frac{3}{16}$ in. reamer through. File the flange oval, and you have the same result as if using a casting. Poke the $\frac{3}{8}$ in. end through the hole in the frame, from the inside; hold the flange tightly to the frame, so that it is vertical. Put the No. 41 drill through the screw holes, making countersinks on the flange. Remove, drill No. 48, tap $\frac{3}{32}$ in. or 7 BA, replace, and secure by screws (any shaped head you fancy) running through the clearing holes in frame, into the tapped holes in the flange.

Details of the slip-eccentric gear, showing the valve rod, eccentric strap and rod, rocking shaft and guide bar bracket.

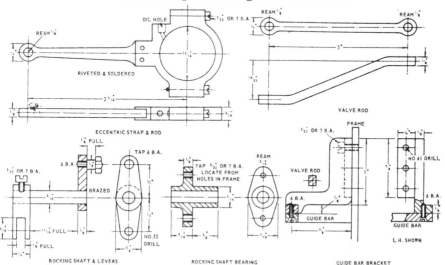

The rocker spindles are merely pieces of $\frac{3}{16}$ in. round silver-steel $1\frac{1}{2}$ in. long. The outside arm, or crank, is filed up from a piece of $\frac{1}{8}$ in. flat steel $\frac{3}{8}$ in. wide. To prevent what the kiddies would call "wobblisation", the holes must go through dead square; so mark them off at the end of a piece of rod long enough to hold in your hand while drilling the holes either on a drilling machine or in the lathe, by the methods previously described. The big hole is drilled No. 14; the smaller one drilled No. 44, and tapped 6 BA. Saw off the drilled and tapped piece, and file to the shape shown; then squeeze the spindle into it, by the same method as you squeezed the crankpins into the wheels. If the spindle really is a squeeze fit, it will not shift under ordinary working stresses; but if the fit is doubtful, the arm can easily be brazed or silver-soldered to the spindle, as shown in the sectional illustration. A small blowlamp or air-gas blowpipe, supplies plenty of heat for these small jobs, and a suitable brazing pan can be made from a small tin lid filled with coke or asbestos cubes. When at my old home at Norbury I used a discarded metal soap dish. The hole should be countersunk on the outside of the arm, and the spindle should project about $\frac{1}{32}$ in. Cover the place with some wet flux, such as Boron Compo mixed to a paste with water; blow up to bright red and touch the joint with a bit of thin soft brass wire, which will melt and fill up the countersink. Silver-solder may be used, in which case only a dull red heat will be needed. Let cool to black, quench in cold water, file the projecting bit of spindle flush with the face of the arm and clean and polish up the whole doings with a strip of fine emery cloth. The arm should then be "shift-proof", and the outside perfectly smooth, a brass ring showing the location of the filled-up countersink.

The inner arm is adjustable, for valve-setting purposes. It is made from a piece of $\frac{3}{8}$ in. by $\frac{1}{4}$ in. mild steel, and is marked out similarly to the outside ram. Drill the small hole No. 32, and the larger one No. 14 as before; then make use of one lesson already learned and slot the end of the rod to a depth of $\frac{5}{16}$ in., by the same process as described for slotting the end of the pump ram. We are now approaching the stage when you can start to realise that "experience teaches", even if the experience is only a few weeks old! Saw off the piece, file to shape, and drill a No. 48 hole in the end as shown, tapping for a $\frac{3}{32}$ in. or 7 BA set-screw. Put the shafts through the bearings and put the inner arm on temporarily; see that the shaft rocks easily. The spindle should fit the bearing exactly, but without shake. A small oil-hole may be drilled in the bearing, if desired, close to the frame.

Eccentric Strap and Rod

Here again, you can draw on your newly-acquired experience, for the method of machining up the eccentric strap, and making the rod and fitting it, is exactly the same as described for the eccentric strap and rod used for the pump. The only difference in personal appearance is that this one has the joint between the two halves of the strap, at top and bottom, instead of being on the slant. To repeat very briefly the sequence of operations, first clean the castings up (that is, if they need it; some are clean enough without needing any filing at all), drill the lugs, saw across, screw the parts together again, chuck in four-jaw, face one side, bore, face other side, slot the lug for the rod, make and fit the rod, and drill and ream the eye. This can be case-hardened, or bronze-bushed, just as preferred. Distance between centres of strap and eye is $2\frac{5}{16}$ in. Take off the inner rocking arm; place the eye of the eccentric rod in the slot, slightly taper the end of a piece of $\frac{1}{8}$ in. silver-steel, drive it through the lot, cut off and file flush each end. Then put the eccentric straps on the loose tumblers, same as mounting the pump eccentric strap, and at the same time replace the arms on the end of the rocker spindles. That completes the work inside the frames.

Valve Rod and Fork

In the drawings of the cylinders, a wide-jawed valve fork or crosshead was shown, and a description of how to make it was added. The wide jaws not being needed for the loose-eccentric gear a narrow-jawed fork is substituted, as shown in the accompanying illustration. It is made exactly as described for the other one, so I need not repeat the details. The material needed is a piece of $\frac{1}{4}$ in. square mild steel rod. Before slotting, drill the cross-hole with No. 44 drill; after slotting tap one side 6 BA and open out the other side with No. 30 drill, as shown.

To make the valve crosshead pin, chuck a piece of $\frac{3}{16}$ in. hexagon steel rod in three-jaw. Face the end and turn down $\frac{3}{16}$ in. length to $\frac{1}{8}$ in. diameter; further reduce a bare $\frac{1}{8}$ in. to $\frac{3}{32}$ in. diameter, and screw 6 BA. Part off to leave a head $\frac{3}{32}$ in. thick; reverse in chuck, and chamfer the corners of the hexagon. The pin for the outside arm of the rocking shaft is made in exactly the same way, except that the plain part is only a full $\frac{1}{8}$ in. long. An alternative way of making the pins is to use $\frac{1}{8}$ in. round silver-steel, turning and screwing both ends and fitting a nut permanently to one end. Pins made thus are very long-wearing; the "natural" finish of silver-steel resists wear to a remarkable degree.

The valve rod is made from $\frac{1}{4}$ in. by $\frac{1}{8}$ in. flat steel rod. Note that the distance between the centres of eyes is 2 in. after the rod has been set over as shown; so when you mark out the rod on the flat piece, set the distance between pinholes farther apart to allow for bending. The approximate distance "in the flat" is $2\frac{1}{8}$ in. There is no need to go to the refinement of "mike" measurements, because we have two means of adjustment, viz. the set-screwed inner arm of the rocking shaft, and the screwed spindle working in the tapped nut actuating the slide valve.

The method of making the valve rods is pretty much the same as making the coupling rods; they may either be milled or filed, as per the instructions given for coupling rods. The eyes may be bronze-bushed, if you care to take the trouble, same as the coupling rod, except that the bushes would be filed flush each side. They will run for a very long time before showing signs of wear if merely reamed and left soft; also they may be case-hardened, as previously described. When bending, merely grip the eye in the bench vice, putting a couple of pieces of soft metal between the rough steel jaws and valve rod. If your fingers aren't strong enough for the bending job use a pair of pliers, but again put a bit of soft metal over the rod to prevent marking it. Just bend until the angle tallies with the scaled illustration shown, and you are literally "all set". Then all that remains is to connect one end of the valve rod to the outside arm of the rocking shaft, and put the other end in the slot in the valve fork, securing them with the pins already made as given above. If the inner arm of the rocking shaft is set exactly opposite to the outer one, the set-screw tightened, and the set-screws in the stop-collars also tightened, the valve gear should operate perfectly when the wheels are turned by hand in either direction.

Guide Bar Brackets

Before setting the valves, the outer ends of the guide bars should be supported, and this is done by aid of a couple of small brackets, cast for preference, though they may be made from plate material. Cast brackets merely need cleaning up with a file. A true surface on the contact side of the flange by which the bracket is attached to the frame, can be obtained by laying a flat file on the bench and rubbing the flange on it; simple, but exceedingly effective. It was young Curly's pet method of getting a true surface on the rubbing faces and port blocks of his little toy oscillating cylinders. The underside of the lug to which the guide bar is attached must be exactly at right-angles to this; and if you put the stock of your try-square against the trued-up back of the flange, the blade will soon show if the underside of the lug is true, or otherwise. Judicious use of a file will soon put it right, if it is out of square. The lug could also be end-milled very easily if the casting is clamped under the slide-rest toolholder with the flange resting on the top of the slide. If you set the flange parallel with the lathe bed, the underside of the lug will be at right-angles to it; and if run across and an end-mill or slot-drill held in the three-jaw, the result will be O.K. in every way. Don't forget that one right-hand and one left-hand bracket will be required.

Erection of the bracket is very simple. First, pull out the piston rod to its full extent by putting the crank on back dead centre; the crosshead will then be at the extreme end of its movement and the guide bar should be perfectly free in it. Stand the bracket on the end of the bar, and hold it there by aid of a toolmaker's clamp put over flange and frame. With a bent scriber put through the screw hole in the end of the bar, mark a little circle on the underside of the lug; or if you don't mind taking the trouble, disconnect the little-end of the connecting rod from the crosshead, drop the rod clear, and make a countersink on the lug by means of a No. 34 drill put through the hole in the bar. Remove the bracket, and if a circle has been scribed, centre-pop the middle of it, and drill it—or the countersink, as the case may be—with No. 44 drill. Tap 6 BA, replace the bracket and secure with a 6 BA countersunk screw; also replace the connecting rod, if it has been disconnected. Turn the wheels by hand to make sure everything is quite free; stop with the crosshead as far away from the cylinder as it will go. Temporarily clamp the flange to the frame again; run the No. 41 drill through the screw holes in the flange, and make countersinks on the frame. Follow up with No. 48, drilling through frame, tap $\frac{3}{32}$ in. or 7 BA, put screws in, any heads you fancy, and the job is done.

A plate bracket can be built up by cutting out a piece of $\frac{3}{32}$ in. steel to the shape shown, silver-soldering on a little brass block to form the lug, and attaching the bracket to the frame by a piece of $\frac{1}{4}$ in. by $\frac{1}{16}$ in. brass angle riveted to the bracket and screwed to the frame as described above.

How to Set the Valves

Valve setting on this engine with the loose-eccentric gear is quite easy. Proceed as follows: Take off the steam chest covers. See that the rocker arms are exactly opposite, and the set-screws in the inner arms tightened up, also the stop-collar set screws. The collars may be in any position for the kick-off. Turn the wheels by hand until the outer arm of the rocking shaft is in mid-travel; then adjust the valve spindle in the nut until the valve is also in mid-travel, the lap extending an equal distance beyond the ports at each end. This can be set "by eye", the valve fork pin being removed, to enable the fork to be turned. Replace pin, and turn the wheels by hand, noting if the ports open an equal amount at each end of the valve travel. If they don't, either make further adjustment on the nut and spindle, or on the inner rocker arm, whichever you like. Now slack the set-screws in the stop-collars and put one of the main cracks on front dead centre; that is, with the piston rod right home. Turn the stop-collar by hand in a forward direction until the valve goes as far as possible to the front end of the steam chest. Continue turning slowly, and watch the valve carefully as it starts on its return journey. As soon as it starts to uncover the port, shown by a black line appearing at the lap of the valve, tighten up the set-screw.

Now turn the wheels by hand in a forward direction, and watch the valve. Note the position of the crankpin when the black line appears at the other end of the valve. If the crank is exactly on the back dead centre, the valve is set correctly and the length is right. If the black line doesn't appear until the crank has passed dead centre, the valve is too long, and a shade must be filed off both laps to keep the exhaust cavity in the middle. If the line appears before the crank reaches dead centre the valve is too short, and beginners had better make another valve; but this is not likely to occur if the instructions have been followed.

Having got that right, turn the wheels backwards, so that the other end of the shoulder of the stop-collar drives the eccentric. If the black line of the port shows at each dead centre position of the crank, the setting is O.K. If it shows before dead centre, the shoulder needs a little taking off it; a small chisel will do the needful. If the line shows after the crank passes dead centres, the shoulder needs making up a bit; and a small bit of brass soldered to it at the place where it catches the eccentric pin is all that is necessary. When both ports "crack", as the enginemen would say, on each dead centre in both directions of movement, the valve setting is as near perfect as is possible to get; and the steam chest covers can be fixed "for keeps" with the joint washers or gaskets between the contact surfaces, as detailed out in the instructions for assembling the cylinders.

Walschaerts' Valve Gear

Before going into details of the Walschaerts' gear for our weeny four-wheeler, maybe it would be as well if I explained to our beginner friends the how and why of it. Most folk can do a better job if they know exactly what they are doing; though you would be surprised at the number of good folk who have made up one of my engines "in blind faith", had the shock of their lives when it ran all right at first time of steaming, and then proceeded to find out why it did, after the excitement had died down. Well, this is how it happened. Egide Walschaerts was a Belgian locomotive foreman, and it appears that (like many of his confrères in early days in this country) he was nearly driven daft by the antics of some of the weird and wonderful valve gear arrangements fitted to the locomotives in his charge. Old Abner Baker had the same sort of experience in U.S.A., only in his case it was traction engines. Anyway, friend Egide thought it was high time somebody had a shot at designing a valve gear that wouldn't give trouble; so, believing in the old saying that if you want a job done properly, the best thing is to do it yourself, he set to work on the problem. Naturally, on a job of that kind, it was a case of trial and error; and our Belgian friend didn't get it right first time, by long chalks. He produced and tried out several different forms of valve gears, just like old man Abner, mentioned above, when he was bitten by the same kind of insect; but in due course they both hit the bull's eye, Abner with the Baker gear and Egide with the Walschaerts. Incidentally, this was another case of history repeating itself, for the Belgian did his job very many years before the American.

It would take too much space here, to describe how the Walschaerts' gear, as we know it today, was "evoluted" from Egide's first design, so I will just describe it as he finally perfected it. He aimed at producing a valve gear in which each part did one job, and one job only; different from cases where one part had to perform two or more functions, and hashed up half of them. The gear is divided into two distinct parts; the part determining the direction in which the engine travels, and the part which attends to the lap-and-lead movement of the valve. If you take a stick of wood, drive a nail through the middle, and loosely attach it to the garden fence, for example, you can see in an instant how the reversing part works. If you waggle the bottom of the stick from side to side, the top part waggles an equal amount, but in the opposite direction. Suppose the bottom end is worked from a fixed eccentric on the driving axle of an engine, and you have another rod, connected to the slide valve, which you can attach either to the top or bottom of the stick. If you connect it to the bottom of the stick, the valve rod would move in unison with the eccentric, and the engine would go, say, forward. If you connect the valve rod to the upper end of the stick, it goes exactly the opposite way to the eccentric and the engine would go backwards. Substitute a slotted link for the stick; connect the valve rod to a die-block sliding in the slot, so that it can readily be moved from one end to the other; replace the eccentric by a return crank set at right-angles to the main crank, and you have one of the fundamental parts of a Walschaerts' gear.

Lap-and-Lead Movement

If the valve is exactly the same length as the distance between the outside edges of the steam ports, and thus has no lap, the simple arrangement described above would be all that was needed; but the valve has to be moved over a greater distance, so that the lap at each end starts to uncover the port at the instant the crank reaches the dead centre. This is easily done by a simple connection from the main crosshead. We won't bother about inside admission piston valves for the time being, but merely concern ourselves with the simple slide valves as fitted to *Tich*. Now, instead of the rod which connects the die-block with the valve (called the radius rod) going direct to the valve spindle, it is connected to a hanging lever which itself is connected to the end of the valve spindle a short distance above. The lower end of the hanging lever (called the combination lever) is connected to the crosshead by a drop-arm and a short link (called the union link) which arrangement is clearly shown in the accompanying illustrations.

Now take a look at the elevation of the gear. When the die-block is dead in the middle of the expansion link, as shown, it is obvious that however much the link is waggled back and forth, the die-block—and consequently the radius

General arrangement of the Walschaert's valve gear.
(NB. Reverse arm is fitted to right side of locomotive.)

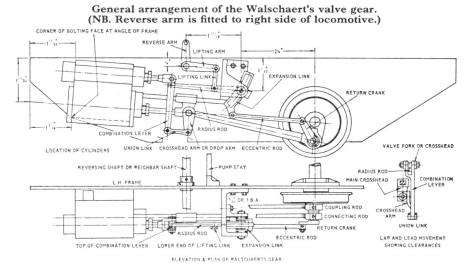

rod attached to it—will not move, for the simple reason that the block is in line with the pivots, or trunnions, on which the link oscillates. Therefore, the point at which the other end of the radius rod is attached to the combination lever is also a temporary fixture. Now, if the wheels are turned so that the crosshead is right up against the cylinder cover, the union link will push the bottom of the combination lever forward (towards the cylinder); and the radius rod connection not being able to move, for the reasons stated above, the combination lever will turn on it, and the upper part will move away from the cylinder, taking the valve spindle with it, and thus moving the valve sufficiently to start opening the front port. Conversely, when the crosshead is as far away from the cylinder as possible (back dead centre) the combination lever will be tilted in the opposite direction, and the top of it will move far enough toward the cylinder to push in the valve spindle far enough to allow the valve to "crack" the back port. Therefore, with the die-block in the middle of the link, the ports "crack" on each dead centre at every turn of the wheels.

Combined Movement

We have already learned, from studying the loose-eccentric valve gear, that for correct timing the "crack" of the port must take place on each dead centre. Now, if we put the Walschaerts' gear engine's crank on dead centre, and take a look at the link, we find it is exactly vertical and the die-block can be shifted from top to bottom of the link without moving the valve spindle. We have also seen, that with the crosshead at either extreme—that is, when the crank is on front or back dead centre—that the combination lever is in the position to "crack" the port. We now see that with the Walschaerts' gear, it doesn't matter a bean what position the die-block occupies in the link—top, bottom, or any place in between—the ports will "crack" on each dead centre when the link arrives at the vertical position; and as the amount of the crack constitutes the "lead opening", to give it the correct title, the lead will be constant for full forward gear, full back gear, or any notched-up position of the gear. The action of the drop-arm, union link and combination lever is just to make sure that the valve starts to open the port at each dead centre, and nothing else.

The rest of the port opening is done by the oscillation of the link. Naturally, if the die-block is at the end of the slot, it will move farther, and give a greater port opening, than when it is near the middle. Also, if it is at the bottom of the link, it will move in unison with the return crank, and cause the engine to move in one direction. If it is at the top—or, in fact, any place above the link bearings—it will move in the opposite direction, and so reverse the direction of movement of the engine. Either movement, of course, is transmitted to the valve by the radius rod, the top of the combination lever, and the valve spindle. We thus see that the link, die-block, and radius rod control the amount of port opening, and the distance of movement; and the drop-arm, union link and combination lever advance the valve to the "lead" position at each dead centre, irrespective of the direction of movement, or the amount of port opening. The two movements, acting together, give the correct valve events.

There is one more desirable feature about the Walschaerts' gear and that is the quick release of the exhaust steam. The sudden reversal of the valve as the combination lever "does its stuff" just before the end of the stroke, causes the edge of the exhaust cavity in the valve, to uncover the inner edge of the steam port all-of-a-sudden-Peggy, and away goes the spent steam, up the blastpipe and out of the chimney, with great alacrity. No "go-slow" movement there! This is the reason why a "King" or "Castle", pulling a heavy load out of Paddington, tries to blow the chimney off the smokebox, and dislodge the girders of Bishop's Road Bridge. My own little engines perform exactly the same antics; none of the feeble "chiss-chiss" that we used to hear before the advent of the "real live steamers". It isn't so much the amount of steam which produces the bark, but the speed at which it leaves the blast nozzle. The old small port-no-lead-straight-slide engines had a loud puff, but it was "dead as ditchwater" in a manner of speaking; the engines sounded as if they were choking themselves, as indeed they were!

Bearing in mind the above explanation, the rawest recruit can take a look at the drawings of the Walschaerts' valve gear for *Tich* and understand them perfectly. You'll see that the expansion link is carried by a bracket bolted to the frames, and the bracket also supports the outer end of the guide bar. A return crank, or "eccentric crank" as it is known in U.S.A. and Canada, is fixed to the main crank, and connected to the link tail by an eccentric rod, thus performing the waggling act. The wide-jawed fork or crosshead on the valve spindle carries the slotted head of the combination lever, the bottom of which is operated by the connection to the main crosshead. One end of the radius rod is pinned to the combination lever in the slot, the other end carries a die-block working in the link slot. The die-block is lifted and lowered and held in any position in the link slot by a small drop link actuated by an arm on the reverse shaft. This shaft carried a vertical arm at the right-hand end, which is connected to a hand lever in the cab, by a straight rod called the reverse rod or reach rod.

If the lever in the cab is pushed forward, the reverse arm will also move forward, and the lifting arm will move up, lifting the die-block to the top of the slot in the expansion link so if we want the engine to run the same way as the inclination of the lever, we must arrange for the upper half of the link to be set for forward motion, and the lower half for backing. This is easily done. If you remember, the loose-eccentric gear drove through a rocking shaft with directly opposed levers; and when the engine was going ahead, the eccentric (driven by the stop collar) was following the crank. The expansion link being pivoted in the centre, will act exactly in the same way as the rocker, when the die-block is at the top. As the eccentric rod is connected to the lower end, all we have to do is to set the return crank in the same relationship to it, as the loose-eccentric is to the rocking shaft in forward motion; that is, following. Look at the elevation of the Walschaerts' gear, and you will see, whatever the position of the main crankpin, the return crankpin is a quarter-turn behind it.

When one speaks of an eccentric or return crank as "leading" or "following" this always refers to its position in forward gear; easy enough to remember!

The above explanation of the "Whys and Wherefores" may not be very "scientific", anyway it isn't intended to be, but I fancy it will convey more to the average beginner than the "learned treatise" type of description. So much for that; let's get busy, and see if we can put what we have learned to practical use.

Link Brackets for Walschaerts' Gear

The link brackets are about the best things for the beginner to start on. They can be made up from castings, or built up from plate material; don't forget you will need one right-hand, and one left-hand. The left-hand one is shown in the illustrations. If a casting is used, smooth off the broad face of it with a file; then, to true it up, lay a sheet of fairly coarse emery cloth or other abrasive, on something flat and rub the face on it, same as truing port faces. The sides must be right-angles to the front; if a milling machine is available, it is a simple job to clamp the casting in the machine vice on the miller table, set it truly with a square, and take off the surplus metal from each side, with a small slabbing cutter on the arbor of the machine. If not, use the lathe again, milling each side of the casting in the same manner described for the pump-stay. Alternatively, the humble file will do the trick, if carefully handled. Test with a try-square, putting the stock against the wide face of the casting, and the inner side of the blade against each side in turn. You'll soon see if any wants to come off, and exactly where to file, if you hold it up to the light and look between blade and casting. The little boss at the bottom, for attachment of guide bar, should also have its contact surface at right-angles to the front of the casting.

A piece of brass or steel channel, $1\frac{1}{2}$ in. wide with $\frac{7}{8}$ in. sides, and $\frac{1}{8}$ in. thick, would make a fine bracket that needed no machining. But a casting would merely need sawing and filing to the shape and size shown in the illustrations, and drilling for the bolts and bushes. A little block of brass or steel, as the case may be, $\frac{1}{4}$ in. long, $\frac{3}{16}$ in. wide, and $\frac{1}{8}$ in. thick, would have to be silver-soldered on, for attachment of the guide bar at the position shown in the drawings. The slot for the radius rod should be cut out in the same way as the openings for the hornblocks were cut in the main frames. The bracket could also be made from a piece of $\frac{1}{8}$ in. plate, $1\frac{1}{2}$ in. long and $1\frac{1}{8}$ in. wide, slotted as shown, with a piece $1\frac{1}{8}$ in. by $\frac{3}{4}$ in. by $\frac{1}{8}$ in. thick, at one side. and another piece, shaped and drilled as shown at the other side, both pieces being brazed on if steel, or silver-soldered if brass. Whether the bracket is cast, made of channel, or built up, the hole for the link trunnion bush must go through dead square; so very carefully mark it off, centre-pop, and drill first with a $\frac{1}{8}$ in. drill, either on a machine, or else in the lathe, with the drill in three-jaw, and the bracket held against a drilling pad, or the end of the tailstock barrel, with centre removed. Open out to $\frac{15}{64}$ in. or with letter "C" drill, but don't ream yet.

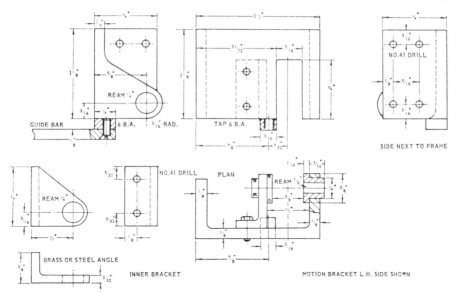

The combined guide bar bracket and link bearing.

The small bracket carrying the inner link trunnion is made from a piece of $\frac{3}{4}$ in. by $\frac{3}{8}$ in. by $\frac{3}{32}$ in. brass or steel angle. If unequal angle is not available, use $\frac{3}{4}$ in. and saw away the unwanted part. Cut off a piece of full $\frac{3}{4}$ in. long, file to shape, drill the screw holes, and for the link trunnion bush, drill a $\frac{1}{8}$ in. hole, opening out to $\frac{15}{64}$ in. or letter C as above. Clamp this bracket temporarily in position on the larger one, $\frac{1}{2}$ in. from the outer side, as shown in dotted lines on the drawing showing the front of the bracket, and more clearly in the plan view; a toolmaker's clamp will do the needful, but before tightening it, put the shank end of the drill through both the holes for bushes, to line them up. The drill should fit easily enough to turn with finger and thumb; if it goes stiff, the holes are not truly in line. Put the No. 41 drill through the two screw holes and make countersinks on the large brackets; follow up with No. 48, going right through, tap $\frac{3}{32}$ in. or 7 BA, and put a couple of screws in, hexagon-headed for preference. Finally, put a $\frac{1}{4}$ in. parallel reamer through both the bush holes at once, which naturally ensures that they will both be dead in line.

These two holes are bushed to take the link trunnions. Chuck a bit of good hard $\frac{3}{8}$ in. round bronze rod in the three-jaw; face the end, centre, and drill down about $\frac{5}{16}$ in. depth with No. 34 drill. Turn down $\frac{3}{16}$ in. of the outside, to a press fit in the reamed holes in the bracket, recollecting your previous experience of turning press fits for crankpins and wheel seats. Part off at a little over $\frac{1}{16}$ in. from the shoulder, and repeat process, making all four whilst at the job. Reverse in chuck, and face off each head to a bare $\frac{1}{16}$ in. width; then press into place. Note which side the heads go; see plan view. Take off the small bracket to do this job, and replace when both bushes are pressed

home. Replace the small bracket and put the screws in tightly; then put a
$\frac{1}{8}$ in. parallel reamer through both bushes together, thus ensuring that they
will be in line, and the link will be able to swing back and forth perfectly easy,
but without any shake. Much of the bad valve setting and syncopated exhaust
beats, found on club and other tracks, is due to the expansion links being
sloppy in their bearings.

How to Erect the Brackets

This job is easy enough; it only requires a little care. Take another look at
the plan and elevation drawings, and you will see that the little block underneath the bracket is right at the end of the guide bar. Set your bracket on it,
thus; but have the crank on back dead centre, with piston rod fully extended,
and the crosshead as near to the end of the guide bar as possible. That will
ensure that the bar is itself in correct position and not forced down, or to one
side, by the bracket, whilst same is being fitted. Put a toolmaker's clamp over
the side of the bracket, and the frame, and screw up tightly. Turn the wheels
by hand and make sure the crosshead is free to slide its full movement along
the guide bar.

Now, carefully check the position of the link trunnion hole in the bracket.
The centre of this should be $2\frac{1}{4}$ in. ahead of the centre-line of the driving
axle and $1\frac{1}{32}$ in. from the top of the frame. If you have followed the "words
and music" correctly thus far, the measurements will be as given. If it is
slightly out there isn't any cause for alarm and despondency. A thirty-second
or so above or below the vertical measurement won't affect the working of the
engine to any appreciable extent. Any slight variation in the distance from the
vertical centre-line of the driving axle can be put right by adjusting the position of the bracket; as long as the little block supporting the guide bar doesn't
foul the crosshead at the end of the stroke its exact position on the bar doesn't
matter, within reason. Tighten the clamp and run the No. 41 drill through the
frame, using the holes in the bracket as guides. The top two are plain sailing;
the bottom one opposite the bushes, can be got at by poking the drill through
the bushes; but the other one is obstructed by the outer side of the bracket,
so you'll have to put a bent scriber through the hole, make a little circle on the
frame, remove the bracket, centre-pop the middle of the circle and drill the
hole. That is, of course, unless you get up to one of your humble servant's
wangles! For making countersinks through holes where an ordinary straight
drill won't reach, I use a broken bit of drill soldered into a short length of
steel spring, into the other end of which is fixed a short length of silver-steel,
about the same size as the drill. This is held in the chuck of a Millers Falls
hand-brace. The point of the drill is inserted in the guide hole, and the bit
acts the same way as a flexible shaft, allowing the drill to turn, although out
of line with the chuck. Naturally, you can't put much pressure on the drill,
but it answers O.K. for jobs such as mentioned above.

After drilling all the holes and filing off any burrs around the edges, fix the

Plate 11

Another view of Mr. Farmer's boiler showing the backhead and dome bush

Below: Mrs. Daltry's "Tich", with boiler prior to mounting in the frames

Plate 12

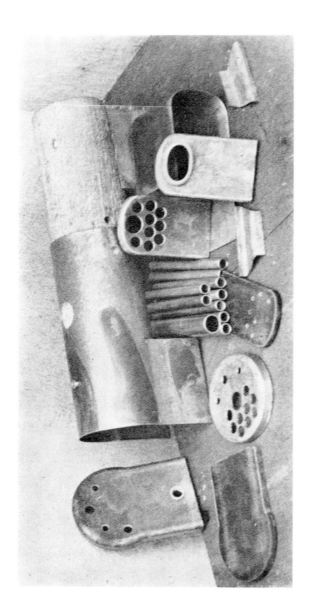

The component parts for a "Tich" boiler made by Mrs. Ruth Daltry: note the wooden former

bracket temporarily in place with a couple of little bolts, $\frac{3}{32}$ in. or 7 BA; no need to put the lot in yet, as the bracket has to come off again when erecting the gear. The bolts can be made by using pieces of $\frac{3}{32}$ in. silver-steel with a nut on each end. Then mark off the position of the hole in the guide bar, on the little block under the bracket, as described for the bracket used with loose-eccentric gear; drill No. 44, and tap 6 BA, and attach the guide bar with a countersunk screw.

Now we are all set to make the various components of the Walschaerts' gear.

Walschaerts' Gear Components

In full-size, these engines have to put up with a lot of rough handling, and get very little in the way of maintenance, so the gear needs to be simple and robust. Despite that, it is in no way clumsy; in fact, if made to the given measurements, it will be far neater than many at present operating on club or other tracks. In making up the levers, rods and links, beginners will have a good opportunity to put into practice the lessons they have already learned, which should save your humble servant much needless repetition, and hasten the job of getting the engine on the road. For example, all the forked ends of the rods and levers, such as the combination lever, union link, eccentric rod and lifting arms, are slotted out by the same method described for slotting the pump ram, viz. clamping the component under the slide-rest toolholder, packed up to centre height, and running it up to a saw-type milling cutter mounted either on a stub mandrel in three-jaw, or on a heavier mandrel between centres. The reduced parts of the combination lever, radius rod and eccentric rod, can be milled from the solid bar, by one of the methods described for milling axleboxes, if a cutter is available. This is run on a stout mandrel between centres, the steel being held in a machine vice, either regular, or improvised out of angle-iron, and packed up to the correct height. If low speed is used, with plenty of cutting oil, the steel can be milled away like cheese, the sharp radii close to the jaws of the forks being finished with a file. The rounded ends can be finished off in the same manner that I described for coupling rods. Where no facilities for doing milling in the lathe are available, or the builder of the engine hasn't any cutters, there is always the humble but very necessary file to fall back on; and this, with the average amount of intelligence behind the handle, can always be relied on to do a satisfactory job.

Combination Levers

Starting from the cylinders, the first job is the combination lever, as we already have the wide-jawed valve forks, or crossheads. This is cut from a piece of $\frac{1}{4}$ in. square mild steel approximately 2 in. long. Mark it off, and drill the holes first, using drilling machine or lathe, as they must go through square with the sides. Next, slot the upper end, as mentioned above; after that, mill or file away the part below the fork, to the size given, then round off the ends.

Some folk like to see a high polish on steel valve gear parts; if you are one of these, rub them on a sheet of fine emery cloth which has previously been rubbed with beeswax. Personally, I prefer the working or "tool" finish, same as on full-size engines in "company" days. They get "finished" in another sense now, sad to say! The same kind of combination lever does for both sides of the engine.

Union Links

Each union link needs a piece of $\frac{7}{32}$ in. or $\frac{1}{4}$ in. square mild steel a little over $\frac{7}{8}$ in. long, to allow for finishing to size. This is an exceedingly simple job. Mark out, drill, and slot the ends as above; round off the ends, then file away the middle, as shown in the plan view, for the sake of appearance. An alternative way, which is a little easier, is to use two separate links made from $\frac{1}{16}$ in. by $\frac{1}{4}$ in. mild steel, cut out and drilled to the same shape and dimensions, as the side view. Instead of the bottom of combination lever, and main crosshead drop arm, entering slots, one of the separate links is put at each side of the lever and arm, and the whole bolted together.

Expansion Links

The expansion links are a little more tricky, but there is nothing at all to scare any beginner. The slots can be machined, but require a special gadget unless you have a drilling-and-milling spindle for the slide-rest of the lathe. If you have, it is a safe bet you will know how to use it; so all I need say on

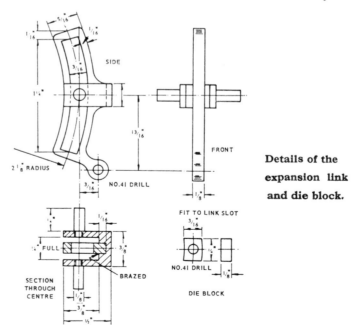

Details of the expansion link and die block.

the subject is that the two link blanks (pieces of ground flat stock, as the steel for gauge-making is known in the trade) should be soldered to a piece of stout brass plate, and bolted to the lathe faceplate at a radius of $2\frac{1}{8}$ in. from centre of mandrel to centre of blanks. Then a $\frac{3}{16}$ in. end-mill or home-made slot drill, in the spindle, will do the trick easily, the slide-rest being run up to the faceplate, the cutter fed into action by the top-slide, and the faceplate moved slowly by hand. Put the back gear in, put the belt on the slowest speed, and pull it by hand very slowly. The resulting slots will naturally have rounded ends, but a small square file will soon bring them to the proper shape, if used with care and discretion.

Beginners who do not possess a milling spindle, can cut the slots by hand quite easily; in fact, although I have a machine which will cut curved slots, more often than not, I do the job by hand, just to see if I haven't lost my "sense of craftsmanship", in a manner of speaking. I guess most folk have heard of the man who described himself as a motor fitter and mechanic, on the strength of ten years at tightening up one nut on car engines as they passed him on a conveyor belt. Locomotive builders get a little more experience than that! Anyway, as I have mentioned before, cut the slots in the blanks first, and then cut the link around the slot. This sounds at first like building a barrel around the bunghole; but if you spoil a slot, it is only a matter of getting another blank and having another shot. If you had cut out a nicely-shaped link, and then spoiled the slot, it would mean a great waste of valuable time, not to mention a probable cataract of railroad Esperanto.

The best material from which to make the links is the stuff mentioned above (gauge steel, or ground flat stock) which is a fine grade of cast steel, and can be hardened and tempered readily. Two pieces are needed, $1\frac{3}{4}$ in. long, $\frac{5}{8}$ in. wide and $\frac{1}{2}$ in. thick. Mark the outline of the expansion link on each; then, on the centre-line of the slot, drill a row of $\frac{5}{32}$ in. or No. 21 holes, practically touching. Run them into a slot by aid of a rat-tail file; then, with a small half-round file, clean up the ragged sides of the slot until a piece of $\frac{3}{16}$ in. round silver-steel can be run from top to bottom of the slot without binding anywhere, and without shake. It isn't as difficult as it may sound; the job just requires a little care, that is all. The ends of the slot can be squared with a small square file. When the slots are O.K. it is an easy job to file the outline and tail. The die-blocks can be filed up from small pieces of the same kind of material, to the dimensions given in the illustration. The curved surfaces at each side should correspond with the curved surfaces of the link slots, and the die-blocks should slide easily from top to bottom of the links, freely but without shake.

The yokes are made from mild steel of $\frac{1}{4}$ in. by $\frac{3}{8}$ in. section; get a piece long enough to clamp under the slide-rest toolholder and square off the ends in the four-jaw. Mill out each end similar to the jaws of the crosshead fork, $\frac{1}{4}$ in. full width and $\frac{3}{8}$ in. depth; this is where the long piece comes in handy, as it is easier to clamp under the slide-rest toolholder. At the bottom of each jaw, and plumb in the middle, mill out a little recess $\frac{1}{16}$ in. deep and a bare

$\frac{1}{8}$ in. wide, so that the expansion link will jam tightly into it. Part off each yoke $\frac{1}{2}$ in. from the end. Jam the tongue at the back of the link, tightly into the little recess, and braze it. Just smear a little wet flux at each side of the link, blow up to bright red and touch the joint with a bit of thin brass wire. Use only very little, or you will have the stuff running all over the link and yoke. Quench out in clean cold water before the redness dies away, and the link will be rendered hard enough to resist wear. The die-blocks can be hardened in a similar manner, at the same time.

On each side of each yoke, exactly opposite the centre of the link slot, make a centre-pop; drill No. 40 and tap 5 BA, using a taper tap, and leaving the threads a shade on the small side. Put a few threads on each end of two pieces of $\frac{1}{8}$ in. round silver-steel and screw them very tightly into the holes in the side of the yoke. File off flush any threads projecting into the space between the jaws; saw off the outside to a shade over $\frac{1}{4}$ in., chuck one in three-jaw, and face off the other to a bare $\frac{1}{4}$ in. length, chamfering slightly. Reverse in chuck and give the other trunnion a dose of the same medicine. The true trunnions should be exactly in line. The complete link should be perfectly clean and smooth, especially inside the slot.

Radius Rods and Lifting Links

The radius rods each need a piece of $\frac{1}{4}$ in. square mild steel approximately $2\frac{1}{2}$ in. long; and as they are machined exactly the same as the combination levers, there is no need for repeating details. Each one carries a pin for accommodating the lower ends of the lifting links. Countersink one end of the middle hole a little, and after squeezing in a pin made from $\frac{3}{32}$ in. silver-steel as shown, rivet over the end into the countersink, and file off flush.

The lifting links are merely pieces of $\frac{1}{4}$ in. by $\frac{3}{32}$ in. strip mild steel, $\frac{7}{8}$ in. full length, drilled and filed to shape shown. The eyes should be case-hardened, as previously described. Put one end of each over the pin in the radius rod; the eye should be an exact fit on the pin; it will be, if the No. 41 drill makes a hole of correct size. Rivet over the end of the pin just sufficiently to stop the link from slipping off, but leave it perfectly free to swing. Only one lifting link can be used on each radius rod as there is no room on the other side, owing to the proximity of the guide bar and crosshead; see plan view of complete assembly.

Return Cranks

The return cranks are made from pieces of $\frac{1}{8}$ in. by $\frac{3}{8}$ in. mild steel a full 1 in. long; another plain filing job. The big hole should be a squeeze fit on the end of the main crankpin. Drill the little hole $\frac{3}{32}$ in. or No. 42, and counter-sink it; this side should be relieved slightly, as shown. Turn a little crankpin from $\frac{1}{8}$ in. silver-steel same as the main crankpins; one end is squeezed into the return crank, riveted over and filed flush whilst the other end is screwed for a nut, to prevent the end of the eccentric rod slipping off. The return

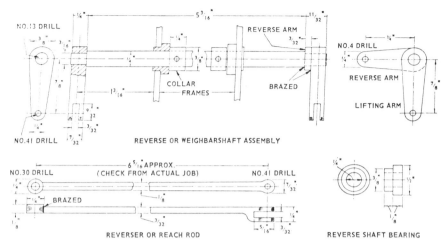

Details of the weighbar shaft and reach rod.

cranks are pressed on to the ends of the main crankpins in the position shown in the view of the complete valve gear, in the previous instalment. Just set them "by eye" for the time being; final adjustment will be made when erecting the gear.

Reverse Shaft Bearings

At $\frac{1}{4}$ in. from the top of the frame at each side and $\frac{5}{16}$ in. to the rear of the vertical centre-line of the leading axle, drill a No. 30 hole in each frame. Put a piece of $\frac{1}{8}$ in. silver-steel through; if the steel lies square and level across the frame enlarge the holes with $\frac{23}{64}$ in. drill, and poke a $\frac{3}{8}$ in. reamer through each. If the test bit of steel isn't square or level, true up the holes with a file and try again with a bigger bit of steel. I usually give the position of the holes for the reverse shaft bearings on the main frame drawings; but in the present instance I wasn't quite certain where it would eventually be.

Chuck a bit of $\frac{1}{2}$ in. round bronze or gunmetal in three-jaw; face the end, centre, and drill down about $\frac{5}{16}$ in. depth with $\frac{15}{64}$ in. or letter C drill. Turn down $\frac{1}{8}$ in. of the outside, to a tight fit in the holes in the frame, and part off at a full $\frac{1}{8}$ in. from the shoulder. Reverse in chuck, skim the face off truly, and put a $\frac{1}{4}$ in. parallel reamer through. Put them in the holes in the frames, with the flanges on the inside.

Reverse Shaft

Another simple job, this. A piece of $\frac{1}{4}$ in. round mild- or silver-steel $5\frac{13}{16}$ in. long, will do the needful. Chuck in three-jaw, face the end, and turn down $\frac{11}{32}$ in. length to a full $\frac{3}{16}$ in. diameter; reverse in chuck, face the other end, and turn that to $\frac{3}{16}$ in. full diameter for $\frac{1}{4}$ in. length. The distance between shoulders should be $5\frac{3}{16}$ in.

Two collars are required; chuck a bit of $\frac{3}{8}$ in. round steel, face, centre, and drill down about $\frac{5}{8}$ in. depth with a $\frac{1}{4}$ in. drill. Part off two $\frac{1}{4}$ in. lengths and fit a $\frac{3}{32}$ in. or 7 BA set-screw to each.

The lifting arms are made from $\frac{1}{4}$ in. by $\frac{3}{8}$ in. steel. Take a piece about 3 in. long, mark off the arms on it at the ends, drill, slot out same as combination lever, and other slotted rods, saw to length, and file to shape. I have shown the arms only $\frac{7}{32}$ in. thick, for the sake of neatness, but they can be left the full $\frac{1}{4}$ in. if you want to save work. The reverse arm is cut from $\frac{3}{32}$ in. by $\frac{3}{8}$ in. mild steel, and drilled as shown. Note: the $\frac{3}{16}$ in. holes in the larger ends of the reverse arm and lifting arms, should be tight on the ends of the shaft, which was why I specified "full" turning.

Put the reverse arm and one of the lifting arms on the longer spigot of the shaft; set them at right-angles, and braze or silver-solder them, same as the expansion link job. Be careful to get this right; with the longer spigot to your right, as shown in the illustration, and the slotted arm pointing towards you, the reverse arm should be vertical, pointing skywards. Clean off all traces of the brazing job; then poke the other end of the shaft through the right-hand bearing in the frame, thread on the two collars between frames, and put the shaft through the other bearing, squeezing on the other lifting arm, as parallel to the first one as you can set "by eye". Then adjust the collars against the bearings, as shown; make sure that the shaft projects an exactly equal amount on each side of frame, and tighten the set-screws. A little hole can be drilled in the shaft, if you like, at the point where each set-screw touches, using No. 41 drill, and the set-screws screwed right down into them; or the collars may be pinned to the shaft.

Assembling the Valve Gear

Note—the pins in the valve gear are plain bits of silver-steel. The bolts are made from bits of silver-steel turned down a shade at each end, screwed, and furnished with nuts; so you'll know what I mean by "pin" or "bolt". Put the bottom of the combination lever in the end of the union link drilled No. 43; squeeze a bit of $\frac{3}{32}$ in. silver-steel through the lot, and file flush both sides. Put the eye of the radius rod in the slotted end of the combination lever opposite the lower hole, and pin that likewise. Don't forget that this has to be assembled right- and left-hand; the side of radius rod carrying the lifting link, goes with the straight side of the combination lever. Put the die block at the bottom of the expansion link slot; pass the fork of the radius rod over it, drive a $\frac{3}{32}$ in. silver-steel pin through the lot, and file flush each side. Take off the inner bearing of the link bracket, and the whole issue can then be put in place, as shown in the view of the complete gear in the previous instalment. The top of the combination lever goes between the jaws of the valve fork, and is secured by a $\frac{1}{2}$ in. silver-steel bolt, made as described above, the ends being turned down to $\frac{3}{32}$ in., and screwed $\frac{3}{32}$ in. or 7 BA. The loose end of the union link is connected to the drop arm on the crosshead by a $\frac{3}{32}$ in. bolt with 8 BA ends; the upper ends of the lifting links go between the jaws of the lifting arms on the reverse shaft, and are secured by similar bolts. Warning: the bolts should be free to turn with your fingers, when the nuts at both ends are hard up against the shoulders; this makes absolutely sure that the forks are not pinched in on the rods, causing binding and friction. Replace the inner link bearing, and we are ready to set the return cranks and make the eccentric rods to the correct length.

How to Set the Return Cranks

Put the main crank on front dead centre, with the piston rod in as far as it will go. Set the expansion link in such a position that the die block may be run up and down the slot, without causing any movement of the valve spindle. Now, with a pair of dividers, take the measurement from the centre of hole in link tail, to the centre of the return crankpin. Next, turn the wheels around until the crank is on back dead centre, but take care not to move the link. Apply the dividers again; if they still touch the centre of link tail hole and return crankpin, the crank are O.K. If they don't, shift the return crank so that the pin moves half the difference, and carry out the test again. When the measurement tallies exactly with the crank on either of the centres, the return cranks are correctly set and the distance between the divider points is the exact length of the eccentric rod between pinhole centres. The eccentric rods can then be made from $\frac{3}{8}$ in. square steel, to the outlines shown, the measurements between holes being taken from the dividers. The link end has an offset fork, same as the combination lever; the other end is made like a weeny coupling rod boss end, as shown. Drill the boss $\frac{3}{16}$ in. and squeeze in a little bush turned from bronze rod; this is reamed $\frac{1}{8}$ in. and should be an exact fit on the return crankpin. Secure that end with an ordinary commercial nut and washer, and put another $\frac{3}{32}$ in. bolt through the forked end and the link tail.

If the gear has been made and assembled correctly, the wheels should turn freely, and the whole of the motion work should operate sweetly without any signs of binding; at the same time it should have no slackness. The engine should reverse readily; no matter what the position of the links, the die blocks should run freely up and down, when the reverse arm is operated. To prevent any movement of the return cranks upsetting the valve operations, drill a No. 48 hole half in the crank, and half in the crankpins, as shown by the dotted circle in the drawing; tap $\frac{3}{32}$ in. or 5 BA, screw in a stub of $\frac{3}{32}$ in. silver-steel, threaded to suit, and file off flush. We will leave the actual valve setting until the reversing lever is made and fitted; the left-hand side lifting arm can also be set to match the brazed one at the same time, and pinned to the shaft, as it is essential that both die blocks occupy exactly similar positions in their respective links at all times. I have seen more than one expensive commercial or professional job in which, with the lever in mid-gear, one die block was above centre, and the other below it—and some folk wonder why they get syncopated beats!

An Inadvertent Test

Everybody being entitled to their own opinion, it only amuses your humble servant when all sorts of prejudiced arguments are put forward to decry my pet frame construction, with buffer-beams made from steel angles; but facts are facts, and the other afternoon, one of my frames inadvertently got a test which proved that my construction can take a knock which would just about cattle up other kinds. It so happened that I needed a small engine on which to carry out some boiler experiments, so I started in to build a *Tich* "on the quick". The frames and angle buffer-beams were duly cut out, assembled, and the joints Sifbronzed up with my oxy-acetylene blowpipe. Just outside the glass lean-to ("Crystal Palace") where my blowpipe work is done, are four steps leading up to the garden, and by the side of them, a brick wall about four feet high. When the doodlebugs were flying around, back in 1944, I used to put my drawing-board, or writing-pad, on top of this wall, and sit on the top step to write or draw. The steps leading to our shelter under the garden are at the end of the wall; and as soon as I heard a whine, I would call to my fair lady, and we would both go down to the shelter, not knowing whether we would ever come up again, but hoping for the best. Incidentally, I made the drawings, and wrote most of the instructions for *Petrolea* under those circumstances, and made far less mistakes than many folk do in the normal way. Whilst I was drawing out the valve gear one afternoon, seven doodlebugs came over in five minutes, all of them exploding within a radius of half a mile or so; yet that valve gear does the job!

Well, after Sifbronzing the frame assembly, I put it on top of the wall to cool down, whilst I disconnected my blowpipe and put it away; I never leave it connected up to the gas cylinders. Just as I had finished, it started to rain. I didn't want the frame to stay out in the rain, so went out to get it; but it had already got wet, and when I picked it up, it slipped through my fingers, and fell cornerwise on the concrete surface four feet below. Judging from the crack it made when it crashed, I thought I was in for a nobby job of straightening out. Anyway, I picked it up, and found it apparently undamaged, so took it into my workshop, wiped all the wet off it, and laid it upside down on my surface plate. You can judge of my relief when I found that there was not the slightest sign of a rock; the frame had remained true. It must have gone down a tidy whack, as the corner of the beam was burred, where it hit the concrete; but a file soon settled that. Any other construction would have either been twisted, or knocked into a rhomboid form.

Incidentally, I don't know whether my time on this job is a record, but I cut the frames out in forty minutes; fitted hornblocks, machined the slots, cut and drilled the buffer-beams, and Sifbronzed the assembly, in three hours; made and fitted the pump complete in three hours, and took the same time turning the wheels, axles, and crankpins, and erecting the lot. I have the tools and machines for the job, and don't have to stop and think what to do, but it may give the good folk who follow these notes, some idea of the way I have to "go for it", if I want to do any locomotive work. I only wish to goodness my poor worn-out noddle would let me do my writing, drawing and correspondence at the same speed!

Reversing Lever

The Walschaerts' gear on our weeny shunting pug is reversed and notched up by what enginemen call a "pole" lever, to distinguish it from the wheel-and-screw type. Among full-size fraternity, anything that operated the gear is called a "lever", and a driver speaks of "notching-up" with a wheel and screw, although there are no actual notches, except some small ones in a little circular catch plate attached to the screw, between the wheel and the stand. A small catch engages with these, to prevent the wheel turning of its own accord (they will!) when the engine is running. Some screw reversers have a double-armed handle, like those on Stroudley regulators, instead of a wheel; and on these, one of the handles is pivoted, and actuates the catch. The Billinton passenger engines on the L.B. & S.C.R. had this type, and it was also found on many Great Western engines; but all goods and shunting engines have a "pole" lever, which is naturally much quicker in action than a screw, and therefore more suitable for shunting.

In the arrangement shown for *Tich*, which is typical of full-size locomotives of this type, the lever is carried by a stand, mounted on a bracket well clear of the boiler, which should be welcome to those with tender fingers. It is long enough to be easily get-at-able when running, gives easy control of the valve gear, is simple to make, and "looks" right. The reverse rod, or reach rod, as it is frequently called because it enables the driver to "reach" the gear, goes straight from the reversing lever to the arm on the weighbar shaft, passing through the side tank. We shall make provision for that, when we come to it.

Stand and Sector Plate

I don't advise the use of a casting for the stand for a "pole" lever, as the latch would soon "make hay" of notches cut in soft metal. Make the stand from $\frac{1}{8}$ in. steel plate. A piece about 3 in. long and $1\frac{1}{2}$ in. wide, will be needed. Mark out on this, the outline shown in the detail drawing, and saw and file it on the given dimensions, all except the curve at the top. Leave that on the large side. Then from another piece of the same kind of steel, mark out the curved sector plate, minus notches, and cut that out as well. I don't have to re-detail out simple jobs like those! Drill a No. 41 hole at each end of the sector plate, then use it as a guide for drilling the corresponding holes in the stand. Temporarily clamp the two pieces together, and put the drill through the lot, taking care to file off any burring. Put a couple of temporary $\frac{3}{32}$ in. or 7 BA screws and nuts in, then remove the clamp, and file the two pieces to the curve as shown. Finish off by draw-filing; that is, hold a fine file by its ends, and draw it lengthwise, backwards and forwards, a few times over the full length of the curve. This will give a very nice finish.

Catch the stand in the bench vice, upside down, with the narrow end just $\frac{7}{8}$ in. above the vice jaws, and bend to a right-angle. Don't hit the foot direct with a hammer, or you will mark it badly; hold a piece of iron or steel bar

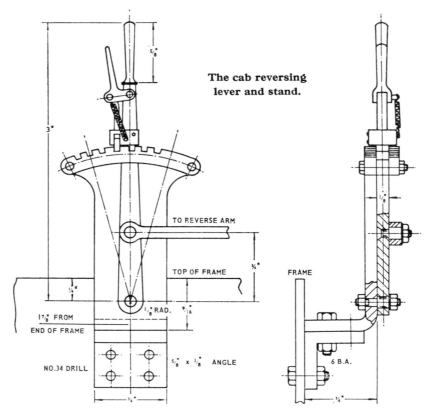

The cab reversing
lever and stand.

TO REVERSE ARM

TOP OF FRAME

FRAME

1⁷⁄₈" FROM
END OF FRAME

NO.34 DRILL

⅛" RAD.

⁵⁄₈" x ⅛" ANGLE

6 B.A.

REVERSING LEVER

against it, and hit that. Also take it easy, or you will crack the steel at the bend. Soft ductile steel will bend without cracking. If the steel you are using appears hard when sawing and filing, anneal it before bending, by heating to red, and letting it cool naturally. If any builder fancies his skill as "the village black-smith", he could bend the angle whilst the metal was still red hot. It merely requires a little dexterity. You want to be mighty quick at setting it in the vice and giving it the O.K. before the redness dies away; quicker than I can write these words. Red-hot steel bends very easily indeed, there is not the slightest risk of fracture, and the job comes out very neat, after the scaly surface has been cleaned up. Beginners might do worse than try their hands on a few odd bits of scrap steel; practice still makes perfect! After bending and cleaning up, trim the foot to size, and drill four No. 34 holes in it, as shown. If anybody makes a slight slip, and finds that the stand is a weeny bit high or low, don't worry, it won't matter; merely make sure that the hole for the fulcrum pin is exactly 1¹¹⁄₁₆ in. from the top of the curve. This hole can now be drilled No. 34, on the centre-line as shown in the illustration.

For the spacer washers, chuck a piece of ³⁄₁₆ in. round steel rod in the three-jaw. Face, centre, and drill down about ½ in. with No. 41 drill. Part off two slices about $\frac{5}{32}$ in. thick; then re-chuck each, and face off each side until they are a full $\frac{1}{8}$ in. thick, so that when the bolts are tight, the sector plate will just allow the lever to slide between it and the stand.

Lever from Solid

The lever itself can be made either from the solid, or built up, the latter being easier. For the solid job, a piece of $\frac{3}{16}$ in. by $\frac{1}{4}$ in. mild steel would be needed, about $3\frac{1}{4}$ in. long. Chuck truly in four-jaw, and turn the handle part with a round-nose tool, setting the top-slide over about 1 deg., if it has a graduated scale; if not, you'll just have to judge the taper. Lucky owners of a milling machine can then grip the embryo lever in the machine vice on the miller table, and with a small slabbing cutter, not less than $\frac{3}{8}$ in. wide, they can mill off first one side of the lever, and then the other, leaving the metal

Details of the cab reversing gear.

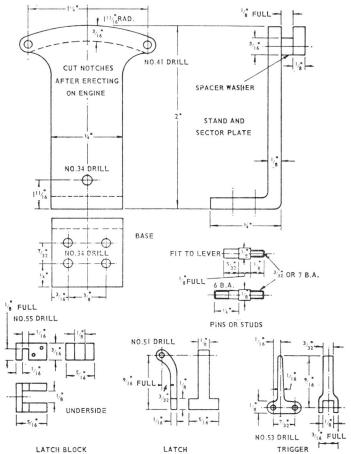

just $\frac{1}{8}$ in. thick. On my own milling machine, which is a No. 4 Burke (exactly similar to a Brown & Sharpe, and a real hefty job) I never have to measure for thickness, as the screws all have finely graduated collars. In the above job, for example, I should set the piece of metal in the machine vice with half its thickness projecting above the jaws. As the bottom of the machine vice is dead true with the table, and I keep a boxful of pieces of parallel packing, all I have to do is to insert enough packing under the metal, to bring it to required height, tighten the vice jaws, and pull the packing away. The metal is then held parallel with the table. If any follower of these notes can't do it that way, he can set the metal "by eye", tighten the vice just sufficiently to hold it, then set his scribing block needle to one end. If the other doesn't tally, a tap or two with a hammer, judiciously applied up or down, as the case may be, will soon level it up. When the bent end of the scriber needle scrapes over each end, with the base resting on the miller table, it is O.K. Tighten the vice jaws, and you're literally "all set".

I set my cut as follows. With $\frac{3}{16}$ in. thickness of metal, we need $\frac{1}{32}$ in. off each side to bring the lever to $\frac{1}{8}$ in. thickness. With the metal under the cutter, I raise the table, and pull the belt by hand backwards, until the teeth of the cutter just touch the metal. Then I run the metal out from under the cutter, and set the graduated collar on the raising and lowering spindle to zero. Next, I run the handle until the 31 marking on the graduated collar lines up with the zero mark on the machine; that indicates that the table has been raised exactly $\frac{1}{32}$ in., and the machine is started, the self-act put in, and in little more time than it takes to write this, the machine has taken $\frac{1}{32}$ in. off the metal at the one traverse, and left a beautiful finish. For lubrication, a small can, with tap and $\frac{1}{8}$ in. pipe, is hung on the overhanging arm of the machine, and a mixture of "Cutmax" (diluted with paraffin for a big job, but used "neat" for small jobs) is allowed to drip on the cutter as it "does its stuff". A repeat performance on the other side of the metal brings the thickness correct.

To get the taper, all you do is to cover one side of the milled surface with the blue or violet marking-out fluid that I have described so often, and mark out on it the taper of the lever. Then catch the lever in the machine vice, with the marked surface at the side, and adjust it until the needle of the scribing block touches the marked line at each end. Tighten jaws, start machine, set the lever into cut, and raise the table until the cutter bites down as far as the marked line. Then traverse the table, and the cutter will do the rest. The end of the lever is rounded off, same as described for coupling rods and similar bosses.

Built-up Lever

The great majority who don't possess milling machines can easily build up their levers as follows. The flat part needs a piece of $\frac{1}{8}$ in. by $\frac{1}{4}$ in. mild steel, $2\frac{1}{2}$ in. long, and a short piece of $\frac{1}{8}$ in. round ditto for the handle. The flat piece of steel is filed up to the shape shown. The handle is turned up as described above, with the bit of round steel held in the three-jaw. Butt the handle and the flat part together on a piece of thick sheet asbestos; this is fairly soft, so that if you press the handle and blade down hard, they will sink slightly into the surface of the asbestos, and will not move when heated. Put a taste of wet flux on the joint, lay the lot in the brazing pan, heat to bright red, and touch it with a bit of brass wire, which will melt and flow in. Coarse-grade silver-solder may be used if desired, in which case a dull red will suffice. Let cool to black, quench in cold water, clean up, and you have a lever that will give as good service as one cut from solid.

Locking Gear

Some arrangement of instantly locking the lever either in mid-gear, full-gear or the notch-up positions, is needed on any engine, big or little; and this is accomplished by the means shown. Beginners who are car owners will note at once that the locking gear differs from that on their handbrake lever, inasmuch as it locks the lever in both directions, and the trigger must be pressed against the handle, to move either way. The parts comprise a trigger, latch, and latch block. To make the trigger, get a piece of mild steel (great stuff, this mild steel!) about $\frac{3}{4}$ in. long, $\frac{3}{8}$ in. wide, and a full $\frac{3}{16}$ in. thick. Mark off on one side the outline of the trigger, as shown in the small detail illustration. First, drill the two No. 53 holes clean through the block. Next, slot right across the drilled end to a depth of $\frac{1}{8}$ in. full, and $\frac{1}{8}$ in. wide, by the method already given for pump ram and the other slotted parts; then saw away the unwanted parts each side of the tongue, or finger grip, and finish off with a file. These little "twiddley-bits" seem to entail a lot of work, but they are quite easy if taken by stages, as above. They remind me of the kiddy who shied at spelling "Constantinople" as one word, but managed it easily enough to what my old granny of beloved memory, always called "silly-billies".

For the latch, you'll need a bit of mild steel of $\frac{1}{4}$ in. by $\frac{5}{16}$ in. section, or nearest available, and $\frac{3}{4}$ in. long. The procedure is pretty much the same; mark off, drill the "bird's eye", saw away the unwanted metal, and file to outline. Alternatively, a piece of thinner metal could be used, and the eye end bent over. The latch-block is the simplest of the lot, being merely a little piece of $\frac{5}{16}$ in. square steel, $\frac{3}{16}$ in. thick. The easiest way to make this component is to take a piece of $\frac{5}{16}$ in. by $\frac{3}{16}$ in. mild steel rod long enough to clamp under the lathe toolholder. Square off the end, then slot it $\frac{1}{8}$ in. wide and $\frac{1}{4}$ in. deep, by method described for pump ram. Then, at $\frac{3}{16}$ in. from the end, make a cross slot $\frac{1}{16}$ in. wide and a full $\frac{1}{8}$ in. deep. Saw or part off $\frac{1}{16}$ in. behind the cross slot, and you have it.

How to Erect the Lever

Drill a No. 30 hole squarely through the bottom end of the lever, and at $\frac{3}{4}$ in. above that, drill a No. 34 hole, countersinking it on one side, Next, turn up two little shouldered pins, as illustrated, from $\frac{1}{8}$ in. silver-steel rod held in three-jaw. Beginners should be able to turn pins with their eyes shut by now! All you do is to use a knife-tool, a drop of cutting oil, and a little care. Turn down a full $\frac{5}{32}$ in. of the rod, to a tight fit in the No. 34 hole in the lever. Part off at $\frac{1}{4}$ in. from the shoulder. Reverse in chuck, and turn down a bare $\frac{1}{8}$ in. of the other end, to a diameter of $\frac{3}{32}$ in. Screw $\frac{3}{32}$ in. or 7 BA. For the fulcrum pin, turn down $\frac{1}{4}$ in. of the rod to $\frac{7}{64}$ in. diameter and screw a full $\frac{1}{8}$ in. of it with 6 BA die; part off, turn and screw the other end exactly as described above. Squeeze the first-mentioned pin into the hole in the lever, as shown, hammering the end into the countersink, and filing off flush. The fulcrum pin is put through the hole at the bottom end of the stand, and secured with a 6 BA nut.

Drill a No. 51 hole through the lever, a bare $\frac{1}{8}$ in. below the handle; smooth off any burring, then put the longer end of the slotted part of the trigger over it, and drive a piece of 16 gauge spoke wire, or $\frac{1}{16}$ in. silver-steel, through the lot, filing off flush each side. I believe that I mentioned a while ago, that cycle spokes from 16 gauge upwards can be purchased cheaply by the dozen at any cycle and motor accessory stores; and the wire from which they are made is excellent for small pins, as used in locomotive building. Several beginners have recently asked what I meant by spoke wire, hence the reminder. Put the "bird's eye" in the other end of the trigger slot, and pin it likewise; but in this case, leave one end of the pin sticking out from the side of the trigger for about $\frac{3}{32}$ in. as we need something to hang the spring on when finishing off the lever, see illustration. Put the latch block over the latch, with the cross slot over the wide part of the latch, as shown; but don't pin the block to the lever yet.

Now remove the sector plate from the stand, and put the lever in position, with the hole in the bottom end over the fulcrum pin, securing it with a commercial nut and washer. When the nut is tight, the lever should be just free to swing. Replace the sector plate, and tighten the bolts. The latch should now be resting on top of the stand and sector plate, the trigger almost touching the handle of the lever. Adjust the latch block so that it just clears the top of the stand and sector plate, as shown in the illustration of the complete bag of tricks, and fix it to the lever in that position with a couple of small rivets. For jobs like these I use bits of domestic blanket-pins, drilling No. 57 holes through block and lever, countersinking them, driving the pins through, snipping off, hammering into the countersinks, and filing flush. If you like, the head end of one end of one of the pins may be left projecting a weeny bit, to take the lower end of the latch spring; it saves putting in a $\frac{1}{16}$ in. or 10 BA screw.

Now we need a bracket on which to mount the whole doings. This is easily made from a bit of $\frac{5}{8}$ in. by $\frac{1}{8}$ in. angle, steel or brass, doesn't matter which. Square off each end, to a length of $\frac{3}{4}$ in., and drill four No. 34 holes in it as shown. Clamp this temporarily to the right-hand frame of the engine, so that the centre of it is $1\frac{7}{8}$ in. from the back end of frame, and the top of it $\frac{9}{16}$ in. below the top of frame; a toolmaker's clamp will do the needful. Drill No. 34

holes through the frame, using those in the angle for a guide; file off any burrs, and secure with four 6 BA bolts. Set the stand carrying the lever on top of this bracket, in the position shown in the assembly drawing, that is, sides of bottom of stand to be flush with sides of bracket, and the edge of the foot of the stand touching the frame. Clamp temporarily in place, drill the bracket to correspond with the holes in the foot of stand, and fix with four 6 BA bolts and nuts. Note—although this size is specified, any other size that builders might have handy can be utilised; but there seem to be millions of 6 BA bolts and nuts still floating about, "surplus" from the war period (somebody gave me a jar full a little while ago, some plated, some tinned, and some rustless) that I thought maybe we might use up a few, as they are O.K. for jobs like this.

Reach Rod

This rod goes straight from the lever to the reversing arm on the weighbar shaft above the valve gear. The lever end is a plain eye; the forward end is an offset fork which engages with the reverse arm. There is no need to cut the whole rod from the solid; a piece of flat steel rod of $\frac{1}{8}$ in. by $\frac{3}{32}$ in. section can be used, with a boss brazed on at the back end, and a block brazed on at the front end, which is machined up to form the fork or clevis. The actual length of the piece of rod would be approximately $6\frac{3}{8}$ in. The little block at the front end is $\frac{1}{2}$ in. long, $\frac{1}{4}$ in. wide, and $\frac{5}{32}$ in. thick. Tie it in place with a piece of iron binding wire; apply a little wet flux, blow to bright red, and touch the joint with a bit of thin brass wire. Quench in cold water; then drill and slot the piece exactly as described for the forked joints in the valve gear and file it up to the shape shown in the illustration.

The boss at the lever end is made by chucking a piece of $\frac{1}{4}$ in. round steel rod, facing off, centring, and drilling with No. 30 drill for about $\frac{3}{16}$ in. depth. Part off a slice about $\frac{5}{32}$ in. thick, reverse in chuck, and face the parted-off side to bring it to the required $\frac{1}{8}$ in. Next, get the actual length of rod between centres. Put the lever exactly vertical, and set the reverse arm on the valve gear in such a position that the die block is exactly in the middle of the link opposite the trunnion pin. Now take the measurement from the centre of the pin in the lever, to the centre of the hole in the reverse arm, and that is the dimension you want. Set the loose boss against the end of the reversing rod, and check the measurement between the centre of that and the hole in the fork. If it doesn't come right, file a little off the end of the reversing rod until you get it. Then very carefully, braze the boss to the rod by the method already described; quench in water, clean up, and the rod is finished. It may appear a little on the fragile side for a $3\frac{1}{2}$ in. gauge engine but there is no need to make a huge clumsy thing, such as I used to see at clubs and exhibitions. The rod cannot whip, as it will go through a tube in the tank. Slip the boss over the pin in the lever, and secure with a commercial nut and washer; put the fork over the reverse arm, and fix that with a little bolt made in the same way as those described for the valve gear. The offset of the fork is on the outside, so that the rod is parallel to the frame, as near as makes no odds, as our rural friends might say.

How to Locate the Notches

First we have to get both sides of the valve gear exactly in unison. Set the die blocks on the lower side exactly in the middle of the link, as stated above, then see if the die block on the other side is also in the middle. If not, adjust until it is; then pin the arm to the shaft by drilling a No. 53 hole through the lot, and squeezing in a bit of $\frac{1}{16}$ in. silver-steel, or 16 gauge spoke wire. Now push the lever as far forward as it will go, and turn the wheels in a forward direction by hand. If the lever doesn't move, note where the latch is resting on the stand and sector plate, carefully mark the spot, and file a notch which is a good fit for the latch. A watchmaker's flat file, or a key-cutter's warding file, will do the trick. If the lever does move, it will go backwards very slightly; file your notch at the point where it comes to rest. The same procedure is followed for the back gear notch, turning the wheels backwards. Having got the two full-gear notches, file another one for mid-gear, with the lever vertical, and the die blocks in the middle of links. Then finally, file four notches, two on each side, spacing them $\frac{1}{16}$ in. apart, as shown in the drawing of the complete assembly. If the lever goes full over, with the wheels in any position, without hesitation or signs of binding, you can reckon you have made a good job of the whole issue. A little wire spring hooked over the pins in the trigger and latch block, completes the job; one made from 28 gauge tinned steel wire is just right.

How to Set the Valves

There is precious little to be done in the way of valve-setting. Merely take off the steam chest covers, turn the wheels by hand with the lever in the middle notch, and watch the valves. If you see the edge of the port just showing as a thin black line at each dead centre, the setting is correct. If one edge shows, and not the other, adjust the valve by taking out the pin at the top of the combination lever and turning the fork. If neither edge shows, the valve is too long; file a shade off both ends, to keep the cavity in the middle. When the valves crack the ports, as the enginemen would say, at each end of the movement, the valve setting is correct; you can put the covers on, with jointing washers, "for keeps". You don't have to bother about port openings, cut-off, or anything else; the valve gear itself looks after that part of the business. It is your humble servant's job to arrange matters so that it does; and that is why most beginners are absolutely astounded when they get up steam for the first time, and the engine kicks off without the least trouble. From my correspondence, I gather that nine-hundred-and-ninety-nine out of every thousand locomotive builders would rather work to guaranteed instructions, or adapt them to their own engines, than "wander off the track" with near-certainty of complete failure; and the odd one never does it again!

Plate 13

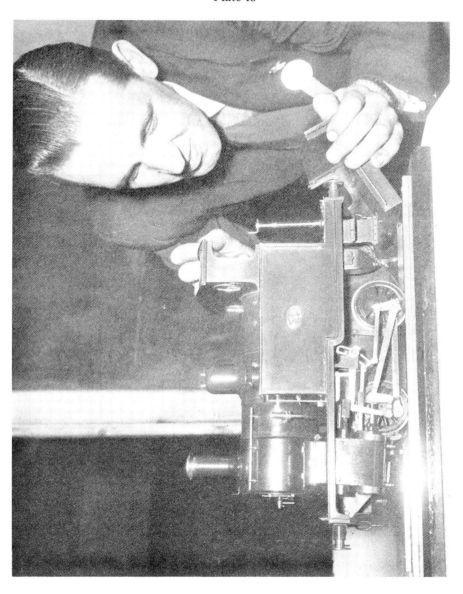

A large-boilered "Tich" built by Mr. J. S. Jackson of Wakefield. A first attempt and an award winner at local exhibitions. Photograph courtesy "Wakefield Express"

Plate 14

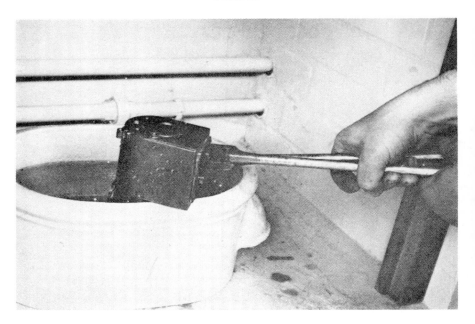

Removing a "Tich" boiler from a "pickle" bath after brazing operations

A view inside the cab of the "Tich" built by Mr. C. Wilkinson of Bradford

CHAPTER SEVEN

Steam pipes and lubricator

Steam Pipes and Lubricator

DURING MY LONG EXPERIENCE in little locomotive building I have seen many weird and wonderful arrangements of steam and exhaust pipes, especially on commercial-made engines. Unions and flange joints in inaccessible places, bits of pipe soldered together, and pipes soldered direct into cylinders and steam chests, are only some of the troubles. One engine which I overhauled for an old friend had the whole of the pipes silver-soldered up into one unit, and it was some unit at that; the late lamented Heath Robinson couldn't have devised a conglomeration to beat it. It was attached to the cylinders by glands, not unions; and to remove it I had to disconnect the motion, take the cylinders off, and dismount the boiler! It is hardly necessary to add that the whole lot was scrapped and replaced by a far simpler arrangement. What we need for *Tich* is something that can easily be made, easily fitted, and easily removed, if for any reason it is necessary to take it off; and the accompanying illustrations show a suitable layout. It is known on the other side of the big pond as "the plumbing"; and plumbing it certainly is, for it was originally suggested by a member of the fraternity who are reputed always to go back to fetch their tools.

Both steam and exhaust cross-connections consist of a central tee-piece which should be a casting, although tees can be built up. Connection between the tee-pieces and the cylinders are made by what our H2O friends actually call "connectors"; that is, pieces of tube having a long screw thread on one end and furnished with a locknut to suit. In the present instance, as there is room to spare between the frames of *Tich*, these connectors also have a blank nut silver-soldered to each of them, near the end of the thread, to enable them to be screwed home into the cylinders without the aid of a pipe wrench, or a "pair of footprints". Mention of that calls to mind how the editor of a weekly illustrated journal once made himself look very ridiculous. He was one of those people who are always trying to take a rise out of somebody or other, by virtue of "superior knowledge"—you know the sort—and reading in the local newspaper that an intruder had stolen, among other things, a pair of footprints, from a tool shed in somebody's garden, he went into ecstasies over it, to the extent of half an editorial column, plus a "thumbnail cartoon" of Bill

Sikes digging up a "Man Friday" type of footprint from the gravel in the garden path; and held up the reporter to scorn for his "ignorance". When his plumber and gas-fitter readers promptly informed him that ignorance was bliss, and not only sent him pictures of the pipe wrenches stamped with the "Footprint" trade mark (hence the nickname) but several pairs of the actual implements, he had to print an apology; and it is hardly necessary to add that no further mention of tools was ever made in the editorial columns of that journal, which has long since ceased publication.

Exhaust and Blast Pipes

Let's take the exhaust first, as that is the easier of the two. The central tee-piece is machined up very similar to that on top of the feed pump, but with internal instead of external threads. Chuck in three-jaw by one of the longer sides, and set the outer end to run truly; face off, centre, and drill right through with $\frac{7}{32}$ in. drill. If your $\frac{1}{4}$ in. by 40 tap is long enough, tap right through the piece; if not, tap about halfway. Take a skim off the outside, to true it up;

Details of the steam and exhaust pipes.

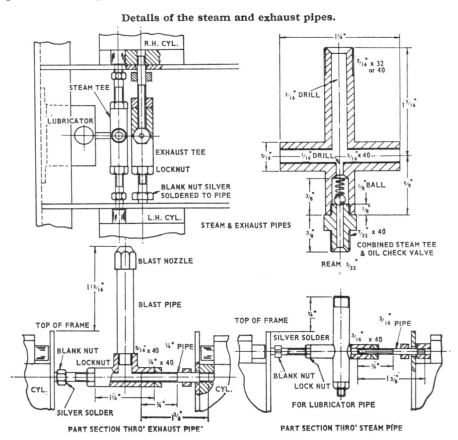

then reverse in chuck, skim off the outside of the other end, to match the first, face off the end, and tap the other half. It doesn't matter about the thread not being continuous, for the cross pipes don't meet in the middle.

There should be a chucking piece cast on, opposite the stem of the tee. Chuck this in the three-jaw, and set the stem to run truly; then face off, centre, drill $\frac{9}{32}$ in. to meet the cross hole, and tap $\frac{5}{16}$ in. by 40. Fine threads are needed for thin pipes. Cut off the chucking piece and smooth the casting with a file. Should a casting not be available, use a piece of $\frac{3}{8}$ in. brass rod $1\frac{1}{4}$ in. long, facing, drilling, and tapping exactly as above. In the centre, drill a hole with letter N or $\frac{19}{64}$ in. drill, as the blast pipe will have to be silver-soldered in.

The two cross pipes, or connectors, are made from pieces of $\frac{1}{4}$ in. by about 22 gauge copper tube, each squared off at the end, in the lathe, to a length of $1\frac{3}{8}$ in. On one side the thread is $\frac{3}{16}$ in. long; on the other, it is $\frac{3}{4}$ in. long. Hold the tube in the chuck and use a $\frac{1}{4}$ in. by 40 die in the tailstock holder, using plenty of cutting oil (same kind as used for turning steel) and pulling the lathe belt back and forth by hand to clear the chippings and get a clean thread. Threads in soft copper tear very easily indeed; but by screwing as stated above, and taking it easy, you should get quite perfect threads. Next we want a couple of nuts "widout anny treds (threads) in thim, begorra!" says Pat. Chuck a piece of $\frac{5}{16}$ in. hexagon rod, face, centre, drill, chamfer the corners and part off a $\frac{1}{8}$ in. slice. Repeat performance and, if the parted off sides are burred, rechuck the other way around, and face that side too. To rechuck truly, quicker than I can write this, put the drill in the tailstock chuck with the nut mounted on it; advance the nut into the jaws of the self-centring chuck on the mandrel, close jaws down on nut, pull the tailstock away, and the nut is chucked truly. Enter the "lead" end of a $\frac{1}{4}$ in. parallel reamer just far enough to make the hole a tight push fit for the $\frac{1}{4}$ in. cross pipe; push same in until the shorter screwed end projects $\frac{3}{8}$ in. beyond the nut. You should be quite an expert at silver-soldering by now, so I need not detail out that job. The locknuts are made the same way, except that they are drilled $\frac{7}{32}$ in. and a $\frac{1}{4}$ in. by 40 tap is run in instead of the reamer.

Put the locknuts on the longer threaded ends of the bits of tube, then anoint all the threads with some plumbers' jointing paste, and screw the longer ends of the connectors right home in the tee-piece. Now hold the tee-piece midway between the frames, with the stem of the tee pointing skywards and the ends of the connectors in line with the tapped exhaust holes in the cylinders. Screw the connectors out of the tee into the tapped holes in cylinders, right to the end of the $\frac{3}{16}$ in. length of thread a little spanner on the silver-soldered nuts will do this job to perfection. Then run the locknuts back against the ends of the tee and tighten them well, but don't overdo it; threads in soft copper strip with little provocation. No packing or jointing is needed on the exhaust pipes. When the locknuts are tightened, the stem of the tee should be held vertically.

The blast pipe is a piece of $\frac{5}{16}$ in. by about 20 gauge copper tube, although it doesn't matter if a little thicker; the length is $2\frac{1}{4}$ in. A few threads of $\frac{5}{16}$ in. by 40 pitch are put on each end, by method described above, and the pipe screwed into the tee, as shown in the illustrations. The blast pipe nozzle, or cap, is made from $\frac{1}{2}$ in. of $\frac{7}{16}$ in. hexagon brass rod. Chuck in three-jaw, face, centre, and drill right through with $\frac{7}{64}$ in. or No. 36 drill. Open out to $\frac{1}{4}$ in. depth with $\frac{9}{32}$ in. drill, and tap $\frac{5}{16}$ in. by 40. Although not actually necessary, it is an advantage to "streamline" the inside of the nozzle, as you get a little more "snap" to the blast without increasing back pressure; so if you feel inclined, make a little taper reamer by turning a cone point $\frac{3}{8}$ in. long on the end of a bit of $\frac{1}{4}$ in. round silver-steel about 3 in. long. File away half the diameter of the cone, finishing with a fine file. Harden by heating to medium red and plunging into clean cold water. Brighten up the flat part by rubbing it on a sheet of fine emery cloth, laid on the edge of your lathe bed, or anything else flat and true, taking great care not to round off the cutting edge. Lay it on a piece of sheet-iron, and hold it over the smallest ring of the domestic gas stove, or a Bunsen or spirit flame, to temper it. Watch it like a cat watching a mouse-hole; as soon as the bright part turns yellow pop it in the cold water again. A rub of the flat face on an oilstone and it is ready for use. Ream by putting it in the tailstock chuck and feeding in same as a drill. Bear in mind the above instructions for making simple little reamers, for the same "technique" applies when making reamers for injector cones, plug cocks and other components having taper holes.

If a piece of rod has been used instead of a tee casting, use a piece of $\frac{5}{16}$ in. tube for the blast pipe, same as above, but $2\frac{1}{2}$ in. long, and only screw one end of it. Ream the hole in the side of the piece of tapped rod and slightly file the plain end of the pipe, until it can be pushed tightly into the hole, for about half the diameter of the rod; then silver-solder it in. Pickle, wash, and clean up; then put a $\frac{7}{32}$ in. drill clean through the rod, to cut away the bit of tube projecting down into the hole through the rod. Also poke a drill down the blast pipe itself, to remove any burrs. Alternatively, a half-round notch can be filed across the bottom of the blast pipe, and any burr scraped off it, before it is inserted into the hole in the rod. The same type of blast nozzle is used as described above, and the assembly is erected in exactly the same way.

Steam Pipes

Whilst the steam pipe assembly bears a family likeness to the exhaust ditto, it differs in dimensions, and also carries the check valve for the oil supply from the mechanical lubricator. In any outside-cylinder engine with a single oil feed, the oil must be delivered at the point where the steam pipes diverge, otherwise one cylinder will get the lot, and the other one nothing at all, like the little pig in the nursery rhyme. A friend, now deceased, once brought to me an engine which had developed such a bad blow on one cylinder that it was all she could do to pull her own tender. She was a $2\frac{1}{2}$ in. gauge job, made by a well-known firm, and cost nearly £60. The boiler was of the water-tube type, and spirit-fired. When I dismantled her I found the trouble, and the cause of it, at one fell swoop. The left-hand cylinder was as dry as a bone;

port face, valve and cylinder bore badly scored, and only a few fluffy fragments left in the packing groove in the piston. The cylinder apparently had received no oil from the time it left the works; whilst its mate on the right-hand side was as in as good a condition as the workmanship on the job allowed. It had not, apparently, been short of oil at all.

The trouble was due to sheer ignorance, carelessness, or perhaps both, on the part of the mechanic who built the engine. The cross steam pipe between the outside cylinders was a straight bit of $\frac{5}{32}$ in. pipe with a rough oval flange on each end, attached to the steam chests by screws. The lubricator was a plain displacement type located between the frames, behind the buffer-beam; and the pipe from this was silver-soldered to the middle of the cross pipe. The trouble was the steam pipe connection. In a water-tube boiler, the steam pipe goes down between inner barrel and shell at one side and returns up the other side. Instead of bringing the end of the pipe around, and connecting it to the middle of the cross pipe, the mechanic had taken it straight to the cross pipe, and connected it close to the left-hand cylinder. Consequently, steam going to the right-hand cylinder blew right past the end of the oil pipe connection and took all the oil with it. Naturally, the oil was unable to force a passage to the left-hand cylinder against the rush of steam, so the right-hand one got the lot. I re-bored the cylinder (incidentally, I had to do the other one as well, to keep both bores the same size), scrapped the pipes, and fitted an exactly similar arrangement to the one shown here, with a mechanical lubricator. I also fitted an oil burner, and did a few more oddments. The engine then worked very well, would do a spot of live passenger hauling, and continued to give every satisfaction.

The ends of the tee carrying the cross steam pipes are machined up in exactly the same way as the exhaust, excepting that they are drilled $\frac{5}{32}$ in. and tapped $\frac{3}{16}$ in. by 40. The tee isn't really a tee at all, says Pat, because what was a chucking-piece on the other one (the exhaust) is utilised on this one as a check valve for the mechanical lubricator; see sectional illustration. Chuck it by that piece, see that the long end runs truly, then centre it deeply, and run a $\frac{3}{16}$ in. drill down it until same breaks into the cross passage at the bottom. Turn the outside to $\frac{5}{16}$ in. diameter, put a few $\frac{5}{16}$ in. by 40 threads on it with a die in the tailstock holder, and skim off any burring at the end; but don't turn away the countersink. If your lathe happens to be on the flimsy side, bring up the tailstock to support the casting whilst you turn the outside of the long stem. The centre-point will fit the countersink.

Reverse in chuck and grip by the long stem. Turn the outside of the erstwhile chucking-piece to $\frac{5}{16}$ in. diameter, and face the end; it should project about $\frac{1}{2}$ in. from the cross piece, but the exact distance doesn't matter a bean. Centre with a small-size centre-drill, and drill right through into the cross passageway with a $\frac{1}{16}$ in. or No. 52 drill. Open out to a full $\frac{3}{8}$ in. depth with a $\frac{3}{16}$ in. drill, slightly countersink the end, tap $\frac{7}{32}$ in. by 40, and skim off any burrs. Chuck a piece of $\frac{5}{16}$ in. hexagon bronze or gunmetal rod in three-jaw; face the end, centre deeply (use letter E centre-drill for all small unions) and drill down about $\frac{5}{8}$ in. depth with No. 43 drill. Turn down $\frac{1}{4}$ in. of the outside to $\frac{7}{32}$ in. diameter and screw it $\frac{7}{32}$ in. by 40. Part off at a full $\frac{9}{16}$ in. from the end. Reverse, and rechuck in a tapped bush held in three-jaw; you should know how to make a tapped bush by now. Keep all you make, and put a dot or figure at the point on the outside of the bush which was opposite to No. 1 jaw when the bush was first made; they can then be used again and again, and will always run truly. I have a box full of them, and find them very handy indeed. After rechucking, turn down $\frac{3}{16}$ in. of the other end to $\frac{7}{32}$ in. diameter and screw $\frac{7}{32}$ in. by 40; put a $\frac{3}{32}$ in. parallel reamer right through, then face off the end until you have just $\frac{1}{8}$ in. of full thread showing beyond the hexagon. If there is any sign of burring, put the reamer through the hole again. I have described how to make simple small reamers from silver-steel, by filing off the end at a long slant, then hardening, tempering and oil-stoning; anybody with shallow pockets should make up a whole set of them, from $\frac{1}{16}$ in. to $\frac{1}{4}$ in.

Seat a $\frac{1}{8}$ in. rustless steel ball on the hole, same as you did when making the bottom fitting for the pump; then assemble in the same way, as shown in the illustration, but with this difference. The tiny ball is so light that it has a tendency to "float" in the thick cylinder oil, which is about the consistency of molasses or golden syrup when cold; so a weeny spring is added, to keep the ball seated when the pump in the lubricator is on the suction stroke. The spring is made from steel wire of about 26 gauge, coiled around a bit of $\frac{3}{32}$ in. wire in the same way as when making the axlebox springs. Touch each end on the emery wheel, when it is running fast, so that it bears fairly on ball and socket. The spring should be just starting to compress as the seating is screwed into the socket.

The fitting is erected in the same way as the exhaust fitting; put the locknuts on the long screws, smear all threads with plumbers' jointing, run the long thread into the tee, hold between the two steam chest bosses, making sure it is central, then running the connector pipes out of the tee into the bosses. Before tightening up the locknuts against the tee, put a few thin strands of asbestos string, or flax, between nuts and tee, tightening up securely, but not enough to strip the threads, which is easily done in soft copper. If a temporary adapter is screwed on to the standpipe of the steam tee, so that a tyre pump can be connected to it, the chassis should dart all over the workshop floor when the pump is operated. If a first-time beginner holds one of the wheels between finger and thumb, and gives the handle of the pump a heavy push, he will get the shock of his life! Not many folk could hold the wheels against about 60 lb. air pressure, and novices will begin to realise why these little engines are capable of pulling such outsize loads.

Tank for Mechanical Lubricator

Now let us turn to a little bit of sheet-metal working. A mechanical lubricator is specified for *Tich*, because it is the most reliable regular-feeding oil supplier that I know of—and I have tried all the other kinds. It operates only

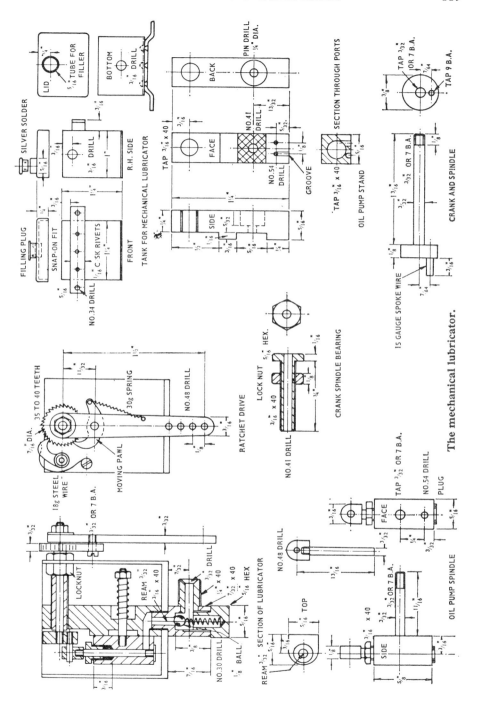

The mechanical lubricator.

when the engine is running, hence no waste. The faster the engine runs, the more oil it gets, a positive amount being delivered at each stroke of the pump. A little extra oil, to help a "cold start", can be injected into the steam pipe by simply turning the ratchet-wheel.

The pump is installed in a small oil tank attached to the front buffer-beam, so we will make the tank first. Cut out a piece of 20 gauge sheet brass or steel, a full $4\frac{1}{2}$ in. long by $1\frac{1}{4}$ in. wide; mark out as shown in the drawing and bend on the dotted lines, to form a rectangle $1\frac{1}{4}$ in. long and 1 in. wide. If the corner persists in springing open, tie a bit of thin iron wire around the lot. Cut out a piece of 16 or 18 gauge sheet metal, same kind as body, about $\frac{1}{16}$ in. larger all around; see that this is perfectly flat. Stand it on the coke in your brazing pan, place the body on top, apply wet flux to the joints, blow to medium red, and touch the joints with a strip of medium-grade silver-solder, paying particular attention to the corner joint. Pickle, wash and clean-up. File the projecting bit at the bottom flush with the sides. Drill a $\frac{3}{16}$ in. hole right in the middle of the bottom plate, and another in one of the shorter sides, $\frac{3}{16}$ in. from the top, and on the centre line.

Cut a strip of 16 gauge metal $\frac{5}{16}$ in. wide and approximately $2\frac{1}{8}$ in. long; bend this to the shape shown in the bottom view of the tank, and attach it to one of the longer sides, at $\frac{3}{16}$ in. from the top. Hold in place with a small clamp whilst the holes are being drilled; countersink those in the strip. Use No. 51 drill, put $\frac{1}{16}$ in. brass or copper rivets through from the inside, hammer the shanks into the countersinks and file flush. To give extra stiffness, the joint can be sweated with solder as well; put some liquid flux (Baker's fluid, killed spirits of salts, or any of the well-known proprietary brands) along each side of the joint, plus a small bead of solder. Hold over a gas or spirit flame with pliers, until the solder melts and disappears into the joint. Wash well in running water to remove all traces of flux. Tip—keep a special old pair of pliers for jobs like these, as it will rust up your best pair. I use a little pair of home-made tongs, which I will describe when we come to the boiler-brazing job—very soon now, if all's well. Don't drill the No. 34 holes in the end tags yet; these are located from the buffer-beam.

For the lid, cut out a piece of metal, same kind as tank, a full $1\frac{3}{4}$ in. long and $1\frac{1}{2}$ in. wide. Scribe lines along all four sides, $\frac{1}{4}$ in. from the edge; cut out the corner bits and bend to right-angles, on the dotted lines, to form a lid for the tank. It should be just a nice push-on fit. At $\frac{1}{4}$ in. from one of the longer sides, and in the middle, drill a $\frac{5}{16}$ in. hole and fit a piece of $\frac{5}{16}$ in. tube about $\frac{3}{16}$ in. long in it. Silver-solder this, and all the four corners, at one heat; but be extra sparing with the silver-solder, or the lid won't fit any more, due to blobs in the corners. Pickle, wash and clean up; turn a little push-in plug for the filler tube from $\frac{7}{16}$ in. brass rod, and the tank is all ready to have the "works" installed.

Oil Pump

Having made the oil tank, we now need a pump to put inside it. Before "standardising" on this particular type of pump, I did a lot of experimenting, as usual, with several types of stationary-barrel pumps operated by slide cranks, eccentrics and cams; but I found that for simplicity and absolute reliability, the oscillating-cylinder pumps had the other kinds well and truly beaten. It will continue to operate, even with leaky clacks, the movement of the cylinder over the ports constituting, in effect, a mechanically-operated valve. If the faces of cylinder and stand are true, it is impossible for steam and water to blow back into the lubricator, as the "entrance to the way out" is completely closed when the pump ram is not forcing oil through it. Beginners can see this plainly enough by noting the action. When the cylinder inclines to the right, the port in same coincides with the left-hand port at the bottom of the stand, the right port being completely closed. The ram being then on its outward stroke, oil is sucked up into the pump barrel via the groove in the bottom of the stand. As the ram arrives at the top of the stroke, the upper part of the pump cylinder swings over to the left, the lower part moving to the right; and by the time the ram begins to descend, and force the oil out of the barrel, the port in the cylinder has moved over to cover the outlet port in the stand. The oil then goes through the port and the little duct behind it, into the clack box under the oil tank; forces down the clack ball, and proceeds along the oil pipe to the check valve under the steam tee. Here it repeats its "get-out-of-the-way" tactics on the check valve ball and mingles with the steam entering the tee from above. The steam atomises it and blows the particles along the cross pipes to the two steam chests, where the oily spray performs its allotted task of keeping the slide valves, pistons and rods in first-class working trim. Well, now we proceed to do a bit of "watchmaking".

Pump Stand

The stand is made from $\frac{5}{16}$ in. square rod; bronze or gunmetal is naturally best, but brass will serve, if nothing better is available. As the pump spends all its working life practically drowned in oil, wear is negligible. Either chuck the rod and part off a $1\frac{1}{4}$ in. length, saw to full length, chuck, and face both ends to correct length. One end must be set to run truly in the four-jaw; then centre, drill to $\frac{5}{32}$ in. full depth with $\frac{5}{32}$ in. or No. 22 drill, tap $\frac{3}{16}$ in. by 40, and skim off any burrs. At $\frac{3}{16}$ in. from the opposite end, on the centre line of one of the facets, make a heavy centre-pop, and drill a $\frac{5}{32}$ in. or No. 22 hole clean through. This job must be done either on a drilling machine or in the lathe, as previously described, because the hole must go through dead square; same applies to the trunnion-pin hole next mentioned. Tap the upper hole $\frac{3}{16}$ in. by 40 using a taper tap to start, so as to ensure a true thread.

Next, on the same centre line, but $\frac{13}{32}$ in. from the bottom of the stand, make another centre-pop and drill it No. 41. This must also be dead square. Then drill the ports; scribe a line across the face, $\frac{5}{32}$ in. from the bottom, and make a centre-pop on it, at $\frac{1}{16}$ in. each side of the centre line. Using a No. 54 drill right through the right-hand pop-mark, into the tapped hole at the bottom of the stand; and be mighty careful as the drill breaks through into the hole, or you'll get a break of another kind—the sort of break, which if repeated too frequently, tends to make you go "broke". Drill the left-hand pop-mark to a depth of about $\frac{1}{16}$ in. only; and with a little chisel made from a bit of silver-steel, cut a groove from the port to the bottom of the stand, as shown in the illustrations.

The face of the stand has now to be rebated to $\frac{1}{16}$ in. depth for $\frac{1}{2}$ in. down from the top, and recessed $\frac{1}{16}$ in. to a width of $\frac{5}{16}$ in. across the trunnion-pin hole. This is just another job where the vertical-slide comes in handy. If the stand is held horizontally in a small machine vice, regular, or improvised with bits of angle as previously described, and attached to the slide, the stand can easily be moved up and down, and past a $\frac{5}{16}$ in. end-mill, or home-made slot-drill, and the recess and rebate cut in two wags of a dog's tail. I made half-a-dozen stands at once, clamp them all together in a machine vice on the table of my milling machine, and run the lot under a $\frac{5}{16}$ in. side-and-face cutter on the arbor. Anybody who has a small planing or shaping machine can catch the stand horizontally in the machine vice, and operate with a square-ended tool in the clapper box. Failing any method of machining, put the stand in the bench vice, with the business side projecting $\frac{1}{16}$ in. above the jaws (no need to bother about "mike" measurements!) and file away the recess and rebate until the file touches the vice jaws. Quit filing at the first scrape of the file on the steel, or you'll need a new file for the next job. Discretion saves file teeth! Finally, with a $\frac{1}{4}$ in. pin-drill having $\frac{3}{32}$ in. pilot-pin, form the circular recess shown in the illustrations, $\frac{5}{32}$ in. deep, in the back of the stand. You'll know about pin-drilling from experience of the leading bosses of the coupling rods. Then true up the working face, exactly the same as described for slide valves and port faces. The stand is then complete.

Pump Cylinder

Cut a piece of $\frac{5}{16}$ in. square rod to a full $\frac{5}{8}$ in. length, as described above. Scribe a line across the middle of one end, and at $\frac{3}{16}$ in. from one end of it, make a centre-pop. Chuck in four-jaw with this mark running truly. Open it with a centre-drill, and drill clean through with No. 43 drill. Open out to $\frac{3}{16}$ in. depth with $\frac{5}{32}$ in. or No. 22 drill and tap $\frac{3}{16}$ in. by 40. Put a $\frac{3}{32}$ in. parallel reamer through the rest of the hole. Home-made reamers do fine for jobs like these; file off the end of a bit of $\frac{3}{32}$ in. round silver-steel on the slant, harden and temper to dark yellow, and rub the oval flat face on an oilstone. Reverse in chuck, and face off the other end; then turn a tiny plug, as shown, from $\frac{3}{16}$ in. brass rod, but before fitting it, drill the port and trunnion holes. Scribe a line down the rubbing face; that is, the one farthest away from the bore. Mark the two spots, one $\frac{3}{32}$ in. from bottom, and the other $\frac{1}{4}$ in. above it. Drill the first one with No. 54 drill, going right into the bore. Drill the other No. 48 but don't pierce the bore; tap it $\frac{3}{32}$ in. or 7 BA instead, and in it fit a trunnion pin made from $\frac{3}{32}$ in. round steel (silver or rustless) cut to length of

$\frac{13}{16}$ in. and screwed at both ends. Poke the $\frac{3}{32}$ in. reamer through again, to cut away any burrs, and remove distortion; then drive the weeny plug in the bottom end and solder it. Soft solder will do.

The gland is made from $\frac{1}{4}$ in. hexagon brass rod, the screwed part being $\frac{1}{8}$ in. long and the head $\frac{1}{16}$ in.; as the process is exactly the same as for the piston rod and valve spindle glands, I don't have to detail that bit out again; you use your experience! The pump ram, or plunger (it both plunges and rams!) is a piece of $\frac{3}{32}$ in. round rod, $\frac{3}{4}$ in. long; rustless or ordinary steel or hard-drawn bronze all do very well. Put a few threads on one end. The little big-end (says Pat) is made from a bit of $\frac{1}{8}$ in. brass, $\frac{1}{16}$ in. wide, filed to the shape shown, drilled and tapped in the thickness, to take the ram, and then cross drilled No. 48 for the crankpin. The easiest way to do the job, is to screw the bit of brass on the end of the ram first, then go ahead and file to shape and drill as shown. Round off the sides of the cylinder, as shown in the plan view; temporarily remove the trunnion pin, true up the rubbing face, as described for slide valves, etc., then replace the pin, assemble as shown, pack the gland with a few strands of graphited yarn, poke the trunnion pin through the hole in the stand, fit a spring wound up from 22 gauge steel wire and secure with a commercial nut and washer.

Crank and Bearing

To make the crank, chuck a piece of $\frac{3}{8}$ in. round brass rod; face the end, centre, drill down about $\frac{1}{4}$ in. with No. 48 drill, and tap $\frac{3}{32}$ in. or 7 BA. Part off a $\frac{1}{8}$ in. slice. At $\frac{7}{64}$ in. from centre, drill a No. 53 hole, tap it 9 BA, and screw in a crankpin made from 15 gauge spoke wire leaving $\frac{3}{16}$ in. projecting. The spindle is merely a piece of $\frac{3}{32}$ in. round steel $1\frac{5}{16}$ in. long with $\frac{1}{8}$ in. of thread on each end, and is screwed into the crank disc.

For the bearing, chuck a piece of $\frac{5}{16}$ in. hexagon brass rod in the three-jaw; face the end, centre, and drill down about $\frac{7}{8}$ in. depth with No. 41 drill. Turn down $\frac{3}{4}$ in. of the outside to $\frac{3}{16}$ in. diameter; screw $\frac{3}{16}$ in. by 40 with die in tailstock holder, part off to leave a head a full $\frac{1}{16}$ in. thick, reverse in chuck, skim the face and chamfer the corners. The nut is just a $\frac{1}{8}$ in. slice of the same rod, drilled $\frac{5}{32}$ in. or No. 22 and tapped $\frac{3}{16}$ in. by 40.

Check Valve

Chuck a piece of $\frac{5}{16}$ in. round rod in three-jaw, face the end, centre, and drill down about $\frac{3}{4}$ in. depth with No. 43 drill. Turn down $\frac{7}{16}$ in. of the outside to $\frac{3}{16}$ in. diameter, and screw $\frac{3}{16}$ in. by 40. Part off at $\frac{7}{16}$ in. from shoulder. Reverse in chuck; open out with $\frac{3}{16}$ in. drill and D-bit to $\frac{3}{8}$ in. depth, slightly countersink the end, tap $\frac{7}{32}$ in. by 40, and skim off any burr. Put a $\frac{3}{32}$ in. parallel reamer through the remnants of the No. 43 hole. Drill a $\frac{3}{16}$ in. hole in the side; and in it, fit a $\frac{1}{4}$ in. union screw. Chuck a bit of $\frac{1}{4}$ in. round rod; face, and centre deeply with size E centre drill. Drill down about $\frac{7}{16}$ in. depth with $\frac{3}{32}$ in. or No. 42 drill. Screw the outside $\frac{1}{4}$ in. by 40 for $\frac{1}{4}$ in. down and part off at $\frac{3}{8}$ in. from the end. Reverse in chuck—you can grip by the threaded part, as long as the chuck jaws are not tightened sufficiently to cut the thread—turn down $\frac{1}{16}$ in. to a tight fit in the hole in the side of the chuck body, squeeze it in, and silver-solder it. Pickle, wash, and clean up; seat a $\frac{1}{8}$ in. rustless ball on the small hole, same method as described for pump. Make a cap for the end, from $\frac{5}{16}$ in. hexagon rod, same process as for glands, but don't drill right through. Only go as far as the middle of the hexagon part. Use No. 30 drill. Wind up a spring from thin steel wire, about 26 gauge, and assemble as shown in the section of the complete lubricator. The spring should just begin to compress as the threads on the cap engage those in the clack body.

Erection

Simple job, this! Put the stand in the middle of the tank, and screw the stem of the clack into it, through the hole in the base. Line up the hole in the top, with the hole in the side of the tank. Poke the end of the bearing through this, put on the lock-nut, and screw the end of the bearing into the top of the stand, until the head of the bearing just touches the side of the tank; don't force it and distort the tank side. Run the lock-nut back and tighten up; then tighten the clack. Note—in the sectional illustration, the clack is shown with the nipple, or union screw, pointing sideways toward the ratchet lever. It is shown this way merely for illustrating the section. On the finished job the clack, when tight, should have the union screw pointing to the back, as shown in the illustration giving a view of the complete pipe assembly.

Ratchet Gear

Suitable ratchet wheels can be purchased. I could give instructions how to cut one on the lathe, but honestly, it isn't worth the trouble of setting up for the job; life's too short! It should be about $\frac{7}{16}$ in. diameter, with from 30 to 40 teeth. The hole in the middle will be small; open it out with a No. 43 drill, then press the end of the crank spindle through until same projects about $\frac{7}{32}$ in. through. Check position from the actual job; hold the crank-disc opposite the end of the bearing inside the tank, with the crankpin through the "big-end", push the spindle through the bearing, and screw it into the disc. When right home tight, there should be the weeniest bit of end play. Warning: be mighty careful to put the wheel on the same way as shown in the view of the ratchet gear, viz. with the buttress (straight) side of the teeth to your left, at the top of the wheel, sloping away to your right, so that the wheel turns clockwise when operated by the pawls. The lubricator can now be tested by pouring some oil into the tank (ordinary motor engine oil will do) and turning the wheel. A distinct resistance should be felt, when the oil forces the clack ball off its seating, on the downward stroke of the ram; and you'll find it impossible to stop oil coming out of the nipple by putting your thumb over it (no matter if you have the strength of half-a-dozen folk of the Hercules type) when the wheel is turned. These lubricators have been tested against 400 lb. pressure, and that was nowhere near the limit.

The rest of the job is plain sailing. The ratchet lever is nothing more formidable than a bit of $\frac{1}{4}$ in. by $\frac{3}{32}$ in. strip steel filed to the shape shown. Drill the upper end No. 41 to take the crank spindle; at $\frac{11}{32}$ in. below that, drill No. 48 and tap $\frac{3}{32}$ in. or 7 BA for the pin carrying the moving pawl. About $\frac{3}{4}$ in. from the bottom drill a $\frac{1}{16}$ in. hole close to the side of the lever, for the end of the pawl spring, and finally, drill four No. 48 holes at the bottom, $\frac{1}{8}$ in. apart, to provide adjustment for the driving fork.

Both pawls are filed up from $\frac{3}{32}$ in. steel, to the shape shown in the drawing, and drilled No. 41 for the pins; the moving one has a $\frac{1}{16}$ in. hole in its tail, and the fixed one (woodpecker head) is slotted or grooved for a wire spring. If possible, make the pawls from gauge steel, same as recommended for expansion links, and harden and temper them to dark yellow. If mild steel is used, case-harden as previously described. The moving pawl is attached to the ratchet lever by a screw with $\frac{3}{32}$ in. of "plain" under the head, as described for valve gear. The stationary one is mounted on a stud, so as to bring it out level with the wheel; see cross-section shown in the small detail sketch. The stud is just a piece of $\frac{5}{32}$ in. round steel rod $\frac{7}{16}$ in. long turned down to $\frac{3}{32}$ in. diameter for $\frac{3}{32}$ in. length at one end, and screwed just sufficiently to take a nut; the other end is turned same diameter for $\frac{1}{2}$ in. length, and screwed likewise. The pawl is mounted on the longer end and secured by a nut and washer; when the nut is tight, the pawl should still be free to move easily. The shorter rod is pushed through a No. 41 hole drilled level with the crank spindle, and about $\frac{1}{8}$ in. from the side of the tank; it is nutted inside from an alarm clock that I bought for a few shillings when I first went to work on the railway; it is still going strong, and keeps good time! The spring is just a bit of 18 gauge steel wire, bent into a swan-neck with a loop at the end, and is secured to the tank by an 8 BA screw (or any near size) nutted inside the tank; a distance piece, made from a bit of $\frac{5}{32}$ in. brass rod, drilled and parted off to $\frac{1}{8}$ in. length, keeps the spring level with the pawl. The end rests in the groove, and keeps the pawl in contact with the teeth, preventing the wheel slipping backwards on the right-hand swing of the lever. The latter is placed on the end of the crank spindle, and secured by a nut and washer; the nut should be tight at the end of the thread, whilst the lever is left free to swing. Before putting the lid on the lubricator, file a segment out of the flange directly above the end of the bearing, so that the lid can sit down on the box and yet clear the hexagon head.

The complete lubricator is attached to the front buffer-beam by two 6 BA screws; drill the No. 34 holes in the beam for same, at $\frac{13}{16}$ in. each side of centre, and $\frac{5}{32}$ in. from the bottom edge of beam. Countersink them on the outside; then, temporarily clamp the lubricator in place and drill the holes in the lugs, using those in the frame as guides. Put two 6 BA countersunk screws in and nut them behind the lugs.

Lubricator Drive

When making the water pump for our little shunting pug, we fitted a special wrist-pin, or gudgeon-pin, to the end of the ram, with an extension at the side for driving the oil pump; so all that remains to be done is to connect this to the ratchet lever, so that the latter will waggle as the ram moves back and forth. The connection is made by a piece of 15 gauge spoke wire, slightly offset, with suitable connections at each end. The eye at the pump end is filed up from a bit of $\frac{1}{8}$ in. brass plate, or from $\frac{1}{8}$ in. by $\frac{1}{4}$ in. flat rod, to the shape shown; the exact size doesn't matter. Drill a No. 41 hole in it, to fit nicely over the extension of the wrist-pan. Drill the end No. 53 for about $\frac{3}{16}$ in. down and tap it 9 BA. The fork at the other end is made by exactly the same process previously described in full for the valve spindle forks; so beginners can make use of their acquired knowledge, and I won't have to repeat the rigmarole. Make the fork to the given size, from $\frac{1}{4}$ in. square rod—either brass or steel will do equally well—slot is a full $\frac{3}{32}$ in. wide and $\frac{3}{8}$ in. deep, to accommodate the end of the ratchet lever easily, and the stem is drilled No. 53 and tapped 9 BA. Note—drill the fork No. 53 before slotting; then tap one side 9 BA, and open out the other side with No. 48 drill after

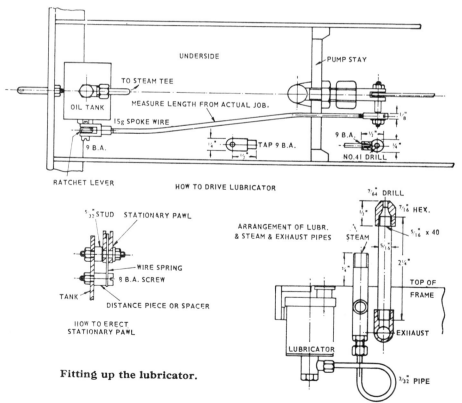

Fitting up the lubricator.

finishing. Make a 9 BA screw from a bit of $\frac{3}{16}$ in. silver-steel, same as valve gear screws, and leave enough "plain" under the head to clear the end of the ratchet lever, and allow the screw to be driven right home without squeezing up the jaws of the fork. This screw is better than a bolt, in the present instance, as it allows of instantaneous disconnections when taking off the lubricator to clean it out, or for any other purpose. An occasional "birthday treat" does the lubricator a world of good, and prevents blockage of the weeny ports, also from minute particles of grit or other unwelcome substance, getting under the clack balls and allowing steam and water to get into the oil pipe.

The length of the rod is found from the actual job. Set the ratchet lever vertical and put the pump ram at half stroke. Bend the piece of cycle spoke as shown, and also set it to clear the pump stay; then cut to required length, allowing a full $\frac{1}{8}$ in. at each end, for screwing into the eye and the fork. Put about $\frac{3}{16}$ in. of 9 BA thread on each end, screw on the eye and fork and erect as shown. The ratchet should click one tooth for every revolution of the wheels. If it doesn't do this with the fork connected to the bottom hole in the ratchet lever, shift the fork up higher until it does.

Mass Production

The union on the check valve under the lubricator is connected to the union under the cross steam pipes, by a bit of $\frac{3}{32}$ in. or $\frac{1}{8}$ in. copper tube, with a union nut and cone on each end. Beginners should make these union nuts a dozen or more at a time, as they are needed for all pipe connections; and if done the following way they can be turned out at the rate of a minute apiece. I have given the instruction before, but they will bear repeating for readers' and beginners' benefit. For $\frac{1}{4}$ in. by 40 unions, you need a piece of $\frac{5}{16}$ in. hexagon brass rod; a centre drill (size E) No. 30 drill (for $\frac{1}{8}$ in. pipe) $\frac{7}{32}$ in. drill and $\frac{1}{4}$ in. by 40 plug tap. If your lathe has the ordinary screw tailstock, put a tap wrench on the tap, right close to the flutes. If the tailstock is not graduated, put a stop on the $\frac{7}{32}$ in. drill a bare $\frac{1}{4}$ in. from the end of the lips; this is just a little collar made from $\frac{3}{8}$ in. brass rod, with a $\frac{3}{32}$ in. set-screw in it. If you have good eyesight and a sensitive touch, merely a mark on the drill would do, or a ring of wire around it, just sprung on.

First operation is to part off your blanks; put the rod in the three-jaw, with about $\frac{5}{8}$ in. projecting, then put a parting tool in the rest, and set it to cut off $\frac{5}{16}$ in. of the rod. Put another piece of rod in your tailstock chuck—any bit handy will do—run up the tailstock until the rod hits the piece in the three-jaw, then tighten the clamp. Now part off; release chuck jaws, pull out the rod until it hits the bit in the tailstock chuck, tighten up, part off again, and ditto repeato until you have the required number of blanks. You can do the whole lot in less time than it takes me to write these instructions.

Now lay out your weapons of offence on the lathe tray or bench, in the order set out above. Put a chamfering tool in the slide-rest; that is, a square-ended tool with the left-hand corner ground off at an angle of about 45 deg. The tool should be backed off below the angle, so that it will cut at the side, and act as a facing tool as well. Pop a blank in the three-jaw; put the centre-drill in the tailstock chuck, and centre the blank; drill it right through with the No. 30; poke the $\frac{7}{32}$ in. drill in, as far as the stop, or mark; then apply the tap, just tightening the tailstock chuck sufficiently to allow the tap shank to slide whilst you hold the tap wrench to prevent it turning. Pull the belt by hand whilst tapping. Finally, chamfer the corners with the tool in the slide-rest; then reverse the nut and chamfer the other end—finis Johnny! The rate at which you can turn out the nuts depends entirely on how quickly you can change the drills and tap in the tailstock chuck. The ideal set-up for a beginner would be to have a turret attachment for the tailstock, which would carry the drills and tap. I have one; gave 17s. 6d. for it at George Adams' old shop in Holborn, soon after the end of the Kaiser's war. Goodness only knows what one would cost now! However, I seldom use it, unless I make (for example) a batch of injectors, and want about half-a-gross or so of nuts; seem to have developed the habit of changing drills, taps and reamers in an "unconscious" manner, just like the girls at the old munition shop used to do. As one gets toward the end of the run over the Great Railroad of Life, the minutes seem absolutely to fly; so the only thing to do is to speed up as much as possible, and fly with them. Maybe it is only fancy; a locomotive or a motor car seems to go ever so much faster at night, yet it takes the same time between stopping points! Still, there it is, as the farmer said when he spotted the Colorado beetle among the "praties".

How to Make Union Cones

Most beginners will probably have seen the commercially-made unions illustrated in the catalogues of various firms, in which the nut is plenty big, and has a separate "lining", as the male or coned part of the union is known in the trade. For a $\frac{1}{8}$ in. pipe, the lining will have to be $\frac{3}{16}$ in. diameter at least, as the pipe fits into it. This necessitates a cone over $\frac{1}{4}$ in. diameter at the base, or widest part, and this in turn means a hexagon nut at least $\frac{3}{8}$ in. across the flats. Well, I've had a fair amount of experience with full-sized engines, but I don't recollect ever seeing a hexagon nut 6 in. across the flats on an oil pipe! The few who have seen my locomotives "in the flesh", and the many who have seen close-up photographs of the working parts, have always remarked on the neatness of the "plumbing", especially the small unions. The reason for this is the complete elimination of the separate union lining. I always put the cone straight on the end of the pipe, and this enables a much smaller nut to be used. It is quite possible to use a nut only $\frac{3}{16}$ in. across the flats, to couple up a $\frac{3}{32}$ in. pipe. However, so as not to make it too fiddling for our tyro friends, we will use the size of nut described in the paragraph above. Cones to suit these are made from $\frac{7}{32}$ in. round rod. This should be copper, if it is available; a copper cone beds in steam-tight, without much tightening of the nut, and the risk of stripped threads. If $\frac{7}{32}$ in. rod isn't procurable, use $\frac{1}{4}$ in. and turn it to size, so that it will just slip in the nut.

Plate 15

This large-boilered "Tich" with open cab was built by Mr. G. F. Collins of Brighton

Cab view of Mr. F. Raw's large-boilered "Tich"

Plate 16

Two views of an interesting variation on "Tich". Mr. G. Sheed of the Eltham Society has disguised his model as an old Great Eastern Tram engine

This is where the four-tool turret comes in handy. All home-workshop lathes should be provided with them as standard fittings. I made my own. It should be furnished with round-nose, knife, combined facing and chamfering (as above) and parting tools. The chamfer tool should have the corner ground off to such an angle that it matches up exactly with the lathe centre-point, or to the angle of a centre-drill held in the three-jaw. Then all you have to do, to make the cones, is to chuck the rod, turning to correct diameter if neccesary. Face the end, centre, and drill down about $\frac{1}{2}$ in. depth with a drill suitable for making a tight-fitting hole for the pipe; say No. 42 for $\frac{3}{32}$ in. pipe, and No. 32 for $\frac{1}{8}$ in. pipe. Feed the chamfering tool "straight at it", coning the end sufficiently to enter the countersink on the check valve connection; don't run the lathe too fast, and apply a drop of cutting oil with a brush. Part off about $\frac{1}{16}$ in. behind the taper part, and there is your cone. Make a dozen or so at a time. If you haven't a four-tool turret, cut several short pieces of rod, chuck each, face and drill both ends of each, then set up your chamfering tool, form all the cones, and finally, set up your parting tool and part them all off.

Cut a bit of tube to reach from the check valve union on the cross pipe fitting, to the clack under the lubricator; put the "piggy tail" in it, as shown in the before-mentioned illustration, to provide flexibility. Put a union nut on each end, then a cone; silver-solder the cones, using the weeniest amount of silver-solder; pickle, wash, and clean up; screw the nuts on, and another job is completed.

Buffers

We might as well fit the buffers and couplings before starting on the boiler, as the couplings, at any rate, will be needed for testing. The guard-irons, and the brake gear, can be left until "the final". Some good folk seem to be under the impression that I leave out or forget the brake gear when designing, and add it as an afterthought, which proves they know little about Curly's methods.

Buffers and couplings.

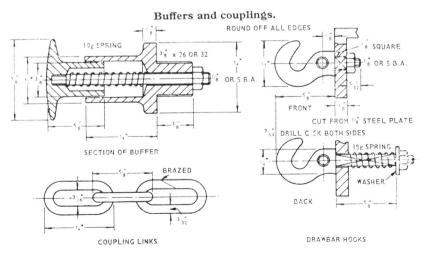

SECTION OF BUFFER

COUPLING LINKS

FRONT

BACK

DRAWBAR HOOKS

My experience of small locomotive builders teaches me one fact, viz. that they would rather get the locomotive on the road, and see the wheels turn, and experience the pleasure of driving it, than spend months, or maybe years, adding what I call "trimmings". I therefore describe the fundamentals first; those who desire, can then doll up the engine as much as ever they desire, meantime having it in working order, to arouse renewed interest whenever they are in danger of getting "browned off".

Castings may be available for the buffers; bronze or gunmetal for the sockets, and nickel-bronze (German silver) for the heads. They can, of course, be made from rod material; brass would do quite well for the sockets, and steel for the heads. Old bolts make swell buffers; young Curly used them—trust that worthy to press any mortal thing into service! A very shallow pocket proved the finest incentive to improvisation. It amused my mother no end, when I begged the brass screwed stopper of the domestic kerosene can, for the chimney cap of a little "Brighton" engine; it was the right shape and size, and the cork I gave her in exchange suited the can just as well as the brass cap. With the turning and fitting experience they have now acquired, beginners should not have the slightest difficulty in making the buffers straight from the drawing. Chuck the socket by the spigot, turn the outside to shape, face the end, centre, drill right through with No. 30 drill, and open out to $\frac{5}{8}$ in. depth with $\frac{3}{8}$ in. drill. Reverse in chuck, turn the spigot to $\frac{3}{8}$ in. diameter, face the back (says Pat) of the flange, screw the spigot $\frac{3}{8}$ in. by 26 or 32, and cut back to $\frac{3}{8}$ in. length.

The heads will probably be cut together, "head on". Chuck by one end, turn to a sliding fit in the socket, face the end, centre, drill to $\frac{3}{8}$ in. depth with $\frac{1}{4}$ in. drill, drill a No. 48 hole at the bottom of the recess, about $\frac{5}{32}$ in. deep, and tap it $\frac{1}{8}$ in. or 5 BA. Reverse in chuck, repeat operation on the other end, then part in the middle. Chuck each piece by the stem and turn the head to shape and size shown. The spindles are $1\frac{5}{8}$ in. lengths of $\frac{1}{8}$ in. round steel, screwed at each end for $\frac{3}{16}$ in. or so; the springs are wound up from 19 gauge steel wire, and the whole assembled as shown. Poke the shanks through the holes in the beams and secure with nuts made from $\frac{3}{16}$ in. slices of $\frac{1}{2}$ in. hexagon rod, drilled and tapped to suit the shanks. The L.B. & S.C. Rly. engines had these hollow-headed buffers, as it gave the springs greater flexibility (they used volute springs) and, wonder of wonders, Hobden described a hollow-headed buffer in the Boy's Own Paper over sixty years ago! To make buffers from rod material, simply cut pieces of suitable sizes of rod to required length, and proceed as above.

Couplings

The coupling hooks are filed up from $\frac{1}{8}$ in. steel. What I usually do, is to mark the outline on a bit of steel left over from frame making—I save the larger scraps—then drill a hole slap in the middle of the hook, sawing down to it, and finishing with a file. Be sure to round off all sharp edges, or they will cut the links. The leading hook only has a short squared part. To erect it, hold the nut between the oil tank and the buffer-beam with a pair of long-nosed pliers (known as "Ally Slopers" in the railway shops) then insert the screwed end of the hook, and start the nut on the thread. If the nut is then turned with a small spanner, the hook will be drawn into place and tightly held. The other hook has a longer shank, with a spring on it, to cushion the sudden pull when the regulator is mishandled by an inexperienced driver. There is no need to set up the hooks in the four-jaw, to turn and screw the ends; just file away the corners of the sqaure, and round off with the file, "by eye". The die will do the rest. The spring for the back drawbar is wound up from 18 gauge steel wire, and secured by an ordinary commercial nut and washer as shown in the illustration.

The three-link couplings are made from $\frac{3}{32}$ in. round silver-steel, and are just a simple exercise in bending; the sizes are given in the drawing. The joints in the links may either be scarfed, as shown, or merely butted together; whichever way you choose, don't forget to put one of the longer links through the hole in the coupling hook before closing the joint. Braze the joints by anointing with wet flux, blowing to bright red, then touching with a bit of thin brass wire, or commonest grade of silver-solder. Let them cool off naturally, otherwise the link will go hard and brittle, and would snap under a sudden jerk. They can either be polished up, hooks and all, or left black or blue; it is very seldom a locomotive of this type has scoured-up hooks and chains! Well, that will be all about the chassis for the time being; now we will see about a suitable boiler.

I propose to give dimensions of two boilers; one, to the size shown on the original drawing, and an alternative with a much larger barrel, to suit the wishes of some beginners who are rather doubtful about their efforts on "the works", and want to make certain of plenty of steam to make up for any inefficiency. Personally, I don't think they have any cause to worry, as the steaming capacity of all my boilers has, up to the present, been more than enough to cope with every demand made on them; but as I'm here to do my best to please as many as possible, I'll fall in with their wishes.

CHAPTER EIGHT

Starting on the boiler

Boiler

IT IS NOW TIME to initiate our beginner friends into the boilersmith's craft; but before doing so, maybe a few words on the subject of boilers in general, and locomotive boilers in particular, may be of assistance to them. In this, as in other branches of locomotive building, I speak from actual personal experience, having long since lost count of the number of boilers I have actually built, well over three figures; and of the whole lot, not one has ever failed to steam, and do all that was required of it, under every condition of service. This is plain honest fact, and no idle boast; hundreds of readers who have built "L.B.S.C.-designed" boilers will confirm that, "with knobs on" as the kiddies would say. The old idea was to put the biggest possible boiler on the chassis, to get the steam required. Now, in my experiments, I found that it wasn't always the biggest boiler that produced the most steam. Many of the "ancient-and-not-so-honourable" designs produced by so-called experts, were absolutely wretched steamers, despite their size. The reason was just this, in a nutshell. To make a boiler steam, and keep steaming, the heating surface must be properly proportioned to the amount of water normally carried in the boiler. This was the principal trouble with the shy steamers just mentioned. The designers had a fixed idea in their noddles, that on no account must the firebox crown be above the centre line of the barrel; consequently, the top part of the firebox was badly restricted, and not only was there not sufficient space for proper combustion, but the large bulk of water above the crown sheet "drowned" the box, in a manner of speaking, and kept the temperature down. Our departed friend Bro. "Iron-Wire" Alexander exploded this fallacy before it was put forward (says Pat), as all his designs had high-crowned fireboxes, and steamed better than he claimed; they would have been better still with a number of small tubes instead of one big tube.

An experience of my childhood days will bear repeating. I was taught to drive a L.B. & S.C. Ry. "Terrier" tank engine before my thirteenth birthday, and was known to many drivers who ran these engines on the London suburban services. One Sunday evening a friendly driver at Victoria invited me to "work my passage home", to Queen's Road, Peckham, saying that his friend on the opposite turn told him I could manage fine with a seven-coach set on the East London line, and he wanted to see how I shaped with a ten-coach set on the South London line. Naturally I eagerly accepted, got up the 1 in 60 to the river bridge in fine style, and made the station stops in a manner which earned the driver's hearty approval. "Old man Billy" said a child could drive any of his engines, and he certainly was right! Well, just after we left Clapham Road, I noticed that there was less than half-a-glass of water, so shut the pump bypass on my side of the footplate. The fireman saw this, and immediately said, "Don't shut it right off, kid, she steams much freer when there isn't so much water to keep hot!" That simple remark solved a problem which had been puzzling me on one of my toy boilers; and it forms the basis of the boilers which I design and build.

The Secret is Temperature

Water boils in a domestic kettle at 212 deg. F., at or near sea level; and as long as the spout or other vent remains open to the atmosphere, the water won't get any hotter, but will be converted into steam, which will escape from the spout as fast as it is generated. If the spout is blocked up so that the steam can't get out, it starts to accumulate under pressure, and the water begins to get hotter. In due course there would be a nobby old bang, and either the lid would blow off, or a new kettle would be needed. Now there is a fixed relationship between the pressure of the steam, and the temperature of the water. Without going into fractions or decimals, by the time the water has reached a temperature of, say 300 deg., the steam pressure will be just over 70 lb.; and another 25 deg. on the water will bring the pressure to over 100 lb.

These simple facts have been known to engineers and scientists "ever since the year dot", to quote the kiddies once again; yet it apparently did not occur to the designers of the inefficient boilers mentioned above, to apply them to their designs. It doesn't need a Sherlock Holmes to deduce that if the temperature of the water can be maintained, you are going to get the steam, whatever the size of the boiler; within reason, of course. To cut a long story short, as Nat Gubbins would remark, all your humble servant did, was to proportion out grate area, heating surface, and water capacity, so that the temperature of the boiler could be maintained whilst sufficient steam was being drawn off to work the engine, and at the same time water was being fed in, to replace that evaporated into steam. It follows that if the cylinders and motion are arranged to do the maximum amount of work with a minimum amount of steam, an outsize in boilers is not needed. If anybody builds a copy, or alleged copy, of any full-sized engine, and puts a proportionately bigger boiler on it than that of its big sister (with or without any excuses!) it always makes me suspicious that the "works" are not quite as efficient as they should be, and therefore require more steam to do a given job. An excessive amount of steam drawn off from a boiler of given size, causes a bigger drop in the temperature than the boiler can sustain; consequently, down goes the steam pressure.

I hope that simple explanation clears the air for all beginners whose ideas

about boilers are hazy. As an example of how it works out in practice, my old
$3\frac{1}{2}$ in. gauge single-wheeler *Ancient Lights* had a boiler with a barrel 15 in. long
and $2\frac{7}{8}$ in. diameter. The firebox is 3 in. and $2\frac{1}{8}$ in. wide; there are seven
$\frac{3}{8}$ in. tubes and a $\frac{5}{8}$ in. superheater flue. The cylinders are a little bigger in the
bore than those of *Tich*, the stroke is a full $1\frac{1}{4}$ in. and the driving wheels are
just over 4 in. diameter. Bear in mind that she is a copy of an ancient type of
express passenger engine, not a "pug" shunter like *Tich*; so, by the good
rights, she should need plenty of steam for sustained high speed. Well, that
old cat will start away, hauling my weight (equal to a load of 320 tons, far
more than any of her full-sized sisters of early Victorian vintage could have
ever shifted) with only 35 lb. on the clock, and a black fire. After the first few
puffs, you can see the needle of the gauge moving around the scale to the
point where it belongs, and long before one circuit of the line has been completed, the firehole door has to be opened, to keep the safety valves (one
spring-balance and one direct acting) from blowing-off "ramping mad" as the
Brighton enginemen used to call it. The reason is, that owing to the boiler
being properly proportioned, the "therms" going into the water are far more
than those being taken out by the steam being used, and the addition of cold
water by the feed pump; consequently, up goes the boiler temperature, and
with it the steam pressure. I know of a *Maid of Kent* which will perform
exactly the same antic with a proportionate load, but one would naturally
expect good results in a modern type of engine in 5 in. gauge, whereas it seems
extraordinary in such a weeny "old iron". Having investigated the whys and
wherefores, let us take a look at the boiler for *Tich*, and then proceed to build it.

Details of the small boiler.

LONGITUDINAL SECTION OF BOILER

BACKHEAD FORMER   SQUEEZE OVAL AFTER TURNING FIREHOLE RING   THROATPLATE   CROSS SECTION AT FIREBOX TUBEPLATE   FIREBOX FORMER   BACKHEAD

A Tiny but Lively Kettle

The construction is as simple as I can possibly make it, the barrel and outer wrapper of the firebox being made from 18 gauge sheet copper, in one piece. The smokebox tubeplate, throatplate and firebox are 16 gauge copper, and the backhead 13 gauge. The barrel is $2\frac{1}{2}$ in. diameter and 4 in. long, and contains five $\frac{3}{8}$ in. tubes and one $\frac{5}{8}$ in. superheater flue. The wrapper has straight sides. The inside firebox also has straight sides, with rounded top corners and a flat roof, all in one piece of 18 gauge copper. It is $2\frac{7}{16}$ in. long, a full $1\frac{7}{8}$ in. wide, and $2\frac{3}{4}$ in. high. There are nine copper stays each side and three at each end, also two longitudinal stays between backhead and smokebox tubeplate. A large bush is fitted to the top of the barrel for the dome, which will contain the regulator, as in full-size practice. The firehole ring (Briggs pattern, forming a stout stay) is $\frac{3}{4}$ in. high and $1\frac{1}{4}$ in. long, oval in shape. As the pump eccentric comes right underneath the firebox when the boiler is erected, I have made special provision for its protection, but will deal with that when we come to it.

All the brazing of this little boiler can be done with a $2\frac{1}{2}$ pint paraffin blow-lamp, or an equivalent air-gas blowpipe operated by fan or bellows. In addition, beginners will need something to use as a brazing pan or forge. An old discarded tea-tray makes an excellent brazing pan, if a piece of sheet iron about 8 or 9 in. wide is bent to the shape of the edge of the tray, and fixed up at the back of it, to stop the coke or breeze from falling overboard. I use a home-made tray from 18 gauge sheet steel, rectangular in shape, and large enough to take a $3\frac{1}{2}$ in. gauge "Pacific" boiler. It is approximately 2 ft. long and 10 in. wide. The front edge is bent up to a height of 3 in., the back to nearly a foot, and the sides slope up from front to back, a few iron rivets holding the lot together at the corners. It stands on top of a pedestal-type cast-iron brazing forge, which I bought from Buck and Ryan's some 20 years ago; when I started in to make bigger boilers, such as $3\frac{1}{2}$ in. gauge *Princess Marina*, the tray proved too small, so we had to kind of "extend the premises". Any beginner could knock up the tray for themselves, mounting it on four legs made of angle-iron, with tie bars riveted at top and near bottom, just like the legs of the domestic kitchen table. It doesn't matter a bean how roughly it is made, as long as it does the job; if made to "mike" measurements, with chromium-plated legs and a rustless steel pan, it wouldn't make the brazing job any better, nor any worse, so why worry? The height should suit the operator's own stature; having it so that you can hold the blowlamp or blow-pipe naturally, without causing fatigue. If too high your arms will ache badly; if too low, you'll literally "get it in the neck".

Tools and Materials

A fair-sized pair of blacksmith's tongs will be needed, to grab the boiler and turn it about when hot; also a small pair which can be home-made. Get two bits of flat steel, say $\frac{1}{8}$ in. by $\frac{3}{8}$ in. or nearest; length about a foot. Grip an inch of one end in the bench vice, and with a hefty pair of pliers, or an adjustable wrench clamped on the bar about $\frac{1}{2}$ in. from the vice, twist the projecting metal at right-angles. Rivet the two pieces together just below the twists with a $\frac{1}{8}$ in. iron rivet, leaving the joint just free enough to move. If the ends above the twist don't meet, bend them a little until they do, and there is your "tongett"—ten minutes work at the outside, and at infinitesimal cost. A piece of $\frac{3}{16}$ in. iron wire about 2 ft. long, one end bent into a ring, and the other filed to a point, serves as a scratching wire, to break up bubbles caused by the flux in the molten metal. For brazing material, used on all the boiler joints except the tubes and bushes, either a good quality easy-running brazing strip, or Johnson-Matthey's B-6 brazing alloy, will be satisfactory. The latter is dearer, as it contains a percentage of silver, but it needs less heat and flows very freely, so maybe some beginners would prefer to use it. As a flux for the former metal, I use Boron Compo, a blue lumpy preparation sold in small tins; for the B-6, the makers sell a special flux called "Tenacity No. 3". For tubes and bushes, either best-grade silver-solder, with powdered borax as flux, or "Easyflo" and the special flux supplied by Johnson-Matthey's for use with it, does very well indeed. Both kinds of material are sold in sheet or strip form, the latter being the more convenient for our purposes; "Easyflo" is also sold as wire, and believe me it is just "the cat's whiskers" for making up boiler fittings. Even the most ham-fisted worker can make jewellery jobs of the fittings, with just ordinary care; but more about that when we come to it. A pair of ordinary pliers—preferably an old pair which have seen their best days on the bench—and a couple of small jars, plus two or three tin lids, completes the outfit. Nothing to be scared of, is it?

The Barrel and Wrapper

First of all, may I assure all beginners that if they carefully follow the detailed notes and instructions for making this little boiler, and it turns out O.K., they need not have the slightest fear about tackling a boiler of any size, within reason. The job is done in exactly the same way; the bigger boiler simply requires harder work to flange and bend the plates, and more heat for the brazing. The first stage of the proceedings is to cut out the plate for the boiler barrel and wrapper sheet, the latter being the boilermaker's term for the outer shell of the firebox. The dimensions of this are shown on the accompanying drawing. The material is sheet copper of 18 gauge, which is a little thinner than $\frac{1}{16}$ in. and the copper should be quite soft, not the bright hard-rolled variety. It can be purchased from any metal merchant's store, over the counter. They sell it by weight. Soft sheet copper of 18 gauge can be cut with an ordinary pair of tinman's shears or snips by anybody whose wrists are of average strength. If you find it hard to cut, rig up an improvised bench shear. Put one handle of the snips in the bench vice and put a length of iron gas pipe over the other handle; this will give enough leverage to enable a kiddy to cut the metal. Cut the edges straight, and note how far the two side cuts extend toward the middle of the sheet; don't make them more or less than shown, as they should come just halfway up the barrel of the finished boiler shell.

If beginners can obtain a piece of hardwood, or anything else fairly strong, about $2\frac{3}{8}$ in. diameter, bending up the shell is just "a piece of cake". Young Curly found a stone ginger-beer bottle very handy for this purpose, and also used an iron sash-weight. Incidentally, the latter makes a fine dolly for riveting up the barrel seam. First bend the whole sheet to semi-circular shape, like a tunnel; then continue bending the shorter end until it is completely circular, the edges overlapping approximately $\frac{1}{4}$ in. The outside diameter should be then $2\frac{1}{2}$ in. but it doesn't matter in the least if it is a little more; it should not be any less. Tie a bit of string or wire around each end, to stop it from springing open; then drill four No. 51 holes through the overlap, at $\frac{3}{4}$ in. centres, starting at $\frac{1}{2}$ in. from the end of the barrel. Put a piece of iron bar in the bench vice, letting it project about 4 in. from one side of the jaws. Put a $\frac{1}{16}$ in. copper rivet through the end holes in the overlap, head inside; rest the head on the bar and hammer down the shank, to hold the overlapping parts into close contact. Ditto repeato with the other holes; then, if you have knocked the barrel out of its proper circular shape in the process, true it up again on the same bit of wood or other material over which you first bent it. The sides of the wrapper sheet should be nice and flat below the curved top.

How to Fit the Throatplate

In a boiler having a curved throatplate—that is, the plate that fills in the space between the sides of the wrapper below the barrel—it would be necessary to cut out the iron forming plate over which the backhead is flanged, and use it to form the throatplate also; but as our little throatplate has straight sides, the flange can be bent in the bench vice. Cut out a piece of 16 gauge copper, $2\frac{7}{8}$ in. long and $2\frac{1}{4}$ in. wide. Scribe a line at $\frac{1}{16}$ in. from each of the shorter sides, grip this strip in the bench vice, the line level with the top of jaws, and bend to a right-angle. Warning: don't hammer direct on the copper to get the bend sharp, but force it down as far as possible with your fingers; this is why we hold the short bit in the vice. Then get a stout bit of square bar, place it over the bend, and you can force the copper into a sharp bend without marking it.

Repeat operations on the other edge; the resulting flanged plate should measure a full $2\frac{3}{8}$ in. over the flanges and should fit nicely in the gap below the barrel. Put it in place and hold it by means of a toolmaker's clamp over the bottom of each flange and the sides of the wrapper. The plates, of course, should be flush at the bottom. Now put a scriber down the barrel and scratch a line on the embryo throatplate, running the scriber point around close to the lower half of the barrel. Remove the plate and cut the piece out, leaving the line just showing. This can be done with a metal-piercing fretsaw, or coping saw, as it is often called; merely a glorified fretsaw. I do jobs like these on my

Driver jigsaw (a thunder-and-lightning edition of a woodmaker's fretsaw machine, which will walk through $\frac{1}{8}$ in. brass plate) but a hand fretsaw with a metal-cutting blade in it, does the job quite well. Anoint the blade with beeswax if it tends to clog or jam. An "Abrafile", which is a piece of thin steel wire with file teeth formed on it, and is held in a hacksaw frame, will take out the superfluous piece of copper in two wags of a dog's tail. If you haven't any of the above, just drill a row of No. 40 or $\frac{3}{32}$ in. holes close to the line, break out the piece (chopping between the holes with a little chisel made from $\frac{3}{16}$ in. silver-steel) and file the rough edge, so that the line is just left showing.

Well clean all around the cut, with coarse emery cloth or similar abrasive, and also clean the edge of the barrel and the front inside edges of the wrapper sheet. The throatplate edges may be cleaned up with a file, second-cut grade for preference. Don't forget that successful brazing needs perfectly clean joints; so wherever I give instructions for fitting parts together for brazing or silver-soldering, "take it as read" that they must be as clean as possible, even though nothing is said about it at the time. As I've remarked before, I give all novices full credit for possessing average "gumption", and it is in cases like this where I assume they exercise it. My old schoolteacher said much the same thing to the class; we kids appreciated his confidence, and took jolly good care never to let him down, which he appreciated in his turn. After cleaning, put the throatplate in place, with the semi-circular edge butting tightly up against the barrel; drill three No. 51 holes in each flange, put a $\frac{1}{16}$ in. copper rivet in from the inside, and rivet up, same as the longitudinal seam. We are then ready for the first brazing job.

Alternative Boiler

Second thoughts are best, says the old saw. Just as I was going to start to describe the first brazing job on the boiler for *Tich*, it occurred to me that as I had already promised to give details of an alternative larger boiler, for those who preferred a larger size in kettles, the obvious thing to do, to save precious time and space, was to give the drawing of the larger boiler right away. As the *modus operandi* is exactly the same for either boiler, one description of how to do the job would cover them both; builders simply work to the sizes given for the boiler of their choice, using the same methods. To enable our beginner friends to make an easy decision, I have drawn out the engine complete with a bigger boiler, so that you can see how it looks. By way of variation, I have altered some of the details; but please note that these can be used for either boiler, larger or smaller. Contrariwise, as Mary would remark, you can use the original fittings and mountings for either job, just as you fancy. It is said that variety is the spice of life—so there must have been an abundance of "spice" on the L.B. & S.C.R. in the days of John Chester Craven. Unofficial history tells us that the principal language spoken was railway Esperanto—and history has certainly repeated itself during the last few years in the same locality. Did I hear somebody quote "and there shall arise in our midst, a Leader"?

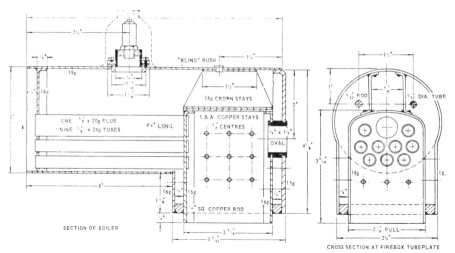

Side and end elevations of the large boiler.

The alternative boiler is exactly the same length as far as barrel and firebox are concerned, and the grate area is only increased by a small amount, due to extra width; but there is more heating surface, due to the firebox being wider at the top and allowing more tubes to be put in. This boiler is a little bigger than that on my old 2-2-2 *Ancient Lights*, and I have already recorded how that one steams, so nobody need have any fear of this one not doing the job, provided that the instructions are followed. When on the rare occasions I hear of one of my specified boilers failing to steam, I am always suspicious of the workmanship, or inattention to details. One, or more usually both, are invariably responsible. Badly made cylinders and motion also waste steam.

The barrel is $\frac{1}{2}$ in. larger in diameter than the original, and contains nine $\frac{3}{8}$ in. tubes and one $\frac{5}{8}$ in. superheater flue. The smokebox is circular and slightly extended; it is mounted on a saddle and bears a resemblance to the Brighton "Terriers" after they were rebuilt, so I thought we might see what a chimney of the pattern fitted to these famous engines would look like on this job. Personally, I prefer the shape shown here, to the original *Tich* chimney, but naturally, I am prejudiced. As some beginners might fight shy of fitting a working spring-balance safety valve, I have substituted an ordinary direct-spring valve, mounted on top of a squat inner dome. The outer casting of the dome is of the usual pattern, but on top of it are two small replicas of the safety valves specified by Dugald Drummond for the L.S.W.R. and other engines. They have no valves fitted, but are drilled straight through. Steam escaping from the valve inside the dome blows through them with a very realistic roar. It did on my $2\frac{1}{2}$ in. gauge *Southern Maid*, anyway. A plain dome could, of course, be used, with a single safety valve in a casing of any desired shape, or without casing at all, just in front of the cab; but the boiler being so short, the top of it would look terribly crowded with a separate safety valve.

The short cab is also just an alternative suggestion; if you prefer the original plain weatherboard, why, just put it on, and that's that. The superheater, backhead fittings and so on, will be the same for either size of boiler.

Slight Variations

For this boiler, a piece of 18 gauge sheet copper measuring 10 in. by 7 in. will be needed. At 3 in. from one long edge, make two cuts with the snips $2\frac{1}{8}$ in. long, similar to the smaller boiler; then from the opposite long edge, cut a $\frac{1}{8}$ in. strip off each end as far as the cuts. After that, carry on exactly the same as described for the $2\frac{1}{2}$ in. diameter boiler, bending the whole lot first to the outline shown in the cross-section, and then continuing with the 4 in. portion until you have formed a complete circle 3 in. outside diameter, the overlap being approximately $\frac{1}{4}$ in. Put a few rivets in it to hold it until brazed, same as the little one. See that the overlapping edges are quite clean; very important, that.

The throatplate needs a piece of 16 gauge copper sheet $3\frac{1}{8}$ in. by $2\frac{1}{4}$ in. If the metal appears to be hard, anneal it by heating to medium red and plunging it into cold water. The sides can be bent over in the bench vice, to form the flanges, same as the smaller one; then put the plate temporarily in position and, putting a scriber down inside the barrel, scribe the radius shown. Cut out the piece as described previously; you will find there is a little tag left at the top of each side flange, so bend this outward to suit the curve of the boiler shell. The throatplate is then put in place, and riveted with a few $\frac{1}{16}$ in. snap-head copper rivets, to hold the parts together in close contact whilst the brazing operation is performed.

How to Braze Boiler Shell

The weather being a little cooler at time of writing, we will now tackle the first brazing job, and beginners will find that it really is easy—like everything else, just a case of knowing how. Young Curly and his boy friend found that out when they brazed up the broken mailcart axle. A minor but important point is, first make sure there is plenty of oil in the blowlamp; or if you are using an air-gas blowpipe working through a slot meter, see that there is no likelihood of the supply failing in the middle of the job. If the source of heat dies out on you, the result is likely to be disappointing, to say the least of it. Also, have everything you need (see my list in the previous dissertation) ready to hand, for the job must be absolutely non-stop; and have the pickle bath handy.

First, mix up some of the flux—Boron Compo or whatever else you are using—to a creamy paste with water, and lay a fillet of the paste all along the joints at each side of the throatplate, around under the barrel and along the barrel seam. Cover all the rivet heads. Then put a layer of coke or breeze in the brazing pan and stand the boiler shell on end in it, with the barrel pointing skywards. Pile the coke or breeze all around the outside, to within $\frac{1}{2}$ in. of the throatplate; also put some inside, to the same height. Now get the blowlamp or blowpipe going good and strong, and start playing the flame on the coke close to the boiler shell. Get it glowing dull red as far around the job as you can. The wet flux will start to bubble, dry out, and presently begin to fuse and form a glaze over the joint. Now concentrate the flame on one bottom corner of the throatplate; and as soon as this part becomes red (bright), dip your stick of easy-running brazing strip in some dry flux—if you hold it in the lamp flame for a few seconds before dipping, a coating of flux will stick to it—and apply it to the hot spot. You will be pleased to see that it immediately melts at the tip, the molten metal running into the joint just like ordinary soft solder. If it doesn't melt and run, the job isn't hot enough, and more "therms" are called for.

Incidentally, those good folk who are not used to a blowlamp invariably try to operate it at too low a pressure. There should be no trace of white in the flame, and it should roar away like nobody's business, the flame being blue nearest the nozzle and slightly orange-violet at the tip. Whilst over in the U.S.A. I had the use of Calvert Holt's workshop, which had a sort of annexe where we did all the soldering and brazing. In addition to air-acetylene equipment, Holt had a huge blowlamp, with a tank about the size of a five-gallon oil drum and a burner about double the size of the average five-pint lamp, which was connected to the oil tank by a flexible metal tube. The row that fearsome bit of apparatus kicked up when going all out is easier imagined than

Further boiler details.

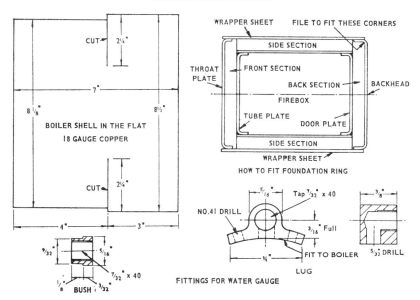

described; and the flame, over 2 ft. long was—well, reminiscent of the nether regions. It practically enveloped most jobs and very little coke packing was needed, even for a $3\frac{1}{2}$ in. gauge boiler.

Scared Stiff!

One day I had this implement of Holts going on a big boiler shell, and was just doing the last bit, when suddenly there was a succession of terrible piercing screams, louder even than the roar of the burner. I shut down mighty quick, thinking that maybe a couple of gangsters had got in and were trying to murder Mrs. Holt before ransacking the place. The screams continued, and then something collided with me and nearly knocked me into the brazing forge. It was Holt's little boy, running around with his eyes shut and yelling blue murder! I picked him up and took him to his mamma. It transpired that he had heard the noise of the blowlamp in the house and had come to investigate; but the sight of the huge flame, the glowing coke, red-hot boiler shell, and behind the lot, your humble servant's face with two green eyes shining out of it (they used to reflect just like an animal's eyes, a phenomenon which persisted up to middle age) and the awful row on top of it all, sent the poor kid into complete panic. It was weeks before he ventured into the workshop again!

Non-stop Run

As soon as the brazing strip melts and runs into the end of the joint, move the blowlamp flame along a weeny bit, then directly that place becomes bright red, give it another dose, continuing the same way until you have filled the full length of the joint with the melted "spelter" (the coppersmith's term for the brazing material) and reached the underside of the barrel. Now note: describing the operation thus, for the sake of making it plain and clear enough for the veriest Billy Muggins to understand, it would appear that the operation is done in jerks, in a manner of speaking. Actually, it isn't, the action being practically continuous, as you'll find out when you come to do it. The heat conductivity of copper is very high, so that the metal close to the lamp flame is very nearly as hot as that actually in the flame; and it needs only a matter of seconds, after you shift the flame, for the fresh section to become hot enough to melt the brazing material. At the same time, the molten metal in the joint just behind the lamp flame, after it is moved, doesn't get time to cool sufficiently to "set", before the next lot comes in and joins it; so that by moving the lamp flame at very slow speed, using care and discretion, you get what is known as a continuous run of metal, unbroken for the full length of the joint. This ensures great strength and complete freedom from leakage. A very small amount of practice will enable anybody with the average amount of "gumption" to get the brazing material to penetrate the full depth of the flange and fill up the crack between the edge of the throatplate and wrapper neat enough to eliminate any need for filing smooth. The condition known as "almond rock" is invariably caused by lack of heat, so that blobs of unmelted spelter cling to the surfaces of the copper, looking just like almonds sticking out of the top of the delectable delicacy just mentioned.

Repeat operations on the other side of the throatplate, starting from the bottom corner and working up to the barrel. This time, when arriving at the barrel, keep the flame on the end of the joint for a few seconds more, and give it a little extra brazing material, so as to ensure a sound joint at the point where barrel and wrapper join. Then work your way around the curved joint between barrel and throatplate, moving the blowlamp flame very slowly and letting a good fillet of the melted spelter run into the joint. When you arrive at the other end, give that an extra dose, same as at the starting end, and see that the metal thoroughly amalgamates.

If there is any sign of bubbling in the melted metal, at any part of the joints, apply the pointed end of the scratching wire in the flame of the lamp. This will break up any borax bubbles caused by moisture in the flux, and there won't be any irritating "pinholes" to plug up in the finished job.

By aid of the big tongs, lift the boiler shell clear of the coke, and lay it down again on its back, with the longitudinal seam under the barrel uppermost. Pile some coke around each side of the barrel, and put some inside as well, about halfway up the diameter; then play the blowlamp flame partly inside and partly outside, so as to get the coke well heated up. Then concentrate on the joint at the end of the barrel; get that well red, apply your strip of brazing material, not forgetting to keep dipping it in the dry flux, and as soon as it starts to melt and run into the seam, work your way very slowly along the full length of the seam, in exactly the same way as you did on the other joints. As the heads of the rivets come within the flame, give each of them a spot of brazing material; don't forget to use the scratching wire as soon as any bubbling takes place. Sometimes you get a job which doesn't show a bubble from start to finish; at other times there are plenty, and it is nothing but scratch and scratch, all along the joints to get rid of them. When the end of the seam is reached, at the throatplate have a special blow, to melt the brazing material on the throatplate joint at this point in order that the metal in the seam may properly amalgamate with it, and ensure that there is no leakage; very important, that!

Make absolutely certain that no places have been missed; then let the shell cool to black, pick it up with the big tongs, and carefully put it in the pickle bath. Mind the splashes! A big sheet of brown paper held between the operator and the pickle bath is a fine interceptor and may save the cost of a new overall, or even new clothes. Acid splashes are very insidious; they don't show any damage at the time, but ere many days are past, a "moth hole" appears at every place where a splash has landed and dried. Liquid ammonia, as used for domestic washing is a good antidote for splashes. If you get any on your skin, wash it off at once, and no harm will come of it; if allowed to dry you will have a red itchy patch, or maybe a raw place which will take a long time to heal. Vaseline, boric acid ointment or any protective agent such as "Rozalex", rubbed into the skin before operating, is good insurance against acid splashes on your skin.

Leave the shell in the pickle bath for about 15 to 20 minutes, then fish it out with the tongs and wash it well in running water. If the acid pickle hasn't dissolved all traces of burnt flux and glazed patches are still showing around the joints, a file which has seen its best days will remove them. If using it in the ordinary way doesn't shift the bits of glazed flux, break off the tip of the file, so as to leave sharp edges, and tap the glaze with it. This will split it up and cause it to flake off. Finally, give the shell a clean up with a handful of steel wool; or if that isn't available, scour it with some of the powder used for cleaning baths, sinks, and the like. Clean copper is much nicer to handle, as I've often remarked; and dirty copper may infect any small cuts or scratches which you may have on your hands. I've usually got a few, though I'm blessed if I know how or when they come!

If our beginner friends manage the job above fully detailed out for their special benefit and get nice clean even joints, with the brazing material showing at the inner edges of the throatplate flanges, and the inner edge of the barrel seam, they need have no fear of not making a successful job of the whole boiler, or in fact any boiler they may tackle at a future date. Larger boilers such as those on *Doris, Pamela, Hielan' Lassie* and so on, are operated on in precisely the same way, the only difference being that more heat is needed to heat up the larger bulk of the metal. It isn't worth while detailing out the oxy-acetylene process in connection with the boiler, because the odds are a million dollars to a pinch of snuff that raw recruits won't possess the necessary outfit. From some of the letters I receive, it appears that equipment is often severely limited, hence my desire to keep the job as inexpensive as possible. Only this week, a letter arrived from a colonial reader who possesses only a few hand tools, begging me to describe in full how to build a locomotive without using a lathe. As the majority of the components of a steam locomotive are finished on a lathe, the cost of buying them ready-made would go far towards purchasing a used sample of that useful machine; maybe any other readers of this book who are in a similar position, will take the tip.

How to Make the Firebox

The firebox is made in three pieces; tubeplate, doorplate and combined sides and crown sheet. The tubeplate and doorplate are flanged up over a forming plate, preferably of iron or steel, though some folk have managed with hardwood formers. They can easily be sawn out of $\frac{1}{4}$ in. iron or steel plate. This isn't quite as formidable as it sounds, as a good make of hacksaw blade, lubricated with the same kind of cutting oil or other compound used for turning steel, will simply walk through the plate, if a speed of about 60 strokes per minute is used, and plenty of pressure put on the saw frame as it is pushed forward—literally throw all your weight into it! The formers for both boilers, larger and smaller, are shown in the illustrations; mark out

Plate 17

This fine example of the large-boilered "Tich" was built by Mr. F. Raw of Stockport

The underside of Mr. J. H. Balleny's "Tich"

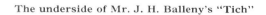

Plate 18

The motion work on the "Tich" built by Michael Holt of Lytham. This engine has slip-eccentric valve gear

This view of Mr. Balleny's engine shows the cab fittings and works plate

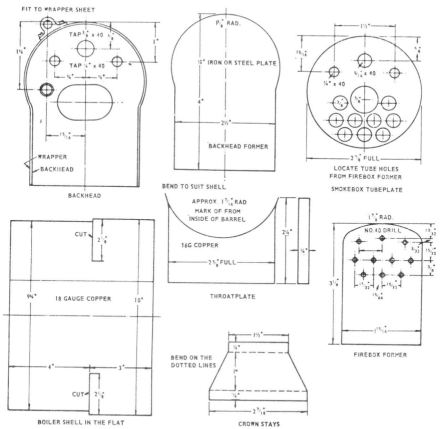

Details of the large boiler.

to the sizes given, saw close to the lines, finish with a file, and round off the sharp edges on one side of the former, so that you get a flange on the copper plate which is rounded, instead of sharp.

The former is also used as a jig for drilling the tube holes. Set out on it the location of the tube holes as shown; make a centre-pop exactly at each point, and drill through the plate with a No. 40 drill. Lay the former on a piece of 16 gauge soft sheet copper, and draw a line around it $\frac{1}{4}$ in. away from the edge, except at the bottom, which needs no flange. Mark out two plates thus, and cut them out. It doesn't matter about trimming with a file, trim up after flanging. If the copper appears hard, heat it to medium red and plunge into cold water, which will soon soften it. Put one of the copper plates in the bench vice, with the former alongside it, and beat down the projecting edge of the copper over the edge of the former. Note: the rounded edge of the former is placed next to the copper. If the copper begins to buckle or crinkle under the beating, re-soften it immediately, as described above, otherwise it will go hard and crack. Before removing the first copper plate from the former, put a No. 40 drill through all holes in it and carry on right through the copper; this will locate the tube holes. The second plate is not drilled, as a big oval hole has to cut in it for the firehole ring. Any raggedness on the edges of the flanges may now be filed off and the flanges themselves cleaned up, all ready for brazing to the sides and crown sheet.

The holes for the large tube, or superheater flue (centre one of the top row) is opened out with a $\frac{39}{64}$ in. drill and reamed with the "lead" end of a $\frac{5}{8}$ in. parallel reamer. If you have no reamer, file it with a small half-round file, until a piece of $\frac{5}{8}$ in. copper tube will fit it tightly; and bevel it a little on the side away from the flange. The other holes are opened out with a $\frac{23}{64}$ in. drill and reamed or filed likewise, using a $\frac{3}{8}$ in. parallel reamer. All the tube holes should be countersunk or bevelled on the side away from the flange, to form a channel around each tube, which is filled up with silver-solder when the firebox and tubes are assembled.

Firehole Ring

The firehole ring is of a special type designed by an old friend and fellow-conspirator of the L.B. & S.C. Rly. It needs no rivets, and forms a very substantial stay between the doorplate and the boiler backhead. To make it, you need a small piece of copper tube $1\frac{1}{4}$ in. outside diameter, $\frac{1}{8}$ in. thick, and about $\frac{9}{16}$ in. long. If the piece of tube is sawn, allow sufficient extra to true up both ends in the lathe, to the given length. Chuck in three-jaw, face the end, and turn a step in it with a knife tool. The step should be $\frac{1}{16}$ in. deep and $\frac{3}{16}$ in. long; a drop of cutting oil on the tool will help to get a clean cut. Now reverse the ring in the chuck and give the other end exactly the same treatment, cutting back far enough to leave the centre piece exactly $\frac{1}{4}$ in. long. Anneal or soften this by heating to red and plunging in cold water, then put it in the bench vice and squeeze it oval, so that the inside measurements will be approximately $\frac{3}{4}$ in. by $1\frac{1}{4}$ in. Lay the now oval ring on the doorplate, $\frac{1}{4}$ in. from the top and midway between the sides, and scratch a line all around it. Drill a row of $\frac{3}{32}$ in. holes all around the inside of the line and break out the piece; smooth the ragged edges with a half-round file until the reduced part of the ring will just fit tightly. One flange will be slightly shorter than the other; push this one through from the opposite side to the doorplate flange and beat the projecting lip outwards and down, into close contact with the doorplate, so that the plate is gripped tightly between the beaten-down lip and the shoulder of the ring. The same size of ring is used for both the alternative boilers.

Sides and Crownsheet

The exact length of the piece of copper needed for the sides and crownsheet of the firebox for either boiler, is obtained from the tubeplate or doorplate by the simple expedient of running a piece of lead wire, or ordinary soft copper wire, right round the flange of either plate and then straightening it out. The width of the piece is $2\frac{7}{16}$ in. for either boiler. Cut it from 18 gauge sheet copper and carefully bend it to the shape of the tube and doorplates; this is easily done by marking on the copper the places where the bends come. Put a piece of round bar, say $\frac{1}{2}$ in. or $\frac{5}{8}$ in. diameter, in the bench vice, with about 3 in. of it projecting from the side of the jaws; lay the piece of copper over it with the marked place resting on the bar, and press downwards. That is all there is to it! I've done dozens of them that way, and still do, if the radius or length is beyond the capacity of my bending machine.

Fit the firebox tubeplate into one end, flange first, and secure it with a few $\frac{1}{16}$ in. snaphead copper rivets at about $\frac{3}{4}$ in. centres, just sufficient to hold the parts together whilst being brazed; ditto repeato on the doorplate end. The plates should be flush each end with the sides and crown, so as to leave a little groove, which is filled up with the brazing material, and makes the firebox as sound as though in one piece.

Crown Stays

Two simple girder-type crownstays are used. These are not only easier to make and fit than a conglomeration of long rodstays, which are difficult to fit satisfactorily to a round-topped firebox wrapper, but are not liable to waste away and give out. Several cases have come to my notice of rodstays wasting away in the middle, breaking and letting the crown sheet down. The whole assembly forms a box girder, which any millwright will tell you is one of the strongest forms of construction. The Britannia Bridge over the Menai Straits is a box girder. Cut out two pieces of 18 gauge sheet copper to the size and shape shown; bend on the dotted lines in opposite directions, and rivet the longer flanges to the top of the firebox, $\frac{3}{4}$ in. apart, as shown in the cross section of the smaller boiler, and $\frac{7}{8}$ in. for the larger one.

Second Brazing Job

The firebox can now be brazed up, using exactly the same "technique" as described above. Cover all the joints with paste flux and stand the firebox on end, firehole ring upwards, in the brazing pan. Pack the coke or breeze around it, and put some inside, to within $\frac{1}{2}$ in. of the ring. Start at one bottom corner, after a general preliminary heating, and work your way right around, taking the ring in your stride, in a manner of speaking, when you come to it. Play the flame directly on the joint between ring and doorplate and run a good fillet of brazing material right around. When through, turn the firebox the other way up and go around the joint between the side and crownsheet and the tubeplate. Warning: keep the flame from playing direct on the narrow bits of metal between the tubeholes, or you may suddenly discover one big ragged hole where previously there were several little round ones!

Finally, stand the firebox right way up in the pan; put a little more flux along the crownstay flanges, and lay a strip of coarse-grade silver-solder along the inner side of each. Heat up the whole issue to medium red; the silver-solder will melt and disappear into the joint, making the flange, to all intents and purposes, solid with the firebox crown, and sealing the rivets. Then, to make assurance doubly sure, as the old saying goes, run some brazing material along the inside of each girder to form a fillet, as shown by the black triangles in the firebox drawings. Let cool to black; pickle, wash off, and clean up as described above. We are then ready to fit the tubes and smokebox tubeplate.

Smokebox Tubeplate

Before fitting the tubes to the firebox we shall need the smokebox tubeplate, to act as spacer and support whilst silver-soldering the ends of the tubes into the firebox. A circular forming plate will be needed for this; anything round, strong and of the right size can be pressed into service. I have used old wheel castings, chuck backplate castings, an old automobile engine piston, a cast-iron cistern weight, and goodness only knows what else. Most scrap pieces as mentioned above, can be turned to the size required, which is $2\frac{9}{32}$ in. diameter for the smaller boiler, and $2\frac{13}{16}$ in. for the larger one. If you have nothing to suit, cut the disc from a piece of $\frac{1}{4}$ in. iron or steel plate; rough-saw it to shape, drill a hole through the middle, clamp it between two nuts on an old bolt, which you can hold in the three-jaw, or run between centres, just as you fancy (the latter is better for light lathes), and the outside can be turned to the correct diameter with a pointed tool with a point rounded off a little (says Pat) and plenty of top rake. Run the lathe slowly, and use plenty of cutting oil. Speaking of lathe tools, I long since discarded the "regulation" pattern; have not used a "text-book" tool for over forty years. I always use raked tools, even for soft brass, which is decidedly "against the rules". During my "term of office" at the munition shop during the Kaiser's war, I took full opportunity to find out which shape of tool gave the best results; and am tickled pink to find out that some of my pet shapes are now used for production work, being independently conceived—"great minds" again! However, joking aside, it is mighty curious how things pan out. Round off one edge of the former, leaving a good radius.

Cut out a circle of sheet copper, 16 gauge, and $\frac{1}{2}$ in. bigger in diameter than the former. Clamp this in the bench vice alongside the former, radius side against the copper, and beat down the edge of the copper disc on to the edge of the former, same as on previous flanging jobs, taking care that the metal is not allowed to become hard enough to crack. The minute it shows signs of crinkling up, or buckling, re-anneal it. When it lies nicely on the former edge all the way around, clean up the flange with a file, before removing the tube-plate from the former. As I explained before, the file scratches form a "key" for the brazing material. In larger boilers, where the barrel is made from a piece of tube, the flange can be turned to a fairly tight fit, using a round-nose tool and a coarse feed, so that the turned surface shall not be too smooth; the ragged edge left by the flanging process may also be turned off smooth. This is not necessary in the little boilers for *Tich*, as the barrels are rolled from sheet metal and have a joint in them; also Inspector Meticulous won't be able to get inside and take a look at the edge of the flange. If it were turned to a millionth part of an inch tolerance, the boiler wouldn't steam one whit the better; so why worry?

Locating the Tube Holes

There is no need to set the tube holes in the smokebox tubeplate by any measurement; simply use the firebox tubeplate former as a jig for drilling the pilot holes. Scribe a line across the middle of the side opposite to the flange and $\frac{3}{8}$ in. from the end of it, make a centre-pop. Lay the firebox tubeplate former on the smokebox tubeplate in such a position that the bottom centre hole is exactly over the centre-pop and you can see the scribed line passing across the middle of the hole directly above it. Clamp the former to the tube-plate by aid of a toolmaker's clamp, then poke the No. 40 drill through the holes in the former and carry on right through the copper. Remove former, then open out the holes exactly as given for the firebox tubeplate, using drills and reamers; but this time, put the reamers well through the holes. If filing to size, either make the holes large enough to allow the tubes to fit easily or, better still, open out with a drill the correct size for each tube, $\frac{3}{8}$ in. and $\frac{5}{8}$ in. respectively, if you have no reamers that size. Countersink all the tube holes on the side opposite the flange.

Mark off the holes for stays and steam pipe according to the drawings of the two alternative tubeplates; the larger one has already been illustrated, and the smaller one is similar. The central hole, for the steam pipe fitting, is drilled $\frac{9}{32}$ in. and tapped $\frac{5}{16}$ in. by 40; the stay holes are drilled $\frac{7}{32}$ in. and tapped $\frac{1}{4}$ in. by 40. See that the taps enter the holes nicely on the square, otherwise the nipples will go in what the kiddies call cockeyed, and the threads will bind.

CHAPTER NINE

Fitting the boiler tubes

Tubes

THE TUBES ON BOTH alternative boilers are the same length, viz. $4\frac{1}{4}$ in. Both have one $\frac{5}{8}$ in. by 20 gauge superheater flue; the larger boiler has nine $\frac{3}{8}$ in. by 24 gauge smoke tubes, and the smaller five only, same kind. The tubes should be of seamless copper; the larger one is a little thicker, as it forms a substantial stay between the firebox and smokebox tubeplates. The small tubes should always be as thin as possible, consistent with adequate strength. We might use thinner still; the tubes in the original boiler of my old engine *Ayesha* were only 26 gauge. and were salvaged from a bus radiator that had come off second-best in a little argument with a street tramway-car. They lasted the life of the boiler. The only wasp in the jampot is that an inexperienced coppersmith is liable to burn up tubes as thin as 26 gauge when silver-soldering them into the firebox.

Always use a hacksaw blade with very fine teeth when cutting thin tubes, and saw straight across, leaving them a little longer than finished length. Chuck each in three-jaw, skim the ends off square with a round-nose tool set crosswise in the rest, and apply a bit of coarse emery cloth or other abrasive, so as to clean the ends with a scratchy surface. Don't be offended if I remind beginners not to forget to spread a piece of paper over the lathe bed, every time emery cloth is used. The lathe will last ever so much longer, and the slides won't need adjusting for many moons. The price things are now, it behoves everbody to take care of what they have; I can assure you that I practice what I preach!

When any beginner has a big nest of tubes to silver-solder into a firebox, the best way is to do the job by instalments, say two rows at a time; but in the case of the present boilers the whole nest can be done at one fell swoop. The set on the smaller boiler is fully exposed; only the two below the superheater flue are covered up in the larger boiler, and these can be seen between the outer tubes, so will be able to receive their share of the heat. Put all the tubes in place in the holes in the firebox tubeplate, letting them project into the firebox for about $\frac{1}{32}$ in. Then put the smokebox tubeplate on the other end; if you put it on with the countersunk side of the tube holes first, it will go on easily. Let it go down over the tubes about $\frac{1}{8}$ in. or so, it will "stay put" by the friction alone. Now, very carefully line up the nest of tubes so that they are parallel with the sides of the firebox, and also with the crown sheet; the whole lot can be adjusted bodily by moving the smokebox tubeplate.

How to Silver-solder the Tubes

Stand the assembly in the brazing pan with the tubes pointing skyward. Pile up coke or breeze all around the firebox to tubeplate level, and fill the firebox to within about $\frac{1}{2}$ in. of the tubeplate. The mixture of flux and water for this job should be fairly thin; put plenty on, so that the whole of the tubes are well covered where they enter the tubeplate. The silver-solder should be of best grade, either No. 1 or "Easyflo" (I use the latter) and is handiest if used in a long thin strip about $\frac{1}{8}$ in. or so in width. Get your blowlamp going good and strong, and carefully heat up the firebox first, blowing all around the outside, and partly inside; keep the flame off the tubes as much as possible. This is where you have to watch your step; it is easy to have a disaster, but at the same time it is just as easy to achieve complete success, which only needs what is popularly known as "common savvy" plus a little patience and care. When the coke is glowing red, and the firebox is well heated, play a little on the tubes; and as soon as a tube glows red, with that portion of the tubeplate in which it is fixed, apply the strip of silver-solder to it. The end will melt off and flash clean around the joint; "Easyflo" is very hot (in more senses than one!) at this game. The silver-solder will not only form a fillet, but penetrate clean through, showing as a silver ring on the inside of the firebox. Give each tube a dose of the same physic; you will find that you canget at the two inner. tubes on the larger boiler through the spaces between those in the bottom row Give the big flue a bit extra for luck. Let cool to black, and whilst this is taking place, pull the smokebox tubeplate off the outer ends of the tubes, which is easily done with a pair of tongs, holding the firebox down with a piece of rod. Apply the blowlamp flame to the ends of the tubes until they are red-hot, so as to soften them all ready for expanding into the smokebox tube-plate when assembling the boiler. Then put the whole lot in the pickle for 15 minutes or so, afterwards well washing in running water (kitchen sink is the best place for this job) and cleaning up.

Tip: silver-solder only requires a medium heat to run perfectly; if the heat is too great it bubbles and becomes porous. I never use my oxy-acetylene out-fit for silver-soldering tubes of the kind described above. All you need is enough heat to make the silver-solder run freely, no more.

First Stage of Assembly

We now have the shell and the firebox and tubes made up as two units, so the next stage of the proceedings is to assemble them into one. First, we shall need the front section of the foundation ring, which isn't a ring at all (says Pat), either on this engine or its full-sized counterpart. On the latter it would, however, be all in one piece, with rounded ends; for our purpose it is easier to make and fit in four separate pieces, which are virtually made continuous by the final brazing or silver-soldering job. A piece of $\frac{1}{4}$ in. square soft copper rod is needed for the front section, which is first to be fitted; this should be just long enough to jam tightly between the bottom edges of the throatplate flange. Round off the corners at each end, where they fit into the flange, so that full-length contact is made with the throatplate bottom. Clean up the copper well, also bottom of throatplate, and slightly bevel the sides of the piece of rod, as shown by the black triangles in the illustrations showing the sections of the boiler. This is to allow the brazing material plenty of room to penetrate. Boilers brazed with ordinary spelter, or bronze-welded, require more grooving than those which are silver-soldered only; this applies also to any joint as well as boilers.

Clean all the parts which will come into contact; then insert the firebox and tube assembly into the shell, as shown in the illustration. The firebox tube-plate should butt up tightly against the piece of foundation ring, nicely in the centre of same, and the top crownstay flanges should be in close contact with the arch of the wrapper sheet for their full length. If they aren't, a little judicious bending is called for. When all O.K. put a toolmaker's clamp over the throatplate, piece of foundation ring, and firebox tubeplate, and another over the wrapper and one of the crownstay flanges. Drill a No. 51 hole clean through bottom of throatplate, foundation ring and firebox tubeplate, at each side of the clamp; put in a couple of $\frac{1}{16}$ in. copper rivets, and rivet over. You needn't bother about fancy heads; in fact, a bit of copper wire would do, well headed over at each end. These rivets are neither for strength nor show; merely to hold the parts together whilst the brazing job is in progress. They can be filed flush afterwards, if you care to take the trouble.

Now drill three No. 51 holes through the wrapper sheet, and the crownstay flange that isn't held by the clamp, and put three short $\frac{1}{16}$ in. copper rivets in, to hold the flange to the wrapper whilst silver-soldering. To hold these up whilst being riveted over, put a short piece of iron bar in the bench vice, with about 3 in. projecting from one side; this makes a fine dolly. To prevent it slipping down whilst you perform with the hammer, take out the inset steel jaws of the vice, usually held by two screws apiece, and rest the bar on the ledges which support the insets. To put the rivets through the holes from the inside of the wrapper, use a strip of tin about $\frac{1}{4}$ in. wide, with a notch in the end like a distant signal. Jam the rivet in the hole, and pull away the strip. When beating down the projecting stem of the rivet, aim carefully and hit the rivet, not the boiler shell; it doesn't have to look as though it had been on an expedition to Korea. Again, no fancy heads are needed, as they are filed flush with the curve of the wrapper when the job has been silver-soldered. After doing one flange, take off the clamp and ditto repeato operations on the other flange. If the job has been properly done, the firebox and tube assembly should now be a tight fit in the shell, the joints of throatplate, crownstay flanges and wrapper all being close, with no gaps.

How to Fit Smokebox Tubeplate

Another job, easy, but requiring care. Insert the tubeplate, flange first, taking care it is up quite straight; a line drawn through the centres of top and bottom holes should be vertical. Gently tap it down until it almost touches the tubes, and then line up each tube with its respective hole by aid of a wooden knitting needle, wooden meat skewer or a blacklead pencil. They will adjust quite easily, being softened by the silver-soldering; but be mighty careful not to distort the end at which you are prodding! When all are lined up, tap down the tubeplate evenly all around, until the tubes are standing about $\frac{1}{32}$ in. proud of the tubeplate; the edge of this should be the same distance from the end of the barrel all the way around. The exact distance doesn't matter a bean as long as it is constant.

The next job is to expand the tube ends. This is done with a taper drift, as in full-size practice when roller expanders are not used. The drift is a tapered steel plug; if you have a drill shank, or something similar which will fit the tube ends, it will save the trouble of making a special drift. Otherwise, take a piece of steel a little bigger than the outside diameter of the tubes and turn a slight taper on it (exact angle doesn't matter; the angle of a drill-shank will do) so that it goes into the tube about $\frac{1}{2}$ in. Polish well with fine emery cloth; the smoother the drift, the easier it will come out. Grease it, and insert in the tube; give it a sharp crack or two with a hammer. This will expand the tube end, bringing it closely into contact with the hole. If the drift doesn't want to come out, a sideways tap will usually teach it good manners; but if especially obstinate, you can prod it out with a rod from the firebox end, though this is very seldom needed. A polished greased drift should fall out of its own free will and accord.

More Perspiration

The next job is to braze in the smokebox tubeplate, silver-solder the tube ends, and silver-solder the crownstay flanges to the wrapper sheet. After beginners' two previous essays at the perspiration job, this one should be quite easy, as you will be getting quite skilful with a blowlamp by this time. To save heating up the whole issue to the melting point of the brazing material, proceed as follows. Get a tin lid, or small tray or other receptacle, any shape will do. Cut a hole in the middle of it, big enough to poke the boiler barrel through. Up-end the boiler in the brazing pan; it might be as well to cover all joints with wet flux before doing this, as the heat travelling down from the smokebox end will dry out the moisture from the flux along the crownstay flanges and make the job quicker. Put plenty around the edge of smokebox tubeplate and around the tube ends. Put the "holey" lid or tray over the end and prop it up each side with something fireproof, so that the end of the barrel is about 2 in. above the tray; then pile up coke or breeze on it, level with the top. Plug all the tube ends with bits of asbestos string or flock, so that the flame doesn't go down inside and burn them just below the tubeplate.

Get the blowlamp going again, and heat up the coke all around the end of the barrel until the whole lot glows red; then concentrate on one point in the circumferential joint—or as Bert Smiff would say: "Ennywhere rahnd the edge'll do"—and keep at it till that glows red too; then apply your stick of easy-running strip and proceed step by step, same as you did the other joints, until the circuit is completed and you are back where you started. Give that point an extra blow-up, to make certain the brazing metal thoroughly runs into a perfect ring, with no break in it. If you like, a coarse-grade silver-solder, such as Johnson-Matthey's B-6, can be used for this job, with the special flux sold with it (Tenacity No. 1); or ordinary No. 3 grade, with borax as flux.

By this time, the flux around the tube ends will have fused and glazed; so play the blowlamp flame direct on the tube ends and touch each with a strip of best-grade silver-solder, or "Easyflo". This will run exactly as it did around the firebox end of the tubes. Now you come to the part where, as the conjurer says, "the quickness of the hand deceives the eye". With the big tongs, pull the "holey" tray or lid off the barrel and put it aside out of the way; lay the boiler on its back quickly in the pan, with the firebox end overhanging. Put something heavy (a firebrick will do) on the barrel to stop it from tipping up. Now cut off two strips of silver-solder a little over $1\frac{1}{2}$ in. long, dip them in the wet flux, and lay them along the outside of the crownstay flanges; the home-made tongs come in handy here. Blow partly outside and partly inside, till the lot becomes red and the silver-solder starts to melt; then give the lamp an extra pump up and blow on the underside, on to what is really the top of the wrapper. Keep it up till the whole issue is bright red, the silver-solder all melted, and sweated right through the joints at each side. Let cool to black, and be very careful how you put the boiler in the pickle, as it is now getting heavy and there is plenty of metal to quench, with corresponding increase in the liability to splash. Leave it about 15 minutes or so as before, then fish it out, wash well, and clean up. There should be a clean silvery ring around both ends of each tube if the job has been properly done. Next stage, final assembly; this will entail the biggest brazing job of the lot, but there isn't the least need to be scared of it, as by now, any beginner with the average amount of gumption, can tackle it with confidence and be assured of success.

Finishing the Boiler

We now have to fit the backhead and foundation ring and do the final brazing job. This is the hottest job of the lot, so you don't need any help from the thermometer. No cause for alarm, I hasten to add; like the rest of the job, it is easy enough when you know how!

The first item needed will be a forming plate for the backhead; and the accompanying illustration will show the exact size to cut it, for either the larger or smaller boiler. Use $\frac{1}{4}$ in. iron or steel plate, unless you can get a cast former, and proceed exactly as given for the firebox former. Lay the finished former on a piece of 13 gauge ($\frac{3}{32}$ in.) soft sheet copper, scribe a line $\frac{5}{16}$ in.

from the edge, all around except at bottom, cut out the piece, and proceed to flange it over the former, same way as you did the end plate of the firebox. You'll find that the 13 gauge copper is easier to flange than the 16 gauge as it has less liability to crinkle or buckle; but anneal it immediately, if it should show any signs of "going hard". Any raggedness on the edge of the flange may be smoothed off with a file, or left, just as you please; it will be out of sight "for ever", and makes no difference to the efficiency of the boiler. But don't forget to clean the actual flange, leaving all the file scratches showing on the contact surface. Also, well clean the metal on the same edge as the flange for about $\frac{1}{2}$ in. up from the bottom edge; this will ensure a good joint when the back section of the foundation ring is fitted.

How to Fit the Backhead

First of all, locate the hole for the lip of the firehole to come through. Measure from the inside of the top of the wrapper sheet, to the firehole; then measure from each side, also to the firehole. Transfer these measurements to the backhead; and mark from them an oval of the same size as the outside of the lip of the firehole ring. Cut the hole, as previously described when dealing with the doorplate of the firebox; but this time, make the hole a little smaller at first kick-off. Now "offer up" the backhead, as the locomotive shopmen would say; that is, hold it in position against the wrapper and see how the hole lines up with the lip of the firehole ring. You will see at a glance how much, and where, to file the hole to make it fit just over the lip when the backhead is in place. Enlarge the hole as indicated; clean all around inside the edge of the wrapper, put the backhead in position, with the lip of the ring coming through the hole, and then flange the lip over the edge of the hole, same as the doorplate end of the ring. Put a stout piece of square or rectangular iron bar in the bench vice, with the end projecting from the side of the jaws for about 3 in. or so—don't forget the tip about taking out the steel inset jaws for this purpose—rest the inner side of the ring on the bar, and beat the lip outwards and downwards, until it is in close contact with the backhead, gripping same firmly and holding it against the shoulder of the ring.

The edge of the wrapper should bed nicely all around against the flange of the backhead; if it doesn't, try gentle persuasion with a light hammer. However, by the general cussedness of things in this benighted world, there will probably be two or three places which refuse to close up. The best way to counteract this antic is to drill a few No. 48 holes around the edge of the wrapper, carrying on right through the backhead flange, spacing them about 1 in. apart; then tap them $\frac{3}{32}$ in. or 7 BA, and screw in pieces of threaded copper wire, squeezing the plates into contact whilst doing this. The copper wire can be held in three-jaw, and the die in the tailstock holder; wet the wire with cutting oil, as used for turning steel. Thread only about $\frac{1}{4}$ in. at a time, screw in the wire to the end of the thread and snip it off flush with wrapper. Don't file it smooth until after the final brazing. I usually fix these "persuaders" at about 1 in. centres, if I find them necessary, which isn't often. After fitting, tap down the edge of the wrapper between them, so that there will be no appreciable gap between the wrapper edge and the backhead flange. Warning—don't, on any account, use brass screws for this job; I'll tell you why in due course.

Foundation Ring

To finish the ring (some "ring"!) the spaces between the firebox, wrapper and backhead, are filled up with pieces of $\frac{1}{4}$ in. square copper rod. This should be well cleaned. First cut a piece to fit the back end, between the backhead and firebox. This will go between the backhead flanges, and the corners should be rounded off, to fit closely in the curves of each flange. The edges should be bevelled off at each side, to form grooves for the brazing material to run in; see the black triangles on the drawings of both larger and smaller boilers. Knock in the piece of square rod, flush with the backhead at bottom; then drill three No. 51 holes clean through the lot—backhead, piece of rod and firebox—and put in three $\frac{1}{16}$ in. copper rivets. If you haven't any long enough use pieces of $\frac{1}{16}$ in. or 16 gauge soft copper wire, hammered over to form heads at each end. It doesn't matter a bean about forming fancy heads, as they can be filed flush after the final brazing.

The spaces between the firebox and wrapper, at each side, are filled up with similar pieces of $\frac{1}{4}$ in. square copper rod, bevelled off in similar fashion. The rivets can be put in at about $\frac{3}{4}$ in. centres; three each side should be plenty, as they are only to hold the parts together whilst being brazed. Tip—if there are any interstices at the ends of the bits of bar, where they join each other, fill them up with splinters of copper driven in, otherwise you'll have the brazing material running down inside, when it is nicely melted, and forming teardrops in the water space.

Bushes

A big bush will be needed on top of the boiler barrel, to carry the inner dome which houses the regulator. Two smaller ones are required, one each side of the boiler barrel near the smokebox, to take the feedwater clacks. I might here remind beginners that cold feedwater should never be introduced into a boiler at the firebox end, but either at the smokebox end, as in the present instance, or else via top feeds on the barrel. It is all right to put the feed from an injector in at the firebox end, because that is always warm, by virtue of the jet of steam condensing in it. It would be advisable also, to put a bush in the backhead, for the bottom fitting of the water-gauge; although the 13 gauge copper is thick enough to take a thread, same is liable to strip very easily, in the event of anybody trying to get the last quarter-turn on the fitting to enable the top and bottom parts of the water-gauge to line up properly. There is no fear of this with the regulator gland, you can stop turning as soon as it is tight.

Wherever possible, bushes should be made either from thick-walled copper tube, when they are large, or copper rod when they are small. The metal from which plumbers' weldable fittings are made, is also very suitable; this is a kind of cast copper. The next best thing is bronze, either cast or drawn. Never use brass bushes in a boiler which has to be brazed or silver-soldered. Most of the "brass" rod sold is an alloy, known in the trade as "screw-rod", and is of a composition that allows it to take very clean screw threads (hence its name) but has a low melting point. I know of several cases where commercial "brass" screws have been used for fixing boiler backheads and securing fittings to a boiler for brazing; and when the job was done, there were only holes left where the screws were originally. The heat of the brazing job had caused them, like the old soldiers in the song, to "simply fade away".

You should be able to purchase either copper or bronze castings, or pieces of suitable tube, for the dome bush on either the larger or smaller boiler; and the method of turning it is exactly same as given for the firehole ring, except that there is only one "step", and it doesn't have to be squeezed oval. Also, you know now how to cut the hole for it in the boiler shell; so all that remains is to remind beginners to set the bush squarely in the hole in the barrel, so that the dome won't emulate the famous Leaning Tower of Pisa when the boiler is erected in the frames.

The holes for the smaller bushes are drilled $\frac{9}{32}$ in. The bushes on the barrel should be on the centre-line, and both the same height; it looks bad when the engine is seen from front or back and one clack box is higher than the other. To avoid this, stand the boiler on something level, putting a bit of wood, or anything else handy, under the barrel to keep it level; then, with a scribing block having the needle set to the height of the centre-line of boiler (easily "sighted" from the smokebox end) scribe a line along each side for an inch or so. At $\frac{7}{8}$ in. from the end of the boiler barrel, on each line, make a centre-pop; don't hit the punch hard enough to dent the barrel. Drill a $\frac{1}{8}$ in. pilot hole, and open out with a $\frac{9}{32}$ in. drill. If you drill direct you'll probably get an oversize polysided hole.

The location of the hole in the backhead is shown in the illustration. The bushes are easily made; chuck the $\frac{5}{16}$ in. rod in three-jaw, face the end, and drill down for about 1 in. depth with $\frac{3}{16}$ in. drill. Tap $\frac{7}{32}$ in. by 40. Turn a $\frac{1}{8}$ in. step at the end, to a tight fit in the holes in the boiler, and part off at a bare $\frac{3}{32}$ in. from the shoulder. Make four of them, in case you spoil one. Reverse in chuck and hold by the step; slightly countersink the end of the hole, skim the face truly and run the tap through again. Squeeze them into the holes in the boiler.

On these small-diameter boilers it is advisable to fit the water gauge up straight, screwing the top fitting to a lug or boss on the wrapper; otherwise you cannot get a glass of reasonable length and of sufficient diameter to obtain correct reading. A $\frac{5}{32}$ in. glass is pretty reliable, but you have to allow for capillary attraction. If beginners don't know what that means, or what its effect is, try the following experiment. Take a short length of glass tube, $\frac{5}{32}$ in. or $\frac{3}{16}$ in. diameter, and 3 in. or 4 in. long; dip it in a cup or glass of water, so as to wet the bore, let the water run out, and then dip it in the water again so that the end of the tube is about 1 in. below the surface. Those who are not wise to the efforts of capillary attraction will be surprised to see the water in the tube rise to about $\frac{1}{8}$ in. above the level of the water in the cup or glass. This is exactly what happens to the water in your boiler gauge; it is always very optimistic about the level in the boiler itself, and I always allow for it. I always try to arrange matters so that as long as you can see water in the glass tube you are quite safe at either extreme; no chance of burning the crown sheet at low level, or excessive priming at high level. Talking of priming, my boilers usually carry a "full pot", as the enginemen say, without priming, provided they are clean inside. The other evening I was running an engine after dark, put the injector on (it is a slow-feeding one) and was so busy watching the lights change on the automatic signals (kid with a new toy, says you!) that I forgot to shut it off at the proper time, and was only reminded of it when she started to throw water from the chimney. The injector knocked off of its own accord at the same time, through water going over with the steam; one of the troubles you get in full-size when the boiler is dirty and the engine starts priming, or foaming, as our cousins over the big pond call it.

In the present instance, the socket for the top fitting of the water gauge is filed up from a small block of bronze, gunmetal or copper; maybe our friends who supply the castings may add this one to the list. The sizes are given in the illustration, and by this time I don't have to tell you any more how to use a file! Drill a $\frac{3}{16}$ in. hole in the wrapper, close to the edge, and attach the fitting to the boiler shell, right over the hole, by a couple of screws, which are turned up from a bit of $\frac{3}{16}$ in. copper or bronze rod. Chuck in three-jaw, face the end, turn down $\frac{1}{4}$ in. length to $\frac{3}{32}$ in. diameter, screw $\frac{3}{32}$ in. or 7 BA, part off $\frac{1}{8}$ in. from the shoulder, and slot the head with a hacksaw. The holes in the fittings are drilled No. 41, and the fitting itself used to locate the screw holes in the boiler.

Final Brazing Job

Now we come to the job which will make you as thirsty as a certain Scottish gentleman who rejoiced in the name of Rab Noolas; and if you spell his moniker backwards it will give you a clue to his trouble. Whilst this job can be done with easy-running brazing strip, same as the previous brazing job, it would be easier for a beginner, or inexperienced coppersmith, to use a coarse-grade silver-solder, such as Johnson Matthey's B-6 alloy, or ordinary silver-solder of No. 3 grade, which is two parts brass and one part silver. With the former, use "Tenacity No. 1" as flux; with the latter, either Boron Compo or powdered borax, mixed to a paste with water as before. Both these materials only need a dull red heat to make them flow; and if only a $2\frac{1}{2}$ pint blowlamp, or equivalent air-gas blowpipe is available, this is an advantage, as there is now a considerable bulk of metal to heat up. Anyway, proceed as before; cover all the joints with the wet flux and lay the boiler on its back in the brazing pan, piling up the coke or breeze almost to the level of the foundation ring. If you have any asbestos cubes, fill the firebox with them, to protect the tube ends from the full force of the flame. If not, put in some bits of asbestos millboard. Have all the necessaries handy, as this must be a non-stop operation.

Heat the whole lot evenly, to a dull red as before; and when the coke glows, concentrate on one corner of the foundation ring, until it is hot enough to melt the strip of silver-solder when same is applied to it. After that, proceed in the same way as the previous jobs; work your way slowly around, running in sufficient of the silver-solder to fill up the grooves where the bits of the ring were bevelled off. Pay particular attention to the rivet heads, giving each one a little dose of silver-solder all to itself, as they come within the flame. When you have been right around, and arrived at the starting point, give an extra blow, to ensure that the metal at the starting and finishing places properly amalgamates and forms a continuous run.

Don't give the boiler time to cool, but grab it with the tongs (the throatplate is the handiest place by which to hold it) and stand it up on end, with the backhead upwards. If there are any bits of coke sticking to the flux, which will be melted and tacky, play the flame on them for a few seconds, and if they don't fall of their own free will and accord knock them off with the scratching wire. Then start blowing on the bottom corner, and go right around in the same way as the doorplate and tubeplate of the firebox was done. Should the blowlamp be on the weak side, and not powerful enough to heat the boiler without aid from the coke packing, try a finer grade of silver-solder; but if still you cannot get it hot enough, the only thing will be to pile the coke all around it to the level of the backhead. However, in the days when I used blowlamps, I never found this necessary, as the heat the boiler received when doing the foundation ring was retained long enough to prevent the radiating away of heat from the blowlamp playing on the backhead joint. The firehole ring flange can be done by playing the flame direct on it and using fine-grade silver-solder or "Easyflo"; same applies to the bush and the lug for the water gauge fitting.

Finally, stand the boiler right way up in the pan; play directly on the dome bush and, as soon as it and the surrounding metal glows red, apply some fine-grade silver-solder, or "Easyflo". Give the two small bushes in the sides of the barrel a dose of the same medicine; then let the whole lot cool to black, and be mighty careful how you put it in the pickle, for it will emulate a volcanic geyser, or an explosion in a submarine for a few seconds after being baptised. Leave it in the pickle for about half-an-hour this time, to get it thoroughly cleaned and all the burnt flux dissolved; then give it a good wash, inside and out, in running water, and clean up the outside as before.

Test for "Pinholes"

The easiest way to test for any weeny leaks in the brazed and silver-soldered joints, is by the same means as used for finding punctures in the inner tubes of cycles or car tyres. First of all, take a good look all around every joint to make sure that there are no bits of burnt or glazed flux sticking to them. They might possibly cover a pinhole, and you wouldn't know anything about it until steaming up; then the heat would melt the flux, out would come the steam and water and a few new words might possibly be added to the dictionary of railroad Esperanto. Next, plug up all the holes except one, with screwed plugs (bits of wood would do, if you don't want to bother about turning up regular metal plugs, and cover the dome hole with a bit of sheet rubber, which might be cut from an old cycle tube. Put a piece of wood, or flat metal, over this and hold it down with a clamp; or if you have not got one big enough, tie it on with string wound over it and around the boiler barrel. Make an adapter to screw in the "excepted" hole; the other end is screwed to fit a tyre pump. Incidentally, I keep an old motor tyre pump expecially for jobs like these; in place of the usual tyre valve connection, it has a $\frac{1}{4}$ in. by 26 union nut and cone on the end of the hose, an adapter to fit any hole or bush can be made in a few minutes.

Connect up the pump, put the boiler in a basin or pail of water, and pump about 20 lb. of air into it; not more, as it is unstayed as yet, and too much pressure would bulge the flat places. If there are any leaks, their position will easily be located by a stream of bubbles. If you happen to be unlucky, don't despair! Drill a No. 55 hole at each spot, tap 10 BA, and screw in a stub of copper wire, with a smear of plumbers' jointing on the threads. Alternatively, the plug can be soldered over. In either case, the plug is filed flush after inserting it. If all O.K. we are now ready for the staying job.

Plate 19

Another view of Mr. J. H. Balleny's small-boilered "Tich"

A close-up of some of the motion work on the "Tich" built by Mr. C. Wilkinson of Bradford

Plate 20

Another view of Mrs. Ruth Daltry's large-boilered "Tich"

Here is an unusual version of "Tich", with Baker valve gear and stovepipe chimney.
It was built by Mr. Williams of Staines

CHAPTER TEN

Staying the boiler

BEGINNERS SOMETIMES ASK WHY it is necessary to stay the firebox and end plates of a small locomotive boiler, when they are sometimes thicker than the unstayed barrel; so maybe a few words of explanation may not come amiss. The answer is, staying is necessary because the surfaces are flat. The strongest natural form is a globe or sphere; the next is a tube. If we could make the boiler in the form of a seamless ball, no stays at all would be needed; and if it were a plain tube, only a hefty stay through the middle, to prevent the ends blowing out, would be all the strengthening required. In the far-off days of childhood, young Curly made a stationary boiler from a discarded cistern float. This was a copper ball, and of very light weight, so that it would float in the tank and operate the water valve; the thickness could not have been more than a few thousandths of an inch. It was made in two halves, each stamped out, and the edge of one-half was slightly enlarged so that the other half would fit into it; the joint was soldered.

The grey matter under the long golden curls realised that a stay would be needed through the middle to prevent steam pressure blowing the halves apart at the joint, and one was fitted, made from brass wire, with square nuts laboriously sawn out of a scrap brass clock-plate. Incidentally, that old brass clock frame, given to me by the local watch and clock repairer, provided material for many jobs, including new port plates for the cylinders of my new toy *Ajax*. It was about ⅛ in. thick and did not have many holes in it. The ball boiler was fitted into the end of a tin can of suitable diameter; holes were cut in the can to ventilate the three-wick lamp, made from a metal-polish tin. The lever safety valve consisted mostly of the brass part of an old-time "batswing" gas burner. The complete bag of tricks made enough steam to keep the small stationary engine, with an oscillating cylinder made from brass tube, going merrily for an hour or so. I wonder how many present-day kiddies would spend their time rigging up such a contraption!

Longitudinal Stays

Two kinds of stays will be required; long ones to hold the backhead and smokebox tubeplate, and short ones between the inside firebox and the plates of the boiler shell. One of the long stays is a solid rod; the other is hollow. I used hollow stays in the boilers made in my early days; one of the first had a plug-cock on the backhead for a regulator, and steam went through the hollow stay, which was merely a piece of tube, to the smokebox end, and thence to the cylinders. John "Iron-wire" Alexander used a hollow stay for carrying the regulator rod, on his single flue loco-type boilers; the regulator was a plug cock in the smokebox, operated by a bit of beloved iron wire running from the handle on the footplate through the stay, to the handle of the cock. It worked quite satisfactorily. Old Bro. J.A.'s engines were crude and ungainly, but they certainly did the job, and "handsome is as handsome does". He was a pioneer. In the case of *Tich*, we use the hollow stay to carry steam for the blower.

It is essential that stays, both bolts and rods, be screwed into the plates. Again, beginners ask why stays cannot be fitted into plain holes, with the head against the outside plate, and the nut against the firebox plate, the heads being soldered over to prevent leakage. This wouldn't do at all, for the simple reason that the expansion and contraction of the boiler would cause the solder to crack, and the plates, heads, and nuts would begin to part company, letting water leak out. If the stays are screwed through the plates; moreover, if the threads are a tight fit, as they should be, no water should come through, though it is advisable to solder over the heads and nuts, as a kind of "insurance against leakage". Threads in soft copper easily tear, both in screwing and tapping, and it is very unlikely that a beginner will get all his screw threads perfect on his first boiler.

It would not only be inconvenient to screw the whole length of a long stay between smokebox tubeplate and backhead, but would weaken it; therefore, I specify these stays to be fixed by screwed nipples, both "blind"—that is, closed at the head end— and "thoroughfare", or open right through. The rod-stay has blind nipples at both ends. The hollow stay carries a thoroughfare nipple at the smokebox end, screwed for a union connecting it to the bent pipe in the smokebox, which carries the blower jet. At the footplate end, the body of the blower valve acts as a fixing nipple, that is shown clearly in the detail drawing.

The solid rod stay is a piece of $\frac{5}{32}$ in. copper rod $6\frac{3}{4}$ in. long; see that both ends are cut off squarely, then chuck in three-jaw, and put about $\frac{3}{8}$ in. of $\frac{5}{32}$ in. by 40 thread on each end, with a die in the tailstock holder. Wet the die, and the end of the rod, with cutting oil, same as used for turning steel, and pull the lathe belt by hand, working it back and forth, to clear chips from the die. It is the chips getting into the threads in the die, that causes the die to tear the threads on the work. The hollow stay is a piece of thick-walled $\frac{5}{32}$ in. copper tube, not less than 20 gauge, or the threads will weaken it enough to make it useless for staying purposes. I use 18 gauge for similar jobs. Cut to same length, and screw in exactly the same way, as the solid stay.

Nipples

To make the blind nipples for the solid stay, chuck a piece of $\frac{5}{16}$ in. hexagon brass rod in the three-jaw. Face the end, centre, and drill down $\frac{5}{16}$ in. depth with No. 30 drill; tap $\frac{5}{32}$ in. by 40. Turn down $\frac{1}{4}$ in. of the outside to $\frac{1}{4}$ in. diameter, and screw $\frac{1}{4}$ in. by 40. Part off at a full $\frac{1}{8}$ in. from the shoulder; reverse in chuck and chamfer the corners of the hexagon. To fix the stay in the boiler, screw one end of it into one of the blind nipples, insert it into the left-hand $\frac{1}{4}$ in. by 40 hole in the backhead, and push it through until it shows at the corresponding hole in the smokebox tubeplate. This might appear to be about as thankless a job as that of the tramway-car driver whose trolley-pole had come off the overhead wire in a dense fog on a pitch-black night; but whereas the unfortunate motorman has to hold the string of the trolley-pole and feel for the wire, you can easily guide the stay to the other hole. What I do, is to put a piece of thin tube, longer than the boiler, through both holes, inserting from the smokebox end; this is easy enough, as you can "sight" the tube at the backhead end and have enough sticking out of the smokebox end to allow for manoeuvring with your fingers. The end of the stay rod is put in the end of the tube, and pushed right home, the nipple being screwed into the backhead. Now, if you pull the tube out at the smokebox end you'll find the end of the stay through the hole; and all you have to do, is to screw the other nipple on it. When the screwed part of the nipple touches the tubeplate, the threads will engage with those in the tapped hole; and being the same pitch as the thread on the rod, the nipple can be screwed home tightly, the heads of both nipples seating against the copper plates, whilst the stay rod is held securely between them.

For the thoroughfare nipple, chuck the $\frac{5}{16}$ in. hexagon rod again, and proceed exactly as described above for the blind nipples; but part off at $\frac{3}{8}$ in. from the shoulder. Rechuck the other way round with the screwed part in a tapped bush held in three-jaw; I have already described how to make tapped bushes. Centre the other end deeply with a size E centre-drill and drill through into the tapped hole with No. 40 or $\frac{3}{32}$ in. drill. Turn down $\frac{1}{4}$ in. of the outside to $\frac{1}{4}$ in. diameter, and screw $\frac{1}{4}$ in. by 40. The resulting fitting will look like the adapter I recently described for testing the boiler for pinholes in the brazing, except that one end is countersunk and the other tapped.

Blower Valve

Chuck the $\frac{5}{16}$ in. rod once more, and proceed yet again as though you were making a blind nipple as described above; this time part off at $\frac{5}{8}$ in. from the shoulder. Reverse, and rechuck in a tapped bush, same as before; then turn down $\frac{1}{4}$ in. of the end to $\frac{1}{4}$ in. diameter, and screw $\frac{1}{4}$ in. by 40. Centre the end, and drill right through into the tapped hole in the other end with No. 48 or $\frac{5}{64}$ in. drill. Open out to $\frac{1}{2}$ in. deep with No. 30 drill and bottom the hole with a $\frac{1}{8}$ in. D-bit, same as pump ball seatings. Further open the hole to $\frac{1}{8}$ in. depth with No. 21 drill, then tap the rest of the No. 30 section with $\frac{5}{32}$ in. tap. If you have $\frac{5}{32}$ in. by 26 and 32, use it, as the coarser threads give a quicker action; if not, then $\frac{5}{32}$ in. by 40, will have to do. Be careful not to put the tap in far enough to damage the seating formed by the D-bit.

At $\frac{1}{4}$ in. from the shoulder, on one of the facets of the hexagon, make a centre-pop, and drill it $\frac{5}{32}$ in. or No. 22, right into the central passageway. A union screw is fitted in this hole; to make it, chuck a piece of $\frac{1}{4}$ in. round brass rod in three-jaw. Face the end and centre deeply; drill down about $\frac{3}{8}$ in. depth with No. 40 or $\frac{3}{32}$ in. drill. Screw the outside for $\frac{1}{4}$ in. length with $\frac{1}{4}$ in. by 40 die; part off at $\frac{5}{16}$ in. from the end, reverse in chuck (you can hold it by the threads if the chuck is not screwed up tightly enough to damage them) and turn a $\frac{1}{16}$ in. long "pip" on the end, to a tight squeeze fit in the hole in the side of the valve body. Squeeze it in, and silver-solder it; after the exercise beginners have had in brazing and silver-soldering the boiler, they should know now how to do that job without further detail. Quench out in pickle, wash off, clean up, and run the tap in again to make certain that no burrs are left.

The valve pin is made from a piece of $\frac{5}{32}$ in. round rustless steel, nickel-bronze, or phosphor-bronze; ordinary brass is too soft, and the valve, if screwed up tightly a few times, would soon begin to leak, as a groove would be formed around the cone point by the valve-seating. Chuck the rod in the three-jaw with about $\frac{3}{8}$ in. projecting; turn down $\frac{5}{32}$ in. length to $\frac{1}{8}$ in. diameter, and form a cone point on the end. I never bother about turning these points, although, as Inspector Meticulous would tell you, the correct way according to the textbook is to set over the top-slide to an angle of about 45 deg. and turn the point with a round-nose tool set at exact centre height. That is, of course, quite O.K., but what your humble servant does, is to take a smooth file, hold it across the end of the rod at the required angle for the cone, and take about half-a-dozen sweeps across, with the lathe running at high speed. That produces a perfect cone in two wags of a dog's tail. Pull the rod a little further out of the chuck; screw the next $\frac{5}{16}$ in. to match the thread in the valve body, with a die in the tailstock holder. Part off at $\frac{7}{8}$ in. from the point.

The handwheel can be turned from any material you fancy; brass, bronze, rustless steel, fibre or plastic. Chuck a bit of rod $\frac{3}{8}$ in. diameter; face the end, centre, and drill down about $\frac{1}{16}$ in. depth with No. 42 or $\frac{3}{32}$ in. drill. Turn away the front, to leave a little boss in the middle, and recess it a little between rim and boss, for the sake of appearance. Set the parting tool to cut off about $\frac{3}{32}$ in. behind the face and feed in about $\frac{1}{8}$ in.; then knurl the edge of the wheel. I never use a knurl, but merely lay a good sharp second-cut file on the rim of the wheel, pull the lathe belt back and forth by hand, and press the file down hard, letting it roll on the wheel. The file teeth cut into the wheel and the result is a nobby knurled edge, providing excellent finger-grip without any chance of slipping. Then part the wheel right off and drill four little holes in the web between rim and boss; about $\frac{5}{64}$ in. or No. 48 drill does fine. The hole through the boss is then squared. To do this, file off the end of a couple of inches of $\frac{3}{32}$ in. square silver-steel, so that it is quite flat and true with the sides. Taper off the other end a little, then harden and temper the squared end, same as I described for D-bits. Lay the wheel on something with a $\frac{5}{32}$ in.

hole in it; I keep a metal disc about $\frac{1}{2}$ in. thick and 2 in. diameter, with a lot of holes of different sizes drilled through it especially for jobs like this. Hold the flat end of the punch squarely over the drilled hole in the wheel and drive it clean through; easy enough if you put the metal block on the vice-jaws, same being partly opened, so that the punch drops between them.

The boss of the wheel will then have a clean-cut square hole in it, and the end of the valve pin is filed to suit. Put the pin in the three-jaw with $\frac{1}{8}$ in. of the plain end projecting; set No. 1 jaw vertical, and with a flat file having a "safe" edge—that is, one edge without any teeth cut in it—file a flat on the end of the pin, keeping the safe edge of the file in contact with the chuck jaw. Repeat operations with the chuck jaw at the three, six, and nine o'clock positions, and there is your squared end. It should be filed to fit the hole in the wheel tightly; the wheel is then pressed on and the projecting end of the pin burred over a little to stop it from coming off.

For the gland nut, chuck a bit of $\frac{5}{16}$ in. hexagon brass rod in three-jaw; face, centre, drill down about $\frac{5}{16}$ in. with No. 21 drill, open out to $\frac{3}{16}$ in. depth with $\frac{7}{32}$ in. or No. 3 drill, and tap $\frac{1}{4}$ in. by 40. Part off at a full $\frac{1}{4}$ in. from the end, reverse in chuck, and chamfer both ends.

How to Fit the Hollow Stay

Screw the body of the blower valve on to the end of the hollow stay, putting a smear of plumbers' jointing on the threads; be mighty careful not to let any of the jointing material get inside either the valve or the pipe. Now insert the stay in the right-hand hole in the backhead, guiding it to the hole in the smokebox tubeplate, exactly as described for the solid stay, and screw the valve right home. Put a little more of the jointing paste on the projecting threads of the stay, also on the threads at the tapped end of the thoroughfare nipple; screw the latter on to the end of the stay until it seats hard against the smokebox tubeplate. Note that when the blower valve is right home, the union screw on it should be standing vertically.

Firebox Stays

The firebox stays are made from $\frac{1}{8}$ in. copper rod, headed over on the outside and nutted on the inside. Mark out all the stayholes, as given in the longitudinal and cross sections of both larger and smaller boilers, make a small centre-pop at each point—if you hit too hard you will distort the thin copper —and drill No. 40 holes clean through both plates, taking care to keep the drill at right-angles to the plate. Tap them all 5 BA with one of the special staybolt taps supplied by the trade; these special taps have a $\frac{3}{32}$ in. pilot pin which guides the tap through the holes in both plates, and forms a thread which will allow the stay itself to fit properly in both plates when screwed right home. A taste of the same cutting oil as used for turning steel, applied to both drill and tap, will ensure clean threads.

Cut six pieces of $\frac{1}{8}$ in. round soft copper rod about 4 in. long; square off the ends and screw them 5 BA for $\frac{1}{2}$ in. at both ends, holding them in the three-jaw and using a die in the tailstock holder, with some cutting oil on both die and rod. Clamp a tap-wrench in the middle and screw the end of the rod into a stayhole; as it comes through, hold a 5 BA brass locknut against it and let the end of the stay screw into the nut. When the stay is screwed in to the end of the thread, snip it off a full $\frac{3}{32}$ in. from the boiler shell (a pair of top-cutting pliers is the tool for this job) and tighten up the locknut with a small spanner. If any of the stay projects through the locknut, snip that off too. When you have used up all the screwed ends, re-screw them another $\frac{1}{2}$ in. and repeat performance until the lot are in. Note.—The threads for the stays in the back-head must be a little longer, say $\frac{9}{16}$ in.

Put a piece of iron bar in the bench vice, letting it project a little from one side of the jaws. Put the firebox over it, resting one of the stay nuts on it; and using the ball end of the hammer head, rivet over the bit of copper rod projecting from the boiler shell into a neat rounded head. Take great care to hit the stay and not the boiler. This process will flatten out any stay end which may be sticking out beyond the nut of the firebox. Give all the nuts a final tighten up with a small spanner, but take care not to strip the threads, which is easily done, as the copper staybolts are soft.

How to Sweat the Heads and Nuts

Make a little wire brush by putting a little bundle of thin iron wires into the end of a bit of $\frac{5}{16}$ in. copper tube and flattening it, so that the wires are tightly held, and fit a wooden handle. Use this to brush some liquid soldering flux all over the stay heads and nuts. Don't use a paste flux for this job, on any account; if any gets inside the boiler, you'll never get it out, and the boiler will be always priming—that is, blowing water from the chimney and safety valves. I use Baker's soldering fluid; but any good preparation of similar kind, or chloride of zinc, or killed "spirit of salts" (muriatic acid with bits of zinc dissolved in it) will do the job.

Heat the boiler, in the brazing pan, until a stick of solder applied to it will melt at the end and deposit a blob among the stayheads. Plumbers' solder, which has a high melting point, is best; babbit metal, as used for bearings, is also suitable, but ordinary tinman's solder may be used. Keep up the heat and brush the melted solder all over the stayheads and nuts until every one is covered. Keep dipping the brush in the flux, add more solder as necessary, and don't get the fumes down your throat. The whole of the inside firebox should be completely tinned over. When all the lot are covered, let the boiler cool off a bit, then well wash it in running water to remove all traces of flux. We are then ready for the water-pressure test, which will show whether your boilersmithing is good, bad or indifferent. For this, we shall need the engine's own emergency hand pump; so, all being well, I will next describe how this is made.

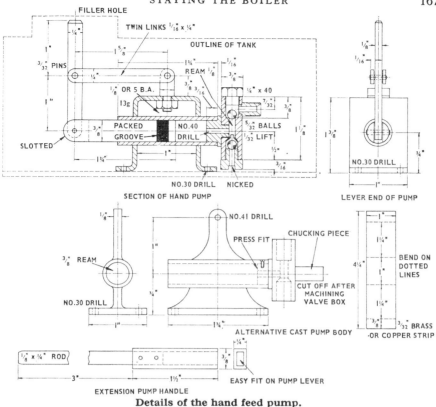

Details of the hand feed pump.

How to Test the Boiler

Before putting any fittings on the boiler of *Tich* it will be necessary to see if the workmanship is good enough to stand the working pressure. Just to cheer up any beginner who feels a little uneasy, I might add that the only failures that have come to my notice, in boilers of this kind, have been nothing worse than the sprouting of a few Welsh vegetables; and small leaks are easily stopped. Even if a plate or seam failed, there isn't the slightest danger of an explosion, as the failure would immediately release the pressure of water; you might hear a faint click, but that would be all. In the case of a boiler giving way under steam pressure, it is the sudden expansion of the steam, from bursting pressure down to atmospheric pressure, that causes the bang; and if the boiler stands the water-pressure test all right—as it will, if the instructions have been followed—there won't be any fear of that happening!

Hand Pump Construction

The "ingredients" needed for the test, are as follows: a pump, for creating pressure; a gauge to register it; a couple of adapters for connecting up the pump and the gauge to the boiler, and plugs for the holes not being used. The hand pump, which I specify for emergency use, and which will be installed in one of the side tanks, will do fine; so I will describe how to make it, right away. The gauge should read to about 250 lb. per sq. in. or over; I use a pressure-gauge of the kind fitted to full-sized engines. This has a central hand and reads to 360 lb. The same adapters used for the "pinholes" test can be once more pressed into service, but you'll need proper screwed metal plugs, as wooden ones would blow out under the test pressure. They can be made by following the method described for blind nipples, but need not be drilled up and tapped, as only the outside threads are needed. Odd scraps of round rod make nobby plugs; slot the heads with a hacksaw and put them in with a screwdriver instead of a spanner. In these times of mounting prices, it behoves us not to waste anything that can be made use of!

Pump Stand and Barrel

The pump can be made without castings, or a cast stand, barrel, and valve box can be used; please your own fancy. In the former case, a piece of 13 gauge ($\frac{3}{32}$ in.) brass or copper will be needed, 1 in. wide and approximately $4\frac{1}{4}$ in. long. This is bent to the shape of the Brunel era on the Great Western. The diagrams show how to bend it in the bench vice. Mark out the strip as shown; then grip it in the bench vice with the second line just showing above the jaws—this will be one of the top bends—and bend over at right-angles, by aid of a hammer used judiciously. Now put a bit of steel bar, 1 in. wide, in the angle thus formed; grip in the vice as shown, and make the second bend. Now put the forming block at the place where the bends for the lugs or feet are needed, and grip the embryo stand in the bench vice, upside down, with the two bits which will form the feet projecting above the jaws. Knock these outwards and downwards until they are flat on top of the vice jaws, and Bob's your uncle.

On the vertical centre-line of each side, at $\frac{3}{4}$ in. from the bottom, drill a No. 30 hole. If beginners centre-pop the first side, set the needle of the scribing block to the pop mark, then turn the stand around and make a scratch across the vertical centre-line without shifting the scriber needle, they will be sure of getting pop No. 2 in the right place, and the two drill holes will be exactly level. Open out both of them with a $\frac{3}{8}$ in. drill. Right in the middle of the top, drill a No. 30 hole; then drill two similar holes in each foot, for the holding-down screws. File off any burrs.

The best material for the barrel is a bit of $\frac{7}{16}$ in. brass treblet tube, squared off at each end in the lathe, to a length of $1\frac{3}{4}$ in. For beginners' special benefit I might repeat that treblet tube has been three times through the drawplate—hence its name—and will be smooth and true enough inside to be suitable for a pump barrel, or even a small steam cylinder, without any further treatment. If this particular material isn't available, use ordinary tube. Square off to length, as above; then put a bit of round wood in the three-jaw, with sufficient emery cloth or similar abrasive wound around it to make it fit the tube loosely. Put the bit of tube over it, run the lathe as fast as you can without causing the workshop to rock or collapse, and slide the tube up and down the improvised lap, holding it loosely, so that it kind of "floats". It takes very little of that treatment to get the bore suitable for the pump barrel. Ream or file the holes in the pump stand until the tube can be gently driven through without fear of distortion. It should project at one end approximately $\frac{1}{4}$ in.

Valve Box

Chuck a bit of $\frac{7}{16}$ in. round brass rod in the three-jaw, face the end, centre, and drill down to about $\frac{1}{2}$ in. depth with No. 40 drill. Turn down $\frac{3}{16}$ in. of the end to a tight fit in the pump barrel. Part off at $\frac{3}{16}$ in. behind the shoulder. Reverse in chuck and turn down $\frac{1}{8}$ in. of the other end to $\frac{3}{16}$ in. diameter; screw $\frac{3}{16}$ in. by 40. This forms the connecting piece between pump barrel and valve box. Part off a piece of $\frac{3}{8}$ in. brass rod to a full $1\frac{1}{8}$ in. length; chuck in three-jaw, centre, and drill right through with No. 34 drill. Open out and bottom one end to $\frac{3}{8}$ in. depth with $\frac{7}{32}$ in. drill and D-bit, same as for the eccentric-driven pump and tap $\frac{1}{4}$ in. by 40. Slightly countersink the end and face off any burr. Repeat operations on the other end, except that the hole is left as drilled, the D-bit not being needed; instead, nick the small hole as shown. At $\frac{5}{8}$ in. from the D-bitted end, drill a $\frac{5}{32}$ in. hole in the side of the valve box, piercing the central passage, and tap it $\frac{3}{16}$ in. by 40. Diametrically opposite, at $\frac{7}{32}$ in. from the D-bitted end, drill another $\frac{5}{32}$ in. hole and tap $\frac{3}{16}$ in. by 40; in this, fit a $\frac{1}{4}$ in. by 40 union screw. Chuck a piece of $\frac{1}{4}$ in. brass rod in three-jaw; face the end, centre deeply, and drill down about $\frac{7}{16}$ in. depth with No. 40 drill. Screw $\frac{1}{4}$ in. of the outside with $\frac{1}{4}$ in. by 40 die in tailstock holder; part off at $\frac{7}{16}$ in. from the end. Reverse in chuck, turn down $\frac{1}{8}$ in. of the end to $\frac{3}{16}$ in. diameter, and screw $\frac{3}{16}$ in. by 40. Screw this into the upper hole in the valve box. It will project slightly into the tapped hole, so chuck the valve box in the three-jaw again, enter the D-bit in just far enough to cut away the projection, and follow up with the $\frac{1}{4}$ in. by 40 tap. Put a $\frac{1}{8}$ in. parallel reamer through the remnants of the No. 34 hole at the bottom.

Press the spigot of the connecting piece into the end of the pump barrel which projects farthest from the stand; screw the valve box on to the screwed pipe and set it so that it is vertical, with the union screw at the top. Then solder over the two screwed joints, the place where the connecting piece joins the barrel, and the places where the barrel passes through the stand. Beginners may want to know why the connecting piece and the union screw are not made press fits in the valve box, and the whole bag of tricks silver-soldered. The reason is, that if you make the barrel red hot it will go soft, and probably distort a little; in which case it won't be suitable for a pump barrel any more. Anybody who so desires can silver-solder the connecting piece and the union screw into the valve box, in which case there would be no need to screw them; but the connecting piece would still have to be pressed into the barrel and soft-soldered, and the barrel soldered around the holes in the stand, which makes the job equivalent to taking two bites at a cherry.

The valve balls are fitted in the same way as those on the eccentric-driven pump, so that job can soon be disposed of. Drop a $\frac{5}{32}$ in. rustless steel ball into the D-bitted end of the valve box and seat it with a hammer-blow via a bit of brass rod, as described for the other pump. Gauge the depth as before; chuck a bit of $\frac{7}{16}$ in. or $\frac{3}{8}$ in. hexagon brass rod in three-jaw, and turn down to $\frac{1}{4}$ in. diameter, a length equal to the depth just measured. Screw $\frac{1}{4}$ in. by 40, slightly cone the end as shown in the illustration, and skim $\frac{1}{32}$ in. off the face, to allow the ball that amount of lift. Part off a full $\frac{1}{8}$ in. from the shoulder; reverse in chuck, holding in a tapped bush, and chamfer the corners of the hexagon, then screw the plug home.

Turn the doings upside down and drop another ball in the nicked end, taking the depth as before. Chuck the $\frac{6}{16}$ in. or $\frac{3}{8}$ in. rod again, turning down a length equal to the gauged depth to $\frac{1}{4}$ in. diameter, and screwing $\frac{1}{4}$ in. by 40. Centre, and drill down about $\frac{1}{2}$ in. depth with No. 34 drill; ream $\frac{1}{8}$ in. then take a skim off the end, to get it perfectly true. Part off at $\frac{3}{16}$ in. from the shoulder; reverse in chuck, and chamfer the corners of the hexagon. File a nick about $\frac{1}{16}$ in. wide, right across the end of the hole. Stand the gadget on something solid, put a $\frac{5}{32}$ in. rustless steel ball in the faced end, give it a crack with a bit of soft metal between ball and hammer to seat it, then screw home as shown.

Ram, Lever and Links

If you have a piece of $\frac{3}{8}$ in. round rustless steel or bronze that will slide easily in the pump barrel, no "turning to fit" will be required. The overall length is a bare 2 in. Chuck in three-jaw, face the end, and turn a groove $\frac{3}{16}$ in. wide and $\frac{1}{8}$ in. deep at $\frac{1}{8}$ in. from the end. Reverse in chuck and round off the other end a little. At $1\frac{1}{4}$ in. from the grooved end, drill a No. 43 hole right across the diameter; then cut a $\frac{1}{8}$ in. slot in it, $\frac{1}{2}$ in. deep, by the same means fully described for the eccentric-driven pump.

The lever is merely a $2\frac{1}{8}$ in. length of $\frac{1}{8}$ in. by $\frac{1}{4}$ in. hard brass or nickel-bronze (German silver) with one end rounded off, and a No. 41 hole drilled through it. At 1 in. above this hole drill another similar. Slightly bevel the top as shown.

The links are two pieces of similar metal, $\frac{1}{4}$ in. wide and $\frac{1}{16}$ in. thick, and a bare 2 in. long. Make two centre-pops $1\frac{5}{8}$ in. apart, clamp the bits together, drill through both at once with No. 43 drill and round off the ends. There is no need to worry about Inspector Meticulous when finishing off these jobs, as he can't see inside the tank, and the pump would work just as well if the ends of the lever and links were left absolutely rough-cut; but you don't want to leave them like that—there is a medium in all things! However, life is short, and there is no need to waste it by spending hours on "spit-and-polish" when nobody sees the result and it doesn't improve the working of the engine by one-millionth per cent!

To make the anchor lug, chuck a bit of $\frac{1}{8}$ in. by $\frac{1}{4}$ in. rod in four-jaw, set to run truly, turn down $\frac{5}{16}$ in. of the end to $\frac{1}{8}$ in. diameter, and screw $\frac{1}{8}$ in. or 5 BA. Part off at a full $\frac{1}{2}$ in. from the shoulder; drill a No. 41 hole through at $\frac{3}{8}$ in. from the shoulder, and round off the end.

How to Assemble

Put a link each side of the middle hole in the lever and drive a bit of $\frac{3}{32}$ in. rustless steel or hard bronze wire through the lot, leaving just a weeny bit sticking out each side, which may be slightly riveted over. Put the anchor lug between the links at the other end and ditto repeato the pinning. Put the bottom of the lever in the slot in the ram and pin that likewise. The links should hug the lever and the anchor lug like a teddy bear, so that the lever doesn't flop sideways when erected. Pack the groove with a few turns of hydraulic packing, which can be obtained by unravelling a short bit of the stuff used for the glands of full-sized water pumps. If this is not available, graphited yarn can be used. Don't forget that the packing doesn't need to be so confoundedly tight that there is a risk of bending the lever when operating; all it needs, is to seal any tiny leak between ram and barrel. As the pump is "drowned" in the tank when in place on the engine, a small whimper doesn't make the slightest difference to the working, and the pump is only for emergency use, anyway.

Insert the ram into the pump barrel, prodding in the packing in the same way as described for the engine cylinders. Put the screwed end of the anchor lug through the hole in the top of the stand and secure it with a brass nut underneath, as shown in the illustration; the job is then completed.

Variation for Cast Pump

If using castings for the pump stand and body and the valve box, there is not much difference in the machining work. The body, or barrel and stand, will be all in one piece, with the anchor lug on top. Valve box and connecting piece will be combined in a separate casting. First of all, smooth off the base of the stand and the sides of the anchor lug with a file; drill the holes as shown. The casting can then be mounted on an angle-plate, as described for cylinders, and fixed by four $\frac{1}{8}$ in. bolts through the holes in the base, or clamped down by a couple of toolmaker's clamps, just as you fancy. Set the barrel to run truly; face the end, centre, drill right through with $\frac{23}{64}$ in. drill, and follow with a $\frac{3}{8}$ in. parallel reamer. If this end is used for attachment of valve box, there is no need to set up for machining the other end in which the ram will fit; it may either be left as it is, or smoothed with a file.

Chuck the valve box by one end, set the other end to run truly, and proceed exactly as described for the valve box made from rod material. When the D-bitted end is finished, the casting won't run truly enough to do the other end if merely reversed in chuck; so chuck any old bit of metal above $\frac{3}{8}$ in.

diameter, turn down about $\frac{3}{16}$ in. length to $\frac{1}{4}$ in. diameter, screw $\frac{1}{4}$ in. by 40, and screw the tapped end of the valve box on to it. It will then run truly, and the other end can be opened out, drilled and tapped, as described above.

Chuck the casting in the three-jaw by the chucking piece on the back and turn the boss which forms the connecting piece to a tight fit in the faced-off end of the pump barrel. Centre, and drill right through with No. 40 drill until it breaks into the central hole in the valve box. Fit a $\frac{1}{4}$ in. by 40 union screw in the side of the D-bitted end, same as for the built-up valve box; then press the connecting boss into the barrel, set the valve box up straight, and solder over the joint and the place where the union screw is attached. If the boss isn't a very tight squeeze fit in the barrel, put a $\frac{3}{32}$ in. or 7 BA brass set-screw in, as shown in the illustration. Saw off the chucking piece and file the stub flush with the valve box, rounding it off to match the circumference.

Details

The valves, valve caps, ram, lever and links are made and fitted in exactly the same way as specified for the built-up pump. An extension handle for either type of pump is made by rounding off the end of a piece of $\frac{1}{8}$ in. by $\frac{1}{4}$ in. rod, about $3\frac{1}{2}$ in. to 4 in. long, and fitting a socket to the end. The socket may be either a piece of rectangular tube which will just fit easily over the lever (this is a commercial article) or else it can be made by wrapping a piece of 18 gauge sheet brass around a piece of rod of the same section as the handle. If tube is used, push the rod into it for about $\frac{1}{2}$ in. and put a couple of $\frac{1}{16}$ in. brass rivets through the lot. If the socket is made from sheet, slide it on to the handle for about $\frac{1}{2}$ in. and silver-solder it, sealing up the corner joint at the same time. When the pump is erected in the engine tank it is operated by putting the extension handle over the pump lever, which is arranged to come exactly under the filler hole. No unsightly slot is needed in the tank top.

Efficient Pumps

Beginners and new readers may be interested to learn that I have used and specified this type of pump for many years past. The old commercial pumps had a huge gland, which the packed ram renders unnecessary; and they also had levers pivoted at the bottom, below the ram. This necessitated huge long slots in the tank tops, as the end of the handle sometimes had to travel over $3\frac{1}{2}$ in. to get less than 1 in. stroke of the ram. I have here at the present moment, a rebuilt commercial $2\frac{1}{2}$ in. gauge engine which originally cost over £130; and in its original state, it had a 4 in. slot in the tank top, with a huge permanent handle projecting through it, yet the pump itself was only $\frac{3}{8}$ in. bore and 1 in. stroke. It is hardly necessary to add that this was scrapped and replaced by an efficient pump, similar to that described above. I might add that my pumps with upper pivot and packed ram, have been pretty extensively copied!

How to Test the Boiler

Having made the pump, the actual testing of the boiler is just a piece of cake. The procedure to follow goes like this. Plug all the holes except two; the dome hole may be covered by a disc of brass $\frac{1}{8}$ in. thick, same diameter as the boiler bush. This is best attached by six 8 BA brass screws in exactly the same way as a cylinder cover, with a Hallite or similar jointing gasket between disc and bush. Be careful to keep this handy after the testing, for you'll need it to use as a jig to drill the dome flange; otherwise you won't get the screw holes in the flange to match those in the bush. Two adapters are needed, as described previously for the "pinhole" test, but one end of each is countersunk for a union.

The boiler is filled right up with cold water and the big gauge attached by a piece of pipe with a union at both ends to one adapter fitting; the pump is attached to the other, and placed in a pan or tray with water in it. You will find it extremely easy to pump against pressure, by aid of the long extension handle; a few strokes will send the big gauge up to 50 lb. Stop here and take a look to see if all is O.K.; if so, go up to 100 lb. and take another look. Don't worry if the firebox crown or side sheets move $\frac{1}{32}$ in. or so, as it will only be the soft copper settling itself into the best position to resist pressure. If still O.K. go to 130 lb. and then finally to 160 lb., which is twice the working pressure; don't go higher, as it is unnecessary, and you only put undue strain on the boiler. If still O.K., leave the pressure on for a little while; then release it by unscrewing a union, drain out the boiler, and pause for a cup of the engineman's best friend (or something a little more potent, according to taste!) for you have well and truly earned it. Should a leak show, stop the test and put it right before proceeding further. We are then ready to adorn the boiler with the necessary fittings and mountings.

CHAPTER ELEVEN

Making the smokebox

BEFORE MAKING THE BOILER fittings, maybe it would be as well to make and fit the smokebox, so I'll deal with that component right away. The smokeboxes shown for the large and small boilers are rather different in construction. That for the smaller boiler is of what is sometimes known as the Victoria type; the wrapper, or outer sheet, comes right down to the frames, and is attached directly to them. It may be waisted in at the sides, as shown, or it may come down straight-sided, like the sides of the firebox. The first plate is flat, and fits closely to the contour of the smokebox, whether straight-sided or waisted. The smokebox for the larger boiler is of modern type, circular in shape, and supported on a saddle which is attached to the frames above the cylinders; the front of this one is a flanged circular plate, turned to a push fit in the shell. The door of each type of smokebox is of the same pattern, though of different size, the fastening is also the same. When scheming out the design, I thought maybe that some builders who are fitting the smaller boiler might prefer a circular smokebox with saddle, and vice-versa; those fitting the larger boiler might prefer the older pattern. If anybody wants to work either of these wheezes, it is perfectly easy; all you do is follow the instructions for making and fitting the kind required, but change over the measurement and use those appropriate to the size of the boiler.

Making it Easy

In full-size, a smokebox of the older pattern would be made in a different way to the construction I shall specify. The smokebox tubeplate, instead of being like we made ours, would be a flat plate, of the same shape as the smokebox front, and the barrel would be attached to it by means of an angle ring. On the smokebox side of the plate, it would be flanged—this would require a specially-shaped former—or else a shaped piece of angle would be riveted around the edge, and the wrapper sheet riveted to this in turn. The front plate of the smokebox would also be either flanged, or have the shaped angle attached, and it would be fixed to the wrapper sheet in the same way. The bottom of the smokebox would be closed by a flat plate; the whole would entail a lot of work; and unless all the joints were brazed, it would be difficult to keep airtight.

We can get over all this trouble by the simple expedient of using a bit of tube pushed on to the end of the boiler barrel and forming an extension of same. The wrapper sheet of the smokebox is simply wrapped around this, the lower part being left either straight or waisted in, as desired, then bent outwards and attached to the frames by a strip of metal at each side. No bottom plate is, of course, needed. The front is a piece of plate cut to shape, with a ring silver-soldered to it; the ring is cut to fit the end of the tube, and when pushed in, with a taste of plumbers' jointing smeared around it, the joint is airtight. One of the accompanying drawings shows the whole issue in section.

The first requirement is a piece of 16 gauge brass or copper tube, $2\frac{5}{8}$ in. outside diameter and a full $1\frac{7}{8}$ in. long. Steel tube could be used, as there is normally no water in contact with the metal; but I have found with steel smokeboxes, that sometimes when the engine is moved cold, a few drops of water come out of the blastpipe and fall among the slight residue of ashes usually found clinging to the bottom of the smokebox. A corroding action is set up, and if the engine is not steamed for some time, the bottom of the smokebox becomes first pitted, then goes into holes, which admit air, destroy the smokebox vacuum, and the engine fails to steam. I have just had to put a new bottom in the domestic coal pail, owing to the corrosion action of damp coke, which rotted the old one clean out. If a piece of tube is not available, roll up a piece of 16 gauge sheet metal, put a couple of rivets through the lap joint, and braze it, the process being the same as described for the boiler barrel.

Beginners should remember that whenever a piece of tube larger in diameter

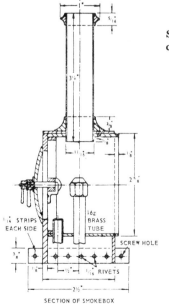

Smokebox, smokebox door and chimney for the small engine.

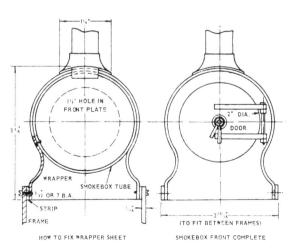

than the hole through the chuck body is gripped in a three- or four-jaw chuck, using either set of jaws, the tube must be supported on the inside, to resist the gripping pressure of the chuck jaws. If it is held unsupported, it will fly out of the jaws as soon as the turning-tool starts operations on the end; and it will not only be badly distorted but may damage your personal anatomy, or wreck the workshop window. Avoid trouble by putting something in the gripped end of the tube, a disc of wood, an old wheel, chuck plate or anything else that will fit. You can then tighten the chuck jaws down, and the tube will be gripped so firmly that it will "stay put" whilst the ends of the tube are squared off to length. I have squared off the ends of a 4 in. by 12 in. boiler barrel quite easily this way, although beginners would probably need a "steady" for a job that length, similar to that described for facing off long firetubes and superheater flues. Use a round-nose tool set crosswise in the rest, and a drop of cutting oil; and don't run the lathe too fast. "Slow and sure" is the motto for this job.

After facing off the second end, bringing the tube to a length of $1\frac{3}{4}$ in., round off the edge as shown; rough-turn it with the round-nose tool, then smooth it off to shape by holding a file to it. Don't drill any holes in it yet.

Wrapper Sheet

The outer wrapper sheet may be brass, copper, or steel, of 16 gauge. Cut a strip $1\frac{3}{4}$ in. wide and 9 in. long, then bend it around the smokebox tube, to the shape shown in the illustration, leaving the sides straight or waisted, as desired. The squared-off end of the smokebox barrel should be $\frac{1}{8}$ in. inside the wrapper sheet, and the rounded-off end should project $\frac{1}{8}$ in. beyond the wrapper sheet at the other extremity. Just above the place at each side where the wrapper sheet leaves the tube, put in three $\frac{1}{16}$ in. countersunk rivets, to hold the sheet in close contact with the tube. If the riveting has distorted the bends, put them right again before proceeding further. I use a couple of small toolmakers' clamps to hold one side in position whilst riveting, then remove them, pull the strip of metal tightly against the barrel, and put the clamps on at the opposite side. After riveting, which is done in the same way as the lap seam of the barrel, heads inside, the stems hammered flush into countersunk holes outside, and filed flush, the bends are fettled up; and if one side is longer than the other, it is cut to correct length, so that the smokebox will stand up perfectly straight on a level surface. This is important; otherwise the chimney will either emulate the Leaning Tower of Pisa, or be off centre, which looks worse still when the engine is viewed from the front.

Stand the embryo smokebox on something level and put a square against the front, adjusting same until the distance from the edge of the square's blade, is exactly the same to either side of the smokebox, at the centre line. Now, exactly where the edge of the square rests against the top of the smokebox, make a mark; and from that, draw a line along the top. This will indicate the extreme top; halfway along, make a centre-pop, which indicates the exact

Plate 21

F. Whitehand of King's Lynn tries out his "Tich" at Eaton Park, Norwich

Below: Here are some of LBSC's other engines

Plate 22

A large-boilered "Tich" built by Mr. C. Wilkinson of Bradford

Mrs. Daltry's "Tich" is seen here coupled to the underframe for a model milk tank wagon

spot to drill the hole for the chimney. From this, scribe a circle $\frac{11}{16}$ in. diameter, with a pair of dividers; make a good deep scratch. Drill a $\frac{1}{8}$ in. hole at the marked spot, and follow with $\frac{1}{2}$ in. drill; you'll probably find that the drill has wandered, and the hole isn't in the middle of the circle. Correct it with a file, then put a bigger drill through; or if you like, file out the hole until you just barely touch the line and finish with an $\frac{11}{16}$ in. parallel reamer, put through by hand. A lot of fuss, maybe, but it is worth it to get the chimney up straight; you'd say so, if you had seen what I have seen!

Stand the smokebox up again, apply square, and mark off the bottom centre-line by a similar process. Make a centre-pop in the middle and another one at $\frac{1}{2}$ in. toward the front. These are for steam and exhaust pipes; drill and ream as above, finishing to $\frac{5}{16}$ in. diameter. It is important to get the hole for the blast pipe exactly under the chimney.

Smokebox Front

The front of the smokebox may be a casting, or made up from $\frac{1}{8}$ in. brass plate, with a ring silver-soldered to it. If a casting is used, chuck it by the door hole, putting the inside jaws of the chuck through the hole, and opening them out. The ring may then be turned to a tight push fit in the smokebox barrel using a knife tool. Next, chuck the casting the other way around, gripping the turned ring in the outside jaws, setting it to run truly. Face off the whole of the front with a round-nose tool set crosswise in the rest. The edge can be cleaned up with a file to the contour of the wrapper, so that it fits neatly when the ring is pressed into the barrel.

To make a built-up front plate, stand the smokebox end-up on a piece of smooth flat $\frac{1}{8}$ in. brass plate, and scribe a line around the outside. By the good rights, the line should be scribed around the inside, but the barrel gets in the way. Anyhow, it is easy enough to mark out another line inside the scribed one at a distance of $\frac{1}{16}$ in. away. Saw the plate roughly to shape, and finish with a file until it fits exactly in the front of the smokebox wrapper, bedding up against the end of the barrel. Leave it in, turn the smokebox the other way up, and scribe a line on the plate, all around the inside of the barrel. This circular scriber mark shows the exact place to put the ring. Find the centre of it, either by trial and error with a pair of dividers, or by the geometry method you were taught at school, or the same way as your humble servant does, viz. put a rule across it vertically and horizontally, so that the edge of the rule crosses the approximate centre, making a scratch "by eye" as near the middle as possible, in both directions. Put one point of the dividers at the middle of the cross, set the other to the circle, and the odds are that you will be within $\frac{1}{16}$ in. of the true centre when you sweep the dividers around. If you haven't hit the true centre, you'll see at a glance where it is! Make a centre-pop on it; and from that, scribe another circle $1\frac{3}{4}$ in. diameter. Either cut out the piece with a metal fretsaw, or drill a circle of holes inside the line and break out the piece, filing away the ragged edge. My own pet wheeze is to chuck the plate in the four-jaw, with the scribed circle running truly, and cut it out with a parting-tool set crosswise in the rest. This leaves a very clean hole which needs no filing, except to take off the sharp edges.

Soften a bit of $\frac{3}{16}$ in. square brass rod about $8\frac{1}{4}$ in. long, by heating to red and plunging into cold water. Bend it to a circle $2\frac{5}{8}$ in. outside diameter. Clean it up, lay the smokebox front in the brazing pan with the ring on it—this should come practically flush with the edge of the circular part—and silver-solder it, using best-grade silver-solder or "Easyflo". After the practice beginners have had in brazing up the boiler, they should all find that job as easy as eating a piece of cake; merely anoint the joint with wet flux, blow up to medium red, and apply the silver-solder. Tip: use a big diffused flame, to heat the work evenly; if you don't, the front plate will buckle. By the same token, says Pat, let the job cool to black before dropping it in the pickle; otherwise, it will go all shapes.

If you should happen to be unlucky, don't despair, but just lay it on something nice and flat, and do what Bert Smiff calls " 'it it wiv an 'ammer", but use care and discretion. Outside my workshop door is a small blacksmith's anvil on a wooden stand, which comes in handy when anything wants a good "biffing", and is just the berries for a job like this. Incidentally, when I first put it there, one of my few personal friends promptly chalked GRETNA on it, saying that any run-away couple in this locality needn't waste their money on a train journey on the L.M.S.; the inscription stayed until finally Jupiter Pluvious washed it off. Young Curly's first "anvil" was a discarded flat-iron, begged off mother, and mounted upside down minus the handle, on a block of wood.

The front plate, with the ring silver-soldered to it, is now the equivalent of a casting as mentioned above, and it is treated the same way, chucking by the hole, turning the ring, then reversing and truing up the front. We will fill in the back and fit the side strips when we come to the erecting job.

Smokebox for the Larger Boiler

As the door and hinges, dart and crossbar fastening, and locking handles are made in the same way for both the larger and smaller smokeboxes, one description will do for both, so if I now describe the larger smokebox shell and front, builders of both sizes can then go right ahead. The shell of the larger smokebox is merely a piece of $3\frac{1}{8}$ in. diameter brass or copper tube, 16 gauge, and a little over $2\frac{1}{4}$ in. long. Chuck it in the three-jaw, using a disc, or other packing, pressed into the end which is being held in the chuck, and square off each end until the piece of tube is exactly $2\frac{1}{4}$ in. long. Scribe a line across it, and in the middle of the line make a centre-pop; from that, scribe a $\frac{5}{8}$ in. circle and make a $\frac{5}{8}$ in. hole exactly as described above for the chimney of the smaller smokebox. Exactly opposite, scribe another line across the shell. I have a very flexible steel rule, almost like a piece of metal tape, which can be wrapped around even a small-diameter tube. I usually measure the circum-

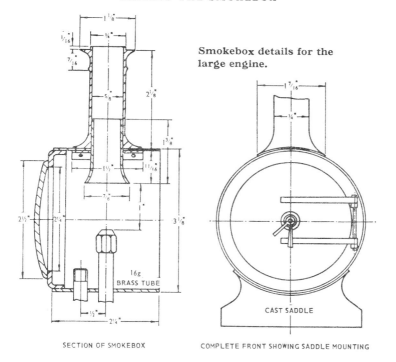

Smokebox details for the large engine.

SECTION OF SMOKEBOX   COMPLETE FRONT SHOWING SADDLE MOUNTING

ference of the smokebox shell with this, then it is easy enough to mark off half the dimension, measuring from the centre of the chimney hole, or from the centre-pop before the hole is drilled. A tape measure, as used by your wife, sister or girl friend, as the case may be, will serve the same purpose.

In the middle of the line, make a centre-pop, and another one $\frac{1}{2}$ in. away; both these are drilled and opened out to $\frac{5}{16}$ in. diameter for the steam and exhaust pipes, same as previously described for the smaller smokebox. No outer wrapper sheet is needed, as the smokebox is supported by a separate cast saddle, as shown.

Smokebox Front

The front may be either a casting or flanged up from plate. In the former case, chuck it on the inside jaws of the three-jaw, by the hole; turn up the outside edge to a tight push fit in the smokebox shell. Round off the edge, as shown. Reverse in chuck and grip by the turned flange, convex side outwards. Face the full diameter with a round nose tool set crosswise in the rest. If the front has hinge lugs cast on, it prevents the whole front being faced off, and there are two courses open to the builder. If the casting is at all rough, it would be best to make a clean sweep of the whole lot, and face the entire front, cutting off the cast-on lugs in the process. Separate lugs can be fitted after-wards, as will be described for the flanged-plate front. If the casting is clean, leave the lugs on, and just face off a section $2\frac{1}{2}$ in. full diameter, just big enough to accommodate the door. If the hole is ragged, true it up with a boring tool.

To make a flanged-plate front, cut out a circle of $\frac{1}{8}$ in. brass (doesn't matter if it is a little thinner; 12 gauge would do) to $3\frac{3}{4}$ in. diameter; or use a commercial stamped brass blank, same as I usually do. Soften it, and flange it exactly as described for the smokebox tubeplate. It will probably need annealing three or four times during the flanging process; brass is more brittle than copper, and is, therefore, more liable to crack. When you have a nice flange, chuck in three-jaw, flange outwards, using the outside jaws, and face off the ragged edge. Then reverse in the chuck and hold it on the outer edge of the outside jaws. It cannot be mounted on the inside jaws, as you will find if you try it! Put a parting tool in the slide-rest, setting it crosswise, a weeny bit above centre, and cut a hole in the plate $2\frac{1}{4}$ in. diameter, using low speed and plenty of cutting oil. As there is plenty of clearance behind the plate, you needn't fear a broken tool when it breaks through. Then face off the rest of the front of the plate; turn the flange to a tight fit in the smokebox shell, and round off the edge. Bevel it with the turning-tool and finish off with a file, with the lathe running at medium speed.

Smokebox Door

If a casting is used for the smokebox door, it will have a chucking piece cast on, in the middle of the convex side. Grip this in the three-jaw, set the casting to run as truly as possible, then face off the edge of the door until you have a true circle approximately $\frac{1}{8}$ in. wide, which will close airtight against the smokebox front when the door is erected. An airtight joint is essential; if the air leaks in, the vacuum in the smokebox is destroyed and no air will be drawn through the fire, which will either burn very dull or go out altogether. If the hinge straps are cast on the door it will not be possible to true up the outside of it in the lathe. Centre the door with a centre drill before removing it from the chuck, and drill a No. 30 hole well into the chucking piece. Remove door, saw off the chucking piece, and clean up the outside of the door with a file, finishing with emery cloth. Drill a No. 51 hole through each boss on the ends of the hinge straps, to accommodate the pin.

A Plate Door

A door may also be made from a disc of $\frac{1}{8}$ in. sheet brass, or a commercial stamped brass blank of similar thickness. This should be a little larger in diameter than the size of door required; say, $2\frac{1}{4}$ in. diameter for the smaller boiler, and $2\frac{3}{4}$ in. for the larger. First job is to "dish" the blank; that is, alter its personal appearance from flat to saucer shape. Make it red hot and plunge into cold water; then lay it on a block of lead and hit it with the ball end of the hammer, starting from the middle and working outwards, all around, until you get the desired shape. Some folk say the dishing should be started from the edge of the disc, different folk have different fancies—all I can say is that

I always start from the middle, and there is nothing amiss with the smokebox doors on any of my engines. When the "saucer" is complete, chuck it in the three-jaw, with the concave side outwards, setting it to run truly. Centre it, and drill right through with No. 30 drill; then face off a little piece around the hole to about ¾ in. diameter. Chuck an odd stub of brass rod, about ½ in. diameter, in the three-jaw and turn a pip on the end, about ⅛ in. long, to a tight fit in the hole in the embryo door.

Squeeze it in, making sure that the shoulder around the pip is in close contact with the faced-off bit of the door. Put a drop of Baker's fluid, or other liquid soldering flux, around the stub, and a bead of solder alongside it. Hold the lot over a gas or spirit flame until the solder melts and forms a fillet all around the stub. When cool, wash in water (if any soldering fluid gets on to the chuck jaws, they will go rusty) then chuck the stub in the three-jaw. If the stub has been properly fitted, the dished plate will run truly; if not, a judicious tap or two with a lead or hide-faced hammer (what the engine shopmen of my generation used to call a "bacon-rind" hammer) will teach it better manners. The whole issue can then be finished off at the one chucking.

Finishing

Turn the outer edge to diameter with a round-nose tool; face the contact edge either with a left-hand knife-tool, or a parting-tool carefully fed straight in; and the outside can be roughed with a round-nose tool set crosswise in the rest, operating both slide-rest handles together. Beginners won't be able to get a smooth finish by that method—nor very few experienced workers could, either!—and the way I finish mine, is to put a bit of bar in the rest. Next you'll need a graver, which is a hand turning-tool made by grinding off the end of a bit of square tool steel to a diamond shape, rested on the bar and the cutting edge applied to the convex surface of the door. A little judicious manipulation soon makes hay of the " 'umps and 'ollers", and a piece of fine emery cloth, or other abrasive, puts a finishing touch to the job.

Heat it up again to the melting point of solder, pull out the stub, wipe off any superfluous solder, and we are all ready to fit the hinges and fastenings.

CHAPTER TWELVE

The regulator and superheater

Regulator for Small-boilered "Tich"

AS THE SMALLER BOILER has a very big dome, we might as well take full advantage of it, and fit a proper regulator; so I have shown one of the simplest type, similar to those used on the Stroudley engines of the L.B. & S.C. Rly. My engines *Grosvenor* and *Jeanie Deans* have exactly the same type, their domes being fairly high, and they give every satisfaction. The whole outfit merely consists of a stand, with a circular port face at the upper end, over which a valve oscillates, opening and closing the ports in a manner somewhat similar to the action of the mechanical lubricator. The valve is operated from a double-armed lever on the regulator rod, via two connecting links like weeny coupling rods. The regulator rod goes out through a gland on the backhead, and is operated by the usual type of single-crank handle.

Regulator Stand

The stand may be a casting or built up; the machining and fitting is just the same for either type of stand. To build up, you simply need a piece of $\frac{1}{4}$ in. by $\frac{5}{16}$ in. brass rod $2\frac{1}{16}$ in. long, at the top of which is filed or milled a $\frac{1}{16}$ in. rebate $\frac{1}{2}$ in. deep, like that at the top of the stand for the mechanical pump. Attach a $\frac{1}{8}$ in. slice of $\frac{1}{2}$ in. round brass rod to this, by a $\frac{1}{16}$ in. brass screw. On the same side, at the bottom, similarly attach another small slice of brass rod $\frac{1}{4}$ in. diameter and $\frac{1}{8}$ in. thick. On the opposite side, at the bottom, attach a block of brass sawn and filed up to the shape and size given. Silver-solder all three joints at one heat, using best-grade silver-solder or "Easyflo". Pickle, wash off, and clean up, and you have the equivalent of the casting, but the use of a casting saves work.

Drilling the Column

First of all, put a No. 30 drill right down the middle of the column, going to within $\frac{1}{16}$ in. of the bottom. If you haven't a bench drilling machine, don't attempt this job by hand, or it is a million dollars to a pinch of snuff that the drill will wander, and maybe break out at the side. Centre-pop the top and chuck the column in the four-jaw, with the pop mark running truly; and use

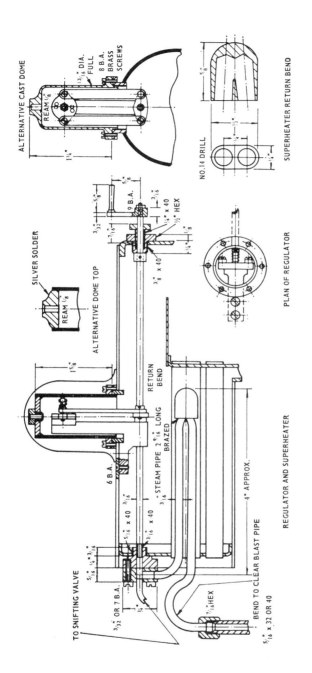

These drawings show how to fit up the regulator, superheater elements and the main steam pipe.

the tailstock chuck to hold the drill in the usual way. On a built-up stand, chucking would be easier if the drilling is done before attaching the bits of the column. Tap the upper end $\frac{5}{32}$ in. by 40 for about $\frac{1}{8}$ in. or so down; plug it, and solder over the plug. Make a centre-pop in the middle of the port face, and two more at $\frac{11}{64}$ in. above and below it. Drill the middle one No. 48, slightly countersink, and tap $\frac{3}{32}$ in. or 7 BA. The other two are also drilled No. 48, going right through into the central hole in the column.

At $\frac{7}{16}$ in. from the top of the step which fits against the inside of the boiler shell when the regulator is erected, drill a $\frac{5}{32}$ in. hole as shown, breaking into the hole in the column. Tap this $\frac{3}{16}$ in. by 40 for the steam pipe. Next, drill a No. 30 hole in the little boss, to take the end of the regulator rod. The easiest way to get this true, is to chuck a bit of $\frac{1}{16}$ in. round rod in three-jaw, and put a few $\frac{3}{16}$ in. by 40 threads on the end, with a die in the tailstock holder. Screw the tapped steampipe hole on to this; the little boss should then run truly, and may be faced off, centred, and drilled as shown. Be careful not to pierce the column too deeply, and break into the central hole; but if you are unlucky, don't worry—you won't be the first, and it is a pretty safe bet you won't be the last! Open out the hole to $\frac{3}{16}$ in. and squeeze in a "blind" bush made from a bit of $\frac{3}{16}$ in. round brass rod. Solder it, to prevent any steam and water going where it shouldn't.

File out the little recess in the block to clear the underside of the dome bush, and then true up the port face. This can be done in the manner described for truing up the cylinder port faces and the stand of the mechanical lubricator. Take pains to have this about right, for a leaky regulator is—well, any full-size driver will give you the exact definition! Tip: when facing a surface at the end of a component, as in the present instance, apply the rubbing pressure as nearly as possible at the centre of the surface to be faced; that is, press the port face to the emery cloth (or other abrasive) by putting your finger on the column, opposite to the trunnion pin hole. Finish off with pumice-powder and water, or a scrape of your oilstone, on a piece of plate glass, or ground flat steel.

The Valve

This is cut from a piece of $\frac{1}{8}$ in. brass plate, to the shape shown in the illustration, which also gives the location of the holes. The two in the ears or lugs are drilled No. 51 and tapped 8 BA. The steam ports are drilled No. 48, at $\frac{1}{16}$ in. off centre-line. and the trunnion pin hole is drilled No. 41 and countersunk on the side that makes contact with the port face. Be careful to face this truly, too! The trunnion pin itself is a $\frac{9}{16}$ in. length of $\frac{3}{32}$ in. round phosphorbronze—brass will do, at a pinch, but something better is to be preferred—with about $\frac{3}{32}$ in. of thread on each end. Screw this into the centre hole in the port face, with a taste of plumbers' jointing on the threads; put a spot of cylinder oil on the rubbing face of the valve, and assemble as shown, using a light spring of bronze or hard brass wire, about 26 gauge, and an ordinary commercial brass nut.

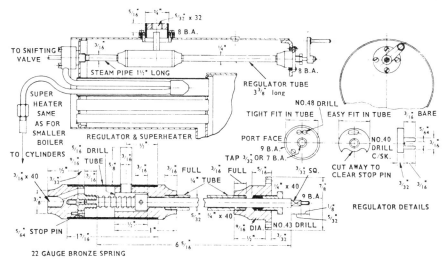

Regulator and superheater for the large engine.

Lever and Links

The double-armed lever at the bottom of the stand is filed from $\frac{3}{32}$ in. sheet brass. Drill the holes No. 43, then file the middle one square, with a watchmaker's square file, until a piece of $\frac{1}{8}$ in. square steel will just go through. The two outer holes here should, however, be drilled and tapped 8 BA. Give both sides a rub on a fine file, to remove any burrs. The connecting links are only a few minutes' work, being merely $1\frac{7}{8}$ in. lengths of $\frac{3}{16}$ in. by $\frac{1}{16}$ in. strip metal (nickel bronze if possible, though anything non-rustable will do as long as it isn't soft) with No. 43 holes drilled at $1\frac{5}{8}$ in. centres, and the ends rounded off. Don't use commercial screws for connecting up; make your own. Chuck a bit of $\frac{3}{16}$ in. round bronze rod in three-jaw, face the end, and turn down a full $\frac{3}{16}$ in. length to a nice fit in the holes in the connecting links. Slip one of the links over the turned part, then screw with an 8 BA die in the tailstock holder, until the die barely touches the link. This leaves enough "plain" under the head for the link to work on. Part off at $\frac{1}{8}$ in. from the shoulder; reverse in chuck, round off the head, and slot it with a fine saw. Connect the links to the lever, but not to the valve; this is done after erection.

How to Fix the Stand

Drill two No. 34 holes in the boiler shell, one about $\frac{1}{8}$ in. ahead of the dome bush, and the other about $\frac{5}{16}$ in. in front of that; countersink both. Insert regulator stand, block first, through the bush; you'll find it enters quite easily if it is tipped up. Then hold it vertically, with the front edge of the little recess hard up against the dome bush; see illustration of complete assembly. Put the No. 34 drill down the holes in the shell, and make marks on the block, or else scribe circles through the holes. Remove regulator stand, drill the block

No. 44 at the marked spots tap 6 BA, replace block, and secure with two 6 BA brass countersunk screws. Either use a smear of plumbers' jointing under the heads, or sweat them over like stayheads.

Steam Pipe and Flange

The steam pipe is a $2\frac{9}{16}$ in. length of $\frac{3}{16}$ in. copper tube not less than 22 gauge, with $\frac{3}{16}$ in. of 40-pitch thread on one end and $\frac{5}{16}$ in. ditto on the other. Give each end a taste of plumbers' jointing, and insert the shorter-threaded end, through the hole in the smokebox tubeplate, screwing it home into the tapped hole in the regulator block. If you insert the end of a small round file into the free end of the tube and use it as you would use a screwdriver, the tube will screw home easily. The file will free itself when turned the other way, leaving the tube in position.

To make the flange, chuck a piece of $\frac{3}{4}$ in. round brass rod in three-jaw. Face the end, centre, and drill down about $\frac{5}{8}$ in. depth with No. 22 or $\frac{5}{32}$ in. drill; tap $\frac{3}{16}$ in. by 40. Turn down $\frac{1}{4}$ in. of the outside to $\frac{1}{2}$ in. diameter; further reduce $\frac{3}{16}$ in. length to $\frac{5}{16}$ in. diameter, and screw $\frac{5}{16}$ in. by 40. Part off at a full $\frac{3}{16}$ in. from the shoulder; reverse in chuck and take a fine skim off the face to true it up. Put some plumbers' jointing on the threads, start it on the end of the steam pipe which should just be standing clear of the tubeplate, and screw it right home, until the outside threads engage with the tapped hole in the tubeplate and the shoulder beds home tightly against it. See complete assembly drawing.

Operating Gear

The regulator rod is a $4\frac{3}{4}$ in. length of $\frac{5}{32}$ in. round bronze rod, phosphor or nickel, it doesn't matter which. Turn down $\frac{1}{8}$ in. length to $\frac{1}{8}$ in. diameter, and file the next $\frac{3}{32}$ in. square, by method previously described, to a nice fit in the hole in the double-armed lever. At the opposite end, turn down $\frac{1}{8}$ in. length to $\frac{5}{64}$ in. diameter, and screw it 9 BA. File a $\frac{3}{32}$ in. square next to this, $\frac{5}{16}$ in. long. Chuck a piece of $\frac{5}{16}$ in. round brass rod in three-jaw; face, centre, drill down about $\frac{1}{4}$ in. depth with No. 23 drill, and part off a $\frac{3}{16}$ in. slice.

For the stuffing box, chuck a piece of $\frac{1}{2}$ in. hexagon brass rod in three-jaw; face the end, centre, and drill down about $\frac{1}{2}$ in. depth with No. 21 drill. Turn down $\frac{1}{4}$ in. of the outside to $\frac{3}{8}$ in. diameter and screw $\frac{3}{8}$ in. by 40. Part off to leave a head $\frac{1}{8}$ in. thick. Reverse in chuck and hold in a tapped bush (you should know how to make these by now!), open out to $\frac{5}{16}$ in. depth with $\frac{7}{32}$ in. drill and tap $\frac{1}{4}$ in. by 40. Make a gland from a piece of $\frac{3}{8}$ in. round or hexagon rod, same as described for piston rod and valve spindle glands; as we progress, you profit by experience gained in building up the chassis, and I don't have to repeat every operation in full detail.

Now watch your step over the next bit. Take the two links, with double-armed lever attached, and drop the lever down in place, behind the little boss at the bottom of the stand, then couple the upper ends of the links to the lugs at each side of the valve. Take care the screws don't push the valve off the port face, as they will if they go too far through. If you are unlucky, shorten the screws slightly, and reface the valve in case it has become burred around the screw holes. Push the collar on to the regulator rod until it is approximately $\frac{3}{4}$ in. from the shoulder where the smaller square starts, at the handle end. Insert the other end through the hole in the backhead, and guide the front end through the hole in the double-armed lever into the hole in the little boss, the squared part engaging the squared hole in lever. Next, put the stuffing box on and screw it right home. When tight up against the backhead, there should be a bare $\frac{1}{32}$ in. end-play in the regulator rod. If tight, the collar wants moving forward a shade; if loose, shift the collar back. It is a case of trial and error. When you have it right, remove the rod, drill a No. 53 hole through collar and rod, and drive in a piece of $\frac{1}{16}$ in. hard bronze or brass wire. Replace rod, screw home the stuffing box with a taste of plumbers' jointing on the threads, and pack the gland with a few turns of graphited yarn.

The handle is filed up from a bit of $\frac{1}{4}$ in. by $\frac{3}{32}$ in. nickel-bronze strip. I have shown a short one for the sake of neatness, but it can be made any length desired. For the boss, chuck a bit of $\frac{1}{4}$ in. round rod, face, centre, drill $\frac{3}{32}$ in. or No. 43 for about $\frac{1}{8}$ in. down, and part off a $\frac{3}{32}$ in. slice. Silver-solder this to the lower end of the handle, which is filed taper, and drilled $\frac{1}{16}$ in. at the narrow end. The grip is turned from a bit of $\frac{1}{8}$ in. rod, to shape shown, leaving a $\frac{1}{16}$ in. pip on the end. Drive the pip through the narrow end of the handle, and rivet over. Continue drilling the boss with $\frac{3}{32}$ in. drill right through the handle; then file the hole square, to fit the end of the rod. Note—put the

Details of the regulator.

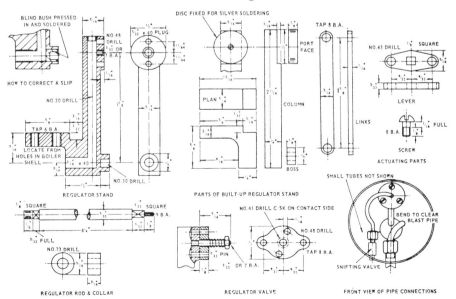

regulator valve in the "open" position, with the holes in the valve coinciding with the ports; then file them square, so that when placed on the square on the rod, the handle inclines 45 deg. to the left. When the handle is moved to a similar inclination on the right, the ports should be completely covered by the valve. Put the handle on the square, secure it with a 9 BA commercial nut, and Bob's your uncle once more!

Superheater

Heat is the source of power; have your steam plenty hot, and you not only get power, also speed, but you get them with the minimum consumption of fuel and water. The superheater looks after the heat business; and the type shown for *Tich* is a simplified edition of full-size practice. The elements are two pieces of $\frac{3}{16}$ in. copper tube of about 22 gauge; one approximately $3\frac{3}{4}$ in. long, and the other about 2 in. longer. One end of each piece is joined by a "return bend". This is made from a piece of $\frac{1}{2}$ in. by $\frac{1}{4}$ in. copper rod, $\frac{5}{8}$ in. long. On one end, make two centre-pops $\frac{1}{4}$ in. apart, and drill them with a No. 14 drill, inclining same towards the centre-line of the block so that the holes break into one another about $\frac{3}{16}$ in. inside the block. Keep on drilling until there is free communication between the holes, as shown in the section of the block. Round off the sides and ends as shown; then drive one end of each element into one of the holes, about $\frac{1}{8}$ in. or so, and braze them. Note—silver-soldering is not advisable for this job. Apply some wet flux, then blow up to a good bright red, and apply a piece of soft brass wire, or Sifbronze rod. This will melt and form a fillet around each tube. Soften the other ends whilst on the job, then quench the lot in acid pickle, and wash off in running water. Bend the ends of the tubes as shown; a piece of steel rod pushed in the end, will provide enough leverage to enable this to be done with your fingers.

The Header

To make this part, chuck a piece of $\frac{3}{4}$ in. round brass rod in three-jaw; face the end, centre, and drill down $\frac{3}{8}$ in. depth with No. 33 drill. Open out to $\frac{1}{4}$ in. depth with No. 22 drill, and part off at $\frac{5}{16}$ in. from the end. Drill a No. 14 hole in the thickness, breaking into the centre hole as shown in the section; also drill three No. 40 holes for the screws. These holes are $\frac{1}{8}$ in. from the edge, and equally spaced. This header is fitted on the bent-up end of the upper element. In the centre hole, fit a piece of $\frac{3}{32}$ in. copper tube approximately $2\frac{1}{2}$ in. long, for the snifting valve.

The swan-necked end of the lower element carries a union nut and cone for coupling up to the vertical member of the cross fitting connecting the steam pipe to the cylinders. The nut and cone are made in the same way as those on the oil pipe which connects the mechanical lubricator to the underside of the cross fittings, except that they are larger, the nut being made from $\frac{7}{16}$ in. hexagon rod, drilled No. 10 to clear the steam pipe, and tapped $\frac{5}{16}$ in.

by 32 or 40, to match the screw on which it fits. The cone is made from $\frac{1}{4}$ in. round bronze rod, drilled through with No. 30 drill and opened out with No. 14 drill, to fit on the $\frac{3}{16}$ in. pipe. Warning—don't forget to put the nut on the pipe before fitting the cone; I've seen the nut left off, quite a number of times, and it is easy to be forgetful! Silver-solder the two pipes into the header, and the cone on the swan-neck, at the same heating; also, it would save time if you fit the $\frac{1}{4}$ in. by 40 union nut and cone on the snifter pipe, and fix that in like manner at the same time. Pickle, clean up, and well wash in running water, letting the water run through the elements to remove any grit or scale that may have accumulated when the pipes were hot.

To fit the superheater is a matter of minutes only. Push the element into the flue, and if the header doesn't line up with the flange on the steam pipe, bend the element until it does. Then poke the No. 40 drill through one of the screw holes, make a countersink on the flange, remove the superheater, drill the countersink No. 48 and tap $\frac{3}{32}$ in. or 7 BA. Replace superheater, put a screw in to hold the bits together, then ditto repeato operations on the other two holes. Finally, assemble with a $\frac{1}{64}$ in. Hallite or similar jointing gasket between the faces—and don't forget to punch a hole in the middle, for the steam to go through. I recollect sticking on the bank halfway between Sydenham and the Crystal Palace about 5.30 a.m. on a winter's morning when the rails were covered with ice, and the fitter who cleaned the sand pipes and valves had put gaskets between the flange joints without making any holes in them. The heat from his ears should not only have melted the ice, but the rails as well! Yes, I know what you are going to say—but he only put the pipes back about two minutes before we left the depot, and the yard foreman chased us out of it before we had a chance to see if all was O.K.

Inner Dome

This may be built up, or turned from a casting. To build up, you need a piece of 22 or 20 gauge copper tube $1\frac{3}{4}$ in. long and $\frac{15}{16}$ in. outside diameter. If not available, either bend it up from sheet copper or use a piece of 1 in. by $\frac{3}{32}$ in. turned down at one end to fit the dome bush. The upper end is plugged by a disc of $\frac{3}{32}$ in. sheet copper with a $\frac{1}{4}$ in. by 40 tapped hole in the middle; or a piece of 1 in. brass rod can be chucked in three-jaw, and a cover turned to fit as shown, with the hole for the safety valve in it. Turn about $\frac{3}{8}$ in. length to a tight fit in the tube, and part off at $\frac{5}{16}$ in. from the end. Hold $\frac{1}{8}$ in. of this in the chuck, and set to run truly. Centre, drill through with No. 34 drill, ream $\frac{1}{8}$ in. and slightly countersink the end with a centre-drill; then round off the top; similar to the shape of the cast dome shown, and press into the end of the tube.

Now take the disc you used to cover the dome hole when testing; chuck in three-jaw, centre, drill to $\frac{3}{4}$ in. in about three stages (if you try to put a $\frac{3}{4}$ in. drill through right away, it will chatter badly) and bore out to fit tightly on the outside of the tube. Press it on at $\frac{1}{8}$ in. from the bottom, and silver-solder both

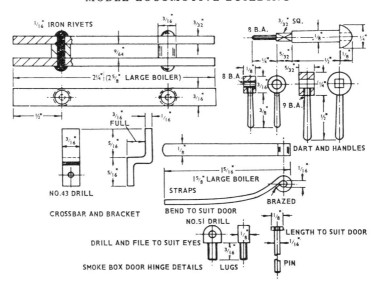

The smokebox fittings.

top and bottom at the one heat. Pickle, wash, and clean up. Put it temporarily in place with a couple of screws, to protect the regulator whilst putting on the rest of the blobs and gadgets. We will fit the safety valve later.

A cast dome should be chucked in three-jaw with the flange outward. Turn the spigot to an easy fit in the dome bush, face the flange, and turn to diameter; then bore the inside to $\frac{13}{16}$ in. full diameter, same as boring cylinders. Mount on a mandrel, a bit of hard wood turned to fit, does fine; hold the mandrel in the chuck and turn the outside to the shape shown. Face the boss on the end, centre, drill No. 34, ream $\frac{1}{8}$ in. and countersink slightly for the safety valve. Bore the testing disc as mentioned above, until it becomes a ring which will slip on the spigot; then use the holes in it as a jig to drill the flange, running the drill through the holes in the ring, and carrying on through the flange. Clamp them tightly together with a toolmaker's clamp, so that the holes coincide exactly, and will thus match up with the holes in the dome bush.

Smokebox Accessories

Before continuing the regulator instructions, let's insert the "missing links", which aren't links at all, says Pat, but the adornments for the smokebox doors. A door knocked up from a blank, and turned on the outside or a turned casting, will need a separate pair of hinges riveted on. The easiest way to make the straps, is to bend them up from pieces of strip metal about 20 gauge. I have used both nickel-bronze and rustless steel, but ordinary steel does quite well; if blue steel is used, and bright hinges are required—cleaner boys on the L.B. & S.C. Railway always scoured up the smokebox door hinges and handles—the blue finish is soon rubbed off with a piece of fine emery cloth.

I cut my strips from ordinary sheet, using a pair of snips before I had the Diacro shear. It is easy enough to cut along a straight line if you are careful. The strips should be $\frac{1}{8}$ in. wide for either door; cut them a little over finished width, and bring to size with a smooth file. Bend the end over like a hook, with a pair of round-nose pliers; then put a piece of $\frac{1}{16}$ in. steel wire in the hook, and continue bending the metal around the wire, until you have a complete loop. The joint is then brazed; just put a dab of wet flux in the joint, heat to bright red, and touch it with a bit of thin brass wire. If the eye becomes stopped up by feeding in too much brass, it doesn't matter a Continental, just poke a No. 51 drill through it.

For the small smokebox, cut off the strips at $1\frac{5}{16}$ in. from the outside of the eye or loop; for the larger one, $1\frac{5}{8}$ in. is just right. Round off the ends, then apply one of the hinge straps to the door, $\frac{5}{16}$ in. above centre-line for the smaller one, and $\frac{3}{8}$ in. for the larger one. You'll then see exactly how it needs bending, to lie in close contact with the door. Do the needful, then drill three holes in it, to suit the fattest domestic pins that your wife, girl friend, or "mum" keeps in her work-basket. I use No. 57 drill, and have a supply of blanket pins; they are iron, but very soft, and make excellent rivets. One hole should be near each end of the strap, and one in the middle; countersink them. Put the strap in place on the door, holding it with a clamp, drill corresponding holes in the door, drive the pins through, snip off about $\frac{1}{16}$ in. from strap, and inside the door, and carefully rivet over the projecting bits of pin, hammering the outside ends well down into the countersink. I always use a bit of $\frac{1}{2}$ in. rod held vertically in the bench vice, as a riveting stake or dolly for this job; if the end of the pin is rested on the dolly, there is no risk of distorting the door. If it is distorted, it won't close airtight, and then I'll have umpteen letters telling me the boiler won't steam. When the straps are smoothed with a fine file, the rivets should be quite invisible.

Hinge Lugs and Pins

The lugs are made from $\frac{1}{8}$ in. by $\frac{3}{16}$ in. rod, nickel-bronze or brass. Chuck truly in four-jaw, and turn down $\frac{3}{16}$ in. length to $\frac{7}{64}$ in. diameter; screw 6 BA. Part off at $\frac{3}{16}$ in. from the shoulder, and round off the sharp corners. Now be careful about the next bit. Put the smokebox door in place and fix it temporarily; this is easily done by cutting a bit of brass or steel rod, say about $\frac{3}{8}$ in. by $\frac{1}{8}$ in. section, a little longer than the diameter of the hole in the smokebox front. Drill a No. 40 hole in the middle and tap $\frac{1}{8}$ in. or 5 BA. Put this across the inside of the smokebox front, in the same position that the crossbar will occupy, and run an ordinary screw into it, through the hole in the door. Tighten up just sufficiently to hold the door tightly in place without distorting it. See that the door is absolutely slap in the middle of the smokebox front; a door put on "cockeyed" is a sign of sheer carelessness. The eyes on the ends of the straps should touch the smokebox front; in full-size they are clear of it, but they are far smaller in proportion to size, and if ours stick out a mile or so, it spoils the neatness. With the door in this position, make a centre-pop in line with the holes through the eyes, and $\frac{1}{16}$ in. below them.

Remove door, drill the centre-pop No. 44, tap 6 BA, and screw the lugs in; then replace door, poke a No. 51 drill down the holes in the eyes, and continue right through the lugs. I can almost hear some beginners asking how the merry dickens are they going to do that, when the drill chuck won't clear the smokebox front. As I often say, everything is easy when you know how. Chuck a piece of $\frac{1}{8}$ in., or even $\frac{3}{32}$ in., round rod in three-jaw; brass, bronze or steel, doesn't matter which. Face it, centre, and drill down about $\frac{1}{4}$ in. with No. 52 drill. Hold a No. 51 drill in the bench vice, point downward, between two clamps, soft copper for preference, with just over $\frac{1}{4}$ in. of the shank projecting. Carefully drive the drilled end of the bit of rod on to the shank, and you have an extension drill that will do the required job like the girl on the flying trapeze.

When the drill has gone through the upper lug, don't pull it out, but push it straight down into the lower one, and carry on with the drilling, the upper eye and lug acting as a drilling steady. Warning—be careful not to move the brace to either side, or you'll either break the drill, or bend the shank just above the extension piece. If the drill doesn't fit tightly in the extension, just solder it. If I happen to break a drill (which is a rare occurrence, though it happens sometimes, as I am still a human being, and not driving the *Astral Belle* yet) the Scottish part of my ancestry won't let me throw it away. I make an extension for the point end, and regrind the shank end, which does for rough jobs, so I then have two drills in place of one, ye ken—hoots, mon, awa' wi' ye!

The hinge pin is made from $\frac{1}{16}$ in. round silver-steel. Chuck in three-jaw, and put about three or four threads on the end, $\frac{1}{16}$ in. or 10 BA. Chuck a bit of $\frac{1}{8}$ in. round rod, centre, and drill it about $\frac{3}{16}$ in. deep with No. 55 drill, and part off at $\frac{1}{8}$ in. from the end. Tap the hole to match the pin, screw it on tightly, chuck in three-jaw again, and trim up the head to a flat button shape. Cut the pin off just long enough to project about $\frac{1}{16}$ in. below the bottom lug when in place; round off the end. Finally, carefully trim off with a fine file any part of the lugs which is projecting beyond the eyes, so that eyes and lugs are same width, as shown in the illustrations. This makes a nice neat finish.

Dart and Crossbar

The dart, which is the engineman's name for the locking bolt, can either be turned from the solid, or built up. In the former case, chuck a piece of $\frac{1}{4}$ in. round steel rod in three-jaw; face the end, and turn down a full $\frac{1}{4}$ in. to a bare $\frac{3}{32}$ in. diameter. Turn down the next $\frac{21}{32}$ in. to $\frac{1}{8}$ in. diameter; then push the rod back into the chuck jaws until only $\frac{5}{32}$ in. of the $\frac{1}{8}$ in. part projects, and file that square. I have already described how to file true squares, using one of the chuck jaws as a guide, so need not go over all that rigmarole again. Screw the little end piece with an 8 BA die in the tailstock holder, then pull

Plate 23

Outer boiler and firebox shell, firebox and tubes built by Mr. G. F. Collins of Brighton

"Tich" under construction by Mrs. Ruth Daltry
Below: Some of the boiler fittings of Mrs. Daltry's engine

Plate 24

Underside view of the "Tich" built by Mr. W. Ducklin. Note the brake gear

the rod out of the chuck jaws again, far enough to part off at $\frac{1}{8}$ in. behind the shoulder, leaving a round head $\frac{1}{8}$ in. thick. File this flat both sides, to the same thickness as the round part, then finish it off to the shape shown in the illustration, and the job is done.

To build up the dart, simply chuck a bit of $\frac{1}{8}$ in. round rod, turn down $\frac{1}{4}$ in. of the end, and screw as above. File the next $\frac{5}{32}$ in. to a square, also as above, then part off at $\frac{5}{8}$ in. from the squared part. Reverse in chuck and turn $\frac{1}{8}$ in. of the end to $\frac{1}{16}$ in. diameter. File the head from any odd scrap of steel $\frac{1}{8}$ in. thick, then drill a $\frac{1}{16}$ in. hole in the middle of the long straight side. Push in the $\frac{1}{16}$ in. end of the spindle, and braze the joint with brass wire; clean up, and the result is as good as one made from solid.

For the key, chuck the $\frac{1}{4}$ in. rod, centre, and drill a $\frac{3}{32}$ in. hole about $\frac{3}{16}$ in. deep; part off a $\frac{5}{32}$ in. slice, and file the hole square, with a watchmaker's square file, until it fits easily on the squared part of the dart. For the locking handle, chuck a bit of $\frac{3}{16}$ in. steel rod, face, centre, and drill about $\frac{3}{16}$ in. depth with No. 51 drill; part off a $\frac{1}{4}$ in. slice, and tap it 8 BA. Drill a No. 53 hole in the thickness of each, and tap it 9 BA. The handles are made from bits of $\frac{3}{32}$ in. silver-steel, or rustless steel if you so desire, filed slightly taper whilst running at high speed in the lathe; the smaller end is screwed 9 BA to fit the tapped holes in the round bosses, and the outer ends are slightly rounded off. The illustrations show the assembly.

The crossbar is an exceedingly simple job, being composed of two bits of $\frac{3}{32}$ in. by $\frac{3}{16}$ in. steel rod, cut to length to suit smokebox. At $\frac{1}{2}$ in. from each end, drill a No. 51 hole in one of the bars, and use it as a jig to drill the other. For the spacers, chuck a piece of $\frac{3}{16}$ in. round steel rod; centre, drill about $\frac{3}{8}$ in. depth with No. 51 drill, and part off two slices $\frac{9}{64}$ in. thick. Put these between the bars, opposite the holes, put $\frac{1}{16}$ in. iron rivets through and rivet up as shown.

The brackets are bent up from $\frac{1}{16}$ in. by $\frac{3}{16}$ in. steel strip; take a cut off any odd scraps of 16 gauge sheet that may be lying around. I keep three boxes handy, and throw into them any "trimmings" of sheet steel, copper and brass, that are left over after doing any sheet-metal job. Since I had the Diacro shear and bending gadgets, these boxes have supplied jolly nearly all the bits of angle, channel, etc. that I have needed, and in double-quick time, too. The illustration gives the measurements. To erect the brackets, put the crossbar in position and set the bracket to it. Shut the door, hold the crossbar in position horizontally across the hole, poke the dart through the crossbar, and through the hole in the middle of the door. First put on a $\frac{1}{8}$ in. steel washer, then the square-hole key with the handle hanging down; finally, the locking handle, screwing it up tightly enough to hold the crossbar in place. Then all you have to do is to put a bracket at each end of the bar and attach the bracket to the back of the smokebox front (says Pat) with an 8 BA screw. If any of the screw sticks out beyond the front of the plate, file off flush. The whole assembly is shown in the illustration of the complete smokeboxes. If preferred, the brackets may be riveted to the plate, at each side of the door hole, but if you rivet, take good care not to give the plate an accidental clout which might distort it. If the door doesn't close airtight, you won't get any steam.

Smokebox Attachments

It doesn't really matter about making provision for attaching the smoke-boxes to frames, until we are ready to erect the boiler; but if the job is done now, they will be all ready. The smaller smokebox needs a strip of 16 gauge metal, $2\frac{1}{2}$ in. long and $\frac{3}{8}$ in. wide, riveted along each side, flush with the bottom, as shown in the recently illustrated section. This not only increases the overall width to the required distance between frames, but allows the whole bag of tricks to be fixed to the frames by a screw at each corner, where the side strips project beyond the smokebox.

The larger smokebox is supported by a cast saddle. All the casting needs is cleaning up with a file. The smokebox shell should bed nicely down into the seating; a half-round file will soon remove any roughness. If a piece of medium emery cloth is wrapped around the smokebox shell, and the saddle rubbed up and down it a few times, the seating will match the curve of the smokebox barrel—not exactly, I hasten to add for the benefit of Inspector Meticulous, but near enough to allow the smokebox to seat well home. The sizes and ends may also be introduced to the emery cloth, after filing off any roughness, if a posh finish is desired; the saddle should just fit nicely between the frames, not tightly enough to push them apart, but tight enough to "stay put" without slipping down. It is not fixed to the smokebox until the erection job is in hand.

Regulator for Larger Boiler

Owing to the squat inner dome carrying a direct-action safety valve, we cannot use the high type of regulator described for the smaller boiler; so here is another type which will be O.K. for the job in hand, as it requires practically no headroom. It is of the "disc-in-a-tube" pattern; and this particular version of it was schemed out by your humble servant many years ago, to obviate the need for making the tube full diameter for its full length, like that described in the Live Steam Book. The long tube, with a lot of "pinholes" in the top, to collect steam, is, however, ideal for a watertube boiler which has no dome at all. The dome on the outer casting of watertube boilers, is usually a dummy. Incidentally, the arrangement shown is another one of many items described in these notes, which have been adopted commercially, in certain instances without as much as a by-your-leave, or even a word of acknowledgment.

The barrel consists of a piece of $\frac{9}{16}$ in. thin brass or copper tube (treblet tube if available) squared off at both ends in the lathe, to a length of $1\frac{7}{16}$ in. For the throttle block, chuck a piece of $\frac{9}{16}$ in. round bronze or gunmetal rod in three-jaw. Face the end, centre deeply enough to make a countersink, and drill to $\frac{3}{16}$ in. depth with No. 48 drill; tap $\frac{3}{32}$ in. or 7 BA. Turn down $\frac{3}{16}$ in. of the outside to a tight fit in the barrel; part off at $\frac{1}{2}$ in. from the end. Reverse in chuck, gripping by the reduced part, then turn the end to the outline shown, centre, drill $\frac{5}{32}$ in. or No. 22 for $\frac{1}{4}$ in. depth, and tap $\frac{3}{16}$ in. by 40. Now watch your step very carefully; at a bare $\frac{3}{32}$ in. from the edge of the faced end, make two centre-pops a bare $\frac{3}{32}$ in. apart; and from them, drill two No. 48 holes slantwise into the tapped hole. The easiest way for beginners to get a fair start, is to drill straight in until the drill has just entered to its full diameter, no more and no less. Then shift the handbrace until the drill points towards the tapped hole, and carry on. Be extra careful as the drill is breaking through, or that won't be the only break! I advise hand drilling for beginners on this job, although it is fairly easy for them on a machine, the block being held in a machine vice on the table, and the table tilted to correct angle. If the table doesn't tilt (mine doesn't) simply put the block in the machine vice at correct angle, sighting it against the drill, exactly as I described for drilling passage-ways in the cylinders.

On the opposite side of the face, approximately $\frac{1}{8}$ in. off centre, and close to the edge, drill a No. 53 hole and tap it 9 BA for the stop pin, which is just a bit of 15 gauge wire (bronze or rustless steel) screwed to suit. It should project $\frac{3}{32}$ in. from the face. The pivot pin is similar, but $\frac{3}{32}$ in. diameter. Before screwing in these pins "for keeps", face off the surface exactly as described for the slide valves, and be mighty careful not to tilt the block when rubbing it on the emery cloth, or you'll never get a true face in a thousand years.

For the valve, chuck a bit of $\frac{1}{2}$ in. rod of a different grade from that of the block. Face the end, turn down $\frac{3}{16}$ in. length to $\frac{3}{16}$ in. diameter, and part off at a bare $\frac{1}{4}$ in. from the shoulder. Reverse in chuck, centre deeply to form a countersink, then drill down about $\frac{1}{8}$ in. with No. 40 drill, as the valve needs to be very easy on the pivot pin. Face off the end; then slot the boss to a full $\frac{1}{16}$ in. width, which is easily done by cutting with a hacksaw and finishing with a watchmaker's flat file. Drill two No. 48 holes as close together as possible, corresponding with those in the port face, but run them into a slot, as shown, by aid of a rat-tailed file. Finally, file a segment out of the bottom, as shown, to allow the stop pin to regulate the movement; the exact length of the segment is a matter for trial and error. When the valve is turned in an anti-clockwise direction, the end of the gap should be against the pin, when the slot is exactly coinciding with the two holes in the port face. When the valve is turned clockwise, the pin should be at the other end of the gap, after the hole has moved off the ports and travelled about $\frac{1}{32}$ in. beyond them, so that they are overlapped by that amount of metal. When you have the gap O.K., face off the valve, same as the port face. Put a spot of cylinder oil on the faces, and they will stick together and be quite steamtight, if the facing has been properly done.

Guide for Regulator Rod

The plug at the opposite end of the tube forms a guide for the regulator rod as well as a socket for the tube carrying the rod. Chuck the $\frac{9}{16}$ in. rod again, or a similar-sized piece of brass rod; face the end, centre, and drill down about $1\frac{1}{8}$ in. depth with No. 21 drill. Open out to $\frac{1}{2}$ in. depth with $\frac{5}{16}$ in. drill, turn $\frac{11}{16}$ in. of the outside to a tight fit in the tube, and part off at 1 in. from the end. Reverse in chuck, turn the outside to outline shown, open out the centre hole for $\frac{3}{16}$ in. depth with No. 3 or $\frac{7}{32}$ in. drill, and tap $\frac{1}{4}$ in. by 40. Squeeze this into one end of the barrel; then at $\frac{1}{2}$ in. from the end of the barrel (that is, $\frac{13}{16}$ in. from the extreme end) drill a $\frac{5}{32}$ in. hole through tube and plug, right into the enlarged hole in the plug (see section) and tap it $\frac{3}{16}$ in. by 40 for the dry steam pipe going up into the dome. This is a $\frac{3}{4}$ in. length of $\frac{3}{16}$ in. tube with a few $\frac{3}{16}$ in. by 40 threads on one end, and is not attached until the regulator is erected in the boiler, when it is screwed in through the dome bush.

The regulator rod is a piece of $\frac{5}{32}$ in. round rod, phosphor-bronze or rust-less steel, $6\frac{3}{4}$ in. long. One end is squared and screwed exactly as described for the rod in the smaller boiler, and will need a similar handle. File two flats on the opposite end, leaving a tongue between, which is an easy fit in the slot in the boss of the valve, but not slack. This tongue should be $\frac{1}{32}$ in. less than the length of the slot and is filed in the same manner as a square, but only on opposite sides instead of on four sides. For the collar, chuck a bit of $\frac{1}{4}$ in. round brass rod in three-jaw, face, centre, drill about $\frac{1}{4}$ in. depth with No. 23 drill, and part off a $\frac{3}{16}$ in. slice. Press this on to the tongued end of the regu-lator rod, so that it is approximately $\frac{5}{8}$ in. from the tongue; it should be a fairly tight fit. Put the rod, longer end first, down the regulator tube until the tongue is just about to enter; then put the valve and throttle block on it, the slot in the boss going over the tongue, and press right home. If the rod has about $\frac{1}{32}$ in. end play, and can be twisted either way until the ends of the gap in the valve hit the stop pin, the collar is set correctly. If too much end play, shift the collar further away from the tongue; if not enough play, shift it nearer. The $\frac{1}{32}$ in. end play is needed to allow for expansion.

When you have it right, take out the rod, pin the collar to it with a $\frac{1}{16}$ in. pin made of bronze wire driven through a No. 53 hole drilled through collar and rod. Replace rod, valve and throttle block; but this time put a spring, wound up from 22 gauge hard bronze or brass wire around a $\frac{3}{16}$ in. rod, between valve and collar, and see that the steam ports in the block are level with the hole for the vertical steam pipe in the tube. When the block is pressed right home the valve should work easily by operating the rod between finger and thumb. The illustration clearly shows the assembly.

Gland Fitting

If a casting isn't available for the gland fitting, turn it from $\frac{7}{8}$ in. brass rod held in three-jaw. Face, centre, and drill down about $\frac{5}{8}$ in. depth with No. 21 drill. Open out to $\frac{3}{16}$ in. depth with $\frac{7}{32}$ in. drill and tap $\frac{1}{4}$ in. by 40. Turn down $\frac{1}{2}$ in. of the outside to $\frac{9}{16}$ in. diameter and further reduce $\frac{5}{16}$ in. length to out-line shown. Part off at $\frac{5}{8}$ in. from the end. Reverse in chuck, open out with $\frac{7}{32}$ in. drill to $\frac{5}{16}$ in. depth, tap $\frac{1}{4}$ in. by 40, then fit a gland as described for the other regulator. Drill four No. 43 holes in the flange for the fixing screws, and scrape off any burrs. Cut a piece of $\frac{1}{4}$ in. brass or copper tube $3\frac{3}{8}$ in. long; the hole through this must be big enough to let the regulator rod pass through easily. Put about $\frac{3}{16}$ in. of $\frac{1}{4}$ in. by 40 thread on each end; push it over the rod, and screw into the guide at the end of the regulator barrel. Screw the gland fitting on the other end. Cut a $1\frac{1}{2}$ in. length of $\frac{3}{16}$ in. copper tube, put about $\frac{3}{16}$ in. of $\frac{3}{16}$ in. by 40 thread on one end, and $\frac{5}{16}$ in. on the other; screw the shorter-threaded end into the throttle block, with a taste of plumbers' jointing on the threads, and the regulator is ready for erection.

How to Erect

Open out the $\frac{3}{8}$ in. hole in the backhead to $\frac{9}{16}$ in. diameter with drill and reamer. Insert regulator until the flange of the gland fitting comes up against backhead. See that the steam pipe hole comes under the dome bush; put the vertical steam pipe temporarily in place, making sure it stands quite upright. Then locate, drill and tap the screw holes on the backhead, exactly the same as fitting a cylinder cover; remove regulator and then replace with a $\frac{1}{64}$ in. Hallite or other jointing gasket between the flange and backhead, and secure the flange with four 8 BA brass roundhead screws, smearing the threads with plumbers' jointing. Pack the gland with graphited yarn and fit the handle, exactly the same as for the smaller boiler. Screw in the vertical steam pipe; make and fit a steam flange at the smokebox end, exactly as described for the smaller boiler, and the job is done. The superheater is made and fitted exactly as described for the smaller boiler; the dome will be described, all being well, along with the safety valve.

CHAPTER THIRTEEN

Starting on the boiler fittings

Safety Valves

OUR WORTHY FRIENDS WHO are building *Tich* will find that I have designed a spring-balance type of safety valve for the smaller boiler, and an ordinary direct-acting spring-loaded valve on the larger one; but if anybody wants to change them over, it will be quite all right. However, builders of the smaller boiler will have to cut down the height of the inner dome and use the regulator described for the larger boiler; whilst the larger boiler fraternity will have to increase the height of the inner dome, or use a long bush, to bring the height of the valve seating to the top of the dome casting. My honest advice is to leave them as they are. If any builder who is using the smaller boiler doesn't care for the spring balance, he can put the direct-acting valve in place of the dummy whistle and shift the latter to the cab roof. Many full-size engines carry whistles on the cab roof, at the front edge, close to the weatherboard.

The Spring-balance Type

The spring-balance safety valve is an interesting piece of apparatus. It is one of the oldest forms of locomotive safety valve and a direct descendant of the weighted lever, which was at one time practically universal for stationary boilers. It was obviously impossible to use a weighted lever on a locomotive, owing to the vibration when running; and the natural thing to do, was to substitute a spring for the weight. The great defect in the earlier type of spring-balance valves was too much leverage; the distance between fulcrum and valve, and valve and spring, was far too great, and the valve could only lift the weeniest amount. To overcome the leverage, a large valve and a weak spring were necessary; and the valve, once it opened, remained open until the pressure had dropped a fair amount below the normal working pressure. This "dribbling" annoyed the old-time engine drivers so much that they got up to all sorts of antics to prevent it, most of which considerably increased the working pressure; and as there were no high-pressure boilers in those days, there were a few boiler casualties, more or less serious. It was these circumstances which led to the introduction of the "lock-up" valve, which consisted of a direct spring-loaded valve, in a casing which usually resembled a cross between a Victorian mantleshelf ornament and a tea urn; and it was so arranged that the drivers could not interfere with it.

It was Stroudley who discarded the long-leverage valve, and substituted the short one with success. When he came from the Highland Railway to Brighton, he tried a type of valve known as the Adams' patent safety valve on the boiler barrels of his first tender engines. They proved unreliable, and would allow pressure to rise above the working limit, when they suddenly blew off like a modern pop safety valve; but unlike the latter, they had a trick of sticking open. He therefore designed a spring-balance valve with short leverage, which was so successful that his successor, R. J. Billinton, continued to fit the same type until the middle of 1901. I remember when one of the "nobody's darlings" (radial tanks) appeared with no balances, but a pair of Ashton pop safety valves over the firebox. The next one had a pair of Brighton-made direct-acting spring valves in brass columns, also over the firebox; and that type became standard from then onwards. However, the old spring-balance already in existence gave excellent service for a good many years after that; and it is this type which I am specifying for *Tich*.

The Action of the Valve

The rawest of tyros will understand the action, from the illustration of the complete assembly. The wing valve, which is countersunk, is held down by a "depressor" pinned to the lever. The latter is pivoted to a fork screwed into the dome, and the outer end is held down by a variation of the well-known

The spring-balance type safety-valve.

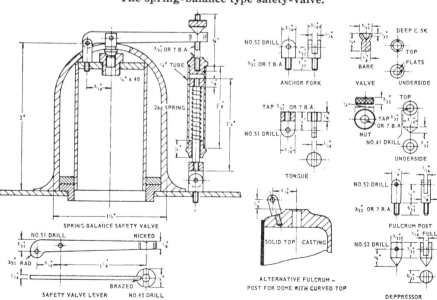

Salter weighing balance. In the present case, this is a long thin cylinder made of tube, with covers, pistons and rod complete; and a spiral spring is wound around the piston rod, pressing against the piston and the bottom cover. The top cover has a rod screwed into it, and this passes through an eye in the end of the lever; the pull on the lever can be adjusted by means of a knurled nut bearing on a wedge-shaped washer. The piston rod passes through the bottom cover and terminates in a tongue which is pinned to a fork screwed into the boiler. Pressure accumulating under the valve tries to force the lever upward; but the pressure of the spring on the bottom cover holds the lever down via the tube cylinder and the upper spindle. When there is enough force at the end of the lever, to overcome the spring, the lever lifts, and the steam escapes from the valve. The short amount of leverage, a little over $3\frac{1}{2}$ to 1, allows a spring of sufficient flexibility to ensure a quick release of excess pressure, and a quick shut-down as soon as the pressure falls; it also admits of a smaller valve, with greater lift, than was possible with the old long-leverage valves.

How to Make the Parts

When describing the dome tops, I mentioned that the holes in the cast one, or a solid top for a tube one, were drilled No. 34, reamed $\frac{1}{8}$ in. and slightly countersunk with a centre drill. The separate seating shown in the complete assembly is drilled and reamed likewise; it is made exactly like a cylinder gland, from $\frac{5}{16}$ in. hexagon rod, so needs no repetition. The valve is made from a piece of $\frac{5}{32}$ in. round bronze rod held in three-jaw. First turn down $\frac{1}{8}$ in. length to an easy sliding fit in the $\frac{1}{8}$ in. hole mentioned above; then turn the coned part to match the valve seat. The cone on the valve, and the coned seating, must, of course, be turned to the same angle, and it is quite possible for you to set a tool to do this, by chucking the centre-drill in the three-jaw and adjusting the tool so that its edge touches the cone on the centre-drill. If you have a four-way toolholder—which should be a standard fitting on all home-workshop lathes—set the chamfering tool in it, to the centre-drill, before starting the valve; then you only have to swing the tool-holder around to the correct station for forming the cone, after turning the shank with a knife-tool. If your toolholder is of the one-at-a-time variety, set a tool and use it both to turn the shank and form the coned part. The tool must be set in sufficiently to form a little undercut, otherwise the valve will always be leaky. When turning the valve, use a spot of cutting oil, it helps a lot to get a nice surface on hard bronze. Tip: if the tool chatters when forming the cone—as it will, if the lathe is at all flimsy—pull the belt by hand and feed very gently until the chatter marks disappear.

Next, with a file having a safe edge (one edge with no teeth cut on it) file a flat on the shank, opposite each jaw of the chuck. Don't file enough away so that the end looks like a triangle with three sharp points, leave a little bit of "round" between each flat. Then part off at $\frac{1}{4}$ in. from the end, reverse in chuck, gripping by the shank end—very important this—letting the chuck jaws bear on the bits of "round" between the flats; otherwise the valve won't run truly. Centre lightly, and then form the countersink with an arrow-head drill. The exact angle doesn't matter; and if you haven't an arrow-head drill, you can make one in a few minutes. Turn the end of a bit of $\frac{5}{32}$ in. round silver-steel to a cone point, about 60 deg. angle; file it flat on both sides, back off the edges, and harden and temper, same as I described for D-bits. This is also useful for centring, where the little hole formed by an ordinary centre-drill is not required.

Hold the shank in the bench vice, using two bits of sheet copper or brass as clams to stop the vice jaws from marking the shank. With a fine hacksaw, or a jeweller's saw, cut a nick across the countersink, but don't go deep enough to cut into the coned part. This is to take a screwdriver for grinding-in purposes, and the valve can be ground in right away. Beginners who own cars and do their own decarbonising and valve grinding won't find this quite as arduous! A weeny taste of pumice powder and water, or a scraping off your oilstone, on the valve seating, will do the trick. It only needs a very few twiddles with a screwdriver to get a perfect seating; but be mighty careful to wash away all traces of the abrasive with a spot of paraffin.

Lever and Accessories

The lever is filed up from a $1\frac{1}{2}$ in. length of $\frac{1}{4}$ in. by $\frac{1}{16}$ in. flat steel. Rustless steel could be used here with advantage, as the lever gets plenty wet, through steam blowing past it. My boilers have a reputation for blowing-off; thank goodness it isn't for blowing-up! Nickel bronze (German silver) could also be used, but ordinary mild steel will do, if nothing better is available. The eye is separate, and brazed on. Chuck a bit of $\frac{1}{4}$ in. round rod in three-jaw, same material as lever, face, centre, drill No. 40 for about $\frac{3}{16}$ in. depth, and part off a $\frac{1}{8}$ in. slice. File, mill or plane a $\frac{1}{16}$ in. nick in the edge; press the end of the lever in it and braze or silver-solder the joint, as described for other similar jobs. After cleaning up the lever, file a nick across the top of the eye, as shown, for the edge of the wedge washer to rest in. The angle needs to be fairly wide, so use a small square file. Drill the fulcrum pinhole only.

The fulcrum post is turned out of a bit of $\frac{1}{8}$ in. square steel; and in making it, beginners can put their acquired knowledge to use, as the drilling, slotting, etc., are the same as described for valve gear forks. After parting off, reverse in chuck, turn down $\frac{5}{32}$ in. of the end to $\frac{3}{32}$ in. diameter, and screw $\frac{3}{32}$ in. or 7 BA. An alternative fulcrum post for a cast inner dome, or a built-up one with rounded top, is also shown, and is self-explanatory.

The little slotted and pointed gadget which holds down the valve is made from a bit of $\frac{5}{32}$ in. round steel, rustless if possible. Cross-drill and slot the end, same as the fulcrum post; part off to full length, reverse in chuck, and turn a cone point on the end to a slightly sharper taper than the countersink in the valve. Note that from centre of pinhole to the point is $\frac{1}{4}$ in. Did I bless these finicky little jobs when making the twin valves for *Grosvenor*! Yet some folk delight in them.

Pin the tail of the lever in the slot in the fulcrum post with a bit of $\frac{1}{16}$ in. wire. At $\frac{5}{16}$ in. ahead of the centre of the valve hole in the dome, drill a No. 48 hole and tap it to suit the screw on the post. Screw in the post, with a taste of plumbers' jointing on the threads, and be careful to avoid bending the lever. When the post is screwed right home the lever should lie right across the centre of the valve. Hold the depressing gadget vertically, with the point in the countersink in the valve, and drop the lever into the slot. Set it so that the top is horizontal, then put the No. 52 drill in the hole in the depressor and make a countersink on the lever. Drill this No. 51, and pin the gadget to the lever. This joint should not be too free; but the fulcrum joint should be quite easy. When pinning these little joints, I cut a bit of wire about twice the length required and ease one end with a fine file, with the wire in three-jaw, and lathe running fast. This is easily passed through the drive-fit holes in the forks; it is then squeezed home with a pair of pliers until tight in the forks, and the surplus cut off. Don't forget a spot of oil.

Spring Balance

The casing of the spring balance may either be a piece of $\frac{1}{4}$ in. thin brass tube, squared off to $1\frac{1}{8}$ in. length, or a piece of $\frac{1}{4}$ in. brass rod of same length, drilled right through with $\frac{13}{64}$ in. drill. Both ends are turned from $\frac{5}{16}$ in. brass rod. Chuck in three-jaw, face, centre, and drill down about $\frac{5}{16}$ in. with No. 41 drill. Turn $\frac{1}{8}$ in. of the outside to a press fit in the case. To do this, take a weeny scrape out of the end of the tube with a taper broach, then turn the rod so that it will just start entering if the sharp edge is taken off. The rest will then require a good squeeze to get it home, which is as it should be. Part off at $\frac{1}{4}$ in. from the end, reverse in chuck, and turn the outside to the shape shown, or as near as you can get it. For the upper plug or cover, repeat the turning part, but don't drill. Part off at $\frac{1}{4}$ in. from the end, as before, then reverse in chuck and turn the outside; after which, centre, drill No. 48 for $\frac{3}{16}$ in. depth, and tap $\frac{3}{32}$ in. or 7 BA. This end can be pressed into the case and a $\frac{3}{4}$ in. length of $\frac{3}{32}$ in. rod, threaded as shown, screwed into it.

The piston rod is a $1\frac{1}{4}$ in. length of $\frac{3}{32}$ in. rod with $\frac{1}{8}$ in. of thread on each end. Screw a $\frac{1}{8}$ in. slice of $\frac{1}{4}$ in. rod on one end, chuck in three-jaw, and turn down to an easy sliding fit in the case. Wind up a spring from 26 gauge tinned steel, or hard brass or bronze wire, around a $\frac{3}{32}$ in. mandrel; slip it over the piston rod, place in the case, and press in the bottom cover. The spring should just start to compress as the cover enters. Chuck a piece of $\frac{3}{16}$ in. rod, face the end, centre, drill down $\frac{1}{8}$ in. with No. 48 drill, and tap to match the screwed end of piston rod. Part off at $\frac{11}{32}$ in. from the end; screw this on to the end of the piston rod, file flat each side to form a $\frac{1}{16}$ in. tongue, round off, and drill No. 51. The anchor fork, into which the tongue fits, is made in the same way as the fulcrum post, only $\frac{3}{16}$ in. square rod is used instead of $\frac{1}{8}$ in.

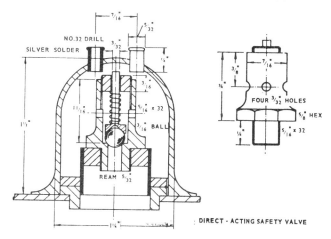

DIRECT - ACTING SAFETY VALVE

For the nut, chuck the $\frac{1}{4}$ in. rod again; face, centre, and drill No. 48 for about $\frac{5}{32}$ in. depth. At $\frac{3}{32}$ in. from the end, run a parting tool in about $\frac{1}{32}$ in. forming a groove. Between the groove and the end, knurl the rod by holding a flat second-cut file hard down on it, whilst pulling the lathe belt back and forth by hand. I find this method gives a better knurl than the regulation little wheel in the holder. Part off, and tap the nut $\frac{3}{32}$ in. or 7 BA to match the spindle on top of the case. The wedge washer is merely an ordinary washer $\frac{3}{32}$ in. thick, filed away at each side to form a very blunt wedge, as shown in the illustration.

How to Assemble

At $1\frac{1}{8}$ in. from the centre of the dome, on top centre-line of the boiler, drill a No. 48 hole, tap $\frac{3}{32}$ in. or 7 BA to suit the anchor fork, and screw same in, with the slot parallel to centre-line of boiler. It may be sweated also, like a stayhead. Put the spindle on top of the balance casing through the hole in the eye of the lever and put on the wedge washer and nut, the ridge of the washer sitting in the nick in the eye. Put the tongue of the piston rod in the slot in the anchor fork, secure it with a pin, and you're through. If desired, one side of the hole through the anchor fork can be tapped $\frac{1}{16}$ in. or 10 BA, the other drilled No. 51, and a screw used instead of a pin, for securing the tongue to the fork. Adjustment of blowing-off pressure is made by screwing the knurled nut up or down the spindle, as required.

Direct-acting Safety Valve

This is a simple job, with no finicky parts attached to it. The body of the valve is made either from a casting, or from $\frac{5}{8}$ in. hexagon-bronze or gunmetal rod. For the latter, chuck the rod in three-jaw, and turn down $\frac{1}{4}$ in. of the end to $\frac{5}{16}$ in. diameter; screw $\frac{5}{16}$ in. by 32. Face the end truly, and part off at $\frac{3}{4}$ in. from the shoulder. Reverse, and rechuck in a tapped bush held in three-jaw. If a casting is used, chuck by the larger end, and machine the screwed end same way. Then for either kind, centre the end, drill right through with No. 24 drill, open out to about $\frac{1}{2}$ in. depth with $\frac{9}{32}$ in. drill, and bottom to $\frac{11}{16}$ in. depth with a D-bit same size. Tap $\frac{5}{16}$ in. by 32 for about $\frac{5}{16}$ in. down, and put a $\frac{5}{32}$ in. parallel reamer through the remains of the little hole at the bottom. Turn down the outside to $\frac{7}{16}$ in. diameter, just far enough to leave about $\frac{5}{32}$ in. of hexagon next to the screw, so that a spanner can be used for tightening up when screwing the valve into the squat dome. At $\frac{3}{8}$ in. from the top, drill four $\frac{3}{32}$ in. or No. 40 holes through the sides, to let the steam out into the dome casing, from whence it will escape through the tubes at the top.

For the nipple, chuck a piece of $\frac{5}{16}$ in. round rod in three-jaw, face the end, centre, and drill No. 40 for $\frac{1}{4}$ in. depth. Screw $\frac{1}{4}$ in. of the outside $\frac{5}{16}$ in. by 32 and part off a $\frac{3}{16}$ in. slice. Make a hacksaw cut across one end, like the slot in a cheesehead screw, so that a notched screwdriver may be used to turn the nipple when setting the valve to blow off at correct pressure. To make the plunger, chuck a bit of $\frac{1}{4}$ in. round rod in three-jaw and turn $\frac{9}{16}$ in. length to $\frac{3}{32}$ in. diameter; take two or three fine cuts at high speed when finishing to size. Part off at $\frac{11}{16}$ in. from the end. Reverse in chuck, take a skim off the boss, to bring it to $\frac{7}{32}$ in. diameter, then centre it, and countersink it as shown. If you have any centre-drills with the tips broken off, they do very well for jobs like this; otherwise, an arrow-head drill can be made, as described for the spring-balance valve, with a rather more obtuse angle than an ordinary drill. However, an ordinary $\frac{3}{16}$ in. drill will do the trick if a proper countersink isn't available, but don't go too deep.

To assemble the valve, simply seat a $\frac{3}{16}$ in. rustless steel ball on the hole, same as when making the pump valves, put a 22 gauge spring (wound up from tinned steel wire around a $\frac{3}{32}$ in. mandrel) on the spindle, and place on the ball as shown; then screw in the nipple. The ends of the spring should be touched on a fast-running emery wheel, to square off the ends, otherwise the valve will have a tendency to dribble; if the spring doesn't press the cup down "fair and square", the ball doesn't seat properly.

Dome Covers

Both larger and smaller dome covers can be machined same way. All I do, is to hold the bodies in three-jaw, flange outwards, and bore just like boring a cylinder, until they are a tight push fit on the dome bush. The bore extends the full length of the parallel part. A bit of hard wood is then turned to a tight fit in the bore, driven in, chucked in three-jaw, and casting set to run truly. The big dome can be centre-drilled at the top, when running truly, with a centre-drill in the tailstock chuck, and the tailstock centre used to support the casting whilst turning the outside. I rough-turn mine with a round-nose tool in the slide-rest and finish off the round part with a hand graver utilised for finishing the smokebox door. The bottom part of the flange, which cannot be turned, is finished off with a half-round file and emery cloth, whilst the job is still in the chuck.

If there is any roughness on the curved base which sits on the boiler, clean off with a half-round file. To finish the saddling, get something which is round, and of the same diameter as the boiler; wood, metal, or even a bottle would do, if truly circular. Lay a piece of emery cloth over it and rub the base of the dome on same, pressing well down; this will soon form a curved seating, true enough to suit our requirements. I have described several ways of machining these seatings, by milling, flycutting, and so on, any of which would form a seating that would earn the approval of Inspector Meticulous; but they are not essential for the job in hand.

Drill a $\frac{3}{8}$ in. hole in the top of the larger dome; then, with a round file, slot this out sufficiently to clear the fulcrum post. To put the dome in place, take a knurled nut and washer off the spring-balance spindle and turn the lever up vertically; the dome can easily be slipped over the lot and the lever replaced in its correct position.

Dummy Valves

The smaller dome needs adorning with a couple of dummy Drummond-type safety valves, which aren't exactly 100 per cent dummy, as they actually let the surplus steam out. Drill two $\frac{5}{32}$ in. holes in the dome casing at $\frac{7}{16}$ in. centres, as shown. Note—these holes are not at right-angles to the surface of the dome, but vertical; beginners may find it easier to drill $\frac{9}{64}$ in. or No. 24 holes straight in and then hand-ream them with a $\frac{5}{32}$ in. reamer, holding same vertical when turning it with a tap wrench. The two little columns are turned from $\frac{5}{16}$ in. rod; after the experience you have now had in turning, this should be just a kiddy's practice job needing no detailing. Make them a tight squeeze fit in the holes in the dome and they will "stay put" without further fixing. If they are at all slack, silver-solder them. Alternatively, the holes in the dome could be tapped $\frac{5}{32}$ in. by 40 (using No. 30 drill) and the lower part of the pillars threaded to suit, and screwed in.

Backhead Fittings

The next stage is making fittings for the backheads, and here you see the two of them, for large and smaller boilers, all-present-and-correct-sergeant. One thing I love to see on any locomotive, big or little, is a neat arrangement of the backhead adornments. In days gone by, when I visited exhibitions (the last I attended was in 1935) the fittings I saw on the footplates of even the prize winners, gave me the proverbial pain in the neck. Huge great square-bodied water gauges, with ridiculously small passages through them, and "taps" that either stuck or leaked; check valves or clacks with equally un-sightly bodies; massive wheel valves, with just the same bodies; there must have been a mania for using square rod in those days; whacking great unions, enormous regulator handles with unsightly stops at each end of a quadrant like the top of a tunnel, all mounted as though any place where they could be squeezed in would do. There was no need for it, because for years I had been describing how to make small, neat and efficient fittings; but tradition dies hard, for the same kind of fittings are being made commercially at the present time. Castings are available for water gauge fittings, valve bodies, and so on; they may be used if desired. Otherwise make the fittings from rod material, turning, drilling and screwing as indicated, and silver-soldering the joints, same as I usually make them.

Different Whistle Valves

Apart from the regulator gland, which I have already described, the only other variation between layouts on the larger and smaller boilers is in the combined steam turret (or fountain) and the whistle valve. I have shown a vertical one on the smaller boiler and a horizontal one on the larger boiler; in the latter case, the whistle valve handle would be too close to the cab roof if a vertical fitting were used. If anybody fancies the horizontal type on the smaller boiler, why, just go right ahead and fit it. Apart from the way steam gets into the valve there is no fundamental difference in the two fittings. Steam and water gauges and firehole door, are the same for both boilers; so is the blower valve, which I have already described, as it forms one fixing for the hollow stay. On the larger boiler I have shown the pipe, which leads down to the whistle, curved to dodge the cab window, as the driver stands on that side, and the window is smaller than on the engine with a smaller boiler. "Variety is the spice of life!" The drawings of the two backheads show clearly the arrangement of the fittings, without any detailed explanation being needed, so all we have to do is to make and erect them as shown.

Water Gauge

First of all, I must call attention to one particular point. The face of the socket into which the fitting of the water gauge is screwed, and the bush in the backhead which receives the bottom fitting, are not in the same plane. The socket is level with the wrapper sheet, whilst the bush sticks out beyond the backhead. This is shown in the side view of the gauge. Therefore, the lengths of the top and bottom fittings have to be made to suit; the top one will be longer than the bottom, in order to get the parts which carry the glass tube into a straight line. It isn't any use my giving a definite measurement for this, because it may vary, according to the degree of workmanship in different boilers; some may have the backhead projecting more than others, and some bushes may have a thicker flange. Well, all you have to do, is to put your steel rule edge-wise across the bush, with the upper part passing across the face of the socket, and measure the gap between the socket and rule. Simple, sure-lie, as they say down Sussex way. Add this to $\frac{1}{4}$ in. and you get the length of the top fitting between shoulders.

If you can get gunmetal or bronze rod for the fittings, use it; if not, brass will do, as there is no movement and no wear. Chuck a piece of $\frac{1}{4}$ in. round rod in the three-jaw, face the end, centre, and drill $\frac{5}{8}$ in. deep with No. 21 drill.

Screw the end $\frac{1}{4}$ in. by 40 for about $\frac{1}{8}$ in. length, with a die in the tailstock holder, and part off at $\frac{9}{16}$ in. from the end. Reverse in chuck, tap the other end $\frac{3}{16}$ in. by 40 for about $\frac{3}{16}$ in. down; slightly countersink the end and skim off any burr. At $\frac{1}{4}$ in. from the tapped end, make a centre-pop—be careful how you hit the punch, or the fitting will be distorted—and drill it $\frac{5}{32}$ in. or No. 21.

Chuck a piece of $\frac{5}{16}$ in. round rod in three-jaw; face the end, centre, and drill to about $\frac{3}{4}$ in. depth with No. 40 drill. Turn down $\frac{3}{16}$ in. of the end to $\frac{7}{32}$ in. diameter and screw $\frac{7}{32}$ in. by 40. Part off at a full $\frac{1}{2}$ in. from the shoulder. Reverse and rechuck in a tapped bush. For this, chuck any odd bit of rod $\frac{5}{16}$ in. diameter or larger. Face the end, centre, and if a short bit ($\frac{1}{2}$ in. length is ample), drill right through with $\frac{3}{16}$ in. or No. 12 drill, tap $\frac{7}{32}$ in. by 40, countersink the end and skim off any burr. Make a dot on it opposite No. 1 jaw, so that when removed from the chuck, it may be replaced again in same position. Screw the fitting into the bush and turn down enough of the outside, to $\frac{1}{4}$ in. diameter, to leave a flange $\frac{3}{32}$ in. thick. Then further turn down the end to a tight fit in the hole in the side of the piece that holds the glass. Don't forget that the length between the face of the shoulder at the screwed end, and that on the smaller end, must be $\frac{1}{4}$ in. plus the distance marked "A" in the side view. When you have got that right, face off the surplus, to leave the spigot $\frac{1}{16}$ in. long. This is then pressed into the hole in the side of the piece made previously. Put it aside until the bottom fitting is made, so that you can silver-solder them both at the same heat.

For the bottom fitting, chuck the $\frac{5}{16}$ in. rod again; face, centre, and drill down to $\frac{5}{8}$ in. depth with No. 40 drill. Turn down $\frac{3}{16}$ in. of the end to $\frac{7}{32}$ in. diameter as before, and screw $\frac{7}{32}$ in. by 40. Part off at a full $\frac{7}{8}$ in. from the shoulder. Put your tapped bush in the chuck again, and screw the fitting into it. If you have replaced the bush correctly, the fitting will run truly. Centre the end, and drill No. 48 until the drill breaks into the No. 40 hole drilled from the other end. Open out to $\frac{1}{4}$ in. depth with No. 30 drill, and bottom the hole to $\frac{5}{16}$ in. depth with $\frac{1}{8}$ in. D-bit. Tap $\frac{5}{32}$ in. by 32 or 40, and be careful not to let the tap scrape the seating.

If you have the coarser thread, use it, as the valve is quicker-acting. Slightly chamfer the end of the fitting for sake of appearance.

Be careful over the next bit. At $\frac{3}{8}$ in. from the shoulder, make a centre-pop; at $\frac{1}{4}$ in. from the tapped end, exactly opposite to the first, make another. The easiest way to get them directly opposite is to mark the spots before taking the fitting out of the tapped bush. Make one mark opposite a chuck jaw set vertically, at its highest point; then turn the lathe mandrel half-a-turn, so that the chuck jaw is vertical again, but at its lowest point. If the second mark is now made on top of the fitting, it must of necessity be opposite to the first one. Centre-pop both marks and drill them $\frac{5}{32}$ in. or 21, letting the drill pierce the centre passages.

By this time you know how to make union screws, having made them for the mechanical lubricator, and so on; so fit one, made from $\frac{7}{32}$ in. round rod, and screwed $\frac{7}{32}$ in. by 40, into the hole in the tapped end of the fitting; see sectional illustration. In the other hole a very similar nipple is fitted, to carry the bottom end of the glass. Chuck the $\frac{1}{4}$ in. rod in three-jaw; face the end, centre, and drill No. 40 for about $\frac{5}{16}$ in. depth. Open out with No. 21 drill for $\frac{3}{32}$ in. depth. Screw $\frac{1}{8}$ in. of the outside with $\frac{1}{4}$ in. by 40 die and part off at $\frac{7}{32}$ in. from the end. Reverse in chuck, and grip by the threaded part, which will be all right as long as you don't tighten the chuck sufficiently to damage the threads; then turn down $\frac{1}{16}$ in. of the end to a tight fit in the hole nearest the screwed end, and squeeze it in.

The joints in both fittings can then be silver-soldered; simply apply wet flux, heat to medium red, touch the joints with a thin strip of silver-solder, of best grade, let cool to black, pickle, wash off and clean up. I always use "Easyflo", and the special flux sold for use with it, on jobs like these. To clean up, I just hold the piece against the tip of a small revolving wire brush, mounted on a spindle which is stuck into a taper hole in the shaft of my electric grinder. As the grinding spindle runs at near 3,000 r.p.m. it only needs a few seconds treatment to make the fittings bobby-dazzle, as the cleaner boys on the L.B. & S.C. Railway used to say. Alas, both boys and railway are now just a legend; I knew a few who would have made the full-sized *Britannia* resplendent in a way that even Mr. Riddles would never have imagined! They just couldn't have resisted turning that shapely little chimney into a gleaming silver ornament, for a start; and no signalman would ever have had any excuse for not seeing the numbers on the smokebox door. Those were the days!

Valve and Gland Nuts

The valve pin can be made from $\frac{3}{32}$ in. rustless steel, or nickel or phosphor-bronze. Chuck in three-jaw, and turn $\frac{5}{32}$ in. length to $\frac{1}{8}$ in. diameter; form a cone point on the end, by the method described for the depressor pin of the spring-balance safety valve. Screw the next $\frac{1}{4}$ in. length $\frac{5}{32}$ in. by 32 or 40 to match the tapped hole in the fitting, and part off at $\frac{7}{16}$ in. from the shoulder. Drill a No. 53 cross hole in the end and squeeze in a piece of $\frac{1}{16}$ in. steel, rustless for preference. The end of the valve pin should be chamfered, and the ends of the cross pin rounded off, to save any risk of skinned fingers.

For the nuts, chuck a piece of $\frac{5}{16}$ in. hexagon rod in three-jaw; face, centre, drill down with No. 21 drill for about $\frac{5}{8}$ in. depth (this is enough for the two) open out to $\frac{5}{32}$ in. depth with $\frac{7}{32}$ in. or No. 3 drill, tap $\frac{1}{4}$ in. by 40, and part off a full $\frac{7}{32}$ in. from the end. Chamfer the corners of the hexagon at both ends. The plug for the top fitting is made from $\frac{1}{4}$ in. hexagon rod. Face off, turn down $\frac{1}{8}$ in. length to $\frac{3}{16}$ in. diameter, screw $\frac{3}{16}$ in. by 40, part off at $\frac{1}{4}$ in. from the end, reverse in chuck and chamfer the hexagon.

How to Erect the Gauge

Smear the threads with plumbers' jointing, and screw the top part into the socket, and the bottom into the bush. Line them up with a $\frac{5}{32}$ in. drill, or a

Plate 25

Raising steam on K. S. Entwhistle's "Tich"
Below: LBSC's "engine-shed" below the stairs. In the foreground is "Mabel", his
L.N.W.R. 2-4-0

Plate 26

A small-boilered "Tich" with Walschaerts valve gear built by Mr. W. Ducklin

Close-up view of part of the Walschaerts valve gear on Mr. Ducklin's engine

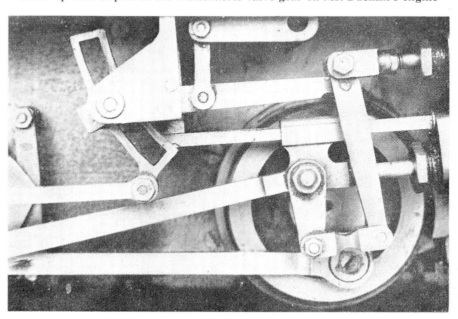

piece of $\frac{5}{32}$ in. silver-steel (which is usually straight) so that when the drill or rod is inserted through the top fitting, it drops easily into the recess in the bottom one. If they won't line up without risk of stripping the threads, either file a weeny shade off the bush and socket faces, or use one or two shim washers made from copper or brass foil. Cut a piece of glass tube $\frac{5}{32}$ in. diameter, by nicking it with a three-cornered or half-round file and snapping off, to such a length that when dropped in place, it rests in the bottom recess, and comes almost up to the hole in the top fitting, as shown in the section.

I use rubber rings for packing, putting a piece of rubber tube about $\frac{3}{4}$ in. long on a short bit of $\frac{5}{32}$ in. rod, and holding same in three-jaw. The lathe is then run at high speed and a piece of fine glass paper held against the rubber tube until it is reduced sufficiently to enter the gland nuts. A wetted safety-razor blade is then applied to the tube at $\frac{3}{32}$ in. intervals. When you push the tube off the rod it falls into rings. Wet the glass tube, push it through the top fitting, put on a wet ring, then the two nuts back to back, then another wet ring. Let the tube drop into the recess, slide the bottom ring down and screw the nut over it. Push the upper ring as high as it will go and screw the other nut over that. The nuts want to be only just a little more than finger-tight, otherwise the glass may break through not being able to expand. Finally, screw the plug in the top, with a smear of plumbers' jointing on the threads—don't get any into the glass tube, on any account—and Bob's your uncle as far as the water gauge is concerned. Tip—if the glass is too tight in the fittings when you first try it in place, either poke a $\frac{5}{32}$ in. reamer down, right into the recess, or put a size larger drill in, say, No. 20. Glass tube is decidedly not made to "mike" measurements, and some kinds are larger than others, although nominally the same size; and sometimes it is a wee bit oval. It must not be tight, either in the fittings or the nuts, or breakages will be frequent; whereas a properly-fitted glass will last for years.

Boiler Fittings

The next item to be made is the combined whistle valve and turret, or steam fountain. When drawing and describing this, I often recall, with a smile, the tiny alleged whistle on my five-shilling tin Ajax of over three-score years ago. It looked like a split marble, perched on a small plug cock with a long wide handle bent over at the end. As the sound produced was only a good imitation of a rat with its tail caught in a trap, it was useless for whistling purposes, but was handy for trying if steam was up. Glorified editions with a bell top are still sold commercially; in fact, I have some specimens here now, which I keep as curiosities, remembrances of the old Aldgate firm of "Model Dockyard" fame. Apparently nobody thought of hiding a big whistle underneath the engine!

For making the vertical turret, chuck a piece of $\frac{5}{16}$ in. round rod, face the end truly, and part off a piece a full $\frac{7}{8}$ in. long. Chuck with the parted end outwards; centre, and drill right through with No. 44 drill. Open out to about

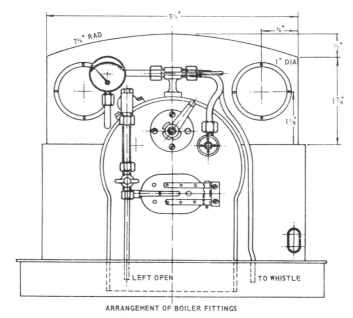

ARRANGEMENT OF BOILER FITTINGS

This drawing shows the layout in the cab on the large engine.

$\frac{1}{4}$ in. depth with $\frac{3}{16}$ in. drill and bottom the hole to $\frac{3}{8}$ in. depth with $\frac{3}{16}$ in. D-bit, similar to the way in which you formed the ball seats in the pumps. Slightly countersink the end and tap it $\frac{7}{32}$ in. by 40 for about halfway down. Take a slight skim off the end to true it up. Then reverse in chuck, and repeat operations, except that the D-bit is not needed; just put the $\frac{3}{16}$ in. drill in to the full $\frac{3}{8}$ in. depth. Next, at $\frac{3}{16}$ in. from the D-bitted end, make a centre-pop. At $\frac{7}{16}$ in. farther along—that is, at $\frac{1}{4}$ in. from the other end, make another one, in line with it. Using $\frac{5}{32}$ in. or No. 22 drill, drill clean through the piece of rod at the first centre-pop; but only drill the second one until the drill breaks through into the centre hole. File or scrape off any burring; then fit a union screw or nipple into each hole. These are made as previously described for mechanical lubricator and other fittings, so repetition is unnecessary. The two opposite nipples at the bottom of the fitting, are screwed $\frac{1}{4}$ in. by 40, and the upper one $\frac{7}{32}$ in. by 40. The spigots should, of course, be a tight fit in the holes in the body of the fitting; they are drilled No. 40.

Silver-solder them in, same as the water gauge parts; wash off and clean up. Then put a $\frac{3}{32}$ in. parallel reamer through the remains of the No. 44 hole in the middle. If you haven't one, file off the end of a couple of inches of $\frac{3}{32}$ in. silver-steel on the slant, so that it looks like a long oval. Harden and temper, in the same way that I described for D-bits, pin drills and so on; rub the oval end on your oilstone until the edges of the oval are sharp, and you now have a serviceable reamer, which will do the trick as well as one purchased in the tool store at an outrageous price, which, incidentally, is no fault of the unfortunate tool merchant. He had to buy it first! Don't put the reamer through by hand; chuck the body, and put the reamer in the tailstock chuck.

To make the bottom plug, chuck a piece of $\frac{5}{16}$ in. hexagon rod in the three-jaw. Turn down $\frac{3}{16}$ in. of the end to $\frac{3}{16}$ in. diameter and screw $\frac{3}{16}$ in. by 40. Face the end off truly. Part off at $\frac{1}{4}$ in. from the shoulder. Reverse in chuck, holding, either in a tapped bush or by the hexagon, whichever you like. Turn down $\frac{1}{8}$ in. of the end to $\frac{7}{32}$ in. diameter and screw $\frac{7}{32}$ in. by 40. Tip: I've mentioned this before, but it will bear repeating. If your die is what the kiddies call "a bit wonky", and is inclined to tear the first thread or two when starting a cut, turn the job over-length, for a kick-off. Then when the screwing is completed, you can face off the damaged threads until the screwed part is of the desired length, with a good thread all the way.

Centre, and drill right through with No. 40 drill; then open out to a bare $\frac{1}{4}$ in. depth with No. 24 drill, and chamfer the corners of the hexagon. Seat a $\frac{1}{8}$ in. rustless steel ball on the D-bitted end of the $\frac{3}{32}$ in. reamed hole, same as described for pumps. Wind up a spring from 24 or 26 gauge bronze or hard brass wire, on a No. 48 drill shank, if you like, or around a bit of 14 gauge spoke wire; the spring should be an easy sliding fit in the socket. File both ends of the spring off square and assemble as shown in the sectional illustration. The spring should just start to compress as the threads engage, and a smear of plumbers' jointing on the last couple of threads nearest the shoulder, will render it steamtight.

To allow steam to pass to the whistle, the ball is pushed off its seating by a little plunger operated by a handle, as shown in the drawing. Chuck a piece of $\frac{3}{8}$ in. hexagon rod in three-jaw; face the end, centre, and drill down a bare $\frac{1}{2}$ in. with No. 48 drill. Turn down $\frac{3}{16}$ in. of the end to $\frac{7}{32}$ in. diameter and screw $\frac{7}{32}$ in. by 40; part off at a full $\frac{7}{32}$ in. from the shoulder. Cut a $\frac{1}{16}$ in. slot $\frac{5}{32}$ in. deep, right across two of the flats; this may be milled by any of the methods already given, or cut on a planer or shaper with a $\frac{1}{16}$ in. parting tool in the clapper box. It can also be cut by hand; an Eclipse 4S tool is the boy for this job, with a $\frac{1}{16}$ in. slotting blade in it, or you can make a slot with two hacksaw blades side by side in the frame, and finish with a thin flat file. Many routes lead to the same destination! File off the two corners of the hexagon opposite the slot, so as to leave the end oblong, as shown in the view of the cab fittings.

The lever is made from $\frac{3}{16}$ in. round rod. Nickel-bronze (German silver) is the best for this, as far as appearance goes, but other non-rusting metals will serve. A bit about $1\frac{1}{8}$ in. long is needed; chuck in three-jaw, and turn the grip to size and shape shown. The rest is filed flat, to fit easily in the groove in the end cap. Note the way the end is filed (like the ends of the arms in the old L.B. & S.C.R. slotted-post signals) the idea being that this catches on the bottom of the groove or slot, and prevents the lever flying right back and letting the pin come out. Two or three of the "foreigners" who have run on my road have lost their whistle plunger pins for lack of this precaution.

The pin is just a short length of 15 gauge bronze or hard brass rod, the length being obtained from the actual job. It should stand up above the bottom of the groove, about $\frac{1}{32}$ in. or so. Drill a weeny hole (I use 57 drill) across one corner of the plug, put the lever in place with the tail just clearing the groove, and the side of the flat part touching the plunger. Make a mark on the lever by putting the drill through the corner hole. Remove lever, drill the mark one size larger, replace lever and pin it with a piece of wire; I use a piece of domestic blanket pin, which is a drive fit in a 57 hole, and a working fit in a 56. If the lever is depressed, the ball is forced off its seat, but will reseat again as soon as the lever is released. It does so with such alacrity, that if you don't put the tail on the lever it will fly right back, and the plunger will promptly emulate a rocket on Guy Fawkes' night.

How to Erect

On top of the backhead, directly above the regulator rod, drill a $\frac{5}{32}$ in. hole in the wrapper, close to the edge, so that the hole goes through the backhead flange. Tap $\frac{3}{16}$ in. by 40, holding the tap vertical, and screw in the turret with a smear of plumbers' jointing on the threads. When tight, the handle should be square with the boiler and parallel to the backhead; ditto the three unions. Be careful not to strip the thread in an endeavour to get it around to correct position; if more than one-third of a turn is required, file the hole slightly flat (says Pat) on top of the wrapper. Incidentally, did you know that Pat's definition of nothing was a bunghole with no barrel around it?

The illustration of the backheads of both larger and smaller boilers given previously show clearly how the unions are connected up. It would be best to purchase the steam gauge from one of our approved advertisers. I have given instructions for making gauges, and many of the more experienced locomotive builders have made their own; but it is a ticklish job for a beginner, and anyway you would need a full-sized steam gauge to calibrate the little one—and thereby a tale hangs. In my early locomotive-building days, the fitter at the locomotive sheds, whose particular job was to attend to defective steam and air gauges on our engines, asked what was the relationship between the pressure indicated by the gauge on my little engine, to that on a full-sized one. I told him the little gauge showed absolute pressure, same as full-size; but he laughed derisively at the idea of 80 lb. per sq. in. in a boiler about 3 in. diameter. I said, "all right, Mr. Cleverdick, you borrow a full-size gauge and bring it around home; and I'll bet you what you like, that if it is connected up to my little boiler, it will show exactly the same pressure as the little one." He thought I was pulling his leg, but finally consented. When I got up steam, with the big gauge connected, and the hand on the big gauge began to walk around the scale, the look on his face was what the school kiddies called "worth a guinea a box"; and when the safety valve finally lifted with his gauge showing 85 lb. and mine 80 lb. only (it proved to be a wee bit "slow") he gave me best. However, I had to explain the difference between pressure and volume (something the "scale pressure" merchants haven't grasped, to this day!) before he could thoroughly understand how a given pressure was equal both in a weeny boiler and its full-sized relatives.

A piece of $\frac{1}{8}$ in. copper pipe is used to connect the gauge to the union on the turret, and this needs a U-shaped bend in it, which is known as a syphon, though it doesn't syphon anything, says Pat. After the first steam-up, the bend is full of condensate water, which remains in it and prevents hot steam getting to the gauge and affecting the accuracy of "the works". If the flattened C-shaped tube in the gauge becomes overheated, it loses some of its springiness, and will not return the gauge needle to what the kiddies call "freezo" when the boiler is cold; a very common fault with small steam gauges. Steam presses on one end of the water in the syphon and the water transfers the pressure to the C-tube, allowing same to remain cool. One end of the syphon pipe has a $\frac{1}{4}$ in. union nut and cone, made in the same way as those described for the mechanical lubricator oil pipe; this is connected to the left-hand union nipple in the turret. The purchased gauge will have what the catalogue calls a "nut and tail pipe" attached, the nut being just an ordinary union nut, usually 2 BA on most $\frac{3}{4}$ in. commercial gauges; the tail pipe is a bit of $\frac{3}{32}$ in. tube about $\frac{1}{4}$ in. long, with either a cone or flat collar on the end inside the nut. This is supposed to be attached to the end of the syphon pipe, but it looks rather botchy if attached thus, so I usually dispense altogether with the tail pipe, and connect the gauge directly to the syphon, in the following simple way.

Chuck the nut in the three-jaw and put a No. 30 drill through the hole where the tail pipe went through. File the end of the syphon pipe off square, poke it through the hole in the nut, and bell it out slightly by driving in something with a blunt taper end; the point of your punch will do the trick. Note—it only requires belling out enough to fit in the threaded part of the nut; if you overdo it, file off a little around the outside of the bell. Pull it down inside the nut, screw same on to the gauge, and Bob's your uncle once more. The belled-out part, being soft, will make a steamtight joint with the bottom of the gauge screw. Curiously enough, although I used the wheeze long before the invention of that wonderful machine which has been prostituted into the greatest curse of mankind, a similar difference being that the end of the screwed part is pointed, and fits the belled-out part of the pipe, the nut crushing the bell on to the cone.

The connection between the right-hand union and the blower valve is made in the same way as the oil pipe on the mechanical lubricator, except that the nuts and cones are made to suit the larger nipples; see illustrations of backheads.

Variation for Horizontal Turret

The only differences in the construction of the horizontal turret are that the end plug is solid, and a third connection is made between the two bottom union nipples for screwing into the boiler. Make the body part as described above, but in between the two bottom holes drill a third one at right-angles.

Chuck a bit of $\frac{5}{16}$ in. hexagon rod in three-jaw; face, centre, and drill down about $\frac{5}{8}$ in. depth with No. 40 drill. Turn down $\frac{3}{16}$ in. of the end to $\frac{3}{16}$ in. diameter and screw $\frac{3}{16}$ in. by 40. Part off at $\frac{3}{8}$ in. from the shoulder. Reverse in chuck holding in a tapped bush; turn down the outside to about $\frac{7}{32}$ in. diameter, leaving $\frac{1}{8}$ in. of the hexagon at the end nearest the screw, Turn down $\frac{1}{16}$ in. of the outer end to a tight fit in the third hole in the body of the fitting; press it in and silver-solder it at the same heat as the union nipples. The end plug is made as shown in the part section, which needs no description, as the end is machined exactly the same way as the larger end of the thoroughfare plug. The turret is screwed into a tapped hole on top of the wrapper and connected up, just the same as the vertical one.

Check Valves

Check valves or back-pressure valves, are usually known as clacks, or clack-boxes, from the noise they make when working. Two are required for *Tich*, to be fitted into the two bushes at the front end of the boiler barrel. To make them, beginners will be able to put their acquired knowledge and experience

Cab layout for the small engine, and details of the water gauge, turret and by-pass valve.

to practical use, for the complete operations have already been fully described; so now let's see what you can do if I give the sequence of those operations. Chuck a piece of $\frac{5}{16}$ in. round rod, face the end, turn and screw $\frac{1}{4}$ in. by 40— then drill for $\frac{1}{4}$ in. depth with No. 34 drill. Part off at $\frac{5}{8}$ in. from the end, reverse in chuck and open out, bottom and tap as described for whistle valve. Ream $\frac{1}{8}$ in., then drill a $\frac{5}{32}$ in. hole in the side, and make and fit a side connection, same as the bottom one in the horizontal turret, or the top fitting of the water gauge, silver-soldering it in.

After cleaning up, seat a $\frac{5}{32}$ in. rustless ball on the hole as shown, then turn and fit the top cap, taking depth of ball and allowing for $\frac{1}{32}$ in. lift, same as for the pumps. Make the cap from round stuff instead of hexagon, and part off $\frac{3}{16}$ in. from the shoulder; then chuck it in a tapped bush and file a $\frac{3}{16}$ in. square on the end, by the same process described for the squares on the ends of the valve pins, where the wheels fit. Most big engines with clacks on the side of the boiler have squared covers to the clacks; all ours on the L.B. & S.C.R. were made thus. When you have made them both, screw them into the bushes on the boiler barrel with a smear of plumbers' jointing on the threads. If they are more than $\frac{1}{4}$ in. turn out of vertical when tight, don't strain the threads, but file a shade off the contact faces of the bushes, or take off a scrape with a $\frac{3}{8}$ in. pin drill.

CHAPTER FOURTEEN

Making the grate and ashpan

WHEN THE OUTLINE DRAWING of *Tich* first appeared, and it was mentioned that an eccentric for driving the pump would be mounted on the driving axle, I received the usual crop of letters from the good folk who are never happy unless they are finding fault with something or other. In this case, the awful moan was that, being right under the firebox, the eccentric would be smothered with ash and grit, and wouldn't last the proverbial five minutes. That didn't worry your humble servant in the slightest, as I have built enough locomotives during my lifetime to know what I am about; in fact, I believe I've built more than the sum total of all the critics, some of whose achievements in that line are precisely and exactly nil. Anyway, it was my original intention to dispense with the usual type of ashpan; and in lieu, use a shield over the trailing horn-blocks, axleboxes and eccentric, in a manner somewhat similar to the successful scheme I employed on the gauge "O" *Sir Morris de Cowley*, which is now 25 years old and still going well, although she hasn't grown much! However, when I came to build my own *Tich*, I found that there was enough room for a simple grate and ashpan of the usual type; and as it was an easier job than fitting the shield, and the grate could be made to dump and reset without turning the engine upside down, here is the whole doings, for beginners to follow suit.

The ashpan is of the ordinary box type, open at the back only, but it has a sloping bottom, which not only allows the eccentric plenty of clearance (see dotted line in the erection drawing, which shows the eccentric in its highest position) but renders it self-cleaning, any residue falling out clear of the eccentric and axleboxes. The "moaners" will probably say that when running bunker first the eccentric might catch some grit; but how often will she run bunker first—she is intended for passenger-hauling, and if you put her bunker first at the leading end of your flat car, how are you going to drive and fire? Well, let's get to business.

Firehole Door

First we need a firehole door; this may be a casting with the hinges and straps already on it, or it may be built up from sheet metal, as shown in the illustration. A casting will have the boss on it, for attachment of the baffle plate. Chuck in four-jaw with the boss outwards, set same to run truly, then

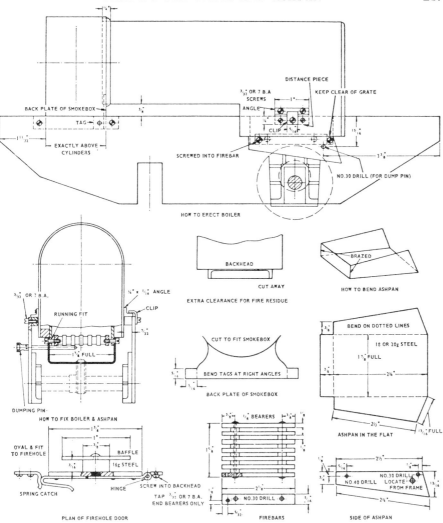

How to assemble the boiler, and arrange the grate and ashpan.

turn down about $\frac{1}{8}$ in. of it to $\frac{1}{8}$ in. diameter. Cut out a piece of 16 gauge steel
steel to an oval shape, approximately $\frac{9}{16}$ in. by 1 in., drill a No. 30 hole in the
middle, and put it on the pip, riveting over the end. The hinges being cast on,
it is only necessary to drill the lugs with $\frac{1}{16}$ in. drill. Rivet on a handle, as
described below, and drill three $\frac{3}{32}$ in. air holes in the door as shown in the
illustrations of the complete backhead.

The built-up door is an oval of 16 gauge steel, measuring $1\frac{3}{8}$ in. by $\frac{7}{8}$ in.
approximately, the baffle being the same as above; the distance-piece is turned
from $\frac{3}{8}$ in. rod, with a pip on each end, the door and baffle being attached to
it as shown in the illustration. The hinges are made from $\frac{1}{8}$ in. strips of 18 or

20 gauge metal, in a similar way to those on the smokebox door, and riveted on with bits of domestic pins; the handle is a similar piece of strip, bent as shown in the plan. The hinge lug, shown in the backhead illustrations, can be filed from an odd bit of brass of suitable size, or made from 20 gauge sheet metal, the piece fitting between the ends of the straps being bent into a loop, same as the strap ends shown in plan. The hinge pin is a piece of 16 gauge wire. The spring catch may either be made from a piece of spring steel, or hard bronze; I use the same stuff as is used for dynamo and motor brush springs, which is easily cut and bent with ordinary snips and pliers, yet keeps springy enough to do the job. The shape is shown in the plan. The whole issue is attached to the backhead by 8 BA screws, which should be home-made from a bit of $\frac{3}{16}$ in. phosphor-bronze rod. It is only a matter of a few minutes' work to make them—I've previously detailed the simple process—and it saves the annoyance of having the heads of ordinary commercial "brass" screws rotting and breaking off. Bend the spring catch so that there is just sufficient pressure on the door handle to prevent the door coming open on its own; no more is needed. You can then do the same as Curly does when firing on the run, viz. flick the door open with the fireman's shovel, and bang it shut again with the same implement.

Grate

If you can get a cast iron grate, I recommend its use, as it saves work and will last much longer than one made up from cut steel firebars. For a built-up grate for the smaller boiler, seven pieces of $\frac{5}{16}$ in. by $\frac{1}{8}$ in. black strip steel will be needed, each $2\frac{1}{8}$ in. long; the larger boiler requires one more, as its firebox is a little wider. In one of the pieces drill two No. 30 holes at $\frac{3}{8}$ in. from each end, and use it as a jig or guide to drill all the others; all the holes must line up or the bearers won't go through them.

The smaller grate needs twelve spacers; and the larger one, fourteen. Chuck a piece of $\frac{1}{4}$ in. round mild steel in three-jaw; face, centre, drill as deeply as you can with No. 30 drill, part off $\frac{1}{8}$ in. slices until you reach the end of the hole, then ditto repeato until you have the required number of spacers. To assemble the grate, take a piece of soft steel wire (rustless, if you like; it lasts longer than ordinary steel, only it must be soft; iron wire would do) and grip it vertically in the bench vice, leaving about 2 in. above the jaws. Countersink the holes on one side of one of the bars and put this on the wire, with the countersink downwards; then a spacer, then another bar, repeating operations until you have the required number of bars on; seven or eight as the case may be. Countersink the holes in the last bar, and put it on with the countersinks upwards. Cut off the wire about $\frac{1}{8}$ in. from the top bar and carefully rivet over the end, so that it fills the countersink and projects a wee bit, as shown in the illustration. Now remove the assembly from the vice, taking care that the bars don't fall off the other end, otherwise the dictionary of railway Esperanto might need revision and additions. Turn it the other way up, rest the head you have already made on something solid—my bench vice has a hammering block cast on it—cut off the other end, same as above, and repeat riveting process. Leave it loose enough to allow the bars to swivel whilst you thread the second bearer through, and put the spacer on; rivet the second up tightly, then finish tightening the first one, and there is your grate. If the ends look a bit ragged and uneven, a few judicious strokes with a file will smarten them up a bit.

Ashpan

The ashpan is made from 18 or 20 gauge steel. Cut out the piece of sheet to the shape and size shown and bend on the dotted line, so that it looks like the prospective sketch. Braze the front corners; merely stand it end-up in the pan, apply wet flux (Boron Compo for preference), blow up to bright red, and touch the joints with a bit of soft brass wire. I use a 100 litre tip in my Alda blow-pipe, plus a touch of Sifbronze, for these jobs. Quench in water and knock off the burnt flux. Tip: to save scratches on your hands later on, round off slightly all the sharp edges and corners. Young Curly learned that the hard way, children's fingers being thin-skinned and soft! Drill the holes shown, near the upper edge of the ashpan, making sure that both sides are in line, or you'll have trouble in fitting; but leave the one for the dumping pin until the boiler is erected.

How to Erect Grate and Ashpan

Now watch your step carefully on the next bit. On either a cast or built-up grate, procedure is the same. At $\frac{5}{32}$ in. from the front end of each outside firebar, and $\frac{1}{8}$ in. from the underside, drill a No. 48 hole and tap it $\frac{3}{32}$ in. or 7 BA. Now make two screws, from $\frac{3}{16}$ in. rustless steel if you have any; if not, mild steel will have to serve. Chuck in three-jaw and turn down $\frac{3}{8}$ in. length to $\frac{3}{32}$ in. diameter; screw half of it only, with $\frac{3}{32}$ in. or 7 BA die, leaving $\frac{3}{16}$ in. of plain, between thread and shoulder. Part off at $\frac{1}{8}$ in. from the shoulder, and slot the head with a thin hacksaw blade. Next, cut away most of the projecting bottom of the inside back firebox plate, to allow the maximum amount of room for clearing out the clinkers and other residue when the grate is down. Grate and ashpan can then be erected, and this calls for a little jerrywangling. Put the ashpan over the projecting bottom of the firebox; this is easily done if the boiler is placed upside down on the bench, supported on two chocks, or on the partly-opened jaws of the bench vice. Then insert the No. 40 drill through the ditto hole in the front end of the ashpan side and drill through the firebox plate. Put a bit of $\frac{3}{32}$ in. wire or a screw, temporarily through the two holes, whilst you repeat operations on the other side.

Now comes the little bit of patience testing. Insert the grate, with a pair of long-nosed pliers, and line up the tapped hole in the outside bar with the one just drilled; then put one of the special screws in. Repeat operations on other side. Both screws should go right home to the end of the thread in the firebars, as shown in the end view and part section. Run the No. 40 drill through the hole at the other end, but only make a countersink on the firebox plate; follow with No. 48, tap $\frac{3}{32}$ in. or 7 BA and put a couple of ordinary screws in. The ashpan is now held tightly in place against the underside of the foundation ring; but the grate pivots on the two special screws and the back end will drop down into the ashpan when the boiler is right way up.

Backplate for Smaller Smokebox

All you need to close in the back of the smaller smokebox is a piece of 16 gauge steel sheet cut to fit the space, as shown in the illustration. The actual shape of this is ascertained from the smokebox itself; it should be a nice fit, naturally. Leave a small tag at each bottom corner, as shown; these are bent at right-angles to the plate and riveted to the inside of the wrapper, as shown in the erection drawing. If there is a rivet in the way knock it out, continue the hole through the tag, and put a longer rivet through.

How to Erect the Small Boiler

All plain sailing now! To keep the firebox amidships, as our nautical friends would put it, two distance pieces or spacers are needed, attached to the inside of the frames, level with the top and just over the driving horn-blocks. The exact position doesn't matter. They are 1 in. lengths of $\frac{1}{4}$ in. square rod with a full $\frac{1}{32}$ in. filed off one facet, as shown in the cross-section, and are attached by two $\frac{3}{32}$ in. or 7 BA screws put through clearing holes in the frame (No. 40 drill) into tapped holes in the pieces of rod; a simple job requiring no detailing. *Tich* builders should be getting quite expert at jobs like these, at this stage! Put a smear of plumbers' jointing around the opening at the back of the smokebox, and push the boiler barrel in for $\frac{1}{4}$ in. depth. No further fixing is needed if a fairly tight push fit, as it should be. Look at it endwise, and see that the chimney is vertical when compared with the dome behind it. Then take off the blastpipe cap and carefully drop the complete assembly into position, firebox between spacers, and the smokebox wrapper between the frames at the front end, the side strips being level with the tops of frames, as shown in the side view of the whole doings. Put a piece of $\frac{3}{8}$ in. rod, square for preference, across the frames just in front of the firebox, and let the boiler barrel sit down on it. Adjust boiler lengthwise until the smokebox is exactly level with the cylinders, as shown, and you are literally all set.

The smokebox end can be attached to the frames by screws at each side, put through clearing holes in the frame into tapped holes in the ends of the strips. Or you can drill clearing holes through the lot, and use $\frac{3}{32}$ in. or 7 BA bolts, or screws and nuts. The back end has to have expansion joints, as the boiler lengthens when in steam. Cut two 1 in. lengths of $\frac{1}{4}$ in. by $\frac{1}{16}$ in. angle, or bend up two bits of sheet brass, thus making your own angle. Drill two No. 40 holes in each, rest them on top of the distance pieces as shown, attach to the boiler with $\frac{3}{32}$ in. or 7 BA brass screws, and sweat them over, same as the stayheads. Now cut two strips of 16 or 18 gauge sheet brass or copper, and bend one end over to form a clip. Drill a No. 40 hole in each, put the clip over the angle, and attach by a $\frac{3}{32}$ in. or 7 BA screw running into a tapped hole in the frame and distance piece, as shown in the end view and part cross-section. Take away the bit of rod from under the barrel and the boiler should be quite firm on the frames.

The No. 30 hole for the dumping pin is drilled $3\frac{3}{8}$ in. from back of frame and $\frac{13}{16}$ in. from the top. Hold the hand brace level, and continue drilling through the side of the ashpan. The pin itself is simply a $1\frac{1}{4}$ in. length of $\frac{1}{8}$ in. round steel, one end rounded and the other furnished with a turned knob screwed on. No matter what Inspector Meticulous says about "one-side support", it will do the job, otherwise I shouldn't specify it!

How to Erect the Larger Boiler

Although there isn't such a wonderful lot of difference between the actual erection of the bigger boiler and the smaller edition, there are a few points which will need watching; so to prevent any of our tyro friends falling into error, I will briefly run over the process. The grate and ashpan will, of course, have to be a little wider, to suit the wider firebox. The grate is illustrated, along with the smaller one, and the construction is exactly the same, the only actual difference being that the larger grate has one extra bar; so it won't be necessary to dilate any further on that subject. The wider ashpan is shown laid flat, in the illustration, and is very similar to the smaller one previously

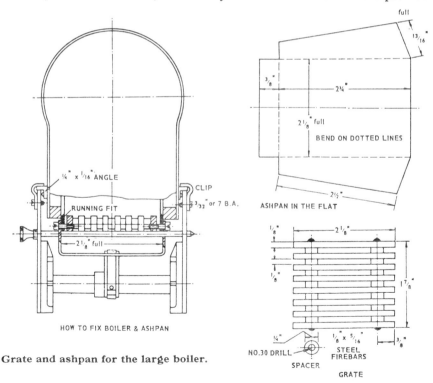

Grate and ashpan for the large boiler.

HOW TO FIX BOILER & ASHPAN

ASHPAN IN THE FLAT

GRATE

described. Mark the outline on a piece of 18 or 20 gauge soft blue sheet; cut to shape, then bend on the dotted lines as indicated. It should fit closely over the projecting part of the firebox below the foundation ring. The side view of the ashpan is exactly the same as shown in the illustration of the smaller one, and three similar holes are drilled in it at each side.

The attachment is also the same as the smaller one. Turn up the two special screws, as shown, from $\frac{3}{16}$ in. round steel rod; drill and tap the two end fire-bars to take them, then put the ashpan in place, drill the clearing holes through the projecting part of the firebox sides, and erect as shown. The screws should be an easy running fit in the ashpan and firebox plates, but the threads should be tight, so that they don't come slack on the road. The back end of the ashpan is held up by two ordinary $\frac{3}{32}$ in. or 7 BA screws running through the clearing holes in the ashpan into tapped holes in the firebox plate. When the whole bag of tricks is erected, the firebars should drop down on the back part of the ash-pan, and be quite free to move up and down. This is one of the places where slack fitting is desirable; unless the screws are quite free they will soon ex-pand and seize up, due to the heat of the fire, and the grate will become a fixture.

Erection of Smokebox Saddle

No. 1 variation in the larger boiler job is that the smokebox saddle is separate, so that merchant must be erected before the boiler and smokebox can be dropped into position on the chassis. There is a clearance between the steam chests and frames which would enable small screws to be put through holes in the frame, direct into the sides of the saddle, but it would be a rather awkward job. Ease and accessibility being our watchwords (eh? Oh, no— you'll find watchworks in gauge "O"!) the simplest way of making the screws easily get-at-able, is to set them far enough apart to miss the ends of the steam chests. The drawing shows how this can be done. Either cut four $\frac{5}{16}$ in. lengths of commercial angle, of $\frac{1}{16}$ in. by $\frac{3}{8}$ in. section, or bend them up from

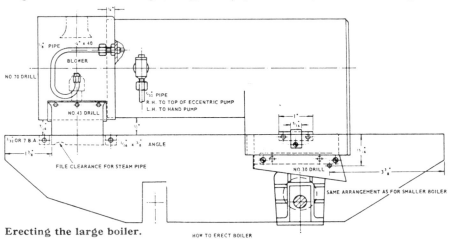

Erecting the large boiler.   HOW TO ERECT BOILER

a piece of 16 gauge metal $\frac{5}{16}$ in. wide; a job easily done in the bench vice. Rivet one at each corner of the smokebox saddle, level with the bottom, and flush with the sides, so that they project "fore and aft". These angles are shown by dotted lines in the illustration. Hold each in place with a toolmaker's clamp, drill a couple of No. 51 holes through angle and saddle, and put $\frac{1}{16}$ in. rivets in, brass or charcoal iron for preference. They remain tight much longer than copper.

Next, at $\frac{5}{32}$ in. from the top of frame, at each side, drill a No. 41 hole at a full $1\frac{1}{8}$ in. from front end of frame. Level with it, and a bare 2 in. farther along, drill another at each side of frame. Then put the saddle in place (don't forget to clean off any burring around the drill holes) and set it so that the leading end is just $1\frac{3}{8}$ in. from the front end of frames, and the bottom of the radius in which the smokebox rests is $\frac{7}{16}$ in. above the tops of frames. Run the 41 drill in the holes, make countersinks on the angle, follow with No. 48, tap $\frac{3}{32}$ in. or 7 BA and put screws in to suit. Any kind of head will do; the running-boards hide them, anyway, which is consolation to those good folk who are scared stiff of Inspector Meticulous! If the threads are at all slack in the angles, put locknuts on the screws inside frames.

If you haven't already drilled the holes in the bottom of the smokebox for the steam and exhaust pipes, do it now; they are indicated in the separate illustration of the smokebox. Take off the blastpipe nozzle. Smear a small amount of plumbers' jointing—if you haven't any, red lead and gold size, or boiled oil, mixed to a paste, will do—around the back edge of the inside of the smokebox, and push the end of the boiler barrel $\frac{1}{4}$ in. into it. Take care you don't get it lopsided; when the chimney is vertical, the sides of the firebox should be ditto, and when you look at the chimney from the front end, there should be an equal portion of dome visible at each side of it. Lay a piece of $\frac{1}{2}$ in. rod, square for preference, across the frames at about $3\frac{3}{4}$ in. behind the saddle. Then carefully drop the boiler and smokebox into place. The blast-pipe and steam pipe, going through the holes in the smokebox, locate the boiler longitudinally (two more words like that, and my Swan will need re-filling!) the saddle settles the height of the smokebox, and the bit of rod ensures that the boiler barrel is the correct height above the tops of the frames. Could anything be easier—I ask you!

Run your scriber along each side of the firebox wrapper, pressing it on the top edge of frames for a guide. Then lift the boiler off again. Cut two 1 in. lengths of $\frac{1}{4}$ in. by $\frac{1}{16}$ in. angle, or bend up the angles from $\frac{1}{16}$ in. sheet, and drill No. 41 holes in each, about $\frac{5}{32}$ in. in from the end. Now watch your step here, as a slip is easily made. When erecting the smaller boiler, we used a distance piece at each side, and a piece of angle, resting on it, for an expansion bracket. This boiler has a wider firebox wrapper, only $\frac{3}{16}$ in. narrower than the distance between frames; and instead of using separate distance pieces, all we need do, is to turn the angles upside down, and let them serve the pur-pose, with slightly projecting screwheads to make up the odd $\frac{1}{32}$ in. each side. It is in the attachment of the angles that a slip might be made, as it is the inside edge of the angle that needs to be set to the scribed line along the wrapper. The best way of making certain that a beginner gets it right, would be to scribe a line a little over 1 in. long at a carefully measured $\frac{1}{16}$ in. above the line already scribed across the side of the wrapper sheets. Set the piece of angle right in the middle of the wrapper sheet, midway between throatplate and backhead, with the outer edge level with the short-scribed line mentioned above. Tack it with a blob of solder, if you like, which is simple and does the trick, but it needs a good hot soldering bit. Slightly countersink the holes in the angle; run the No. 41 drill in, make countersinks on the wrapper, follow it with No. 48, tap $\frac{3}{32}$ in. or 7 BA, and put countersunk brass screws in. Sweat over both angles, just the same as if they were stayheads. If the screwheads project too far, and the boiler won't go down in position, file them off till they stand a little under $\frac{1}{32}$ in. from the angles.

Before fitting the clips, there is one other little duty to perform at the smokebox end, viz. drilling the saddle flange for screws. If you are sweet on lots of hexagon heads, now is the chance to let yourself go, for you can drill a line of No. 51 holes close to the edge of the saddle flange and fill them all with $\frac{1}{16}$ in. or 10 BA hexagon-head screws, when the smokebox is on "for keeps". However, if, like myself, you believe in utility, as it isn't ugly (like a "Spam can", for example, or a "Q1" class 0-6-0!) just drill three or four No. 43 holes in the saddle flange, and use 8 BA round-head screws. When the slots are filled up with paint, they look like rivets! The boiler can now be dropped into position and a couple of clips attached to the frame, at the firebox end, to hold it down, yet allow for expansion, just as described for the smaller boiler. They are clearly shown in the illustrations, and no further detailing should be needed for that simple job. At the smokebox end, run the clearing drill through the holes in the saddle flange, making countersinks in the smokebox; follow with No. 55 for the hexagon-head screws, or No. 51 for the round-heads. Tap $\frac{1}{16}$ in., or 8 BA, according to your choice, and put the screws in. That settles that!

Finally, drill the necessary holes for the dumping pin which supports the grate when the engine is at work. In this instance, as the grate is wider, I have shown the pin going right across the chassis. Mark off and drill the holes in the frame on both sides of the engine, continuing right through the sides of the ashpan. Make the pin from $3\frac{3}{8}$ in. length of $\frac{1}{8}$ in. round steel; or the iron wire beloved of our late friend J. A. Alexander, would do fine. Fit a turned knob on one end, and form the other to a rounded point (says Pat) by filing in the lathe. When inserting the pin, you won't have any trouble in "finding the other side", as the hole in the ashpan acts as a guide. It would not be possible to put a tube across the ashpan, otherwise the grate would not dump when the pin was pulled out.

Pipe Connections in Smokebox

The pipes are arranged in the same way in both larger and smaller boilers.

Plate 27

"Model Engineer" Editorial Director "Dicky" Dickson has a drive behind
LBSC's o-6-2 tank engine "Mona". The track was the author's line at Purley
Oaks. Note the "full-size" L.B.S.C.R. signal in rear

Plate 28

A view inside LBSC's "locomotive works" at Purley Oaks. The locomotive on the bench is a free-lance 4-6-0 named "Swanhilde". Note
"boiler" and pressure gauge below the bench

First of all, connect up the union on the end of the superheater to the vertical pipe which is attached to the cross steam pipe; and—very important this—don't screw it up so tightly that you either distort the cross pipe right away, or else run the risk of it happening on any future occasion, when it might be necessary to take off the boiler. A copper cone requires very little pressure to enable it to sit steamtight on a countersink made by a centre-drill. Next item is the blower pipe and jet. This is just a length of $\frac{1}{8}$ in. pipe with a union nut and cone on one end, and a very small edition of the blastpipe cap on the other. The pipe should be approximately 3 in. long for the larger boiler, and $2\frac{1}{2}$ in. for the smaller one. Make a union cone and silver-solder it on one end of the pipe; that job, also the union nut, should be easy enough without further detailed explanation; most beginners who have progressed thus far successfully, should be quite experienced by now! The other end of the pipe is screwed 5 BA, and on it is screwed a flea-size edition of the blastpipe nozzle, made in exactly the same way, but using $\frac{3}{16}$ in. hexagon rod. Face, centre, drill No. 40 for $\frac{1}{8}$ in. depth, tap 5 BA (any other fine thread may be used), chamfer, part off at $\frac{3}{16}$ in. from the end, reverse in chuck and chamfer again to form the coned top. Reverse again in chuck and carefully put a No. 70 drill down the tapped hole, feeding steadily until it breaks through.

Screw the union on to the end of the thoroughfare nipple, on the smokebox end of the hollow stay. For jobs like these, I use a special home-made spanner, which is first made like an ordinary single-ended spanner, but with a long handle. This is easily filed up from an old bit of $\frac{1}{8}$ in. frame steel, and the spanner jaws fitted to a nut. The end is then bent at right-angles, and the other end bent to the opposite angle, to give the necessary leverage; the jaws are then case-hardened, and we have a mighty useful tool at practically no cost—something not to be sneezed at in these days of sky-high prices. The nozzle end of the pipe is bent to a curve, to enable the little nozzle to cuddle against the blast nozzle and direct the tiny jet of steam up the liner and chimney. The layout is shown in the illustration.

The blastpipe nozzle is then set to direct the exhaust steam slap up the middle of the chimney; and the easiest way of doing this, is to use a piece of silver-steel, which is usually dead straight, of a size that just fits the hole in the nozzle. Put it down the chimney, into the nozzle; if it doesn't stand in the middle of the chimney, like a sweep's rod with the brush knocked off, carefully bend the blastpipe until it does. Then seal the interstices around the bottom of the blastpipe and steam pipe with a few turns of asbestos string anointed with plumbers' jointing, or some asbestos "putty" made by kneading up some scraps of asbestos millboard with a little water. This can be applied like putty, and sets hard when dry.

Finally, smear a little plumbers' jointing, or red lead and goldsize, around the inner edge of the smokebox barrel, and press the complete front home. The shape of the smaller front automatically locates it, but the circular one should be carefully set so that the smokebox hinge straps are horizontal; it looks awful if they are skew-whiff. Next stage, running boards and side tanks.

CHAPTER FIFTEEN

Starting on the platework

Running-boards

FOR THE RUNNING-BOARDS, or side platforms as they are sometimes called, we shall need two strips of sheet metal, 16 or 18 gauge, $13\frac{1}{4}$ in. long and $1\frac{11}{16}$ in. wide. As long as the metal is nice and flat, it doesn't matter whether it is brass or steel; I prefer hard-rolled brass. Both edges must be perfectly parallel, and the ends truly square, so a little judicious filing will be called for. Test the ends with a try-square. The right-hand running-board will require two "bites" taken out of it; one to clear the bracket supporting the reverse lever, with an additional clearance for the lever itself, and a small one to clear the clip holding down the expansion bracket on the boiler. A hole is also needed for the reverse arm to pass through. The left-hand one only requires the small clearance. The exact location of these bits to be cut out, is best obtained by measurements from the actual engine. The sides of the bigger one can be sawn down, a row of No. 40 holes drilled along the connecting line, the piece broken out with pliers, and the ragged edges trimmed to size with a file. The smaller clearances require filing only. When measuring for clearances, note that the running-boards overhang the buffer-beams by $\frac{1}{16}$ in. at each end.

Valances

The valances, as the edgings below the running-board are usually called, are in three pieces; the central straight part is made from $\frac{1}{16}$ in. by $\frac{1}{4}$ in. angle, and the curved ends are made from sheet. Use brass angle if obtainable. The pieces of angle are approximately 12 in. long, and riveted to the underside of the running-boards at $\frac{1}{16}$ in. from the edge, leaving $\frac{5}{8}$ in. at front and back. Clamp in place with a toolmaker's clamp at each end, and use $\frac{1}{16}$ in. brass rivets at about $\frac{1}{2}$ in. centres, countersinking the holes (No. 51 drill) on top of the running-board, hammering the rivets flush and smoothing off with a file, so as to prevent an unbroken surface for the enginemen to walk on, same as we had on the L.B. & S.C. Railway engines. Alternatively, if you happen to be one of those good folk who would love to see a long row of pimples along the edge of the running-board, why, bless your heart and soul, go right ahead and enjoy yourself. Space the rivets about $\frac{3}{16}$ in. apart, put them in from the top, and rest the head on a dolly held in the bench vice. This is just a bit of round or square steel rod, about $\frac{1}{4}$ in. diameter, with the end truly squared off, and a recess for the rivet-head formed in it. Just make a countersink with a $\frac{5}{32}$ in. drill, put a $\frac{5}{32}$ in. cycle ball in the countersink, and give it two or three heavy biffs with a heavy hammer. This will turn the countersink into a cup recess, about the right size for a $\frac{1}{16}$ in. rivet head. Rest the head in this, and you can then hammer down the projecting stem of the rivet inside the valance without destroying the pristine beauty of its noddle. Final tip—for goodness sake keep the line of rivet heads dead straight; if any are out of line, the net result is what the kiddies would call "worse'n awful".

The end pieces which curve down to the buffer-beams will need four pieces of 16 or 18 gauge sheet metal, each 1 in. long and $\frac{7}{16}$ in. wide. Mark them out as shown in the illustration, leaving a tag $\frac{5}{16}$ in. wide above the curved outline. Bend this at right-angles, and don't forget you need two right-hand and two left-hand; then rivet them to the underside of the running-board, so that they match up with the angle section and, in effect, form a continuation of it. To keep them in line, I usually solder a little strip of metal, about $\frac{1}{2}$ in. long and $\frac{3}{16}$ in. wide, on the inside, half on the angle and half on the end piece. If the crack, or join, between the two is filled up with solder—it usually fills "on its own", without any help!—and filed off flush, the joint is invisible when the valance is painted.

Side tanks and running-boards.

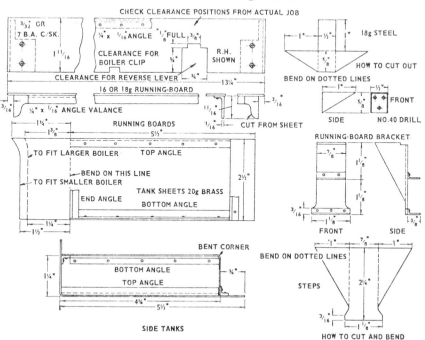

How to Erect Running-Boards

On the plan view, you will notice the outline of the tops of the buffer-beams shown dotted, and two screw heads are shown at each end. They are $\frac{3}{8}$ in. from the ends of the running-boards and approximately $\frac{5}{8}$ in. apart; the exact spacing doesn't matter a Continental. Drill the two No. 41 holes at each end and countersink them. Put the running-board in position and carefully adjust it to get the proper amount of overhang at each end. The inner edge should be level with the top edge of the frame. Poke the No. 41 drill through the holes and make countersinks on the beam tops; hold the running-board in place with a toolmaker's clamp at each end whilst this job is being done. Drill out the countersinks with No. 48 drill, tap the holes $\frac{3}{32}$ in. or 7 BA, and put countersunk screws in. Now put the reverse lever in full forward gear and take a look at the lifting arms on the weighbar shaft. If your workmanship is true to measurements, the ends should just clear the underside of the running-board by about $\frac{1}{64}$ in., which is quite O.K. If, however, there should have been any slight error, and they touch, there is nothing to worry about. Just mark the point of contact and make a clearance by taking off the running-board, drilling a hole about $\frac{3}{16}$ in. diameter at the marked spot and filing it out with a small square file until the lifting arms will clear easily.

There may be a slight gap at the top of the guide-bar bracket, where the running-board passes over it. If so, cut a piece of sheet metal about $\frac{1}{2}$ in. square, and just thick enough to push in between the top of the bracket and the underside of the running-board. If this is simply soldered to the underside of the running-board, it will prevent any tendency to sag.

An extra support will be needed between the guide-bar bracket and the back buffer-beam, and this is provided by a bracket which can be either cast or bent up from sheet metal. Fabrication is used now, to a great extent, in full-size practice, so we may as well follow suit; a fabricated bracket is very strong and light. The illustrations show how to cut out the bracket from 18 gauge steel; a wee bit thicker or thinner metal doesn't matter in the present instance. Mark out as given, cut to shape, and when bent on the dotted lines, you'll have a sort of triangular box, the joints of which are brazed in a matter of a couple of minutes. Apply wet flux (Boron Compo paste), blow up to bright red, touch the joints with a bit of soft brass wire, and Bob's your uncle once again. Drill No. 40 holes in the back of the bracket as shown; set it in place under the running-board about midway between the guide-bar bracket and the back buffer-beam, with the drilled part butting up against the frame and the top part tight up against the underside of the running-board. Attach to frame with three $\frac{3}{32}$ in. or 7 BA screws, any head available will do; you'll know how to locate, drill, and tap screw holes by now! Then drill one solitary No. 40 hole right through the running-board and the top of the bracket; countersink it, put in a countersunk screw ($\frac{3}{32}$ in. or 7 BA) and secure it with a nut underneath. The running-boards should now be perfectly rigid.

The space between the boiler backhead, the two running-boards, and the back of the buffer-beam, can now be filled in by a piece of the same kind of metal as used for the running-boards. The size of this is obtained from the actual engine, so no drawing of it is needed. Nicks are filed in the edge next to the boiler backhead, to form clearance for the pipes, when all the pipe work is completed. It can be fixed to the top of the back buffer-beam by a couple of screws, same as the running-boards; metal of 16 or 18 gauge should be stiff enough to "stay put" without further support at the front end, as it has not the weight of a driver and fireman to carry. If it shows any tendency to sag down, just attach a short bit of angle to the boiler backhead, or toe the frame at each side, doesn't matter which, as long as it holds up the bit of footplate. No drawing is needed for that simple job, either, as our beginner friends should "know their A.B.C." by now, in a manner of speaking.

A similar piece of metal is needed to fill the space in front of the smokebox, and the measurement of this is also obtained from the actual engine; but this differs, inasmuch as it must be made detachable, for the purpose of filling the mechanical lubricator. This is easily done. Drill two holes in it, just as if you were going to screw it down to the front buffer-beam, but use No. 48 drill. Put the piece of metal in place, and make countersinks on the top of the buffer-beam; then remove the metal and drill the holes in the beam, through the countersinks, with No. 40 drill. Instead of screws, cut two bits of $\frac{3}{32}$ in. round wire about $\frac{1}{4}$ in. long; chuck in three-jaw, and turn a full $\frac{1}{16}$ in. of the end, to fit tightly in the No. 48 holes in the plate. Put them in and rivet the ends over. When the plate is dropped into position, the little pegs will go through the holes in the beam and prevent the plate slipping forward; it can't sag down towards the smokebox, as the filler of the mechanical lubricator will hold it up. A lamp iron, made from 18 gauge brass or steel, and set in the centre of the front edge, will serve as a lifting handle; or better still, permanently fit a dummy lamp in the same position, and you'll have something bigger to catch hold of, and probably get a hearty pat on the back from Inspector Meticulous in the bargain!

The steps are made from 16 or 18 gauge sheet metal, in a manner somewhat similar to the brackets for the running-boards; the illustration clearly shows how they are cut out and bent to shape, without further explanation. The treads are bent up from sheet metal also, and may be either riveted or brazed on. They are not fixed to the running-boards until the tanks and bunker are erected, so as to get them exactly in the space between; see general arrangement drawing.

Side Tanks

The tanks form a nobby exercise in neat platework; nice flat smooth sides and properly squared ends are called for, if the little engine is to look like a real good job. The outside sheet, and the front end, are in one piece; the inside sheet and the back end are also in one piece, both being put together by aid of angles, as shown in the illustrations. For the small-boilered engine, the outside sheet needs a piece of 20 gauge sheet brass $7\frac{1}{4}$ in. long and $2\frac{1}{2}$ in. wide;

for the larger boiler it is $\frac{3}{8}$ in. shorter. For the inside sheets of both, the necessary piece is 6 in. by $2\frac{1}{2}$ in. The easiest way of ensuring that the front end fits the curve of the boiler is to make a template from a piece of stiff paper or thin cardboard; this can easily be cut to shape by aid of the domestic scissors, and if you spoil a dozen pieces before getting it O.K. you won't be a farthing the poorer—but sheet metal is both scarce and expensive! When you get it right, lay the cardboard on the metal, run your scriber around the edge, and carefully cut to outline. Then mark off the bending line as shown, and bend to a right-angle in the bench vice. It looks better if the corner is slightly rounded. Don't, on any account, hit the metal with a hammer; hold a piece of wood against it, and hit that. The inside sheet is also bent at right-angles, at $1\frac{1}{4}$ in. from the end. The two pieces are then placed together, as shown in the plan view, and a piece of $\frac{1}{4}$ in. by $\frac{1}{16}$ in. angle, or a bit of home-made angle bent up from sheet, is riveted into each corner. Be very careful to have a true rectangle. The reason for the actual tank being shorter than the outside sheet, is to allow space for the reverse lever, and the bypass fittings. Again, may I remind our worthy friends that one right-hand and one left-hand tank is needed.

Stand the embryo tank on a piece of 16 or 18 gauge sheet brass and run your scriber all around the inside at the bottom; then cut out the marked piece, so that it fits tightly into the bottom of the tank, lying flush with the edges. Cut two pieces of angle to fit along the bottom of each tank, and two to fit along the top edge, as shown. These can be temporarily tacked with solder, whilst the holes for the rivets are drilled No. 51, and $\frac{1}{16}$ in. brass or copper rivets put in. Countersink the rivet holes underneath the tank, hammer the rivets flush, and smooth with a file, as the tanks have to sit down tightly on the running-board. Here again, lovers of millions of rivet heads can let themselves go once more, by close-riveting the top and bottom angles, and letting the heads show on the outside of the tanks; but I personally prefer to see them perfectly smooth. The upper angles are flush with the upper edges of the tanks, as the tank covers have to be screwed down to them. When all the angles are fixed, sweat over all the joints, on the inside of the tanks, with soft solder, same as stayheads, etc., to make the tanks perfectly watertight. Next stage, fitting in the hand pump and the bypass connections and valve.

How to Erect Tanks

Before fitting the tops to the tanks, or putting anything inside them, it would be advisable to erect them on the running-boards. The tops can then be made to an exact fit against the boiler. First of all, drill four No. 40 holes in the bottom of each tank in the position shown in the illustration; these need be approximate only, as the holes in the running-boards are drilled to suit. Now place the left-hand tank in position, as shown. The distance from the outside of the leading buffer-beam to the front end of the tank should be $5\frac{1}{4}$ in. on either the smaller- or larger-boilered engine. On the former, the tanks should be $\frac{1}{8}$ in. from the edge of the running-board; on the latter, a shade less,

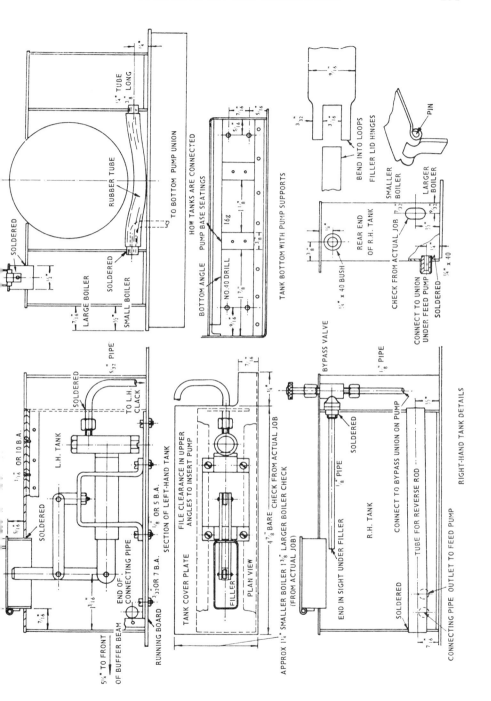

say $\frac{7}{16}$ in., so that the inner side sheet of the tank just misses the boiler. If it touches, some of the heat of the boiler will be dissipated into the tanks, and the boiler will not steam so well. When the tank is correctly located, clamp it temporarily in position; about the easiest way to do this is to lay a stout piece of metal, say a bit of $\frac{1}{4}$ in. by $\frac{1}{2}$ in. bar, across the top at about mid-length. Then put a carpenter's G-clamp over it, the curved part going under the running-board and the screw pressing on the cross-piece. Put a No. 40 drill with extended shank—I've already explained how to fit short ends into pieces of $\frac{3}{16}$ in. rod, to make extension drills—through the holes in the bottom of the tank, and carry on right through the running-board. Clean off any burrs underneath, and put brass screws in either $\frac{3}{32}$ in. or 7 BA. Nut them over underneath, then solder over the heads, to prevent water leaking through. Beginners who are inexperienced with soldering-irons, and who might manage to let the solder get down between the running-board and tank bottom, thus making a permanent fixture of the whole works, had better remove the tank, put the screws through the holes, and solder them whilst the tank is off the running-board. Any surplus solder that creeps through can be scraped off, or else removed with any old rough file that has seen better days.

The primary object of drilling clearing holes in the running-board and using nutted screws, is to render the whole tank easily removable; all that is needed, is to take off the nuts and lift the tank clear. The soldered-over heads not only prevent leakage, but retain the screws in position, and prevent them turning when the nuts are slacked off.

How to Erect the Hand Pump

First make a solid base for it by cutting two pieces of 16 gauge brass or copper, $\frac{3}{8}$ in. wide, and just long enough to fit between the angles at the bottom of the tank. They can be fixed by a couple of $\frac{1}{16}$ in. rivets in each, or soldered, or both. The position is shown in the detail illustration. The pump can then be put in. As the stand is wider than the distance between the top angles, a clearance will have to be filed at each side, to admit it. Set the pump handle vertical, and then adjust the pump in the tank, so that the centre of the handle is approximately $1\frac{3}{16}$ in. from the front end of the tank. No need to bother about "mike measurements", but the pump should be central between the tank sides. Make countersinks on the seating or base, by aid of an extension drill (No. 30), put through the holes in the lugs at the bottom of the pump stand. Remove pump, drill right through the base pieces, tank bottom, and running-board with No. 30 drill; scrape off any burrs and replace pump, fixing it temporarily with a couple of 5 BA screws and nuts.

Be careful about the next bit. Measure from sides and bottom of tank to the centre of the union nipple on the pump valve box. Transfer these measurements to the outside of the back end of the tank; mark the spot, and drill a No. 41 hole. Poke a bit of $\frac{3}{32}$ in. wire, or a drill shank, through the hole; this should go straight into the hole in the union nipple. If it doesn't, a little judicious administration of a small rat-tail file will be necessary to line up the hole with the union; when this is O.K., open out the hole with a $\frac{5}{32}$ in. or No. 22 drill.

The next item needed, is a piece of $\frac{5}{32}$ in. copper pipe approximately $10\frac{1}{2}$ in. long. One end of this is furnished with a $\frac{1}{4}$ in. by 40 union nut and cone, a job which should not need detailing out again, as it was dealt with along with boiler fittings; you should be well able to draw on your experience by now! When silver-soldering the cone to the pipe, heat the whole pipe to dull red, quench the lot in the acid pickle, and run some water through it before cleaning up. This will make it ductile enough to be easily bent by finger pressure alone. Remove pump, poke the pipe through the hole in the end of the tank, from the inside (it may be bent a little for this purpose) then put the pump back temporarily again, and couple up the union. Remove the tank, solder around the pipe where it comes through, then bend it right around. as shown in the illustration, so that it points forward. Replace tank temporarily and adjust the pipe bends so that the pipe runs along inside the frame, turns upwards under the left-hand clackbox, and meets it. Take off the tank again, and fit a union nut and cone ($\frac{1}{4}$ in. by 40 as before) to the upturned end of the pipe.

Whilst the tank is off, drill a $\frac{1}{4}$ in. hole in the inside sheet, about $\frac{1}{4}$ in. from the bottom, and just clear of the vertical corner angle. In this, solder a piece of $\frac{1}{4}$ in. pipe about $\frac{3}{8}$ in. long, to form part of the connection between the two tanks. The tank can then be replaced and permanently fixed by nutting the screws under the running-board, and fixing the pump by four $\frac{1}{8}$ in. or 5 BA brass screws with a smear of plumbers' jointing under the heads. Couple up the union on the front end of the pipe to the left-hand clackbox.

Right-hand Tank

To erect the right-hand tank, take off the reversing rod temporarily, and proceed in a manner similar to that described for the left-hand merchant; then, whilst it is in place, check off on each end the location of the tube through which the reversing rod passes. The centre of this should be $\frac{1}{2}$ in. above the frame at the back end, and $\frac{7}{16}$ in. at the front, as shown in the illustration; on the smaller-boilered engine it should be approximately $\frac{7}{32}$ in. from the outside sheet, and on the larger, $\frac{9}{32}$ in., as the tanks are a wee bit farther apart. Then take off the tank and fit the tube. For this you need a bit of thin $\frac{5}{16}$ in. copper tube $4\frac{7}{8}$ in. long. Soften it by heating to red and plunging into water; clean the ends, then put it between the vice jaws and squeeze it oval. To get an even squeeze without making marks on the pipe—not that it would matter, as Inspector Meticulous can't see through the tank sheets!—put the tube between two bits of wood 5 in. long or a little over, and put the whole lot in the vice jaws. If you put the end of the tube against the tank and run a scriber around it you'll get the exact shape of the necessary hole. Drill a round one in the middle of the marked spot, with a $\frac{3}{16}$ in. drill, and file to outline. Then push the tube through, solder both ends from the outside, and add a fillet of solder inside. It doesn't matter if the tube projects a little to the rear, but file the front almost flush with the end of the tank.

Make a bush from $\frac{3}{8}$ in. rod—brass will do for this—turning the "step" to $\frac{11}{32}$ in. diameter, drilling $\frac{7}{32}$ in. and tapping $\frac{1}{4}$ in. by 40; same process as used for the backhead bush. At the position shown, viz. $\frac{1}{4}$ in. from top, and $\frac{3}{8}$ in. from inside sheet, drill a hole with a $\frac{11}{32}$ in. drill, and solder the bush into it. This bush carries the by-pass valve, by which the water delivered by the eccentric-driven pump is returned to the tanks when not required for the boiler. Our Stroudley tank engines on the L.B. & S.C. Rly. had a similar arrangement, except that the valves were inside the tank, and were operated by small handles, with quadrant and locking screw, on the ends of the tanks inside the cab. The pumps, like the one on *Tich*, were always pumping water, and the amount going into the boiler could be regulated to a nicety.

By-pass Valve

The valve itself is made in the same way as the blower-valve, as you can see by the section shown here. Part off a piece of $\frac{5}{16}$ in. rod, round or hexagon, 1 in. long. Chuck in three-jaw, face, centre deeply with E-size centre-drill, and put a $\frac{3}{32}$ in. or No. 43 hole clean through. Turn down $\frac{1}{4}$ in. length to $\frac{1}{4}$ in. diameter, and screw $\frac{1}{4}$ in. by 40. Reverse in chuck and ditto repeato turning and screwing operations. Open out to a bare $\frac{5}{8}$ in. depth with No. 30 drill; if you have a D-bit that size, it would be a slight advantage to bottom the hole with it, although it doesn't really matter on a small water valve. Further open out to $\frac{3}{16}$ in. depth with No. 21 drill, and tap the No. 30 part either $\frac{5}{32}$ in. by 32 or 40. The coarser thread gives a quicker action to the valve.

In the middle of the body, drill a $\frac{3}{16}$ in. hole, piercing the tapped part; and in this, put a fitting similar to the one at the top of the water gauge, but shorter. This one should only be $\frac{5}{16}$ in. from the shoulder to the centre of the valve, and screwed $\frac{1}{4}$ in. by 40. Drill it $\frac{3}{32}$ in., open out the end for $\frac{3}{16}$ in. depth, to take a 3 in. length of $\frac{1}{8}$ in. thin-walled pipe. Silver-solder both joints at the same heating. After pickling and cleaning up, put the tap down the spindle hole again, to clean off any burring; after which, beginners can put their acquired knowledge and skill to test, by fitting the handwheel, spindle, and gland nut, exactly as I described for the blower valve. You should be getting quite experienced hands by now! Screw the completed fitting into the bush, on the end of the tank, as shown in the illustration; and if it doesn't come up straight when tight, either take a shade off the face of the bush, or else put a thin washer between the bush and shoulder. Washers can be made to any thickness, by parting slices off a drilled rod of suitable diameter, held in the three-jaw.

Now we need two final small items. First, solder a $\frac{3}{8}$ in. length of copper pipe into a hole drilled in the lower front corner of the inside tank sheet (see illustration) for the connecting pipe between the two tanks. Right alongside this, fit a $\frac{1}{4}$ in. by 40 union nipple, made just the same as the ones on the blower valve and whistle turret. This can also be soldered in, as there is neither heat nor pressure to withstand. Before permanently fixing the tank, there is now a little job of plumbing to do. Put the tank temporarily in position; and with bits of lead wire, or soft copper wire, get the exact lengths of your pipes. Measure from the bottom union of the by-pass valve to the back-pointing union on top of the valve box of the eccentric-driven pump; and from the union nipple at the bottom of the tank to the union nipple under the pump valve box. Cut two pieces of $\frac{1}{8}$ in. thin-walled copper tube—I use a 24 gauge tube for these jobs—and fit union cones and nuts to both ends of each; another little job you can do "all by yourself" now. Soften the pipes whilst doing the silver-soldering of the cones. Attach one end of each to the by-pass valve and the outlet union, and bend them carefully so that the pipes will couple up to their respective unions on the pump; then put the tank in place, adjust the pipes to meet the union screws, and couple up the union nuts. Whilst on the plumbing racket, couple up the forward-pointing union on the pump to the union under the right-hand clackbox, with a piece of $\frac{5}{32}$ in. copper tube, with union nuts and cones on each end.

Put the reversing rod, or reach rod, through the "tunnel" in the tank, and couple it up to the reverse lever, and the arm on the weighbar shaft; see if the lever works all right, and if all is O.K., as it should be, put the nuts on the fixing screws under the running-board. Finally, connect the two tanks with a piece of rubber tube slipped over the stub ends of copper pipe at the lower front corners of the tanks. The above instructions apply to engines with Walschaerts' gear; same will do for loose-eccentric engines, but there will, of course, be no need to fit the tube through the right-hand tank, as there will be no reversing rod.

Tank Tops

The rest is just the proverbial "piece of cake". The tank tops are made from 18 or 20 gauge sheet brass, and just overlap the tank sheets at sides and front, sufficiently to form a beading; they should be wide enough to meet the boiler. At the cab end, a piece is cut away, as shown in the plan view of the hand pump in place. At $\frac{1}{2}$ in. from the front end of each, cut a rectangular hole with rounded corners, $1\frac{1}{4}$ in. long and $\frac{1}{2}$ in. wide; or a little wider, if you prefer a big hole to pour the water in. Bend a strip of metal $\frac{1}{2}$ in. wide to the shape of the hole—get the length of this by making a template with a bit of stiff paper; one of young Curly's "Welldon pattern" tricks!—and solder it in, so that $\frac{3}{8}$ in. of it projects above the tank top. The lids are made from the same kind of metal. When cutting them out, leave two tags about $\frac{3}{8}$ in. long, $\frac{3}{32}$ in. wide and $\frac{3}{16}$ in. apart, and bend them into loops with a pair of round-nose pliers. Cut a strip of metal to fit nicely between the loops, and bend one end of that into a loop as well. Line it up with the other loops, and put a pin through the lot; you then have a nobby hinge, as shown in the detail sketch. Pin or solder this to the end of the filler, as shown in the tank connection view. A wire loop handle, or a small turned knob, as desired, can be added, for lifting purposes.

Finally, round off the sharp edges of the tank tops and attach them to the angles at the top of the side sheets by $\frac{1}{16}$ in. or 10 BA brass countersunk screws; or if you are a lover of rivet heads, roundhead screws may be used. Drill the No. 51 holes for the screws at approximately $\frac{7}{32}$ in. from the outer edges, which will allow for the overlap, and the screws will go through the horizontal part of the angles without fouling. About $\frac{3}{4}$ in. centres will do nicely for countersunk screws, but roundheads can be set as closely as you like. Temporarily clamp the top in position, put the No. 51 drill through the holes in the plate, make countersinks on the angles, follow with No. 55 drill, tap $\frac{1}{16}$ in. or 10 BA, put the screws in, and Bob's your uncle. The hand pump, if and when needed, is operated with the extension handle through the left-hand filler, whilst the amount of water being by-passed, can be seen through the right-hand filler. The connecting pipe allows the water in the two tanks to keep at the same level. Next item, cab or weatherboard, and bunker.

Cab and Weatherboard

After the exercise our beginner friends have had on the platework in the side tanks, the cab, or weatherboard, whichever you desire, and the bunker, should present not the slightest difficulty. The specifications call for a plain weatherboard for the smaller job, and a cab for the larger; but there is not the slightest objection to swapping one for the other, in a manner of speaking. The only difference in the construction would be to make the arch-shaped curve at the bottom to suit the different diameter of the boiler.

Let's deal with the weatherboard first. This will require a piece of 16 gauge sheet metal; any kind will do, even aluminium, as there is nothing to be soldered to it. It should measure $4\frac{1}{4}$ in. by $5\frac{1}{4}$ in. The reason for using 16 gauge metal is that the weatherboard has to stand up by its own unaided efforts; there are no side pieces, nor roof, to give it any moral or physical support. First of all, cut out the window openings. These are $1\frac{1}{4}$ in. square, with rounded corners, and are located $\frac{3}{8}$ in. from the sides, and $\frac{1}{2}$ in. from the bottom. Mark them out carefully, then cut them by the same process as described for cutting out the firehole openings in the backhead, and back sheet of the firebox; another chance to test your acquired knowledge. Tip: if you have a metal-piercing saw—just a glorified fretsaw—drill a $\frac{7}{32}$ in. hole at each corner of the marked-out space; then saw from one hole to the next, until the piece comes out. Trim up with a file, and there are your window openings with nicely-rounded corners. It's ever so easy! Whilst on this job, cut out two similar openings in another piece of metal, a little thinner, say 20 gauge, for the window frames. If brass is used, the window frames can be polished; many of the old-time contractors' engines were kept in spotless condition by their drivers and firemen. Cut away the metal around the openings to within $\frac{1}{8}$ in. of the holes, leaving two rectangular frames with rounded corners.

A Template Helps

The next item is to cut out the arch-shaped openings that fit over the boiler; and the easiest way to get a perfect fit is to make a template from a piece of thin cardboard or stout paper, by aid of the domestic scissors. Scribe a circle on it, $2\frac{1}{2}$ in. diameter, with a pair of pencil compasses; draw a line through the middle, then at $\frac{1}{2}$ in. down the line, measuring from the edge of the circle, scribe another line at right-angles to the centre line. Cut across this, then cut out the segment of the circle left on the card or paper. This should fit exactly over the smaller boiler, the straight part of it resting on top of the tank at each side. If it doesn't, you'll see at a glance where to operate with the scissors to get a perfect fit. When you have it, lay the card or paper on the piece of metal, with the straight part each side of the arch, flush with the $5\frac{1}{4}$ in. edge, and exactly in the middle. Run your scriber around the arch, and cut out the marked piece with saw and file; it should fit exactly over the boiler, and no metal will be wasted. Then, at $1\frac{7}{8}$ in. from the bottom, bend over the top of the weatherboard to the angle shown. Clamp it in the bench vice alongside a piece of 1 in. round rod, and finger pressure on the projecting part will give you a perfect bend, without a trace of kinking. Round off the top corners, with snips and file, to approximately $\frac{7}{8}$ in. radius.

Rivet a piece of $\frac{1}{4}$ in. by $\frac{1}{16}$ in. angle along the bottom, at each side of the arch opening. Finally, do the "glazing". Cut two pieces of thin mica, or Perspex, to the size of the window frames; place these over the window openings—inside or outside, just as you prefer—and put the frames over them, riveting through the lot with pieces of domestic pins for rivets. Alternatively, 12 BA roundhead screws could be used, put through clearing holes in the window frames, into tapped holes in the weatherboard. The completed weatherboard is attached to the tops of the side tanks, at $1\frac{5}{8}$ in. from the rear end of the tanks by 8 BA screws run through clearing holes (No. 43 drill) in the angles, into tapped holes in the tank tops, at the point where the angles are fixed inside the tank. This gives a double thickness hold for the screw threads. Alternatively, instead of using pieces of angle along the bottom of the weatherboard, the sides could be made $\frac{1}{4}$ in. longer, and bent over at right-angles, as shown for the cab used with the larger-boilered engine.

Cab

The cab would appear to be more complicated than a weatherboard, but it is just as easy, as the whole lot—sides, front, and extension pieces for fixing—can be made in one piece. Sheet metal of 18 or 20 gauge is thick enough for this. The whole outline, with dimensions, is shown in the accompanying illustration. Mark it out carefully and cut to outline; the exact curve of the cab sides doesn't matter, as long as they are both alike. If you have any big drills, the window openings can be drilled, using a small pilot first, say about $\frac{3}{16}$ in., and finishing with a $\frac{7}{8}$ in. drill. It will be a miracle if this drill finishes the hole plumb in the middle of the marked circle, so the humble but necessary half-round file may be used to true the hole and put the finishing touches. Make two window frames as described above; or if you have a bit of brass tube 1 in. bore, they can be turned, same as I turned round frames for *Jeanie Deans* and *Grosvenor*. A paper or card template can be used to get the arch-shaped opening for the boiler O.K., as described above.

Be careful about what my one and only niece would have called the "bendification job" in her schoolgirl days. The two sides are bent at right-angles to the front, and must be parallel. The bottom tags are bent inwards at right-angles, and the upper tags are bent inwards at an angle to suit the curved cab front. The end-on view showing how the cab is attached to the tank tops should make this quite clear. After bending, try the whole issue in place, and if any adjustments have to be made—some folk fall down over bending; why, goodness only knows!—make them right away. All the bends can easily be made in the bench vice, by putting the metal in with the marked line showing at the jaw tops, and using a piece of hard wood as a buffer between the hammer and the metal. "All right for a biff?" "Indubitably, Buff!" as the British Railways advertisements would put it!

Fit mica or Perspex windows in exactly the same way as described for the square ones in the weatherboard, then erect the cab on the tank tops. Drill a couple of No. 40 holes in each bottom angle, about $\frac{1}{4}$ in. or so from the ends, then put the cab in place with the lower end of the side sheets about $\frac{1}{16}$ in. from the rear edge of the tank tops; see illustration. The screws nearest to the cab front can be tapped into the tank tops, but those at the rear end should be nutted, as shown, as the metal is thin and narrow here. Just continue the No. 40 hole through the tank top, and put the screw in as shown. Hexagon-headed screws may be used if preferred.

A piece of metal $2\frac{1}{4}$ in. wide, and a wee bit over $5\frac{1}{2}$ in. long, will be needed for the cab roof. Bend this to the same radius as the top of the cab front sheet, and round off the corners, as sharp corners are prone to take bits of skin off your fingers at the slightest provocation. Drill four No. 43 holes, two at each side, about $\frac{3}{16}$ in. from the edge, in the position indicated in the side view of the cab erected; countersink them. Larger screws than 8 BA may be used if desired, but those shown are neater. Put the cab top in place, getting it nicely central, and in close contact with the curved top of the cab front, and temporarily fix it with a couple of small clamps, whilst you put the No. 43 drill through the bent-over angles, using the holes in the cab roof as guide. Secure with countersunk screws, nutted underneath, as shown.

I haven't shown any beading to the cab edges, "for the sake of simplicity" as a famous catalogue always points out; but if any builder would prefer a beaded edge, simply solder on a piece of half-round wire, level with the curved edge. This will give a similar appearance to the beading around the bunker.

Bunker

This ought to be spelt "bunkum", as it doesn't carry any coal! To make it,

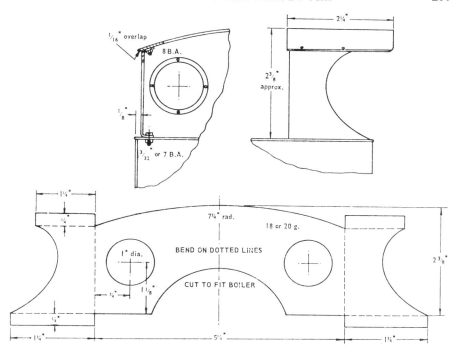

CAB FOR LARGER-BOILERED ENGINE
Some more parts of the "platework".

you'll need a piece of sheet brass or steel, 18 or 20 gauge, $7\frac{3}{4}$ in. long and
$2\frac{9}{16}$ in. wide. Bend it at right-angles, as indicated by the dotted lines, at $1\frac{1}{8}$ in.
from each end; it looks better if the corners are left rounded. Solder a piece
of half-round wire, $\frac{1}{16}$ in. or $\frac{3}{32}$ in., just as you fancy, all along the top edge.
For jobs like this, I use three or four little toolmaker's clamps, made from
$\frac{1}{4}$ in. square brass rod, with $\frac{1}{8}$ in. commercial screws. They only take a few
minutes to make, and are mighty handy. Brass is used, to prevent rusting up
when splashed with soldering fluid, and also when washing off a job with the
clamps still attached. I have already explained how to make these clamps, in
the earlier instalment of this serial. The wire is placed in position, and held by
the clamps, one at each end, and a couple more at what certain folk would
call "strategic points along the route". Solder the wire, in the ordinary way, to
the bunker sheet between the clamps, and be sparing with the solder, so as
to keep the job neat; also keep the solder clear of the clamps. Then remove
them, and solder the places which they covered. Any solder showing beyond
the beading can easily be removed by aid of a square-ended scraper, made
from a small flat file which has outgrown its legitimate job by virtue of *Anno
Domini.* Grind the end off square, and grind the teeth—or what is left of
them—away at each side of the ground end. You won't need any instruction
on how to use this useful gadget, but don't use it without a handle!

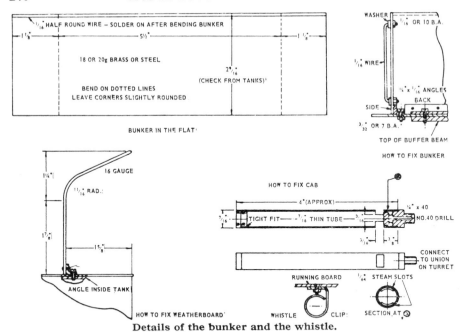

Details of the bunker and the whistle.

Rivet a length of $\frac{1}{4}$ in. by $\frac{1}{16}$ in. angle along the bottom, at the back, and a shorter piece at each side; the note previously addressed to lovers of metallic pimples, applies also in the present instance.

Finally, attach the bunker to the running-boards by $\frac{3}{32}$ in. or 7 BA screws. The two at the sides can be put through clearing holes drilled through the running-board, and nutted underneath. The angle along the back of the bunker comes over the back buffer-beam, so the screws at the back may be screwed into tapped holes in this. Use an extension drill (previously described) to put through the screw holes in the angle, and make countersinks on the footplate; drill these No. 48, clean through footplate and top of back buffer-beam, finally tapping $\frac{3}{32}$ in. or 7 BA.

Before permanently erecting the bunker, fit the grab rails. These are simply pieces of $\frac{1}{16}$ in. or 16 gauge wire, nickel-bronze for preference, about $2\frac{5}{8}$ in. long. Bend over about $\frac{5}{16}$ in. of each end at right-angles, and screw the bends a full $\frac{3}{16}$ in. with either $\frac{1}{16}$ in. or 10 BA die. Screw a tapped washer on to each, or solder on a plain washer, whichever you like. Drill two No. 50 holes at 2 in. centres, about $\frac{3}{16}$ in. from the edge of the bunker; make sure the upper one is exactly above the lower, so that the grab rail will be vertical. Put the screwed ends of the rail through the holes, and secure with commercial nuts. Fit similar grab rails to the back ends of the tank sheets. The bunker can then be erected and screwed down.

Whistle

The whistle is of the organ-pipe pattern with a double slot, which is the next best thing to a regular bell whistle. In these small whistles, the trouble is to keep a "bell" type tube in line with the annular steam slot, without using an outsize spindle. In the whistle shown, two slots are used in place of a complete circular opening; and the metal between the ends of the slots keeps the lot in line. The tube, $\frac{7}{16}$ in. diameter and 4 in. long, is squared off at each end in the lathe; at $\frac{3}{8}$ in. from one end, make two scratches, $\frac{3}{16}$ in. apart, right around it, using a pointed tool. File the slots between these scratches, leaving $\frac{3}{16}$ in. of metal between, as shown in the illustration.

The front end is closed by a simple plug turned from $\frac{7}{16}$ in. brass rod. For the rear end fitting, chuck the $\frac{7}{16}$ in. rod again; face, centre deeply, turn down $\frac{1}{4}$ in. length to $\frac{1}{4}$ in. diameter, screw $\frac{1}{4}$ in. by 40, and part off at $\frac{1}{2}$ in. from the shoulder. Rechuck the other way around, in a tapped bush held in three-jaw, and turn $\frac{3}{8}$ in. length to a tight push fit in the tube. At $\frac{1}{8}$ in. from the end, turn a groove $\frac{1}{8}$ in. wide and about $\frac{1}{8}$ in. deep. Drill a No. 40 hole right across this, and drill another similar hole up the centre of the union screw to meet it. File away a portion of the flange at each side to form steam slots, as shown in the end view of the fitting; then press this into the whistle tube with the steam slots opposite the "noise openings", so that steam issuing from the slots blows across them.

To erect the whistle, make two clips from strips of 20 gauge brass, $\frac{1}{4}$ in. wide, as shown in the illustration, which needs no description; put them on the whistle tube, and attach to the underside of the right-hand running-board by means of nutted screws, as shown. The union is connected to the union screw nearest the whistle-handle on the turret by a $\frac{1}{8}$ in. pipe, with union nuts and cones on each end, which you can make, by this time, without further detailed instruction. The pipe comes down by the side of the wrapper, as shown in the backhead illustrations, passes through the running-board, and is bent around to meet the union screw on the whistle.

CHAPTER SIXTEEN

The final details

Brake Gear

HAVING BUILT A LITTLE locomotive that will go, we might as well follow full-size practice and provide a means of stopping it, or preventing it accidentally moving from rest; and so we come to the final mechanical job, viz. the brake gear. Incidentally, it always amuses your humble servant when somebody or other starts to describe how to build an engine and applies brake gear to the wheels as soon as ever they are on the frames, irrespective of whether the blessed thing will go or not. It reminds me of Mike O'Finnegan, who drives the Ballyma-crackpot express, and always puts the brakes on before he starts, so as to make sure of stopping all right! Another reason why I left the brake gear to the last, was because it is optional; when *Tich* is on a little job of live passenger hauling, the brake on the passenger car will do all that is necessary in the way of stopping, the weight of the engine being far too small to have any appreciable effect in retardation (third programme again!). However, the provision of brake gear gives the finishing touch to the little "contractor's pug"; and for those who desire it, here are the necessary notes and illustrations.

At first sight it would appear that the brake rigging might be the "simplest ever", on a weeny four-wheeler; just blocks and hangers, with simple crossbeams operated by a single central pull rod connected to the drop arm on the brake shaft. Normally, this would suffice; but in the case of *Tich*, the low position of the axles, due to the little wheels, brings the pump down to a level that doesn't admit of a central pull rod. On some full-sized locomotives having small wheels, and inside cylinders, the pull rods are located outside the wheels, as on the old L.B. & S.C. Railway 0-6-0 goods tanks; but again, in the present case, the coupling rods come too low, on the bottom centre, to allow of outside pull rods being fitted. The only alternative is to use double pull rods, arranging matters so that one comes at each side of the pump; and the plan view shows how this can easily be done. The leading and trailing beams are connected by two rods at $1\frac{1}{4}$ in. centres; the two shorter rods in line with them are coupled at their front ends to the back edge of the trailing beam, and at the back ends to a connecting or equalising bar, which in turn is actuated by a single pull rod coupled to the drop arm on the brake shaft. The latter is

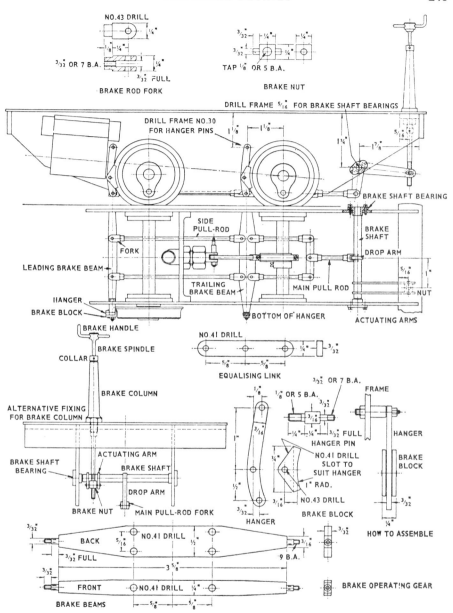

Details of the brakes and the brake operating mechanism.

worked from the footplate, by the brake spindle, which is furnished at its upper end with the usual fireman's muscle-tester, and is supported by a column, screwed to the top of the rear buffer-beam. It projects below the column and is screwed to fit the brake nut. This is a tapped cube, with a pin projecting at each side, the pins working in slots in the ends of two parallel arms attached to the brake shaft. When the handle is turned the nut moves either up or down, taking the parallel arms with it, and partially revolving the brake shaft, which is supported in bearings in the side frames. This causes the drop arm, situated in the middle of the shaft, to move forwards or backwards, according to which way the handle is turned; the movement causes the whole pull rod assembly to move in unison, either applying or releasing the brakes as desired. Any beginner should be able to grasp the principles of action, in two wags of a dog's tail, by looking at the drawings.

As to the making and erecting of the various parts, this should not present the slightest difficulty to any beginner who has thus far completed the building of the little engine. There is only one bit that is at all likely to be ticklish, and that is erecting the leading brake hanger nicely between the cylinder casting and the leading wheel. There is just enough room for it; none to spare.

The First Step

Item No. 1 is to locate the correct positions of the holes for the hanger pins in the main frames. They need not necessarily be "to mike measurements", though care should be taken to get them as nearly correct as is possible. However, the location is just "a piece of cake". The holes are $1\frac{1}{8}$ in. ahead of the axle centre, and $1\frac{1}{8}$ in. from the top of the frame. Now, as the edge of the wheel flange, at axle level, is $1\frac{1}{8}$ in. from the axle centre, all you have to do is to put your try-square with the stock resting on top of the frame, and the edge of the blade just touching the wheel flange; run your scriber along the edge of the blade, making a scratch on the frame. At $1\frac{1}{8}$ in. from the top of the frame, make a centre-dot on the scribed line, and drill it with No. 30 drill. Smooth off any burring. Nothing could be simpler!

To locate the holes for the brake shaft bearings, apply your try-square, with the stock resting on top of the frame again, and the edge of the blade at $1\frac{7}{8}$ in. from the rear end of the frame, inside the buffer-beam. Run your scriber along the edge of the blade, as before; mark off a point on the resulting line at $1\frac{3}{4}$ in. from the top of frame. Centre-dot it, drill a No. 30 pilot hole, and open out to $\frac{5}{16}$ in., removing any burrs left by the drill. Ditto repeato operations on the other side of the frames.

Brake Blocks

Weeny cast-iron brake blocks, same as used on full-sized locomotives, should be available; if so, very little machining will be needed. The big ones are merely drilled for the pins holding them to the hangers; if the little blocks are clean, they won't need any more attention, unless the slot at the back, which fits on the hanger, needs cleaning out, in which case a thin flat file will do the needful. If, however, castings are not available, the blocks can easily be made from four pieces of $\frac{1}{4}$ in. by $\frac{5}{16}$ in. mild steel rod, each $\frac{3}{4}$ in. long. The easiest way to cut them is to chuck a length of rod of the given size in the four-jaw (it doesn't matter about setting it to run exactly true) and part them off to the given length; otherwise they may just be sawn off. If the latter, smooth off any roughness left by the sawing, with a file. The next item needed is a piece of metal about $\frac{1}{8}$ in. thick; note only that as long as the bit of metal is big enough to carry the four blocks, and allow for two attaching bolts, it will do. Scribe a circle, or part of a circle, on the metal, with your divider points set at 1 in. apart; lay the four embryo brake blocks on it, with their ends touching the scribed circle, or part thereof, as the legal fraternity would say, and solder them to the plate. Drill two or more $\frac{1}{4}$ in. clearing holes in the plate, and bolt it to the lathe faceplate by $\frac{1}{4}$ in. bolts, as shown. The scribed circle, or segment of same, must be 1 in. from the lathe centre-line. Set it either to the tip of a pointed tool in the slide-rest toolholder, adjusted so as to be 1 in. from centre; or else stand a scribing block on the lathe bed, with its needle set to 1 in. from lathe centre, and adjust the piece of metal on the faceplate, until it lines up with the scribing block needle; then tighten the bolts.

Put a boring tool in the slide-rest toolholder. This should have a fairly narrow tip, slightly rounded for choice; alternatively, a knife-tool might be used, set cross-wise in the rest in similar fashion. In that case, it should be slightly above centre height, or else have extra clearance below the cutting edge, so that it doesn't rub on the blocks when cutting the radius. The point should also be inclined a little toward the operator. Run the lathe at a slow speed, feed the tool in just the same way as if you were boring a cylinder, don't forget a brushful of cutting oil, and you'll soon have a lovely radius on all the four blocks. Careful feeding is obviously essential; if the block bangs up against the cutting edge, through too "greedy" a cut being attempted, either the block will be knocked off the plate (unofficial history tells us that it was a turner who first used the expression "knock his block off"!) or else the tip of the tool will go west. Continue feeding until the tool cuts a small groove in the plate and clears the edges of the blocks; then unship the plate and melt the blocks off it, wiping off any superfluous solder whilst still melted.

On the centre-line of each block, at $\frac{3}{16}$ in. from the curved edge, drill a No. 43 hole. If you haven't a drilling machine, use the lathe, with the drill in three-jaw, and the work held against a drilling pad in the tailstock barrel, or against a piece of hard wood across the end of it. The holes must be square with the sides of the blocks. Then go ahead and file all the blocks to the shape shown; a job needing more elbow-grease than instruction. If you happen to be the lucky owner of a milling machine, shaper, or planer, put the slots in the back of the brake blocks before trimming the ends to shape. Hold them end-wise in the machine vice on the table of the machine. If milling, use a $\frac{3}{32}$ in.

saw-type slotting cutter on the arbor; one traverse, with the table set at the correct height to cut the depth of slot required, viz. approximately $\frac{1}{4}$ in. will do the trick. The job can be done in the lathe, in similar fashion; I have already fully described the process in connection with other milling jobs.

The block is held in a machine vice, either a regular one, or an improvisation made from two bits of angle connected by bolts which is bolted to the lathe saddle. The block is set at correct height and slotted by traversing under a saw-type cutter on an arbor or mandrel between centres. No cutting oil is needed for cast-iron, but the steel blocks need a good dose for a clean finish; run the lathe slowly. After cutting the grooves, trim off the ends of the blocks at right-angles to the curved face, as shown in the drawing.

Brake Hangers

There are two ways of making the hangers; they may be made from strip steel of the correct section, and bent to shape, or cut out from steel sheet. Curved hangers are necessary, on account of the limited clearance between the backs of the cylinders, and the leading wheels. It would, of course, be possible to use straight hangers for the driving wheel blocks only, but this would be a cock-eyed sort of antic, necessitating separate measurements for erection, and not the slightest gain in efficiency.

The Strip Job

For this, four pieces of $\frac{3}{32}$ in. by $\frac{3}{16}$ in. mild steel, a little over $1\frac{3}{4}$ in. long, will be required. Grip one of these edgewise in the bench vice, with about 1 in. length between the jaws, the remainder projecting from the end of them. With a lead or copper hammer, the projecting end can be judiciously coaxed into the shape in the illustration. If the metal buckles at the start of the bend, as it may do if you hit too hard, just take it out of the vice and flatten it; and before having another go, heat it to medium red and let it cool naturally. When you have one correct, use it as a gauge to bend the rest of the merchants to the same curve. They can then be marked out, drilled, and the ends rounded off, in exactly the same way as described for valve gear components. Mark out one only, drill it, and use as a jig to drill the other three, which not only saves time, but ensures that they are all alike.

If you have any odd bits of steel left over from the frames, the hangers can be cut from them, and no bending will be required; just mark the shape of the hangers on the bits of steel, and saw and file to outline, leaving them a little on the big side (says Pat). Drill one, and use it as a jig to drill the others; then rivet them all together temporarily, and finish the lot to correct outline and dimensions, at one fell swoop. After parting, rub each on a bit of emery cloth laid on the bench, to remove edge burring and put a bit of a finish on them.

The pins which carry the hangers are just a kiddy's practice job. Chuck a bit of $\frac{3}{16}$ in. round mild steel in the three-jaw; face the end, turn down $\frac{1}{4}$ in.

length to $\frac{1}{8}$ in. diameter, and screw $\frac{1}{8}$ in. or 5 BA. Part off a full $\frac{7}{16}$ in. from the shoulder. Turn down a full $\frac{3}{16}$ in. of the other end, to $\frac{3}{32}$ in. diameter; slip one of the hangers over, and run a $\frac{3}{32}$ in. or 7 BA die on until it almost touches the hanger. This will ensure that when the nut is screwed on as far as it will go, the hanger will still be able to move back and forth, without being subject to an attack of side wobblitis.

How to Assemble and Erect

Put the hangers in the grooves in the brake blocks and test for movement with a bit of $\frac{3}{32}$ in. round steel or wire filed to an easy fit in the hole. The block should tilt just a weeny bit each side of centre; just enough to allow it to accommodate itself to the wheel tread when erected, and when the brakes are on. When O.K., drive a bit of $\frac{3}{32}$ in. steel clean through the lot, and file off to leave about $\frac{1}{64}$ in. projecting at each side of the brake block, leaving the block just free enough to seat full length on the wheel tread, but not loose enough to lop over and rub on the tread when the engine is running. Then all you have to do, to erect, is to poke the $\frac{1}{8}$ in. ends of the hanger pins through the holes in the frames, and put nuts on the inside of same; put the hangers on the pins, and secure with ordinary commercial nuts. Next stage, operating gear.

As previously mentioned, we are using ordinary brake beams, but with twin pull rods to clear the pump; so the next item will be the beams. These are different, inasmuch as the leading beam only has to provide for two pull rod attachments, whereas the trailing beam has four; but they are all made in exactly the same way. The leading beam needs a piece of flat mild steel $\frac{1}{4}$ in. by $\frac{3}{32}$ in., and the trailing beam $\frac{1}{2}$ in. by $\frac{3}{32}$ in., both pieces a little over $4\frac{1}{16}$ in. long. Chuck truly in four-jaw, if your lathe mandrel has a hole in it large enough to allow this to be done, with about $\frac{5}{8}$ in. projecting beyond the chuck jaws. If not, the only thing to do, will be to turn the beams between centres. In that case, square off both ends of the piece of flat strip with a file; carefully mark off the centre, make a centre-punch mark, and drill it with the smallest sized centre-drill that you have available. Put a small dog or carrier on the end, and put the piece between centres, so that the pin in the lathe catchplate will drive the tail of the carrier.

Whether chucked, or between centres, the turning job is the same. Turn down a bare $\frac{7}{32}$ in. of the end to $\frac{3}{32}$ in. diameter, using a knife-tool in the slide-rest; then further reduce a full $\frac{3}{32}$ in. length, to $\frac{5}{64}$ in. diameter. If the piece is chucked, screw this small end with a 9 BA die in the tailstock holder; if between centres, leave it as it is for the moment. Now reverse the beam, whether chucked or between centres; if the latter, naturally you'll have to change ends with the carrier as well; then ditto repeato operations on the other end of the beam, making sure that the distance between the shoulders is $3\frac{5}{8}$ in. as shown in the illustration. If the beams have been turned between centres, the extreme ends can now be screwed with a 9 BA die in an ordinary hand-operated die stock. Put the beam vertically in the vice jaws, and take mighty good care to hold the die stock absolutely horizontal, when starting to cut the thread. Work it back and forth carefully, and don't forget a drop of cutting oil, which will ensure clean threads.

The holes for the pins holding the pull rod forks to the beams are drilled $\frac{1}{8}$ in. each side of the centre of the beams, using No. 41 drill. On the front or narrower beam, they are located on the longitudinal centre-line; on the back, or wider beam, they are $\frac{5}{32}$ in. ahead and behind the centre-line, that is, at $\frac{5}{16}$ in. centres, as can be seen in the illustration. Smooth off any burring, then put the beams in position between the hangers, the reduced ends going through the holes at bottom of same; don't bend the hangers when erecting the beams, but just slack the upper hanger nuts sufficiently to allow the ends of the hangers to go over the beams. Use 9 BA commercial nuts and washers to keep the hangers in place on the ends of the beams.

Brake Shaft Assembly

To make the brake shaft, a piece of $\frac{1}{4}$ in. round mild steel, a little over $3\frac{3}{8}$ in. long will be required. Chuck this in the three-jaw; it doesn't matter much if it isn't exactly "spot on", so don't waste time in setting it to run truly with a dial test indicator—life's too short! Face the end, and turn down $\frac{5}{16}$ in. of the end, to $\frac{3}{16}$ in. diameter. Reverse in chuck, and ditto repeato operations on the other end, making sure that the distance between the shoulders is $2\frac{3}{4}$ in. That part is soon settled!

Next, make the arms. The drop arm, which actuates the pull rods and beams, is filed up from a piece of $\frac{1}{8}$ in. by $\frac{3}{8}$ in. flat mild steel. Put a couple of centre-dots on it at $\frac{7}{8}$ in. centres, drill them both No. 30, then enlarge one of them with a $\frac{15}{64}$ in. or letter C drill. Then file up the drop arm to the shape shown, around the holes; I guess you've all heard of the Irish cooper, Tim O'Harrigan, who built a barrel around the bung-hole so that he got it in the right place—well, there's something in that! You'll find that your $\frac{1}{4}$ in. parallel reamer has a slight lead at the business end; if that won't enter the larger hole, enlarge the hole slightly until it will, then carefully ream the hole until the drop arm can be driven or pressed on to the shaft. Note—it doesn't need a "press fit" in the generally-accepted sense of the term; the drop arm just needs to be able to "stay put" while being brazed.

The two actuating arms are made in a similar manner, using $\frac{3}{8}$ in. by $\frac{1}{16}$ in. flat mild steel, and drilling two No. 40 holes at $1\frac{5}{8}$ in. centres. Clamp or solder the two bits of steel together, and drill them both at once; then file to shape. Enlarge the hole at the bigger end, to a tight fit on the shaft, as described above; slot the smaller one with a $\frac{1}{8}$ in. rat-tail file, until it is $\frac{3}{16}$ in. long. Before mounting these on the shaft, the brake nut must be made, as it goes between them. For this, a piece of $\frac{1}{4}$ in. square rod will be needed. On full-size engines, the nut is made from hard bronze, as it has to do considerable work, and is square-threaded, to suit a similar thread on the brake spindle. On the little engine, bronze should be used if available; but as the brake is more for ornament than use, brass will do, and ordinary Whitworth or BA threads are quite suitable. Chuck the rod truly in four-jaw, face the end, and turn down $\frac{3}{32}$ in. length to $\frac{3}{32}$ in. diameter. Part off at a bare $\frac{3}{8}$ in. from the shoulder; reverse in chuck, and turn a similar pip on the other end, leaving $\frac{1}{4}$ in. between the shoulders. Make a centre-pop right in the middle of one of the facets; drill it No. 40, and tap it $\frac{1}{8}$ in. or 5 BA.

The brake shaft is supported in two oval-headed bearings attached to the frames. Use bronze if available, but brass will do if there is nothing better to be had, as the wear is negligible. They can be turned from a piece of $\frac{5}{8}$ in. round rod held in the three-jaw. Face the end, and turn down $\frac{3}{16}$ in. length to $\frac{5}{16}$ in. diameter, a good fit for the holes previously drilled in the frames. Centre, and drill to $\frac{5}{16}$ in. depth with No. 12 drill; then part off at a full $\frac{3}{32}$ in. from the shoulder. File the flange to an oval shape as shown, then drill

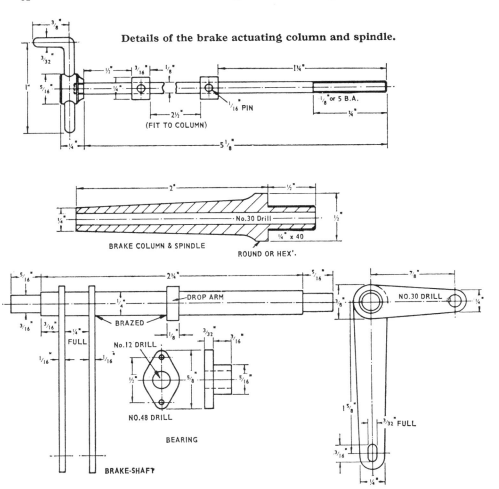

Details of the brake actuating column and spindle.

the two screw holes at $\frac{1}{2}$ in. centres, with No. 48 drill. Rechuck by the round part, and take a facing skim off the flanges with a round-nose tool set cross-wise in the rest.

How to Erect the Shaft

First set the two actuating arms in position on the shaft. The inner one is set at $\frac{1}{2}$ in. from the shoulder; take a look at the illustration, and you'll see the exact spot at which to put it. The other one is pressed on to line up with it; but before setting it in exact position, put the brake nut between the ends, the pips on either side of the nut going through the oval holes in the ends of the arms, as shown in the end view of the assembled gear in the previous in-stalment. Then press on the other arm, until the brake nut is just held between the arms, free to turn, but without any slackness. See that the drop arm is in the middle of the shaft, then set it so that it is at right-angles to the actuating arms; once again, there is no need for "mike measurements", and if you set them by eye alone, it will be quite O.K. The drop arm should hang down when the actuating arms are to your left and pointing towards you; see illustration.

The actuating and drop arms can then be brazed to the shaft; simply anoint the joints with a little wet flux—Boron Compo or similar—blow to bright red, and touch the joints with a piece of soft brass wire, which will melt and run around to form a fillet. Silver-solder may be used instead of brass wire, in which case either borax can be used as a flux, or any special kind, such as "Tenacity", according to the grade of silver-solder used. A coarse grade is quite suitable for such jobs as this. Quench in water only, and clean up with fine emery cloth or similar abrasive.

Erection is easy; insert the ends of the shaft through the holes in the frame, which can be readily done if the plain end of the shaft is pushed through the hole in the right-hand frame from the inside. Hold each reduced end of the shaft in line with the middle of the hole in the frame, then push the end of the bearing through the hole, so that the end of the shaft enters the hole in the bearing; see the plan view in the last instalment. Set the bearing flange parallel with the slope of the frame, run a No. 48 drill through the holes, making countersinks on the frame, follow with No. 53 drill, tap 9 BA, and put screws in to suit. Any heads will do; use whatever is available.

Brake Column and Spindle

The hand-brake column may be made from $\frac{1}{2}$ in. round or hexagon brass rod, or from a casting if available. A piece of rod a full $2\frac{1}{2}$ in. length is needed; chuck this in the three-jaw, face the end, centre, and put a No. 30 drill in, to the full depth of the fluted part of the drill. Keep withdrawing it, and clearing the chippings out of the flutes, otherwise they will choke, cause the drill to seize in the hole, and probably break it. Turn down $\frac{1}{2}$ in. of the outside to $\frac{1}{4}$ in. diameter, and screw it $\frac{1}{4}$ in. by 40. Reverse in chuck, face the other end, centre, and put the No. 30 drill in, until it breaks into the hole first drilled, forming a continuous hole right through the full length of the rod.

Next, make a $\frac{1}{4}$ in. by 40 tapped bush, from any oddment of rod over $\frac{3}{8}$ in. diameter, and $\frac{3}{8}$ in. long or over; you don't need any instruction for that simple job, as I have already described it more than once. After running the tap in, and skimming any burr off the end, screw the embryo brake column into it, and bring up the tailstock, with a centre-point in the hole in the barrel, until the point enters the hole in the outer end of the drilled rod. If the tailstock barrel is now locked, and the tailstock locked to the lathe bed, the column will be firmly supported at both ends, and can be turned without chatter. Don't forget a spot of oil at the tailstock centre. Set over the top-slide a weeny bit, and take a cut along the rod. If your top-slide has a graduated base, set it over 2 deg., and it will turn the taper on the column exactly right, so that when the smaller end is down to $\frac{1}{4}$ in. diameter, the larger end, just against the shoulder, will be $\frac{3}{8}$ in. diameter. If a round-nose tool is used, the radius at the end of the cut will be formed automatically. If your top-slide hasn't a graduated base, it is a case of trial and error. A tin setting template could be made, but it isn't worth the trouble, especially as the taper is merely ornamental, and the exact degree doesn't matter a Continental. If the turning tool leaves marks and scratches along the taper, clean them out with a piece of fine emery cloth, or similar abrasive, for neatness sake, as the column is in view on the footplate.

The brake spindle is made from a piece of $\frac{1}{8}$ in. round steel approximately $5\frac{1}{4}$ in. long. Chuck in three-jaw, and put $\frac{1}{8}$ in. of thread, $\frac{1}{8}$ in. or 5 BA, on one end. Reverse in chuck, and put $\frac{3}{4}$ in. of thread of same pitch, on the other end. Chuck a bit of $\frac{5}{16}$ in. round steel in three-jaw; face the end, centre, drill down about $\frac{5}{32}$ in. with No. 40 drill, and tap $\frac{1}{8}$ in. or 5 BA, same as the spindle. Put a curved chamfer on the edge with a round-nose tool, and part off at $\frac{1}{4}$ in. from the end. Screw this tightly on to the end of the brake spindle; shorter-threaded end, of course. Then chuck the brake spindle with the boss close to the chuck jaws, face off the end, and slightly chamfer it, both for appearance sake, and so that a sharp edge doesn't cut your fingers.

The next item is to drill a No. 43 hole slap across the centre of the little boss, and take care to have this right; because if the cross-handle goes through to one side, it will look what the kiddies call "worse 'n awful"—they always have a name for it, bless their hearts! If you rest the boss in a vee-block, the drill can be "sighted" outside the boss; all I do, is to pull down the handle of the drilling machine, so that the drill comes down in front of the boss, and goes straight into the tip of the groove in the block. If it doesn't, simply shift the block until it does. Don't move the block any more, but move the boss along the groove in the block, until the drill, when pulled down, enters the centre-pop in the boss. Start the drilling machine, pull down the handle steadily, and Bob's your uncle. In passing, a simple job like drilling a hole exactly where you want it seems to stump the very folk you would imagine to be experts at it. I repaired a professionally-made engine for a friend. The engine was only a 2½ in. gauge job, and cost a three-figure price, back in the cheaper days; and believe it or not, as Ripley says, fully 40 per cent of the holes in the frames had been filed oval, or otherwise enlarged, because they were originally drilled in the wrong place. Anyway, when you have drilled your hole truly through the boss, drive in a piece of $\frac{3}{32}$ in. silver-steel. Cut off one end at ½ in. from centre; bend up the other, also ½ in. from centre, and cut off at $\frac{3}{8}$ in. above the bend. Round off the cut ends nicely with a file, and the result should be as shown in the illustration.

To make the collars, chuck a piece of round rod in the three-jaw; ¼ in. diameter brass or steel will do. Face, centre, and drill No. 32 for about ½ in. down. Turn down a full $\frac{3}{16}$ in. length to $\frac{7}{32}$ in. bare diameter, and part off a $\frac{3}{16}$ in. slice; face the end again, and part off another $\frac{3}{16}$ in. slice, the full ¼ in. diameter. Ream both collars slightly until they fit tightly on the brake spindle. Put on the larger one, setting it as ½ in. below the handle; drill a No. 53 hole through collar and spindle, and squeeze in a bit of $\frac{1}{16}$ in. wire, filing flush both sides. Smear the spindle with a taste of oil, put it down the column, and put on the smaller collar, adjusting same so that the spindle turns freely but cannot move up or down; then pin the collar to the spindle, as above mentioned.

Erecting and Connecting Up

At $\frac{5}{16}$ in. from the inner edge of the top of the back buffer-beam, and exactly above the brake nut—that is, at $2\frac{3}{16}$ in. from the left-hand end of the beam— drill either a ¼ in. clearing hole or a $\frac{7}{32}$ in. hole, tapping the latter ¼ in. by 40. Put the bottom end of the brake spindle through the hole and enter it into the brake nut, screwing about halfway through. Note—if a clearing hole has been drilled, a ¼ in. by 40 nut, made from $\frac{5}{16}$ in. hexagon rod, must be slipped over the brake spindle underneath the beam, before entering it into the brake nut. The screwed spigot of the brake column is then poked through the hole in the beam, and secured with the ¼ in. by 40 nut. If the hole in the beam has been tapped, simply screw the spigot into it.

All that remains is to connect up; for this, ten forks are needed, and five pieces of $\frac{3}{32}$ in. round steel, for pull rods. The forks are made from ¼ in. square brass or steel rod, as you fancy; same process as described for valve gear forks, so you can call on your acquired experience for that job. Make nine of them to the sizes given in the last instalment, but make the slot in No. 10 ⅛ in. wide, to fit over the drop arm, and drill it No. 30, to take a ⅛ in. bolt for attaching it to same. An equalising link is also needed, but this is only a few minutes work. It is merely a piece of ¼ in. by $\frac{3}{32}$ in. flat steel strip, 1½ in. long, with two No. 41 holes drilled in it at 1¼ in. centres, and the ends rounded off. A third No. 41 hole is drilled in the middle.

Starting from the back, the main pull rod is a piece of $\frac{3}{32}$ in. rod, 1 in. long, with ⅛ in. of thread ($\frac{3}{32}$ in. or 7 BA) on each end. The wider-jawed fork is screwed on to one end of the rod; and on the other, one of the narrower-jawed forks is pinned to the centre of the equalising link by a bit of $\frac{3}{32}$ in.

silver-steel squeezed through fork and link. The two short pull rods are $1\frac{7}{16}$ in. long, screwed $\frac{1}{8}$ in. full at both ends, and furnished with forks. These are attached to the ends of the equalising link, and the trailing beam, by $\frac{3}{32}$ in. pins, as mentioned above. If the wide-jawed fork is attached to the drop arm by a $\frac{1}{8}$ in. bolt—bit of $\frac{1}{8}$ in. round steel, screwed and nutted at both ends, as in the valve gear—and the brake handle turned, the rear brakes should go on and off nicely.

Now cut two $3\frac{5}{8}$ in. lengths of $\frac{3}{32}$ in. rod, screw as above, and put a fork tightly on one end, pinning same to the leading beam. Screw the forks on the other end finger-tight, and couple up to the trailing beam temporarily with loose-fitting pins. Operate the brake handle. If the rear brakes come on first, screw up the forks a little more; if the front brakes come on first, unscrew a shade. When all four blocks come on together, the adjustment is correct, and you can either pin the forks to the trailing beam as above, or open the holes in the forks to No. 41 size, and use $\frac{3}{32}$ in. bolts, made in the same way as the drop arm bolt. The latter makes any subsequent adjustment easy to carry out; but as the brakes are only for ornament, or to keep the engine from running away when left standing unattended, it is a really unnecessary refinement.

Chimney for Small Boiler

As Pat would remark, the smaller chimney is the biggest, begob! It is a simple built-up job, and needs no liner. The barrel is a piece of $\frac{11}{16}$ in. brass or copper tube of about 22 gauge, squared off in the lathe at both ends, the finished length being $3\frac{1}{4}$ in. Chuck it in the three-jaw, and do the needful with a round-nose tool set cross-wise in the slide-rest. The rim or cap, and the base, may be made from rod, cored stick, or castings. For the cap, a piece of rod or cored stick 1 in. full diameter will be needed, sawn or parted off in the lathe to $\frac{3}{8}$ in. length. Chuck in three-jaw; and if rod is used, centre, drill a pilot hole about $\frac{3}{16}$ in. diameter right through it, then bore it out exactly as described for boring cylinders, until it is a very tight fit on the chimney tube. Cored stick, or a casting, is bored in the same way, but naturally will need no preliminary drilling, as it will have a cored hole through it. Squeeze the bored ring on to one end of the chimney tube; if you have slipped up, and the fit is too easy, silver-solder it. Chuck the tube in the three-jaw and turn the ring to the shape shown, or any other shape that may tickle your fancy, using a round-nose tool with a fairly good radius. I keep a small selection of round-nose tools of different radii, which come in handy for special jobs.

The base will need a piece of metal as above, but a wee bit over the finished diameter of $1\frac{1}{4}$ in. If it is a casting, it will be shaped, or saddled, as usually termed, to fit the smokebox, and will only need cleaning up. The easiest way to do this, is to lay a piece of medium-grade emery cloth or similar kind of abrasive material on the smokebox itself, holding same in close contact with the metal; then put the casting on it and work it back and forth over the emery cloth until the curved underside is smooth, a matter of a couple of minutes only. Inspector Meticulous will immediately tell you that this is all wrong, because the curve of the underside of the casting will be greater than the curve of the smokebox, by the thickness of the emery cloth, and therefore you won't get a perfect fit; but in actual practice, the difference is so small as to be negligible, as you'll find when you fit the chimney to the smokebox.

The outside of the casting will also be shaped; and as the irregular curve cannot be turned on an ordinary lathe, use a file and a piece of emery cloth to smooth it. Drive a piece of wood into the core hole, to serve as a handle, and rest the casting on the vice jaws, partly opened, while first filing off any roughness, and afterwards applying the emery cloth. If preferred, the casting can be mounted on a piece of round wood, held in three-jaw, saddled side towards the chuck, and the finishing touches put by wrapping a piece of emery cloth around your finger and holding it against the revolving casting; one of young Curly's antics. It did the trick all right; but the young "indefatigable" was always mighty careful to keep his fingers clear of the chuck jaws! Finally, chuck the casting in the three-jaw, holding by the edges, and bore it out as mentioned above, to a tight fit on the chimney tube. Press it on so that about $\frac{1}{4}$ in. of the tube projects below the saddled part.

How to Machine a Curved Base

If the base is made from rod or cored stick, it is an easy job to machine the bottom to fit the curve of the smokebox to a nicety. All you need is a home-made flycutter. This merely consists of a piece of $\frac{1}{2}$ in. round steel rod about 3 in. long, with a $\frac{3}{16}$ in. or $\frac{1}{4}$ in. cross-hole drilled $\frac{1}{4}$ in. from one end. Drill down the end to meet this cross-hole using $\frac{13}{64}$ in. or $\frac{7}{32}$ in. drill, and tap either $\frac{1}{4}$ in. Whitworth or $\frac{1}{4}$ in. by 40, or 0 BA if you like; fit a set-screw—preferably hexagon head—to suit. Make a round-nose tool from $\frac{3}{16}$ in. or $\frac{1}{4}$ in. round silver-steel to fit the cross-hole, and you're all set for the job. Clamp the bit of rod or cored stick under the slide-rest toolholder, setting the middle of it level with the lathe centres. Adjust the flycutter so that it projects exactly $1\frac{3}{8}$ in. (half of the smokebox diameter) from the centre of the holder, and put the latter in the three-jaw. Feed up the rod in the slide-rest until it touches the cutter when revolving, then traverse the rod longitudinally by moving either the top-slide or the lathe saddle. As the end of the rod passes the revolving cutter, the latter will chaw out a curved groove in it. Feed in about $\frac{1}{32}$ in. at the beginning of each traverse, and your patience and perseverance will be eventually rewarded by a perfect concavity at the end of the rod, which will fit the smokebox exactly. Owners of milling machines might do worse than make up one of these fly-cutters to fit the taper hole in the mandrel. I have one, the shank being No. 9 B. & S. taper; the cutter holder is $1\frac{1}{4}$ in. diameter, taking $\frac{3}{8}$ in. square cutters. I find it exceedingly useful for cutting curved surfaces of different radii to those of my regular milling cutters. It was made in an hour, at the cost of a shilling or so; goot bithneth, eh? Ye dinna need to spend muckle siller! The set-up was illustrated in one of my articles many years ago; so a "repeat", as the radio folk call it, may be of use to my readers who are tyro locomotive builders.

Chuck the piece of rod in the three-jaw with the concave end outwards; and with a round-nose tool, turn down about $\frac{1}{2}$ in. length to $\frac{3}{4}$ in. full diameter, starting from the edge of the radiused part, and taking care not to cut into it. Centre the concave end, drill a pilot hole, enlarge, and bore to a tight fit on the chimney tube, for about $\frac{1}{2}$ in. depth; then part off at $\frac{3}{8}$ in. from the end of the radius. Mount the base on a piece of wood, to use as a handle; then carefully file away the sharp edges, until the base is the shape shown in the illustration, the edge of the curved part being a little under $\frac{1}{32}$ in. thick all around. If thicker, it will look clumsy. Clean out the file marks with emery cloth, as mentioned above for the casting, and press the base on to the chimney tube at $\frac{1}{4}$ in. from the bottom. If at all slack, silver-solder it. You should be experts at that sort of job by this time!

Erection

The chimney is easily erected, as it only needs four $\frac{1}{16}$ in. or 10 BA brass screws; or a little thicker can be used if desired. Drill four clearing holes (No. 50 for size of screw mentioned) in the chimney base, equally spaced, and about $\frac{1}{8}$ in. clear of the edge. Insert bottom of chimney into the hole in the top of smokebox; set it exactly vertical in all aspects—you can do it "by eye"; they use plumb-lines in full-size practice, sometimes improvising them with big nuts tied to bits of string—then run the No. 50 drill through the holes in the base and make countersinks on the smokebox. Remove chimney, drill out the countersinks with No. 55 drill, tap $\frac{1}{16}$ in. or 10 BA, smear some plumbers' jointing around the chimney tube where it projects below the base, put the chimney in place, and secure with four screws, roundheads or countersunk, as you please. The whole arrangement is shown in the sectional drawing.

Chimney for Larger Boiler

This is machined up from a casting, and mounted on a separate liner made from tube. The liner is made from a piece of $\frac{5}{8}$ in. copper or brass tube about 22 gauge. Square off in the lathe at both ends, to a length of $1\frac{3}{8}$ in. Cut a piece of 18 or 20 gauge sheet brass or copper to $1\frac{1}{2}$ in. square. Drill a pilot hole in the middle, and enlarge to a tight fit on the tube, exactly the same as the holes in the smokebox were made; then bend the square to the radius of the inside of the smokebox. Push the piece of tube halfway through the hole, taking care to see that it goes through fair and square, so that when the plate is attached to the inside of the smokebox, the liner will stand exactly vertical. Silver-solder the joint, using the least possible amount of silver-solder; should any ooze through the joint and form a blob on the convex side of the plate, file it off. Now carefully bell out the bottom end of the liner; this is easily done by driving something tapered into it. A piece of hardwood will do quite well, as the soft tube readily expands under pressure.

Drill four No. 50 holes around the chimney hole on top of the smokebox, so that the screws will come on the corners of the liner plate. Countersink the holes with No. 30 drill. Put the liner in place from inside the smokebox; hold it temporarily in place, then put the drill down the holes in the smokebox again, and carry on right through the plate. Remove liner, and put a good smear of plumbers' jointing around the liner, where it comes through the plate; then replace it, and fix with four $\frac{1}{16}$ in. or 10 BA countersunk brass screws, nutted inside the smokebox. If the screw heads don't sit flush in the countersinks, smooth them off with a file, as the chimney base won't bed down on the smokebox if the screw heads are sticking out at all. Incidentally, weeny nuts are fiddling things to fool around with, inside a little smokebox; an alternative to using them, would be to solder four $\frac{1}{4}$ in. squares of $\frac{3}{32}$ in. sheet brass over the drilled holes, on the concave side of the plate. Drill these No. 55, through the holes on the convex side of the plate; tap $\frac{1}{16}$ in. or 10 BA and then, when the liner is put in position, the screws can be entered through the holes in the smokebox, into the tapped holes mentioned above, and screwed home.

There will be no need to build up the chimney, as castings are available; I have a couple here now, very clean, and with the curved base exact to radius of smokebox. The casting must be bored to fit over the liner; and about the easiest way to chuck it for the boring operation, is to use a split wooden bush. Chuck a bit of hardwood in three-jaw, and turn about $1\frac{1}{2}$ in. of it to a little over $1\frac{1}{2}$ in. diameter. You can use your ordinary slide-rest tools for this job, as "finish" doesn't matter. Then centre it, and poke an $\frac{11}{16}$ in. drill down for same distance. Part off at about $1\frac{3}{8}$ in. from the end, and saw the piece in two, right across the hole. Put the chimney casting between the two halves, with the cap and base projecting from each end; grip the lot in the three-jaw, curved end outward, and bore to a fairly tight fit on the liner, using the same "technique" as for cylinder boring. The curved base can be trued up on a bit of emery cloth, as mentioned above.

The outside of the chimney can be turned on a mandrel, which may either be solid rod, or tube. I have a few mandrels which fit between centres, and they have a very slight taper, which enables them to be driven into whatever is going to be operated on; but a bit of $\frac{5}{8}$ in. rod or tube, with a piece of foil, or even paper wrapped around it so that it fits tightly into the bored chimney, will do. It can be held in three-jaw, chimney cap outwards. A round-nose tool will do the needful on the cap and barrel, and a knife-tool will attend to the lip at the top; the base cannot be tool-finished, owing to its irregular shape; but if you hold a half-round smooth file against it as it revolves, and then a bit of fine or medium emery cloth, all traces of the casting skin will soon be removed. No fixing is required for the chimney; just push it over the liner. If the casting is good gunmetal, the polished top will go a lovely golden colour when the engine is put in steam, and the chimney becomes hot.

CHAPTER SEVENTEEN

Firing and driving the engine

How to Run "Tich"

IT IS NO GOOD owning a Rolls-Royce if you don't know how to drive and look after it. Same applies to locomotives large and small. It takes a full-size driver many years to learn how to handle a locomotive in the most efficient way; in fact, it would not be an exaggeration to say that he has never finished learning. The finest engine ever turned out from Swindon, Crewe, Doncaster or any other big works, cannot give of its best if improperly handled. Readers of these notes may follow implicitly all the instructions I give, and with careful workmanship, produce an excellent engine, capable of doing all I claim—and a bit extra for luck; yet that same locomotive may be an abject failure on the track, simply for lack of knowledge of the proper way to fire and drive her. It has often happened in full-size, that the first engine of a new class has been put into service, and the drivers and firemen who ran her were used to running different classes of engines altogether. The methods used for the older engines did not suit the new one, and she has not performed as well as expected; yet the fault lay, not in the engine herself, but in the engine crews. The L.M.S. Pacifics were a case in point. The enginemen were only used to engines with narrow fireboxes, the wide firebox of the 4-6-2 needed firing in an entirely different manner from that for the narrow boxes, and there were plenty of steaming—or rather no-steaming—troubles until enginemen "learned the trick", in a manner of speaking. When they did, it wasn't only the fur that began to fly!

Facts About Fires

If our beginner friends will get the following few facts well and truly planted in their noddles, they won't have any difficulty in running their little engines successfully.

It is barely necessary to point out that the bigger the fire, the greater its stability. A weeny fire is quickly lit, and brought up to full incandescence, which being interpreted means bright red all over; but the drawback is, that it will die out just as quickly without certain precautions being observed. Item No. 2 is that the fire needs a certain amount of oxygen, which it gets from the air, to keep it burning at the point where it gives out the maximum of heat.

If it doesn't get enough air it burns dully, and the boiler won't make steam. If too much air is drawn through, loose particles are lifted, drawn through the tubes and blown out of the chimney, whilst holes will appear in the fire. Cold air enters through the holes, cools the inside of the firebox, and down goes the "clock" again.

If a small fire is made up too thick, the blast cannot draw sufficient air through it, and it will not only burn dully, but the bottom part of the fire will burn away first, and the ash and other residue will probably choke the air spaces between the firebars, thus kind of "piling on the agony". If the fire is too thin, the effect mentioned in the preceding paragraph will occur. If the fire is heaped in the middle of the box, the sides burn away first, and cold air is drawn in close to the plates. If the fire is thick at the back and thin at the front, or vice versa, same thing happens, as the thinnest part of the fire always goes first. In full-size, the correct way to fire a narrow box, is to fire around the sides, under the door, and against the tubeplate, putting very little in the middle, so that the bulk of the fire is in contact with the firebox plates.

In a little firebox, the best thing is to keep the fire even. You can't "scale" Nature; and the fire acts in exactly the same way, subject to the same natural laws, in a box three inches long as it does in one three yards long. There is such a tiny distance between the middle of the fire, and the firebox plates, that the "saucer" fire would show no advantage, and probably go into holes in the middle. When a grate slopes from back to front, it is usual, in full-size practice, to put more coal on at the back, under the door and in the back corners, than at the tubeplate end, as the movement of the engine tends to shake it down. This applies equally to small size; my single-wheeler *Grosvenor* has a sloping grate exactly the same as her big sister of blessed memory, and she performs best when fired in the same manner.

Making a Draught

We already know that coal requires air to make it burn; and to get the air through the firebox in sufficient quantity, we must create a draught. A pity we can't bottle up some of the confounded draughts that come in through windows, doors and sundry other places, on a winter's night, and make use of them! Many good folk don't realise that there is no natural draught through the firebox of even a full-sized locomotive; the breeze has to be created by blast and blower. Now and again you read in the newspapers of a driver and fireman being burnt—sometimes, alas! fatally—by what the uninitiated reporters call a "blow-back". If a driver inadvertently forgets to open the blower valve before he shuts the regulator, flames will pour from the firehole instead of going into the tubes, and set the enginemen's clothes alight in a fraction of a second. If the engine has a short chimney, and is running chimney first, against the wind, the latter will blow down the chimney and help matters on.

The blast and blower of the tiny engine serve the same purpose, and work exactly the same as in full-size; but whereas a full-sized engine's fire will burn up slowly, of its own accord, after being lit up in the shed, the little one won't do anything of the kind. The big fire burns up on the same principle as the bonfire you may light in the garden, to burn the rubbish, or maybe to amuse the kiddies on Guy Fawkes' night; the combustion is too slow to require any additional draught. This slow-burning fire will get steam up in the full-sized boiler, but very slowly; *Grosvenor*'s big sister took about four hours from all cold. This is quite in order, because if a big locomotive boiler is forced, the expansion will be uneven, and tube and stay leakage will ensue. The slow combustion will not produce enough heat to maintain working steam pressure; but once the boiler has reached the temperature of boiling water all over, it may be forced to any extent within reason, without injuring it in any way. The reason why the big fire can be lit and left to burn up, is because of its bulk. There isn't enough bulk in the little fire, to follow suit. Even if the contents of the firebox (wood or charcoal) are soaked in paraffin, the latter would just burn out—incidentally, you'd need a gas mask!—and there might be a few red embers left, but they would only last a minute or so. But if a current of air is passed through the firebox, the small fire will not only keep alight, but quickly raise enough steam to work the engine's own blower, and bring the pressure to working level. Well, I hope the above explanation hasn't bored our more experienced friends; but if you had read some of the letters I have received, you would agree that it was needed by many of our fraternity who are raw recruits, and totally ignorant of the whys and wherefores.

Simple Auxiliary Blower

The simplest way of creating the necessary draught through the firebox of *Tich*, to get up steam, is by aid of an auxiliary blower. This consists of a piece of tube about 6 in. long, just large enough to be a push fit in the chimney; or a piece of the same diameter as the chimney will do. Bend a piece of 22 gauge sheet brass or copper about 1 in. wide, into a tube that will push into both the chimney and extension tube; silver-solder it into the latter and push the protruding piece into the engine's chimney when using it. A blower jet is fitted in the extension tube about 1 in. from the bottom. Close up the end of a piece of $\frac{1}{8}$ in. or $\frac{5}{32}$ in. tube, by hitting it all around with a hammer; easily enough done if the tube is first softened by heating to red and dipping in cold water. File off the end squarely, and drill a No. 70 hole in it; or the nearest size larger, for which you have a drill. Bend the end over at right-angles, drill a suitable hole in the large tube about 1 in. from the end, insert the bend, and silver-solder it. The jet must stand straight up in the middle of the tube.

The next requirement is a balancing chamber, to keep the stream of air steady. This may be simply a tin can, soldered up airtight; an old coffee or cocoa tin does fine. Drill two holes on opposite sides, close to the top; and in them, solder two pieces of tube, same size as the blower tube in the extension pipe. The third item is a tyre pump; a motor pump is best, but a cycle pump will do at a pinch, though it takes longer to get up steam. The pump is connected to one of the tubes in the can, and the other tube in the can is connected to the blower tube by a piece of stout rubber pipe. A cycle pump connection may be used if desired, adapters for the screwed ends being made from discarded cycle valves silver-soldered to the pipes. The whole outfit is shown in the diagram.

How to Get up Steam

Fill the boiler until the gauge glass shows three parts full, either by taking out the safety valve on the larger boiler and pouring water in, or by using the engines own hand pump. After the first run, there should always be enough water left in the boiler for the next. All the moving parts of the engine should be oiled with any good brand of lubricating oil, but it should not be too thick; I use "Etna heavy medium", a product of the Vacuum Oil Company, having bought a five-gallon drum of it some years ago for my shop machinery. The cylinder lubricator should be three parts filled with a good brand of cylinder oil suitable for superheated steam; Shell "Valvata", Vacuum 600W, or similar. Thin oils are useless; the hot steam will just vaporise them. Put the extension tube in the chimney of the engine; and for the first two or three runs, it would be a help to get somebody to operate the pump. If you are a married man with interested kiddies, that difficulty will soon be solved! Either wood or charcoal can be used for starting the fire; I use charcoal broken up into pieces about $\frac{1}{2}$ in. long, with the dust sifted out. Either small sticks or blocks of wood will do, if charcoal isn't available. Put the charcoal or wood in a tin lid and pour paraffin over it. Shovel some into the firebox, enough to well cover the bars; start the pump going, and throw in a lighted match. The whole lot will catch alight and start roaring merrily. Add some more wood or charcoal, and shut the door for a minute or so. Fill the side tanks, if not already done, with clean water.

The coal should be broken up to the size of peas, and the dust sifted out. Best results are obtained with Welsh steam coal, anthracite, or a mixture of the two; house coal is of very little use. Not only does it make a lot of smoke, and leave a tarry deposit in the tubes, but it hasn't sufficient "therms" in it, to generate steam fast enough for the engine to work at full power. As soon as the wood or charcoal has caught alight all over, and is glowing red, pop on about four shovelfuls of coal and shut the door again. In three or four minutes, depending on how vigorously the air pump is operated, there will be enough steam to work the engine's own blower. Open the valve a little and remove the extension tube. By this time, the charcoal or wood will probably be all burnt away, and the coal will have settled on the firebars; if so, give her another couple of shovelfuls. You will now see the needle of the steam gauge "walking up"; and in a minute or so, the safety valve will lift.

The First Run

Put the lever in full forward gear; or if she has loose eccentrics, move the engine forward one turn, then open the regulator steadily. Steam going into cold cylinders will condense into water, and this may become trapped between piston and cylinder cover, locking the wheels. If this happens, shut the regulator and move the engine by hand for a turn or so. The water will force the slide valves off their seatings and escape up the blast pipe, so don't put your face over the chimney top, or you'll be well and truly christened. The slide valves will not lift with the regulator open, as the steam pressure on them will hold them down. When the engine wheels turn freely again, open the regulator once more. If the wheels still lock, ditto repeato above; but the third time she should be O.K. as the cylinders should then be hot enough. Now be careful, for if you open up too much, the engine will dart away from you like a shot from a gun-barrel; and if she does, you can say good-bye to all your patient endeavours, for she will run off the road and crash. Open up steadily, and she will behave herself like a well-bred locomotive should. If you have a short straight line, let her run up and down, without any load, two or three times; if a continuous track, let her do a complete circuit. Warning—as she will be probably blowing off all the time, as well as using steam for running, look at the gauge glass; and if the water is below half-a-glass, put a drop in with the hand pump. Try to remember always to shut the blower valve after opening the regulator, and to open the blower valve before shutting the regulator. There is no need to have the blower on when the engine is running; it only wastes steam, also you cannot hear the beats properly. They should be sharp and snappy, with no trace of a wheeze in between.

How to Fire and Drive

There are tricks in every trade, and the enginemen's trade is no exception, whatever the size of the locomotive; also what goes for the big one, goes for the little one as well. Couple up your passenger car; and as *Tich* doesn't carry any coal on board, take some in a tin box on the front end of your car. Put a couple of shovelfuls of coal on before starting; take your seat, and open up steadily. Don't tap at the handle; hold it like a full-size driver does, so as to keep full control. If you are of normal weight and the car is an eight-wheeler on ball-bearings, little *Tich* will treat you as the equivalent of a bag of feathers, and move off with all the vim and vigour of the full-size article, with loud even puffs from the chimney, and will begin to blow off almost immediately; so close the by-pass valve, and if she has the full valve gear, bring the lever back next to middle, making certain that the latch drops into the correct notch in the quadrant. The beats will ease off a bit, and she will settle down to a steady pull. Speed is then controlled by the regulator. Watch the gauge glass, and when the water rises to three parts of a glass, open the by-pass valve a little. This valve should be regulated, as near as possible, to keep the level in the boiler as constant as possible; you'll find the correct amount of opening after two or three runs.

Recollect that you are a "one-man crew", and have to fire as well as drive;

so watch the fire. Whatever else you do, don't let it get too low, because such a weeny fire will soon die out if any holes form in it. At the same time, don't fill the box right up to the door, or you will choke the fire. As soon as the engine is well under way, take a look at the fire; the bit that you put on just before starting, should now be well alight. If parts of it are still black, not fully incandescent, shut the door for a minute or so. You'll soon know when it is thoroughly alight, as the safety valves will lift. That is the right time to put a bit more on. Most beginners have the impression that the proper time to make up the fire is when the steam begins to go down; they never made a bigger mistake! When the safety valve blows off is the right time to fire; and the motto is "little and often". When you have about an inch depth, or a little less, depending on the quality of the coal, try to keep it at that. A sprinkling of fresh coal on top of an incandescent mass will not reduce the steam pressure; and the residue, falling through the bars into the ashpan, will lower the level, so that the fire has burned down slightly by the time the next bit goes on. This brings up the level again, and literally "keeps the pot boiling".

If you let the fire down too much, and then smother the top with raw coal, pressure will fall rapidly. If this is done, as frequently happens with inexperienced firing, the best way to recover pressure is to drop the lever a notch or so, making the engine puff harder, and open the by-pass fully, so that no cold water goes into the boiler for a minute or so. The stronger blast will rapidly light up the coal, and the steam pressure will recover much more quickly without the feed; but as soon as full pressure returns, shut the by-pass until the water level is restored, then regulate as before, and don't let the fire down again!

The above instructions apply to non-stop running on a continuous line. If only a straight line is available, don't fire on the run; make up the fire when stopping at the end, always remembering to put a bit more on when the fire is fully incandescent, and the safety valve blowing off. As more steam will be used in constantly starting and stopping, than on continuous running, the by-pass valve will probably have to be closed all the time. When finishing the run, let the fire burn right down; don't run until steam is all gone, but shut down when pressure has dropped to about 30 lb. Dump the remains of the fire by pulling out the dump pin, and wipe off any oil spashes, etc., while the engine is still hot. Don't leave the blower valve open when the engine is cooling down, or ash and grit might choke the nozzle when the steam is all gone, and the vacuum in the boiler starts sucking in air through any available opening.

Accessories for "Tich"

Some of our beginner friends who have visited club and exhibition tracks, have noted that the accessories such as firing tools, oil feeders, etc., even on well-made locomotives, seem to have been added as an afterthought, any old thing that happened to be handy, being pressed into service. One beginner told me that he saw a really fine engine being fired with an improvised salt spoon, and oiled with a battered relic which had evidently once been used on an ancient sewing machine. These "spring-sided" oil cans could, at one time, be bought at any ironmongery store for the princely sum of one penny!

Firing Shovel

The kind of shovel which I use on my own engines has a blade of the same shape as used in full-size, but a longer handle is necessary, as the fireman doesn't ride on the footplate. The first thing needed is a small iron former, similar to that used for flanging boiler plates. Make it of $\frac{1}{4}$ in. iron or steel plate. It is only a few minutes' work to saw out the plate, and file it to shape; and once made, you can make shovels galore on it, if they should be needed.

The blade is knocked up from a piece of 20 gauge steel. Lay the former on the bit of sheet steel, and mark a line all around, a full $\frac{1}{4}$ in. from the edge, except at the narrow straight part. Cut it out—easily done with hand snips— clamp in vice jaws alongside the former, and proceed to beat down the projecting edges of the steel; but here, you'll find things slightly different from flanging a copper plate! As fast as you hammer down one part of the flange, another bit of it will bob up again, and you'll probably find that you have a row of crinkles instead of a smooth flange. Well, don't worry; just keep on pegging away at the crinkles, hammering them down as fast as they come up. In the end, they'll get tired of it and give you best, and you will have a nice flange all around the former. The edge of the flange will be rather ragged, but a file will soon teach that good manners. Round off the front corners of the shovel blade to finish.

The handle is made from iron wire—black, tinned, or galvanised; doesn't matter a bean—about $\frac{5}{32}$ in. diameter. I make mine about 6 in. long, but you can make yours to suit your own ideas. Bend one end into a flattened ring. Hold the other end on something solid, such as an anvil, block of iron, or similar, and give it a few hearty biffs with a hammer to flatten it. File off any raggedness, and make a slight bend at the end of the flattened part.

Put the blade upside down in the brazing pan, set the handle against it (I usually prop mine up with a few bits of coke) apply some wet flux, blow to bright red, and touch the joint with a bit of soft brass wire, which will melt and flow in. Let cool to black, quench in water, knock off any burnt flux which may be sticking to the handle, and there is your shovel. The angle of the handle may be anything you like; just bend it to suit the engine.

Uninitiated readers of the present generation may be amused to learn that the fireman's shovel was, in the really good old days, the principal footplate cooking utensil. The blades were always clean and bright, and in those happy times when we could get as much bacon, meat, etc., as we wanted, enginemen used to fry big rashers and grill huge steaks on the shovel, holding the blade just inside the firehole door. Just fancy—a juicy rasher about $\frac{1}{4}$ in. thick, two new-laid eggs, the top of a cottage loaf, about a quarter pound of fresh butter, a big can of tea, and plenty of time to sit down comfortably in the cab and enjoy it all, before it was time to take the next train out; kind of makes your mouth water, doesn't it? Enginemen of my generation never had any canteens, hostels, etc., and didn't need any. I've attended banquets, in days gone by, at the Café Royal in Regent Street, London, and other swell places, but give me the merry old alfresco footplate lunch every time—it makes you feel equal to pulling the train without any engine!

Oiling Syringe

The driver of a full-sized engine can go underneath with his oil-feeder, and put a drop of oil wherever it is needed; but it would puzzle the driver of a small one to follow suit. As I've often remarked, you can't "scale" Nature! The only thing to do, is to use some more convenient method of putting the oil where you need it. A commercial pressure-feed oiler with a piece of thin tube soldered into the end of the spout, is quite a good wheeze; I have three of them, each holding a different grade of oil. However, these oilers are now fairly expensive, and an alternative is a simple syringe-type oiler which will do the necessary just as well. Any beginner should be able to make one inside of half an hour. The sizes given may, of course, be varied to suit any oddments of tube and rod, that you may have handy.

The barrel is a piece of $\frac{1}{2}$ in. brass or copper tube, squared off at each end, in the lathe, to an approximate length of 4 in. treblet tube is best, as it is smooth inside; but if ordinary tube is used, and the inside is roughened, as it usually is, wind a piece of fine emery cloth around a stick, until it will just go in the tube. Chuck this in the three-jaw, put the tube over it, run the lathe as fast as possible, and run the piece of tube up and down the improvised lap. Very little of this treatment is needed to smooth the inside of the tube.

To make the piston, chuck a piece of $\frac{1}{2}$ in. brass rod in the three-jaw. Face the end, centre, and drill down about $\frac{1}{4}$ in. with No. 30 or $\frac{5}{32}$ in. drill; tap either $\frac{5}{32}$ in. by 40 or $\frac{3}{16}$ in. by 40. Turn down a little over $\frac{3}{4}$ in. length, to a close sliding fit in the tube, same as if you were fitting a steam piston, then part off at $\frac{3}{4}$ in. from the end. Should there be a wire-edge left after parting off, chuck the piston again, plain end outwards, and chamfer the end just sufficiently to remove the sharp edge. Chuck the piece of rod again, repeat the facing, drilling and tapping processes, then turn the outside to the shape of a knob, or handle; and part off. The piston rod is a piece of $\frac{5}{32}$ in. or $\frac{3}{16}$ in. brass rod about $3\frac{1}{2}$ in. long. Chuck in three-jaw, face off and screw about $\frac{1}{4}$ in. at one end, and about $\frac{1}{8}$ in. on the other. Screw the knob tightly on to this end whilst the rod is still in the chuck, and chamfer the knob a little, so that there won't be any sharp edge to cut your fingers. Screw the piston on to the other end.

For the end cap, chuck the piece of $\frac{1}{2}$ in. rod once more, and turn down $\frac{3}{16}$ in. of it to a tight squeeze fit in the end of the tube. Part off at $\frac{5}{16}$ in. from the end. Rechuck by the reduced part; centre the end, drill right through with

$\frac{5}{32}$ in. drill, and tap $\frac{3}{16}$ in. by 40. Skim off any burr. Press the cap into the tube, and solder it in as an extra precaution. Drop a bead of solder down the tube, plus a few spots of Baker's fluid, or any other good liquid soldering flux; heat over a gas or spirit flame, holding the tube with a pair of pliers, almost vertically, so that the flame heats up the cap. In a minute or two, the solder will melt and form a nice fillet all around the end of the cap inside the tube. Wash well in running water, to remove all traces of the soldering flux, which naturally wouldn't be much good for lubricating purposes!

The nozzles can be made from $\frac{1}{8}$ in. or $\frac{3}{32}$ in. tube, to suit different types of locomotives. For an engine like *Tich*, two would be plenty; one with a short tube, and one with a long tube. Chuck a piece of $\frac{1}{4}$ in. hexagon rod in three-jaw, face the end, turn down $\frac{1}{4}$ in. length to $\frac{3}{16}$ in. diameter, and screw $\frac{3}{16}$ in. by 40. Part off at $\frac{1}{4}$ in. from the shoulder. Reverse in chuck, centre, drill right through with $\frac{3}{32}$ in. drill, and if $\frac{1}{8}$ in. tube is used for the nozzle, open out to $\frac{1}{8}$ in. depth with No. 32 drill. Chamfer the corners of the hexagon. Cut a piece of tube the length required for the spout, and silver-solder it into the nipple, heating the tube full length to soften it. Pickle, wash, clean up, screw the gadget into the hole in the cap, and you're all set. To use, pull the piston right out, pour some oil into the tube, replace piston, and press the knob very gently when applying the end of the spout to the part needing oil. The spout, being soft, can be bent as required, to oil around the corners, and get at every moving part. To prevent leakages, the end of the spout can be screwed, and a little blind cap made to fit it. If this is screwed on when the syringe is not in use, no oil will escape, and make a mess on the bench, or wherever you keep the syringe.

Index